D1572043

Linguistic Communication and Speech Acts

Linguistic Communication and Speech Acts

Kent Bach
Robert M. Harnish

The MIT Press
Cambridge, Massachusetts, and
London, England

This book was set in VIP Times Roman by Village Typographers, and printed and bound by Halliday Lithograph Corporation in the United States of America.

Library of Congress Cataloging in Publication Data

Bach, Kent.
  Linguistic communication and speech acts.

  Bibliography: p.
  Includes index.
  1. Speech acts (Linguistics). 2. Languages—Philosophy. 3. Oral communication. I. Harnish, Robert M., joint author. II. Title.
P95.55.B3   410   79–15892
ISBN 0–262–02136–6

For our parents
Karl and Meryl Bach
Robert F. Harnish and Dorothy C. Holmes

Contents

Preface

Extensive work in the study of language has been stimulated by the work of Chomsky on grammar, Grice and Katz on meaning, and Austin and Searle on speech acts. Nevertheless, little has been done to integrate these topics into a general account of linguistic communication, even though it is widely recognized that to communicate linguistically is more than just saying something—what is communicated is determined not merely by what is said. The structure and meaning of the expressions used are essential, but so are the speaker's intention and the hearer's recognition of it. In our view a communicative intention has the peculiar feature that its fulfillment consists in its recognition. The speaker intends the hearer to recognize the point of his utterance not just through (1) content and (2) context but also because (3) the point is intended to be recognized.

The two major alternative theories, Sadock's (1974) and Searle's (1969), fail to do justice to all three factors. Moreover, neither explains just how linguistic structure and speech acts are connected—and how they are not. Sadock focuses on linguistic structure and Searle on speech acts, but both assume (in different ways) that this connection is mostly semantic. Our view is that the connection is inferential, not just for nonliteral and for indirect utterances but even for literal ones. The inference is simplest in the literal case, but each case involves all three factors: content, context, and communicative intention.

These factors require systematic explanation. Accordingly, we attempt to characterize precisely the nature of communicative intentions together with the nature of the inference the hearer makes in identifying them. Within the framework of this account we offer a detailed classification of speech acts and discuss the function of linguistic devices and the role of social conventions in the performance of speech acts. Although our approach is primarily philosophical and linguistic, it intersects with cognitive and social psychology by exploring psychological and social factors that contribute to successful linguistic communication.

Our aim is ambitious: to present a conception of linguistic communication that integrates philosophical, linguistic, and psychological issues. We have profited from the intellectual legacy of the authors cited, as well as from the work and encouragement of our friends Stephen Schiffer, Bruce Fraser, George Spanos, and Chuck Carr. Special thanks go to George E. Smith (for his voluminous comments), Tom Larson (for the index), Claire and Polly Baker, and Judy Miles. Thanks are due also to our many students who have endured cruder versions of our theory and have helped us, either by their questions and suggestions or by their noncomprehension, to produce clearer formulations of our ideas.

Introduction

There is nothing people do more often, in more ways, than talk to one another. For most people, nothing is easier. Sometimes we have to struggle to find the right words or to get them out, sometimes we must pause to discern or decipher what someone else says, but on the whole we speak fluently and understand others effortlessly. Yet using language is a very complex enterprise, as anyone knows who has tried to master a foreign language. Moreover, much goes into using a language besides knowing it and being able to produce and recognize sentences in it. Exchanging words is a social affair, usually taking place within the context of a fairly well-defined social situation. In such a context we rely on one another to share our conception of what the situation is. With people we know, rather than spell everything out we rely on shared understandings to facilitate the process of communicating. What sort of process is it? Linguistic communication is easily accomplished but not so easily explained.

There is a popular and venerable conception of linguistic communication as conveying a message. It dates back at least to John Locke (1691, III, i) and has been stated most recently as follows:

A has in his mind some sort of message (or idea), and he wishes B to form in his head the same message. This message is transformed ultimately into a series of neural impulses that are sent to the muscles responsible for the actual production of speech, which follows immediately . . . The listener, B, must decode A's message by converting the sounds into a semantic representation. (Cairns and Cairns 1976, 17–18)

Even on this popular conception linguistic communication involves more than transmitting a signal; inference on the part of the hearer is required.

Commonsensically: Communication is successful only when the hearer infers the speaker's intentions from the character of the utterance he produced. (Fodor 1975, 103)

In more detailed and sophisticated form the commonsensical view goes like this:

The speaker's message is encoded in the form of a phonetic representation of an utterance by means of the system of linguistic rules with which the speaker is equipped. This encoding then becomes a signal to the speaker's articulatory organs, and he vocalizes an utterance of the proper phonetic shape. This is, in turn, picked up by the hearer's auditory organs. The speech sounds that stimulate these organs are then converted into a neural signal from which a phonetic representation equivalent to the one into which the speaker encoded his message is obtained. This representation is decoded into a representation of the same message that the speaker originally chose to convey by the hearer's equivalent system of linguistic rules. (Katz 1966, 103–104)

This sophisticated rendition of the commonsensical view is highly plausible—as far as it goes. It captures the mechanical, context-independent aspects of linguistic communication, but it leaves much to be accounted for. First, utterances can be ambiguous, so disambiguation must be considered. Second, a person need not speak literally and directly. Instead of meaning just what he says, he may mean something else or something more; to be understood, the utterance requires more than being decoded in the way Katz describes. Third, the commonsensical view neglects the role of shared understandings in successful communication. Finally, it does not tell us what exactly these messages are. Indeed, it gives the impression that linguistic communication is limited to conveying information and ignores acts of making requests, offering apologies, conveying greetings, and so on.

Linguistic communication is *not* exclusively a matter of conveying information, that is, of making statements. J. L. Austin's pioneering investigation (1962) of the variety of speech acts opened philosophers' eyes to the breadth of ways in which language can be used. In presenting a preliminary version of our account of linguistic communication, in chapter 1 we adopt a version of Austin's well-known distinction between locutionary, illocutionary, and perlocutionary acts by characterizing the sorts of intention with which each act is performed. Of special importance is our account of (communicative) illocutionary intentions. They are reflexive intentions, in the sense of H. P. Grice (1957): a reflexive intention is an intention that is intended to be recognized as intended to be recognized. We further restrict illocutionary intentions to those intentions whose fulfillment consists in nothing more than their recognition. The sort of reflexive intention that has this feature is that of expressing an attitude (such as a belief or desire). Accordingly, an act of linguistic communication is successful if the attitude the speaker expresses is identified by the hearer by means of recognizing the reflexive intention to express it. Of course, recognizing that there is some such intention is not to identify the specific attitude expressed—it is identified on the basis of what is said, together with what we call *mutual contextual beliefs*.

What is said is the content of *locutionary acts,* the topic of chapter 2. What the speaker says is largely, but not entirely, a matter of what his words mean. After all, they may be ambiguous and their reference (in the case of referring expressions) underdetermined, and so the hearer must rely on more than just his knowledge of the language (and the supposition that the speaker shares this knowledge) to determine what the speaker is saying. All together, what is said depends on what expression is uttered, what meaning it has in the language, what the speaker means by it, and what things he is referring to. We offer a schematic account of how the hearer identifies these various items. Once he identifies them, he has identified what is said; from that, together with mutual contextual beliefs, he can proceed to the identification of the speaker's illocutionary act, that is, of what attitude the speaker is expressing.

Before representing this phase of the hearer's inference, in chapter 3 we attempt to sharpen and systematize Austin's detailed classification of *illocutionary acts* in order to make explicit the full range of communicative acts to which our account is meant to apply. They are categorized in terms of the kind of attitude each expresses. Then in chapter 4 we spell out the illocutionary phase of the hearer's inference. Our schematization of this inference, which we call the *speech act schema* (SAS), applies not only to literal but also to nonliteral and indirect utterances. In chapter 5 we explain how our theory operates both as an analysis of linguistic communication and as a representation of what it takes (linguistically, psychologically, and socially) to communicate. In our view, then, an act of linguistic communication is an act of expressing an attitude by means of saying something. What type of attitude is expressed determines the kind of illocutionary act being performed. That act is successful—communication has been achieved—if the hearer identifies the attitude expressed in the way the speaker intends him to identify it. This requires the hearer to make an inference, an inference based partly on the supposition that the speaker intends him to make it.

Our intention-and-inference approach contrasts sharply with Austin's view of illocutionary acts as conventional. He neglected to explain what he meant by *conventional,* much less why he considered such acts to be conventional, but John Searle (1969) has since developed this sort of theory, using his controversial notion of constitutive rules. Our theory is thoroughly at odds with Searle's, but we do allow, following P. F. Strawson (1964), that certain kinds of illocutionary acts involve convention rather than intention-and-inference. Those acts are not essentially communicative, however, as the examples of christening, nominating, and acquitting illustrate. It is no coincidence that cases like these influenced Austin's thinking about illocutionary acts in general. In chapter 6 we characterize and categorize conventional illocutionary acts. Chapter 7 deals with assorted topics related to convention, including the difference between rules and conventions, Searle's theory based on constitutive rules, conventions and explicit performatives, and the conventionality of locutionary acts.

The seven chapters of part I present the essentials of our theory of linguistic communication and speech acts. In part II we take up various philosophical, linguistic, and psychological issues raised by our theory. Chapter 8 investigates the concepts of linguistic meaning and speaker meaning, together with the allied notions of presupposition and implication. Clarifying these notions enables us to sharpen our conception of locutionary acts. In general, the linguistic meaning of an utterance does not severely delimit, much less determine, the speaker's communicative illocutionary intent. It does delimit what the speaker says, which in turn provides part of the basis on which the hearer infers the speaker's intent, but because the speaker could be speaking nonliterally or indirectly, the hearer must rely on much more than the linguistic meaning of the utterance to determine the speaker's intent. However, as investigated in chapters 9 and 10, there are certain kinds of linguistic devices that seem directly tied to the performance of particular kinds of illocutionary acts. Explicit performatives, first investigated by Austin, are the most familiar, but there are also the hedged performatives discussed by Fraser (1975) and a variety of constructions investigated by Sadock (1974). Apart from their intrinsic linguistic interest, the relevance of these devices to our theory is that their use short-circuits the pattern of inference followed by the hearer in identifying the speaker's illocutionary intent. This is the phenomenon of *illocutionary standardization,* as we call it. Other theorists have attempted to account for this phenomenon in terms of linguistic meaning (Sadock 1974) or illocutionary convention (Searle 1975a), but we hold that short-circuited inference is still inference—inference compressed by precedent rather than by meaning or convention.

Our account of linguistic communication and speech acts is primarily analytical, not empirical. To be sure, we rely on everyday experience for the extensive variety of communicative phenomena we consider, but the view we present is essentially a conception of what it takes to communicate and to understand. Our view is that linguistic communication essentially involves the speaker's having a special sort of intention (an intention that the hearer make a certain sort of inference) and the hearer's actually making that inference. In proposing this analytical conception of linguistic communication, we could ignore empirical questions and take the stubborn position that if in fact people do not have the intentions and make the inferences we attribute to them, they do not engage in communication when they talk to one another. Then the question would arise, What do they do? We cannot demonstrate that people do what we claim they must do if they communicate, but in chapter 11 we try at least to make this possibility empirically plausible in the light of current investigations in the psychology of language. Moreover, we suggest further directions for empirical research, whose eventual fruitfulness would be one mark in favor of our theory.

Part One   **The Theory**

Chapter One

Linguistic Communication: A Schema for Speech Acts

People don't speak merely to exercise their vocal cords. Generally, the reason people say what they say when they say it is to communicate something to those they are addressing. That is, in saying something a person has a certain intention, and the act of communicating succeeds only if that intention is recognized by the hearer. The intention is recognized partly on the basis of what is said, but only partly. What is said does not fully determine what the speaker is to be taken to be doing. If he says "I'm going to pay you back for that," he could be making a promise or issuing a threat. How does the hearer decide which? And how does the speaker know which way the hearer will take his utterance?

1.1. COMPONENTS OF SPEECH ACTS

Before taking up those questions, we need to distinguish the different aspects of a speech act. If S is the speaker, H the hearer, e an expression (typically a sentence) in language L, and C the context of utterance, the main constituents of S's speech act can be schematically represented as follows:

Utterance Act: S utters e from L to H in C.
Locutionary Act: S says to H in C that so-and-so.
Illocutionary Act: S does such-and-such in C.
Perlocutionary Act: S affects H in a certain way.[1]

These acts are intimately related. In uttering e, S says something to H; in saying something to H, S does something; and by doing something, S affects H. Moreover, the success of the perlocutionary act depends on H's identifying one of the other acts. Our problem is to specify as precisely as possible the nature of these acts as well as their relations to one another.[2]

Clearly there is more to a speech act than saying something (performing a locutionary act), but our preliminary characterization gives no indication of the difference between illocutionary and perlocutionary acts. Austin's distinction in terms of what is done *in* saying something and what is done *by* saying something (1962, lectures IX and X) is suggestive at best, since it does not explain the distinction it marks.[3] Illocutionary and perlocutionary acts can both produce effects on the hearer, but according to Austin (p. 116) a successful illocutionary act brings about "understanding of the meaning and of the force of the locution," that is, it secures *uptake*. Strawson (1964a, 459) suggests that for illocutionary acts, the effectiveness of the speaker's intention requires that the intention be recognized by the hearer: "The illocutionary force of an utterance is essentially something that is intended to be understood." That is, part of the speaker's intention is that the hearer identify the very act the speaker intends to be performing, and successful communication requires fulfillment of that intention.

In general, we cannot rely on our vocabulary of verbs of speech action to mark the distinction between illocutionary and perlocutionary acts. Although Austin's conception of the distinction is different from the one we wish to develop, he himself recognized that "the same word may genuinely be used in both illocutionary and perlocutionary ways and that many illocutionary acts are cases of trying to do some perlocutionary act" (1962, 145–146). For acts like ordering, warning, informing, and assuring, we must distinguish the ultimate perlocutionary effect the speaker is trying to achieve from the illocutionary effect of hearer uptake.

This and the next few chapters will be devoted largely to elaborating this conception of illocutionary acts as being performed with the intention that the hearer identify the very act being performed. In particular, since the hearer's primary, but not exclusive, basis for identifying the speaker's illocutionary intention is what the speaker says, we must spell out the connection between the locutionary and the illocutionary act, such that the hearer can reasonably be expected by the speaker to identify the illocutionary act being performed.

1.2. SIMPLE VERSION OF THE SPEECH ACT SCHEMA (SAS)

We view linguistic communication as an inferential process. The speaker provides, by what he says, a basis for the hearer to infer what the speaker intends to be thereby doing. However, what he says under-determines what he can reasonably expect to be taken to be intending. Suppose S says "I love you like my brother." There are various ways H could take this, depending on what he can infer S's intention to be under the circumstances, given what H believes about S and in particular what H believes S to believe H believes about S. Normally, H can assume that if S says "I love you like my brother," S means that he loves H as he (S) loves his own brother. But if a woman says to a man "I love you like my brother," the man can infer (taking himself to be intended to infer) that the woman has a feeling that is more familial than amorous. Perhaps, however, it is not the kind of love but the amount of love that is in question, as, for example, where two wartime buddies are involved. Or "I love you like my brother" might be uttered by one man to another where it is recognized that the speaker hates his brother. In this case H would no doubt take S as informing H that he hates him.

In general, the inference the hearer makes and takes himself to be intended to make is based not just on what the speaker says but also on *mutual contextual beliefs* (MCBs), as we call such salient contextual information. With the example "I love you like my brother," in one case the crucial MCB is that the woman does not have amorous feelings toward her brother, whereas in another it is that the speaker hates his brother. We call such items of information "beliefs" rather than "knowledge" because they need not be true in order to figure in the speaker's intention and the hearer's inference. We call them "contextual" because they are both relevant to and activated by the context of utterance (or by the utterance itself). And we call them "mutual" because S and H not only both have them, they believe they both have them and believe the other to believe they both have them.[4] The contextual beliefs that figure in speakers' intentions and hearers' inferences must be mutual if communication is to take place. Otherwise, it would not be clear to each that the other is taking this belief into account. For instance, if e is ambiguous and S is not punning or otherwise speaking ambiguously, only one meaning of e will be operative; only one will be intended by S to be recognized by H as relevant. Suppose S utters "I had the book stolen," intending to say that he (S) got someone to steal the book for him—a book that S wanted to acquire. For communication to succeed, H must recognize that that is what S intended to say, and not that S intended to say that S had the book stolen from him (S). To reasonably expect his utterance to be taken this way, S must believe not merely that he wanted to acquire the book but also that H believes this and believes that S believes this. And for H to take the utterance as it is intended, H must believe not only that S wanted to acquire the book but also that S believes this and believes that H believes this. Thus, if the belief that S wanted to acquire the book is mutual, S can reasonably intend H to take, and H can reasonably take, S's utterance as saying that S had someone steal the book.

In general, a mutual contextual belief figures in the speaker's intention and the hearer's inference in the following way: if p is mutually believed between S and H, then (1) not only do S and H believe p, but (2) each believes that the other takes it into account in his thinking, and (3) each, supposing the other to take p into account, supposes the other to take him to take it into account. Whether or not p is something previously believed by S and H (much less previously mutually believed), both S and H cannot but think of p, S in making his utterance and H in hearing it, and therefore each supposes that the other cannot fail to take it into account and also that the other cannot fail to suppose that he takes it into account.

The stolen book example illustrates how an MCB can be utilized by H to close the gap between what the speaker utters and what he says. An MCB can be utilized also to determine the intended type of illocutionary act being performed. An utterance of "I love you like my brother" might, depending on the context, have the force of an assurance, an admission, an answer (to a question), or even a promise. Or it might have merely the force of a simple assertion (and by "force" we simply mean 'illocutionary act type'). Whichever way it is to be taken, the speaker must intend the hearer so to take it on the basis of certain MCBs. For example, it might be intended (and be taken) as an assurance if S and H mutually believed that H doubts that S loves him. It would be intended and be taken as an answer if they mutually believed that H has just asked S how he feels about H.

In short, the hearer relies on, and is intended to rely on, MCBs to determine from the meaning of the sentence uttered what the speaker is saying, and from that the force and content of the speaker's illocutionary act. Accordingly, the inference H makes and is intended to make is of roughly the following form:

	Basis
L1. S is uttering e.	hearing S utter e
L2. S means such-and-such by e.	L1, MCBs
L3. S is saying that so-and-so.	L2, MCBs
L4. S is doing such-and-such.	L3, MCBs

Cast in this preliminary form this inference pattern constitutes what we call the *speech act schema* (SAS).

In addition to mutual contextual beliefs, there are two general mutual beliefs that the hearer relies on to make his inference. They are shared not just between S and H but among members of the linguistic community at large. Pervasive as they are, they may seem almost too obvious to mention, but must be included in the SAS. We call them the *linguistic presumption* (LP) and the *communicative presumption* (CP).

Linguistic Presumption (LP): The mutual belief in the linguistic community C_L that
i. the members of C_L share L, and
ii. that whenever any member S utters any e in L to any other member H, H can identify what S is saying, given that H knows the meaning(s) of e in L and is aware of the appropriate background information.

If the LP did not prevail in C_L, and between S and H in particular, then H could not assume that e means to S what it means to himself, and H could not assume that S assumes he (H) assumes this. Similarly, S could not reasonably intend to be saying that so-and-so to H in virtue of the fact that e means so-and-so to L. Thus, in addition to the first two lines of the SAS (L1 and L2), the LP is needed to license H's inference to L3 of the SAS. To license L4 we need the CP.

Communicative Presumption (CP): The mutual belief in C_L that whenever a member S says something in L to another member H, he is doing so with some recognizable illocutionary intent.

If H does not think the CP is operative in a given context—if, for instance, H thinks S is merely reciting a speech—then H has no reason to infer any particular illocutionary intent from what S utters. The CP does not help H determine what S's illocutionary intent is—H must rely on what S says and on the MCBs for that. The CP licenses only H's conclusion that S has some illocutionary intent or other. Accordingly, we may augment our provisional version of the SAS. S intends H to reason as follows:

	Basis
L1. S is uttering e.	hearing S utter e
L2. S means such-and-such by e.	L1, LP, MCBs
L3. S is saying to H that so-and-so.	L2, LP, MCBs
L4. S is doing such-and-such.	L3, CP, MCBs

In the following section we raise certain issues pertaining to the connection between what S says (L3) and what S means (L2) by what he utters (L1).[5] The relation between the locutionary act (L3) and the illocutionary act (L4) is discussed in section 1.4.

1.3. SAYING AND THE LINGUISTIC PRESUMPTION

Without mutually believing that they share the language they are using, people would not, and perhaps could not, use the language to communicate: the third step in the SAS (L3) would be blocked. Generally, this mutual belief between S and H arises from the linguistic presumption that prevails among members of the community at large. As a matter of social fact, the LP in a community is so strong that not to know the language is often a sign of nonmembership in the community. People presume that if you belong to the community, you know the language. So when S utters something e in L (the language in question), he expects H to understand it. Indeed he expects this not because he thinks H has heard e before or ever learned the meaning of e in particular, but because he thinks H knows L and will, by virtue of knowing L, understand e.[6] Thus, because the LP applies generally to communication situations in C_L, S and H mutually believe that each will understand almost anything in L uttered by the other; unless something happens to show that the LP does not apply, S and H are each in a position to reach L3 of the SAS, H to identify what S is saying and S to intend H to identify what he is saying.

Implicit in our discussion of the LP is the distinction between a group's having a language and their sharing that language. However improbable, a group of people could all have a language without mutually believing they do, in which case they probably would not use the language to communicate—no one would have any reason to believe he would be understood. Because of the distinction between having a language and sharing it, we cannot expect linguistic meaning to be explicated in social terms. It is logically possible for a person to know a language without ever having used it (or heard it used) to perform speech acts.[7] Although the concepts of a language, of knowing a language, and of sharing a language figure in the linguistic presumption (the mutual belief prevailing in a community that a certain language is known and shared), we need not ascribe theoretical understanding of these concepts to ordinary speakers, who, after all, are not philosophers or linguists. Intuitive understanding is enough for them. Though not pertinent here, characterizing what a language is and what it is to know one (linguistic competence) presents tough philosophical problems.

Recall that in the speech act schema, S's uttering a sentence e and the meaning of e are covered by L1 and L2, while what S says is left for L3. L2 is separate from L1 for two reasons: that S means anything at all by e—that S is doing anything over and above the act of uttering—requires further intentions; moreover, what S means by e may not be wholly determined by the semantics of e, since e may be ambiguous. So whereas S's act of uttering e is reported by direct quotation in L1 of the SAS, the operative meaning of e is given in L2. Because linguistic meaning does not in general determine reference, S's locutionary act is represented separately by L3, in the form of indirect quotation: S said that so-and-so. For this, references must be specified. The pattern of inference whereby H identifies what S says will be spelled out in chapter 2.

As familiar as indirect quotation is, so are the problems it gives rise to.[8] Nevertheless, we will provisionally assume that the notion of indirect quotation can be made philosophically acceptable enough to be used in the SAS. For present purposes let what S means by e be represented by a lacuna of undetermined form, "...," and let what S says in uttering e be represented by a dummy indicator for sentence type "*" and "p" for a proposition: "that *(...p...)." This notation is meant to indicate that what is said is a function of the intended meaning ("...") of the expression e. If e is declarative, then what is said may be specified by truth conditions. For other sentence types it may be feasible to generalize the notion of a truth condition and thereby allow a homogeneous semantics for natural languages and a single style of specification for what is said (see Stenius 1967, Lewis 1969, Strawson 1971, and Katz 1972). If e is imperative, the that-clause specifying what S says (that !(...p...)) is not itself imperative but of the form, "that H is to A."

As for interrogative sentences, there seem to be two options. On the one hand it could be argued that sentences like "What time is it?" do not express a proposition and their use is to be reported with "ask"—S asked (H) what time it is. In this view (Schiffer 1972, 114ff) interrogative sentences are conventional means for performing illocutionary acts of just one particular kind, namely, asking a question. If this is correct, then the locutionary step in the SAS ("S said that ...") is simply bypassed in the case of interrogatives, and indirect quotation will be of the form "*S* asked ... ." Nevertheless, such sentences need not be used literally (as when used rhetorically to make a statement) and so an adaptation of the SAS must allow for that. On the other hand it might be suggested (as by Katz 1977c, 205ff.) that what is said when *S* uses an interrogative expression like "What time is it?" is: that *H* is to tell *S* what time it is. In general, the form of the report will be: *S* says that *H* is to tell *S* ——, where the blank is filled in by some expression determined by *e*.[9] On this account questions would be a particular case of requests and would be performed normally via the schema. Since either account is compatible with our overall theory, we will leave the matter as it is for now.

1.4. LITERAL ILLOCUTIONARY ACTS

In the speech act schema L3 represents what the speaker says and L4 what he is thereby doing in saying it. Since the speaker might not be performing any illocutionary act at all, it is only on the presumption that he is (the CP) that the hearer will infer that the speaker is performing some illocutionary act or other. As for identifying what the act is, the hearer relies primarily on what is said, and we find the most straightforward relation between what is said and what is done when the speaker means what he says and nothing else. In this case he is speaking literally and what he does is largely determined by what he says.

Because of nonliteral and indirect illocutionary acts, the slogan "Meaning determines force" is generally false. It is most nearly correct in the case of literal acts—but not quite. Although *what* the speaker does might be determined by what he says, *that* he is performing any illocutionary act at all is not; he could be merely practicing his English or mechanically reciting some lines. Moreover, that he is speaking literally is not determined by what he says. If *S* says, for example, "The sun is shining on me today," he could be talking either about the weather or about his fortunes, depending on whether or not he is speaking literally. Inasmuch as he can use the same sentence literally or nonliterally, how he intends his utterance to be taken is not determined by what he says.

Even allowing for the fact that the meaning of what is uttered does not determine that some illocutionary act is being performed, much less that it is being performed literally, it is not always true that meaning determines the force of literal illocutionary acts. In general, the meaning merely delimits the force. For example, if someone says that he will return, whether he is making a promise or merely a statement of intention, his illocutionary act is literal. So the force (illocutionary act type) of an utterance need not be explicit to be literal. You do not have to say "I accuse . . ." to make an accusation. For that matter, you can use a performative verb nonliterally, as when posing a threat by saying "I promise."

Let us borrow Searle's (1969, 31) notation for representing an illocutionary act by "$F(P)$," where "F" represents the force and "P" the propositional content of the illocutionary act (lowercase "p" represents the proposition in the locutionary act). Now suppose that S utters e, which means '...', and thereby says that *(...p...). His act is *literal,* and represented by "$F*(...p...)$,"[10] just in case the proposition that P is the same as the proposition that p and the illocutionary force F of the utterance is *locutionary-compatible (L-compatible)* with the sentence type and meaning of e. Without giving a definition, we can introduce the notion of L-compatibility by examples. An utterance's being a prediction is L-compatible with the sentence used only if the sentence contains future time reference. If that sentence contains an action verb predicated of S, then the force of the utterance is L-compatible with the sentence whether the sentence is used to make a promise or a prediction.[11] An utterance's being a request or an order is L-compatible only with imperative sentences; analogously, an utterance's being a question is L-compatible only with interrogative sentences. If an utterance has a force L-incompatible with the mood and meaning of the sentence used, it is not literal. Notice that our characterization of literal utterances requires what the speaker says to be the same as what he F's, that is, that p be the same proposition as P. Even though an utterance of the sentence, "I am sorry for stepping on your toes," has the L-compatible force of an apology, the speaker can be apologizing nonliterally (say, for preempting the hearer's authority).

Using our notation we can reformulate our provisional version of the SAS. In so doing we will recast L4 in such a way that it is left open for further inference, whether or not S is speaking literally. S intends H to reason as follows:

	Basis
L1. S is uttering e.	hearing S utter e
L2. S means ... by e.	L1, LP, MCBs
L3. S is saying that *(...p...).	L2, LP, MCBs
L4. S, if speaking literally, is $F*$-ing that p.	L3, CP, MCBs

Only after we spell out the details of these steps and present our taxonomy of illocutionary acts will we be in a position to elaborate the SAS to include the further steps whereby H infers, as S intends him to infer, what illocutionary act is in fact being performed, be it literal or otherwise. As we will see, H relies on the *presumption of literalness* (PL):

Presumption of Literalness (PL): The mutual belief in the linguistic community C_L that whenever any member S utters any e in L to any other member H, if S could (under the circumstances) be speaking literally, then S is speaking literally.

If it is evident to H that S could not be speaking literally, H supposes S to be speaking nonliterally and seeks to identify what that nonliteral illocutionary act is.

1.5. THE COMMUNICATIVE PRESUMPTION AND ILLOCUTIONARY INTENTIONS

The communicative presumption is the mutual belief prevailing in a linguistic community to the effect that whenever someone says something to somebody, he intends to be performing some identifiable illocutionary act. We say "to the effect that" because, of course, people don't have the technical concept of illocutionary acts and therefore do not have beliefs, much less mutual beliefs, about illocutionary acts. But they do mutually believe that speakers speak with overt intentions, and this mutual belief figures in ordinary communication situations. People do rely on others to have identifiable intentions in their utterances, and they expect others to rely on them to have such intentions.

There are all sorts of effects a speaker can intend an utterance to have on the hearer. S may or may not intend H to recognize S's intention to produce a certain effect, and even if he does so intend, H's recognition of S's intention may be incidental to the production of that effect. In general, hearer recognition of perlocutionary intentions is incidental to the production of perlocutionary effects. Even in the special case where identification of the speaker's intention is necessary to the production of a perlocutionary effect—H might believe something or do something because and only because S wants him to—still there is a distinction between the hearer's recognizing that intention and its being fulfilled. The hearer might recognize what effect is intended without its being produced in him. What distinguishes illocutionary intentions, we suggest, is that their fulfillment consists in their recognition.

This general conception of illocutionary acts and intentions is shared by Searle and Strawson (in detail their views differ radically from ours). Searle (1969, 47) points out the connection between the fulfillment of illocutionary intentions and their recognition when, in contrasting illocutionary with perlocutionary acts, he says,

In the case of illocutionary acts we succeed in doing what we are trying to do by getting our audience to recognize what we are trying to do. But the 'effect' on the hearer is not a belief or a response, it consists simply in the hearer understanding the utterance of the speaker. It is this effect that I have been calling the illocutionary effect.

As Strawson puts it (1964, 459),

The understanding of the force of an utterance in all cases involves recognizing what may be called broadly an audience-directed intention and recognizing it as wholly overt, as intended to be recognized.

Their formulations help to spell out Austin's view that successful communication in performing an illocutionary act consists in uptake, that is, in the hearer identifying the illocutionary act being performed. Our later elaboration of the SAS will detail the pattern of inference by which this is accomplished, but first we must consider precisely what sort of intention is such that its fulfillment consists in its recognition. What sort of intention is distinctively illocutionary and communicative?

Both Searle and Strawson suggest that this intention is essentially reflexive and of the sort discovered by Grice (1957). According to Searle (1969, 43),

In speaking I attempt to communicate certain things to my hearer by getting him to recognize my intention to communicate just those things. I achieve the intended effect on the hearer by getting him to recognize my intention to achieve that effect.

Not just any way of achieving that effect will do. Hypnosis or electrical stimulation might "get" the hearer to recognize the speaker's intention, but for this recognition to be the effect of linguistic communication, it must be achieved by an inference from the speaker's utterance, and normally that is how it is accomplished.

Searle criticizes Grice's account of speaker meaning in terms of reflexive intention, that is, in terms of the intention "to produce some

effect in an audience by means of the recognition of this intention"
(Grice 1957, 385). Searle argues that the sorts of effects Grice mentions,
such as beliefs, intentions, and actions, are not produced by means of
recognition of the intention to produce them. For example, the hearer
might recognize that he is to believe something and yet refuse. These
sorts of effects are perlocutionary, and the speaker's illocutionary act,
whose identity he is trying to communicate, can succeed without the
intended perlocutionary effect (if there is one) being produced. So a
reflexive intention is involved in communication, just as Grice claimed,
but the kinds of intended effects he specified are not of the right sort.
Getting the hearer to recognize them does not constitute producing
them. In section 1.6 we consider just what sort of reflexive intention is
fulfilled merely by being recognized.

Grice's account of reflexive intentions in communication neglects the
role of the communicative presumption when the communication is
linguistic.[12] Grice focuses on nonlinguistic examples like drawing a
picture and deliberately frowning.[13] When people do things like these,
there is no presumption that they have a communicative intention, as
there is in the case of linguistic utterances. Because of the CP, when
somebody says something to someone, he cannot but expect—he need
not intend—the hearer to think he has some identifiable illocutionary
intention. Contrary to Grice's nonlinguistic cases, H's reason for
thinking S has some such intention is not that he has spotted anything
special in S's utterance but, because of the CP, merely that S has
uttered something linguistic. S realizes that H routinely assumes that
some recognizable intention is there, so no generic intention to be
performing some such act is necessary. Indeed, if S were mimicking
someone or rehearsing a line and thought this was not evident to H
(with the implicit understanding that the CP was inoperative), S would
have to have a special intention, one that he could reasonably expect H
to recognize, *not* to be performing a full-blown illocutionary act. After
all, being a presumption, the CP is operative unless there is indication
to the contrary (as ordinarily there is when people mimic or recite).

The difference between linguistic communication and Grice's nonlinguistic cases is the presence of a presumption that there is an inference to be drawn as to what the speaker is doing in issuing his
utterance. In Grice's examples part of what the audience has to infer is
that *there is an inference to be drawn*. The SAS, which includes the CP,
represents the nature of this inference for linguistic cases, and the
hearer implements this inference by recognizing what the speaker ut-

ters. That it is a sentence in a shared language is enough to implement the inference. So although reflexive intentions (R-intentions) are essential to linguistic communication, not just any sort of R-intention will do. Linguistic R-intentions are executed pursuant to the communicative presumption, and their fulfillment consists in their recognition. We must now consider what their content can be for this to be true.

1.6. ILLOCUTIONARY INTENTIONS AND EFFECTS

An illocutionary act is communicatively successful if the speaker's illocutionary intention is recognized by the hearer. These intentions are essentially communicative because the fulfillment of illocutionary intentions consists in hearer understanding. Not only are such intentions reflexive, their fulfillment consists in their recognition. Thus the intended effect of an act of communication is not just any effect produced by means of recognition of the intention to produce a certain effect, it is *the recognition of that effect*. There seems to be a reflexive paradox here, but in fact there is none. The effect, the hearer's recognizing the speaker's intention to produce that effect, is not produced by the hearer's recognizing that intention—that would be worse than a paradox, it would be a miracle. Rather, it is produced by the hearer's recognizing that the speaker has an intention to produce a certain effect in him that he is to identify (and thereby have produced in him) partly by recognizing S's intention to produce an identifiable effect. The hearer has to figure out what that intention—the intended effect—is, on the basis primarily of the speaker's utterance, along the lines of the SAS.

   Now what sorts of (intended) illocutionary effects—effects consisting in recognition of R-intentions—can there be? In other words, what can be the content of communicative intentions? It is a commonplace that linguistic communication consists in putting one's thoughts into words. This cliché is correct as far as it goes; the problem is to go further. In our view, to communicate is indeed to express a thought or, more generally, an attitude, be it a belief, an intention, a desire, or even a feeling; but in saying that to communicate is to express an attitude, we mean something very specific by "express."

Expressing: For S to *express* an attitude is for S to R-intend the hearer to take S's utterance as reason to think S has that attitude.

Accordingly, the intended illocutionary effect (or simply illocutionary intent) is for H to recognize that R-intention. In the taxonomy of communicative acts that we develop in chapter 3 many types of illocutionary acts are differentiated by types of attitudes expressed.

For now, consider a couple of simple and common types of illocutionary acts: statements and requests. In the case of statements the speaker expresses two attitudes: belief in a certain proposition and the intention that the hearer believe it as well. That is to say, for S's utterance of e to be a statement that P, S must R-intend H to take the utterance as reason to think (a) that S believes that P and (b) that S intends H to believe that P. Correlatively, for H to understand that S is stating that P in uttering e, H must take S's utterance of e as R-intended to be reason to think (a) and (b). For a statement to have been made and to be successful as an act of communication, it is not necessary that H actually think that S believes that P or that H believe that P himself. These would be perlocutionary effects of S's utterance and are not necessary for the success of the illocutionary act of stating. We might say, speaking loosely, that S's statement was unsuccessful (with respect to a further perlocutionary effect) unless H believed that P (presumably taking S to believe that P); but surely it would be correct to claim that S had successfully made a statement if H understood S's utterance of e, even if H didn't believe that P. It is sufficient that H recognize S's R-intention, S's expressed attitudes. This is what communication is about; anything more is more than just communication.

Similarly, for S's utterance to count as a request that H do A, S must R-intend H to take S's utterance as reason to think (a) that S desires H to do A and (b) that S intends H to do A because of S's desire. His request is successful as an act of communication if H recognizes S's R-intention. Again, anything more—H's actually doing A—is more than just communication.

1.7. PERLOCUTIONARY ACTS AND EFFECTS

Austin (1962, 101) introduces the notion of a perlocutionary act as follows:

Saying something will often, or even normally, produce certain consequential effects upon the feelings, thoughts, or actions of the audience, or of the speaker, or of other persons: and it may be done with the design, intention, or purpose of producing them . . . We shall call the performance of an act of this kind the performance of a *perlocutionary* act.

Since there is virtually no limit to the sorts of things that can result from speech acts—almost anything is possible, from insulting someone to starting a war—it would seem reasonable to restrict the category of perlocutionary acts in whatever ways seem theoretically appropriate. This is a matter of terminological stipulation, of course, but that does not make it arbitrary.

We propose first to limit perlocutionary acts to the *intentional* production of effects on (or in) the hearer. Our reason is that only reference to intended effects is necessary to explain the overall rationale of a given speech act. Utterance, locutionary, and illocutionary acts are all intentional and are generally performed with the primary intention of achieving some perlocutionary effect. To be sure, a speaker can insult, appease, disturb, or excite someone without intending to, but unless this is done intentionally, the fact that it is done does not help explain the speech act. In any case, the vocabulary of verbs of speech actions cannot be relied on to mark the distinction between illocutionary and perlocutionary acts.

We propose further to restrict perlocutionary acts to producing effects from steps of the speech act schema. In our preliminary version of the SAS these steps include the hearer's identification of L1, the utterance of *e;* L2, what *S* meant by *e;* L3, the locutionary act; and L4, the illocutionary act. We will be interested primarily in perlocutionary effects generated from L4, effects that rely on hearer uptake (of course their production involves more than uptake, more than recognition of the intention to produce them). Perlocutionary effects can be generated from other steps of the SAS as well. The utterance of certain words might be intended to offend someone just by their sound or their manner of pronunciation; or perhaps their meaning is what offends. And the locutionary act might have a distinctive perlocutionary effect, such as reminding the hearer of a person or event referred to. When we refine the SAS, we will see that there are other ways, corresponding to steps in the schema as elaborated, in which perlocutionary effects can be generated. For example, the very fact that an illocutionary act is performed nonliterally or indirectly might have a definite perlocutionary effect, such as protecting the hearer's feelings or making him suspicious.

This second restriction, construing as perlocutionary only those intended effects generated off of steps of the SAS, excludes all sorts of other speech acts, which we will survey in section 5.5: joking, manipulating, boring, interrupting, and so on. Some of these speech acts are essentially intentional, some even R-intentional. However, they do not work off of the SAS, and in some cases, such as in telling a joke, they presuppose the suspension of the communicative presumption.

Our characterization of the various aspects of speech acts as well as our formulation of the speech act schema itself should be taken as provisional. In the next chapter we spell out the details of each step as formulated thus far, thereby enabling us to refine our conception of locutionary acts. In chapter 3 we develop a taxonomy of communicative illocutionary acts, followed in chapter 4 by our full formulation of the SAS to cover nonliteral and indirect as well as literal illocutionary acts. In chapter 5, after the SAS is fully elaborated, we explain how it contributes to a philosophical analysis of linguistic communication and provides a framework for the psychological explanation of linguistic communication. The SAS is only a schema, however, and can do only so much. It represents the pattern of inference made by the hearer but it does not represent how the inference is made. In particular, even though mutual contextual beliefs are cited in various lines of the schema and are relied on by the hearer to go from one step to the next, the SAS is not equipped to predict which MCBs are activated and so cannot predict precisely how a given hearer will take a given utterance. Moreover, although it represents the pattern of inference in steps, thereby organizing the mass of information available to the hearer, in practice the hearer often works holistically, both looking ahead and backtracking as he goes along. Our examples often illustrate this, but we will not return to the status of the SAS as a whole until it is spelled out in detail.

Chapter Two

**Elaborating the Schema:
Locutionary Acts**

The locutionary act, the act of saying something, provides the hearer with the core of information from which to infer the speaker's illocutionary (communicative) intent. Other items of information contribute substantially to this identification, especially when S is speaking nonliterally or indirectly. But even when he is speaking literally, such that his illocutionary intent is made more or less explicit by what he says, his intent still has to be inferred by the hearer. Thus, a locutionary act is always distinct from any literal illocutionary act being performed, and until the hearer takes into account other information besides that provided by the locutionary act, all he can infer is what, if any, literal illocutionary act is being performed, as indicated in L4 of the SAS.

2.1. AUSTIN ON LOCUTIONARY ACTS

Austin distinguishes three aspects of the locutionary act.

To say anything is:
(A.a) always to perform the act of uttering certain noises (a 'phonetic' act), and the utterance is a phone;
(A.b) always to perform the act of uttering certain vocables or words, i.e. noises of certain types belonging to and as belonging to a certain vocabulary, in a certain grammar, with a certain intonation, &c. This act we may call a 'phatic' act; and
(A.c) generally to perform the act of using that [sentence] or its constituents with a certain more or less definite 'sense' and a more or less definite 'reference' (which together are equivalent to 'meaning'). This act we may call a 'rhetic' act. (1962, 92–93)

Unfortunately, there are two ways of taking the phrase "with a certain sense and reference" and thus two ways of taking the notion of a rhetic (hence of a locutionary) act. On one reading, the phrase identifies the

operative sense (and denotation) of expressions in case they are ambiguous; on the other it specifies what the speaker means and refers to by
the expressions used. The latter is probably what Austin had in mind
(pp. 114–115, note 1). Even though he did not draw the distinction
clearly, for Austin there is a major break between the phatic act and the
rhetic act, in that specification of the former entails no specification of
what the speaker meant, whereas the latter does. For one thing, identifying the operative sense (and attendant denotations) of the expressions in a sentence uttered does not guarantee that something was *said*
rather than, say, recited. Moreover, because few referring expressions
uniquely pick out particular referents solely in virtue of their meaning,
reference at the level of the phatic act does not in general determine
reference at the level of the rhetic act. Though Austin did not draw
his phatic/rhetic distinction quite right, he had the right ingredients:
the (operative) meaning of ambiguous expressions, what the speaker
meant, and the fixing of referents. But how should these be blended
into a more adequate formulation?

We will attempt to answer this question by spelling out how the
hearer reaches line L3 of the SAS, the step at which he identifies what
the speaker says. As provisionally formulated, the SAS runs as follows.
S intends H to reason:

	Basis
L1. S is uttering e.	hearing S utter e
L2. S means ... by e.	L1, LP, MCBs
L3. S is saying that *(...p...).	L2, LP, MCBs
L4. S, if speaking literally, is F*-ing that p.	L3, CP, MCBs

We will examine the details of the inference from one line to the next.
As we proceed, it should be understood that the speaker's intention
cannot realistically be supposed to include every such detail.

2.2. INFERRING OPERATIVE MEANING

Hearer H, at L1 of the SAS, realizes that S has uttered e.[1] Assuming S
meant anything at all by e, to reach L2 H must determine what S meant
by e, that is, the *operative meaning* of e. Since the linguistic presumption is in effect, H can reasonably suppose that S did mean something
by e and that this is something that e means in L, their shared language.
However, inasmuch as ambiguity is rampant in natural languages, H is

likely to need more than the LP and the identity of *e* to determine what
S meant by *e*. If *e* has two meanings in *L*, *H* has to make an inference of
the following form (how the lacunae are filled—the vexing problem of
representing linguistic meaning—will be discussed in section 8.1):

	Basis
L1. *S* is uttering *e*.	hearing *S* utter *e*
(a) *e* means ... and ____ in *L*.	knowledge of *L*
L2. *S* means ... by *e*.	L1a, LP, ?

Only if *e* is unambiguous can *H* infer L2 on the basis of what *e* means in
L, and even then he must assume, pursuant to the LP, that *S* takes *e* to
mean ... in *L*. Disambiguation is not required in the unusual case where
e is ambiguous but *S* intends both its meanings to be operative. Even
then *H* needs a basis for inferring that both of *e*'s meanings are indeed
operative.

   Consider the case, by far the most common, where *e* is ambiguous
but only one sense is operative. How does *H* infer which meaning is
operative? It would seem that he must reject all but one of the meanings
of *e* as contextually inappropriate and rely on certain mutual contextual
beliefs to do this. Accordingly, his inference would take the following
form:

	Basis
L1. *S* is uttering *e*.	hearing *S* utter *e*
(a) *e* means ... and ____ in *L*.	L1, knowledge of *L*
(b) *S* means ... by *e*, or *S* means ____ by *e*.	L1a, LP
(c) The supposition that *S* means ____ by *e* is contextually less appropriate.	L1b, MCBs
L2. *S* means ... by *e*.	L1b, L1c

We do not claim that contextual selection always represents a psychologically real process (see chapter 11), nor, where real, that selection
necessarily proceeds in just the sequence specified. Usually we seem
just to hear (or read) and understand the expression *e* in the contextually most appropriate way—which is why we often miss subtle puns.
Perhaps, then, the process of understanding an utterance involves
operations that make certain readings more probable, given certain
mutual contextual beliefs, and as hearers we often take these readings
as first hypotheses concerning what *S* meant by *e* unless (or until) they
are defeated by MCBs, future remarks, and so on. For instance, sup-

pose we are discussing a local airport's flight pattern across the university campus and I say "Flying planes sure can be dangerous." Given the supposition that I am being relevant, one of the things I might have meant by e is ruled out—discussing the hazards of piloting would have been irrelevant and would have changed the course of conversation in an illegitimate way (see chapter 4). This leaves the other reading as more plausibly operative. So what we are representing here is the information available to H and its general direction of flow, not the operations underlying H's use of the information. But what would be the structure of H's inference if he made it step by step?

To reach L1(a), H simply relies on his knowledge of L. To reach L1(b) he relies on the LP and supposes that S takes e to have just those meanings that in fact it has in L. Getting to L1(c), at which H must exclude certain meaning(s) of e as inappropriate, is more problematic. Of course, if e is unambiguous, this step is vacuous, and if S seems to mean both ... and _____ by e, this step is bypassed. But in the case of ambiguous expressions uttered with a single operative meaning, H must select one of the disjuncts from L1(b) as the operative one. As the flying planes example illustrates, under the circumstances of the utterance, H may have certain expectations or make certain judgments of appropriateness to decide which meaning of e is operative. If H's conception of the conversational situation is sufficiently determinate or his expectations of the direction of S's utterance sufficiently specific, H may not even go through the process of considering and discarding the inoperative meanings. In any case, if H's antecedent expectations do not settle the matter, then contextual appropriateness must, or H cannot but infer that S is speaking ambiguously. (We are being vague here about what contextual appropriateness is; this notion will be examined at length in our discussion of the illocutionary part of the SAS in chapter 4.)

As the intermediate steps from L1 to L2 are represented in the SAS, H takes for granted that whatever S means by e is one of the meanings of e in L. Or, rather, at L1(c) he does not reject all the meanings of e in L for being contextually inappropriate. Before concluding that the linguistic presumption is inoperative (very unlikely if the utterance occurs in the middle of a conversation), H will ask himself (in effect), "Does S think e means something different from what it means in L, or is he simply speaking nonliterally?" He has followed the SAS to the consequences of literality and, having ruled them out, searches for a nonliteral interpretation of S's utterance. If he can find no such interpretation, he may backtrack to L1(b) and consider the possibility of S's being mistaken about the meanings of e in L. To illustrate how complicated these matters can get, imagine a case like the following, in which S utters "The vote was anonymous." H has four distinct options:

(1) a. S thinks e has the meaning 'It was a secret ballot' in English, S was speaking literally, and this is what he was saying (literal meaning).
b. S was speaking sarcastically, not literally, and was nonliterally stating that it was a public vote (nonliteral meaning).
c. S (mistakenly) thinks "anonymous" means 'unanimous,' and, if speaking literally, was saying that everyone voted for it (false linguistic belief).
d. S meant to utter "unanimous" and to say that everyone voted for it (slip of the tongue).

Such lines of inference can converge, in which case it will not matter which route the hearer has taken. In this example it does not matter which of (1c) or (1d) was followed; the result is the same.

Since we have been concerned with the inference from what the speaker utters to what he means by it under the circumstances, we have looked at the meanings of e from H's point of view. In the example, H's option (1c) involves attributing to S a false belief about the meaning of what he uttered. The reverse can occur too, as is evident if we take S's point of view. Suppose S believes that H takes e to mean ... but does not himself believe that. S can still communicate linguistically by playing along with H's linguistic belief, which he (S) takes to be mistaken. If S is correct about H's belief about e, H won't know the difference and will infer the operative meaning of e even though e has no such meaning in L. Finally, S and H can mistakenly, though mutually, believe that e means ... in L. Perhaps S is the parent of H so that H acquired S's linguistic misconceptions. In such a case neither S nor H would know the difference: S would mean ... by e even though e does not mean ... in L; H would take e to mean ... in L and infer that S means ... by e; and nothing would occur to suspend the linguistic presumption.[2] These various cases in which there is a discrepancy between the operative meaning of e and what e means in L seem to be cases of genuine communication. This being understood, as presented so far the SAS represents only the normal case where what S means by e is one of the meanings of e in L.

2.3. INFERRING LOCUTIONARY ACTS

Hearer H, at L2 of the SAS, has inferred that S means ... by e. From this together with the LP and various MCBs, H must infer that S is saying that *(...p...):

L2. S means ... by e.
L3. S is saying that *(...p...).   L2, LP, MCBs

At L3, H is able to determine *that* something is being said and to identify *what* is being said. Since the LP sanctions the first part of this inference, our problem is to show how the second part works. That is, what is the pattern of inference by which H identifies what S is saying?

To identify what is said is to identify sentence type and propositional content. Three things determine propositional content: operative meaning(s), referent(s), and time(s) specified. On this initial account, to identify what is said would be to identify (in addition to sentence type) what referent(s) are being ascribed what properties (or relations) at what time(s). It is clear that H's knowing the language L and believing that S means ... by e suffices to fix:

1. which type the sentence is (⊢, ?, !),
2. which parts of e can be used to *refer* (the referring expressions in e),
3. which parts specify *times,*
4. the *senses* of the referring expressions,
5. the *properties* and *relations* being ascribed.

Since these are determined by what S means by e, all that is left for H to identify in order to determine what S said is the type of saying (corresponding to the sentence type), the objects being referred to, and the times being specified. With regard to times—except for tenses, whose contribution to what is said H can determine relative to the occasion of utterance—temporal descriptions, pronouns, and adverbs can be subsumed for our purposes under the heading of referring expressions. Accordingly, given that the items listed are fixed by what H takes to be the operative meaning of e, what remains for H to identify in order to determine what S said are sentence type and references.

2.3.1. Sentence Type and Type of Saying

Since sentence type contributes in a regular way to what is said, we adopt the following form for representing this contribution:

Declarative e:
S is saying that ⊢(...p...);
S is saying that it is the case that (...p...).

Imperative e:
S is saying that !(...p...);
S is saying that H is to make it the case that (...p...).

Yes/No Interrogative e:
S is saying that ?(...p...);
S is asking (or saying that H is to tell S) whether or not it is the case that (...p...).

Wh Interrogative e:
S is saying that ?(...Wh-x p...);
S is asking (or saying that H is to tell S) (...Wh-x p...).

For Wh interrogatives, the symbol Wh-x next to p schematizes the identity of the x being questioned. Thus "Who" in "Who discovered the calculus?" becomes: the identity of the person x such that x(discovered the calculus). Putting this all together yields the following locutionary specification: in uttering "Who discovered the calculus?" S is asking (or saying that H is to tell S) the identity of the person x such that x discovered the calculus.

2.3.2. Reference

To identify the referent(s) is to identify what S intends to be referring to. But how does H use the presumptions and MCBs to recognize S's referential intent? The main devices S uses to signal his referential intent are descriptions, pronouns, and proper names, but in general their linguistic meaning does not determine their reference. For each type of referring expression we describe the pattern of inference H makes to identify the referent.

Definite Descriptions
Suppose S utters something of the form: "The so-and-so is . . ."[3] H will be expected to search his memory or the context for some relevant referent that is so-and-so and that can reasonably be thought to be what S intends to pick out. In terms of the SAS:

L1. *S* is uttering "The so-and-so is ..."

L2. (a) *S* means 'some definite so-and-so is ...' by *e*.

(b) "The so-and-so" is a definite referring expression in English. knowledge of *L*

(c) In uttering *e*, *S* intends to pick out some definite *x*.
L2(b), LP

(d) In uttering *e*, *S* intends to pick out some definite *x* that is so-and-so.
L2(a), L2(c), PL

(e) The so-and-so *S* intends to pick out is the such-and-such.[4]
L2(d), MCBs

(f) In uttering *e*, *S* is saying of the such-and-such, under the description of being so-and-so, that it is ...
L2(e), LP

L3. In uttering *e*, *S* is saying that the so-and-so (namely, the such-and-such) is ...
L2(f), LP

The schema now allows for a variety of referential possibilities for descriptions. Line L2(a) allows for different uses of the definite article as contrasted in:

(2) a. The asteroids are small planets. (specific)
   b. The children are asleep. (specific)
(3) a. The Turks invaded Vienna. (nonspecific)
   b. The Chinese have known about porcelain for three thousand years. (nonspecific)
(4) a. The owl is nocturnal. (generic)
   b. The kiwi is extinct. (generic)

In (2a) "the asteroids" is used to refer to the totality of asteroids, whereas in (2b) "the children" is used to refer to a certain group of children (determinable in the context). In both cases it is clear which particular entities are being referred to and which are not. In (3a) context does not help to determine which Turks "the Turks" is used to refer to. An analogous point applies to (3b), and matters are further complicated, in ways we will not take up here, by the fact that no individual Chinese has known anything for three thousand years. Finally, in (4a) a certain *type* of animal is being referred to, and as (4b) makes clear, referring to a type is not equivalent to referring to all the individuals of that type.

Lines L2(d)–L2(f) allow for nonliteral as well as literal uses of descriptions.[5] For instance, S might observe that the last (adult) guests at a party have passed out in the backyard after making fools of themselves and say to H "The children are asleep," intending H to infer that S is saying that the remaining guests are asleep:

L1. S is uttering "The children are asleep."

L2. (a) S means 'The children are sleeping' by "The children are asleep."

(b) 'The children' is a definite referring expression of English.

(c) In uttering "The children are asleep" S intends to pick out some definite x's.

(d) There are no children (so-and-sos) for S to be referring to.

(e) Since the guests were acting like children, the x's S intends to pick out are the remaining guests (the such-and-suches).

(f) In uttering "The children are asleep," S is saying of the remaining guests, under the description of being children, that they are asleep.

L3. In uttering "The children are asleep," S is saying that the children (namely, the remaining guests) are asleep.

S is not saying *that* the remaining guests are asleep but saying *of* the remaining guests, referred to as children, that they are asleep.

Pronouns

We deal here only with personal pronouns in their simplest uses. A comprehensive account would cover demonstrative and relative pronouns, and such phenomena as ostensive and cross reference. Suppose S utters something of the form: "She is . . ." As with descriptions, H will be expected to search his memory or the context for the relevant referent. In terms of the schema:

L1. S is uttering "She is ..."

L2. (a) S means 'some female is ...' by "She is ..."

(b) "She" is a singular definite referring expression in English.

(c) In uttering e, S intends to pick out some definite x.

(d) In uttering e, S intends to pick out some definite female.

(e) In uttering e, S intends to pick out the female who is so-and-so.

L3. In uttering e, S is saying that some definite female (namely, the so-and-so) is ...

As with descriptions, the schema accommodates various uses of the pronoun, for example, "she" used to refer to inanimate objects such as boats or, nonliterally, to males. By providing parameters for speaker and hearer, the schema is able to represent some uses of the pronouns "I" and "You":

(5) a. In uttering "I like you," *S* is saying (to *H*) that *S* likes *H*.
   b. In uttering "Leave the room!" *S* is saying (to *H*) that *H* is to leave the room.
   c. In uttering "What time is it?" *S* is saying (to *H*) that *H* is to tell *S* what time it is.

Proper Names
Suppose *H* hears an expression of the form: "Sam is . . ." *H* will be expected to search his memory or the context for the relevant referent. Inasmuch as proper names lack descriptive content, do they have all of the flexibility of use exhibited by descriptions? What would count as a nonliteral use of a proper name? Perhaps using a name to refer to something it was not the name of. Of course, unless the connection between the object and its pseudoname can be inferred, communication will break down. But if, say, *S* and *H* mutually believe that Sam considers himself to be something of a renaissance man, *S* might utter "Here comes Leonardo," intending *H* to infer that *S* is referring to Sam.

We have completed our schematic look at the inference from what is meant by *e* to what is said. We have made no attempt to deal with the various technical problems generated by particular sorts of referring expressions, such as definite descriptions, personal pronouns, demonstrative pronouns, temporal adverbs, and proper names. Our concern here has been simply to lay out the general pattern of inference from what is meant by *e* to what is said. *H*'s identification of the operative meaning of *e* fixes the operative senses, the predications, and the sentence type. From these, together with mutual contextual beliefs, *H* is to identify what *S* said. That is a matter of determining the type of saying (from the sentence type), time specifications,[6] and what referents under which descriptions are ascribed the properties (and relations) predicated.

2.4. SAYING THAT

There are three constraints on a correct account of L3 in the SAS: (i) the account must render L3 determinable from L2; (ii) since L3 represents the hearer's identification of what the speaker has said, the account should accord with how "said that" is commonly ascribed; and (iii) it must provide an adequate basis for the hearer to reach line L4 of the SAS ("S, if speaking literally, is F^*-ing that p"). We have seen already how (i) is met and in the next section the SAS will be developed so as to meet (iii). But before going further, we should look into (ii) in order to clarify how the hearer specifies what the speaker says.

One problem is that there are two ways of taking said-that sentences: as *referentially opaque* or as *referentially transparent*. When such a sentence is taken opaquely, it makes a difference which referring expressions are used within the scope of "said that." For example, if S utters "The inventor of Yo-Yos died happy," thereby saying that the inventor of Yo-Yos died happy, it is false, on the opaque construction, that S said that the inventor of parking meters died happy, even though the inventor of Yo-Yos also invented parking meters. Even if H were aware of this curious fact, he would not regard S as having said that the inventor of parking meters died happy—though that is nevertheless true if "said-that" is taken transparently. Fortunately, ambiguity can be avoided if "said of" is used instead of the transparent "said that." Thus, H could describe S as having said *of* the inventor of parking meters (whom S referred to as the inventor of Yo-Yos) that he died happy.

The SAS seems to require that "said that" be taken opaquely. Suppose the speaker utters "The man with a martini is a famous poet," where the description is being used to pick out a specific man (S has him in sight). If the man (with a martini) is in fact an unknown poet, it would be incorrect to use (6a), taken opaquely, rather than (6b), to report what S said.

(6) a. S said that the obscure poet with a martini is a famous poet.

b. S said, of the obscure poet with a martini, that he is a famous poet.

For the purposes of the SAS however, (6b) is unhelpful in that it does not reflect S's point of view, which H is presumably trying to represent. Accordingly, we should restrict the specification of what is said by letting the *sense* of the referring expressions play a role in determining what is said. Thus "the present king of Sweden" could be replaced by "the present male monarch of Sweden" but not by "King Gustav." The restriction of H's ascription of "said that" to the opaque interpretation not only seeks to capture S's point of view, it records information that could well affect illocutionary force. Compare (6a) with (6c):

(6) c. S said that the schmuck over there with a martini is a famous poet.

In general, H determines what is said by identifying the operative meanings of the predicates, the operative senses of the referring expressions, the time specifications and the referents (if any), together with sentence type. Problem cases come to mind, many of which are presently the subject of intense philosophical inquiry. Since judgments on them are varied (both between persons and between cases), the following remarks should not be taken as conclusive. Indeed, we will find some special cases in which it is not clear at all what the speaker said.

False Descriptions
Again suppose S utters "The man with a martini is a famous poet." But this time, unbeknownst to S, the man's glass contains nothing but water. Surely S said *of* that man that he is a famous poet, but did S say *that* the man with a martini is a famous poet? So far, the theory does not predict anything specific because we have not yet defined the operative senses of referring expressions. Are they the descriptive content of the referring expressions? The descriptions S believes are true of the referents? Descriptions S believes H thinks are true of the referents? We take "said that" to report the senses of the referring expressions (in this case the descriptive content of the description) as well as the things referred to by S with each of these expressions, but it is not required that these senses *determine* the objects referred to. Thus S is free to pick whatever referring expressions best suit his immediate conversational objectives; in particular, he is free to pick descriptions he believes to be false of the referents. He might believe, for example, that H believes them to be true of the referents. Or he might have reason to expect that H, though also believing them to be false of the referents (perhaps also believing S to believe that), will make the right

identifications. In such case H can still use the description to identify the referents, and nothing in the schema precludes this. Indeed, the schema demands this. Consider the case where S utters the sentence about the man with a martini, believing that the man is drinking water but thinking H believes it is a martini. If S does not want to bother mentioning that the man is drinking water, S can say what he wants to say by exploiting H's false beliefs. In general, the requirement is that H, in representing what S says, pick out the referents in the way he thinks he is intended to.

Proper Names
Suppose that speaker S utters the sentence "The Morning Star is really a planet." Did S say that Venus is really a planet? Suppose S utters the sentence "Venus is really a planet." Did S say that the Morning Star is really a planet? Our account can make no prediction without an account of the sense of proper names and a way of determining which expressions are functioning as proper names. Is H to infer that "the Morning Star" is functioning as a proper name? As a description? As both? And does the language, the speaker, or both determine this? These are hard questions and we have no general doctrine of proper names. However one thing does seem relatively clear. If by "sense" of a referring expression one means 'descriptive content," then proper names do not have sense. But if by "sense" one means 'that which determines reference,' then nonvacuous names would appear to have sense—after all, something must determine their reference; surely there is some sort of connection between such words and things.[7]

So far we have left "sense" open between these two interpretations because it was not clear which conception is required by the ordinary use of "said that." In order to proceed we will adopt the safest policy, one that licenses an identification of what was said only under the most restricted circumstances. The schema may fail to reflect some legitimate inferences, but it will rarely legitimate bad ones. We will assume that proper names have no descriptive content but that they do have something that contributes to their reference potential, and we will call this their sense. However, since what connects a name to an object will usually involve the name itself (there being no meaning), reporting what was said in the utterance of a proper name will require use of the same name or one with the same connections to the referent for the speaker. Any shift in the report from one name to a name not connected in the same way to the same object for the original speaker will be a change in what is said. Thus, the answer to our questions regarding "Venus" and "the Morning Star" is no.

In our earlier Leonardo example, it is unclear what the speaker said in uttering "Here comes Leonardo." If he did not say that there came Leonardo (he was referring to Sam), did he say that there came Sam?

Vacuous Terms

Suppose that speaker S utters "The largest prime number is larger than 100." Since nothing satisfies the description "largest prime number" and there is no contextual clue as to what else might be referred to, what has S said, if anything at all? The same question can be posed for vacuous proper names. Suppose that S utters "Santa Claus lives at the North Pole." What did S say, if anything?

Our account does not yet predict these cases. Furthermore, it is not clear how determinate our pretheoretic use of "said-that" is in such cases. However, if what is said can be a bearer of truth values, then it might be supposed that what was said with the vacuous description can be specified in terms of Russell's (1905) theory of descriptions: there is just one number that is the largest prime and it is larger than 100. How about vacuous proper names? Both ordinary usage and the theory of truth leave that case unsettled.

Pronouns

Suppose that S utters "He is a conservative" referring to William F. Buckley. Did S say that Buckley is a conservative? Suppose S utters "William F. Buckley is a conservative." Did S say that he (referring to Buckley) is a conservative? Surely in the first case S said *of* Buckley that he is a conservative, but did S say *that* Buckley is a conservative?

On the assumption that pronouns like "he," "she," "them," "it," and so on, do have (minimal) descriptive content as their sense, our account predicts that such shifts from proper names to pronouns change what is said. So the answer to our questions is no.

Mistaken Linguistic Beliefs

Suppose that speaker S utters "The milkman is erotic" thinking "erotic" means 'erratic.' Did S say that the milkman was easily aroused (or whatever)? We think not, but this causes no problem for the schema. Although the linguistic basis for the inference to L2 of the SAS is intended to be the hearer's (shared) knowledge of the language, in this case the hearer cannot succeed on this linguistic basis alone. In this case the hearer must rely on another fact as well, that S thinks "erotic" means 'erratic.' What the speaker said is determined as usual by the operative meaning of what was uttered, although that was not one of its meanings in L.

Mistaken Factual Beliefs

Suppose that speaker S, thinking that whales are fish and not mammals, utters "That's not a boat, it's a huge fish that is attacking." Even if H knows better, he could still rightly regard S as having said that a whale was coming.

Nonliteral Utterances

Suppose that S utters "Mac is a fine friend" with obvious insincerity. Did S say that Mac is a fine friend? The answer is complicated. If there is no intonational difference between this utterance and the sincere case, then it seems that S did say that Mac was a fine friend, though again he did not mean it, does not believe it, would not be fairly represented as having committed himself to the truth of it. If, on the other hand, there is an intonational clue to the sarcastic reading, it seems that such an utterance *means* the opposite of what it means without the change of intonation, and so the speaker may well have *said* that Mac was a scoundrel (or whatever). We see no reason to deny that there are characteristic sarcastic intonation contours with semantic effects.

Slips of the Tongue

Suppose speaker S utters "The vote is anonymous," intending to say that the vote is unanimous. Did S say that the vote is anonymous? Yes, but surely, as one might ordinarily remark, he did not mean it (that is, intend to say it). It would be misleading but true to report S as saying that the vote is anonymous without adding some rider to the effect that S intended to say that the vote is unanimous, but has misspoken. For the purposes of the SAS, at any rate, the hearer could make the appropriate adjustment if he recognized what S intended to utter.

Illocutionary Adverbials

An interesting problem for our account of saying is illustrated by an utterance of "Frankly, Bruckner bores me." S is saying at least that Bruckner bores him, but we cannot readily describe him as saying that frankly Bruckner bores him. The reason is that "frankly" does not modify the content of what S is saying but rather his assertion of it. We discuss such illocutionary adverbials in chapter 10.

We may conclude that except for the troublesome cases just mentioned, which generate special problems to be taken up later, what the hearer identifies as represented at line L3 of the SAS is just what would ordinarily be described as "what the speaker said."

2.5. DETERMINING LITERAL ILLOCUTIONARY FORCE POTENTIAL FROM LOCUTIONARY ACTS

At L3 of the SAS, H has inferred that S is saying that *(...p...). How does H infer L4 from L3?

L3. S is saying that *(...p...).
L4. S, if speaking literally, is F*-ing that p.

In other words, what can H infer about any illocutionary act being *literally* performed in the utterance of e? If S is speaking literally, then what S says delimits what his illocutionary act can be, but in general it does not fully determine what that act is. Indeed, it is possible (if the communicative presumption is not in effect) for S to be performing no illocutionary act at all.

In section 1.4 we characterized an illocutionary act as performed literally when the (propositional) content of the locutionary act and illocutionary act are the same, and the illocutionary act type is L-compatible with the sentence type and meaning of e. Because of the connection we have established in section 2.3 between the sentence type and meaning of e and the locutionary act performed in uttering e, we can view L-compatibility simply as a relation between illocutionary and locutionary acts. A certain type of illocutionary act is L-compatible with a given locutionary act only when S has the right sort of communicative intent. Specifically, it is required that

Compatibility Condition (CC):
i. If S is saying that ⊢(...p...), S is expressing the belief that p;
ii. If S is saying that !(...p...), S is expressing the desire that H make it the case that p; and
iii. If S is saying that ?(...p...), S is expressing the desire that H tell S whether or not p.

We will use the phrase "*S* is expressing attitude *A* *(...*p*...) to schematize the connections set down in this definition. In chapter 3 we propose a detailed taxonomy of communicative illocutionary acts in terms of types of expressed attitudes. Various subtle distinctions are drawn there, but the general types of expressed attitudes mentioned in the compatibility condition will suffice for present purposes. We can say that an illocutionary act type *F* is L-compatible with a given locutionary act of saying that *(...*p*...) if the attitude expressed in *F*-ing, as specified in the taxonomy, meets the compatibility condition. From this we get a natural definition of the literal performance of an illocutionary act:

Literal Performance (Lit): *S*'s *F*-ing that *P* in saying that *(...*p*...)
is literal just in case:
i. *P* = (...*p*...), and
ii. *F*-ing is L-compatible with saying that *(...*p*...).

In the schema it is convenient to represent literally performed illocutionary acts with the notation: *F**-ing that *p*. The hearer's inference from L3 to L4 of the SAS can accordingly be represented for the case of declarative utterances, for example, as follows:

L3. *S* is saying that ⊢(...*p*...).

    (a) If *S* is speaking literally, *S* is expressing the belief that *p*.
    L3, CC

    (b) If *S* is speaking literally, *S* is asserting that *p*, or otherwise *F**-ing that *p*.
    L3(a), Lit

L4. *S*, if speaking literally, is asserting that *p*.
    L3(b), CP, MCBs

It should be clear that L4 might well have different content if *H* had a different hypothesis at L3(b), for example, the hypothesis that *S* was making a suggestion rather than an assertion: different types of illocutionary acts could be literally performed in saying that *(...*p*...).

    Consider some sample sentences. Suppose that:

(7) a. In uttering "John will close the door" *S* is saying that it will be the case that John closes the door.
    b. In uttering "Close the door" *S* is saying that *H* is to close the door.[8]

    c. In uttering "Did John close the door?" *S* is asking (or saying that *H* is to tell *S*) whether or not John closed the door.

Looking ahead to the taxonomy we develop in the next chapter, we can see, considering sentence type alone, which illocutionary acts are L-compatible with each of these sayings. In particular, only certain constatives[9] and commissives are L-compatible with *S*'s saying (7a), only certain directives are L-compatible with *S*'s saying (7b), and only questions (a subtype of directives) are L-compatible with *S*'s saying (7c). Considerations involving propositional content (what is said) further narrow down the set of L-compatible illocutionary acts. Performing a predictive, not a retrodictive, is L-compatible with (7a), because a predictive requires future time reference, a retrodictive past time reference. Some commissives (for example, acts of swearing that) are L-compatible with (7a), but others (such as surrendering, inviting, bidding, and volunteering) are not. Having inferred that *S* is saying that it will be the case that John closes the door, *H* is still free (linguistically) to infer that *S* is doing any one of a number of different illocutionary acts. These include predicting, guessing, informing, confirming, conceding, assenting, replying, suggesting, and guaranteeing. To infer which one *S* was performing, *H* needs more information than is available from what *S* has said. These remarks hold true, mutatis mutandis, for (7b) and (7c) as well. L-compatible with *S*'s saying that *H* is to close the door are requesting, demanding, and ordering, but not stating, prohibiting, promising, or congratulating. Moreover, questioning, querying, and inquiring, but virtually no other illocutionary act named in our taxonomy, are L-compatible with *S*'s asking *H* whether or not John closed the door. Finally, it should not be thought that only word order and propositional content contribute to compatibility, for such things as performative verbs and intonation contribute as well. We have very little to say at the moment about intonation,[10] and we discuss the special problem of performatives in chapter 10.

    We will call the linguistic side of L-compatibility *force-determinacy* (F-determinacy). An expression *e* is F-determinate with respect to a particular type *F* of illocutionary act just in case if *S* utters *e* and performs some illocutionary act literally, then *S* is *F*-ing. Notice that a sentence, on a reading, can be more F-determinate than the sentence taken simpliciter. Consider the sentence "I will pay you back (for that)." F-determinacy depends on meaning, but the operative meaning of this sentence can be any of the following:

(8) a. I intend to repay you.
   b. It will be the case that I repay you.
   c. I intend to get even with you.
   d. It will be the case that I get even with you.

Our original sentence is at best constative-or-commissive determinate in virtue of the fact that each of its readings is compatible with a variety of constatives and a variety of commissives.

2.6. CONCLUSION

We have spelled out the pattern of inference H makes in order to identify what S says in uttering something and thereby to determine its literal illocutionary force potential. Schematized as a whole, this phase of the inference goes as follows:

	Basis
L1. S is uttering e.	hearing S utter e
(a) e means ... and ____ in L.	L1, knowledge of L
(b) S means ... or ____ by e.	L1(a), LP
(c) The supposition that S means ____ by e is contextually less appropriate.	L1(b), MCBs
L2. S means ... by e.	L1(b), L1(c)
(a) e contains referring expression(s) R,	knowledge of L
(b) In using R, S is referring to the such-and-such(s).	L2, L2(a), MCBs
L3. S is saying that *(...p...).	L2, L2(b), LP
(a) If S is speaking literally, S is expressing attitude A *(...p...).	L3, CC
(b) If S is speaking literally, S is F^*-ing that p, or ...	L3(a), Lit
L4. S, if speaking literally, is F^*-ing that p.	L3(b), CP, MCBs

The substeps of these inferences need not be specifically intended by S. Rather, they comprise typical patterns of inference that hearers actually make. Only the numbered lines figure in what S needs to intend if he is to communicate linguistically.

In the first section of this chapter, we were left with a certain ambiguity in Austin's characterization of locutionary acts, as exemplified by the phrase, "uttering a sentence with a certain sense and reference." At L2 of the schema, what S means by e is one of the meanings of e in L, as specified at L1(a). At this stage uttering e with a certain sense and reference is merely to intend a certain one of its meanings to be operative and for the referents of its referring expressions to be delimited accordingly. Nothing is yet entailed about what the speaker is saying, which is represented by L3. Only there is it inferred what S is referring to, generally in a way much more determinate that the way referring expressions refer (as a consequence of their senses). So we can resolve the ambiguity in Austin's formulation by letting locutionary acts be represented by L3. Whatever else fits his ambiguous characterizations falls under earlier steps or substeps of the SAS and consequently gets accounted for without being included in the locutionary act itself.[11]

Certain philosophical and linguistic issues remain. For instance, what are the different types of meaning alluded to in the steps from L1 to L2, and how are they to be specified? What is the nature of such phenomena as implication and presupposition, which are closely connected to what is said but are not part of what is said? These issues will be taken up in chapter 8. In the next chapter we develop our taxonomy of communicative illocutionary acts.

Chapter Three   **A Taxonomy of**
                                 Communicative
                                 Illocutionary Acts

Types of illocutionary acts are distinguished by types of illocutionary
intents (intended illocutionary effects). Since illocutionary intents are
fulfilled if the hearer recognizes the attitudes expressed by the speaker,
types of illocutionary intents correspond to types of expressed attitudes. Accordingly, we will classify types of illocutionary acts in terms
of types of expressed attitudes. This will enable us to integrate our
taxonomy with the SAS.

To *express* an attitude in uttering something is, in our conception, to
R-intend that the hearer take one's utterance as reason to believe one
has the attitude. The speaker need not have the attitude expressed, and
the hearer need not form a corresponding attitude. The speaker's having the attitude expressed is the mark of sincerity, but illocutionary or
communicative success does not require sincerity. If the hearer forms a
corresponding attitude that the speaker intended him to form, the
speaker has achieved a perlocutionary effect in addition to illocutionary uptake.

Individuating communicative illocutionary acts in terms of expressed
attitudes leaves ample room for a rich diversity of act types. In most
cases the speaker expresses not only his own (putative) attitude toward
the propositional content but also his intention that the hearer form a
corresponding attitude. For example, to inform someone of something
is not only to express a belief in it but also to express one's intention
that the hearer believe it. Act types are further differentiated by the
reasons for or the strengths of the attitudes expressed. For example,
what we call "confirmatives" are distinguished from assertions generally by *S*'s expressing his belief as being the result of some truth-
seeking procedure. And within the class of what we call "advisories,"
the difference between urging someone to do something and merely

suggesting he do it is marked by the difference in strength in S's expressed intention or desire that H do it. Finally, some act types are picked out by expressed attitudes concerning the context or occasion of utterance: an answer is R-intended to be taken as a response to a question; an apology is R-intended to be taken as occasioned by the speaker's having done some regrettable thing to the hearer. As we develop the taxonomy in detail, just how these various dimensions of expressed attitudes determine illocutionary act types will be made clear and concrete.

Many taxonomies of illocutionary acts have been proposed, but we will not discuss or compare all of them. Austin's original scheme (1962, Lecture XII) included a rich variety of illocutionary act types, but, as Searle (1975b) has argued, there are no clear principles by which Austin collected them into his five classes. All subsequent taxonomies[1] are attempted improvements on Austin's, but only Searle's is tied to a general theory of illocutionary acts. We agree with Searle that a scheme of classification should be principled. Its categories should not overlap[2]—at least not beyond what can be expected from the nature of the subject—and the entries in each category should satisfy the criteria for belonging to that category. Moreover, to be of theoretical interest the scheme's bases of classification must be tied to some systematic account of illocutionary acts.

The fundamental idea behind our taxonomy is that the illocutionary intents, or expressed attitudes, by which types of illocutionary acts are distinguished are all homogeneous with the speech act schema. That is, the SAS represents the general form of illocutionary intention and inference, and the entries in the taxonomy provide the content, as is evident in the concluding step of the SAS: the identification of the illocutionary act being performed. Since such acts are identified by their intents (H's recognition of S's expressed attitudes), the distinguishing features of each illocutionary act type specify the very thing H must identify in the last step of the SAS.

A more obvious merit (we hope) of our taxonomy is its comprehensiveness and explicitness. It covers a great many types of illocutionary acts in detail, not only labeling them but specifying what distinguishes them. We divide illocutionary acts into six general categories. Two of these categories, *effectives* and *verdictives,* are conventional not communicative; they will be discussed in chapter 6. The four main kinds of communicative illocutionary acts are *constatives, directives, commissives,* and *acknowledgments;* these correspond roughly to Austin's ex-

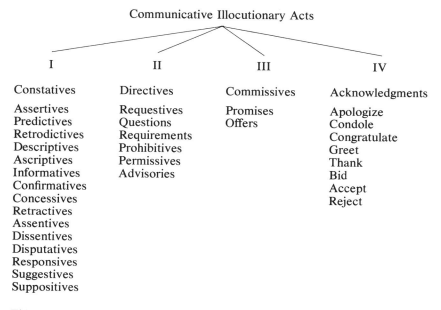

Figure 3.1 Classification of communicative illocutionary acts (in category IV specific verbs are listed)

positives, exercitives, commissives, and behabitives, respectively, and closely to Searle's representatives, directives, commissives, and expressives, although our characterizations of them are different from Searle's.

For us, *constatives* express the speaker's belief and his intention or desire that the hearer have or form a like belief. *Directives* express the speaker's attitude toward some prospective action by the hearer and his intention that his utterance, or the attitude it expresses, be taken as a reason for the hearer's action. *Commissives* express the speaker's intention and belief that his utterance obligates him to do something (perhaps under certain conditions). And *acknowledgments* express feelings regarding the hearer or, in cases where the utterance is clearly perfunctory or formal, the speaker's intention that his utterance satisfy a social expectation to express certain feelings and his belief that it does. Figure 3.1 lists the subcategories falling under these four headings. They will be discussed in detail in the sections to follow, where specific R-intentions will be spelled out, together with, when not obvious, the correlative perlocutionary intentions.

3.1. CONSTATIVES

In general, a constative is the expression of a belief, together with the expression of an intention that the hearer form (or continue to hold) a like belief. The following analyses of various specific kinds of constatives exhibit this pattern.

Assertives (simple): (affirm, allege, assert, aver, avow, claim, declare, deny (assert ... not), indicate, maintain, propound, say, state, submit)
In uttering e, S asserts that P if S expresses:
i. the belief that P, and
ii. the intention that H believe that P.

Predictives: (forecast, predict, prophesy)
In uttering e, S predicts that P if S expresses:
i. the belief that it will be the case that P, and
ii. the intention that H believe that it will be the case that P.

Retrodictives: (recount, report)
In uttering e, S retrodicts that P if S expresses:
i. the belief that it was the case that P, and
ii. the intention that H believe that it was the case that P.

Descriptives: (appraise, assess, call, categorize, characterize, classify, date, describe, diagnose, evaluate, grade, identify, portray, rank)
In uttering e, S describes o as F if S expresses:
i. the belief that o is F, and
ii. the intention that H believe that o is F.

Ascriptives: (ascribe, attribute, predicate)
In uttering e, S ascribes F to o if S expresses:
i. the belief that F applies to o, and
ii. the intention that H believe that F applies to o.

Informatives: (advise, announce, apprise, disclose, inform, insist, notify, point out, report, reveal, tell, testify)
In uttering e, S informs H that P if S expresses:
i. the belief that P, and
ii. the intention that H form the belief that P.

Confirmatives: (appraise, assess, bear witness, certify, conclude, confirm, corroborate, diagnose, find, judge, substantiate, testify, validate, verify, vouch for)

In uttering *e*, *S* confirms (the claim) that *P* if *S* expresses:
i. the belief that *P*, based on some truth-seeking procedure, and
ii. the intention that *H* believe that *P* because *S* has support for *P*.

Concessives: (acknowledge, admit, agree, allow, assent, concede, concur, confess, grant, own)
In uttering *e*, *S* concedes that *P* if *S* expresses:
i. the belief that *P*, contrary to what he would like to believe or contrary to what he previously believed or avowed, and
ii. the intention that *H* believe that *P*.

Retractives: (abjure, correct, deny, disavow, disclaim, disown, recant, renounce, repudiate, retract, take back, withdraw)
In uttering *e*, *S* retracts the claim that *P* if *S* expresses:
i. that he no longer believes that *P*, contrary to what he previously indicated he believed, and
ii. the intention that *H* not believe that *P*.

Assentives: (accept, agree, assent, concur)
In uttering *e*, *S* assents to the claim that *P* if *S* expresses:
i. the belief that *P*, as claimed by *H* (or as otherwise under discussion), and
ii. the intention (perhaps already fulfilled) that *H* believe that *P*.

Dissentives: (differ, disagree, dissent, reject)
In uttering *e*, *S* dissents from the claim that *P* if *S* expresses:
i. the disbelief that *P*, contrary to what was claimed by *H* (or was otherwise under discussion), and
ii. the intention that *H* disbelieve that *P*.

Disputatives: (demur, dispute, object, protest, question)
In uttering *e*, *S* disputes the claim that *P* if *S* expresses:
i. the belief that there is reason not to believe that *P*, contrary to what was claimed by *H* (or was otherwise under discussion), and
ii. the intention that *H* believe that there is reason not to believe that *P*.

Responsives: (answer, reply, respond, retort)
In uttering *e*, *S* responds that *P* if *S* expresses:
i. the belief that *P*, which *H* has inquired about, and
ii. the intention that *H* believe that *P*.

Suggestives: (conjecture, guess, hypothesize, speculate, suggest)
In uttering *e*, *S* suggests that *P* if *S* expresses:

i. the belief that there is reason, but not sufficient reason, to believe that *P,* and
ii. the intention that *H* believe that there is reason, but not sufficient reason, to believe that *P.*

Suppositives: (assume, hypothesize, postulate, stipulate, suppose, theorize)
In uttering *e,* *S* supposes that *P* if *S* expresses:
i. the belief that it is worth considering the consequences of *P,* and
ii. the intention that *H* believe that it is worth considering the consequences of *P.*

We said at the outset that in general, constatives are the expression of a belief, together with the expression of an intention that the hearer form, or continue to hold, a similar belief. Simple *assertives, descriptives,* and *ascriptives* are of this sort. The perlocutionary intention normally accompanying these acts is that the hearer believe, or continue to believe, the proposition (*P*) in question, perhaps by way of believing that the speaker believes it. That is, over and above identifying the belief and the intention expressed, *H* is intended to believe that *S* believes the proposition and, possibly because of this, to believe the proposition himself. Of course, there are cases in which the speaker knows perfectly well that the hearer disbelieves that *P* and will not change his mind just because *S* believes that *P.* Nevertheless, *S* wants *H* to ascribe the belief that *P* to *S,* and, even if he does not intend *H* to believe that *P,* at least he wishes that *H* believe it; in these cases *S* expresses the wish, rather than the intention, that *H* believe that *P.* As we suggested in chapter 1, when in performing an illocutionary act *S* expresses a certain intention regarding *H,* in general he has the corresponding perlocutionary intention. However, if *S* disbelieves that his utterance will have any such perlocutionary effect on *H,* he expresses at most the wish that such an effect result. So *S* may have the perlocutionary intention that *H* attribute to him this wish. Finally, there are cases where *S* thinks *H* won't take his utterance as sincere. That is, *S* expects *H* not to attribute to him the belief and the intention *S* is expressing. In this case *S* cannot expect to have fulfilled, and therefore cannot reasonably form, the perlocutionary intention that *H* believe that he (*S*) believes that *P,* much less the further intention that *H* believe it himself.

The *assertives* listed vary in strength of belief expressed and in the corresponding expressed intention. When one maintains or avows something, one's expressed belief and intention are very strong, whereas the belief and intention expressed when one alleges or submits that something is the case are much weaker. We have reserved the separate categories of *suggestives* and *suppositives* for constative utterances that express not even a weak belief that P, but only the belief that there is reason to believe that P or that (because it is possible or plausible that P is true) it is worth considering the consequences of P.

Some of the verbs listed as *descriptives* are rather specialized in their coverage. Verbs like "appraise," "date," "diagnose," and "grade" apply to restricted categories of things. These verbs are not synonymous, but that does not mean they designate different sorts of illocutionary acts. They don't: not every difference between illocutionary verbs is illocutionary.

What distinguishes *informatives* from simple assertives is that the speaker expresses (in addition to his belief) the intention that the hearer *form* the belief that P. For assertives, S's expressed intention is that H form the belief, or continue to believe, that P. We might say that at the time of utterance, S presumes that H does not believe that P. Here we rely on a notion of *illocutionary presumption:* in his illocutionary intention, S presumes that q if the truth of q is necessary for the rationality of his illocutionary intention. Of course, the notion of rationality is multifarious; all we mean, in speaking of the rationality of illocutionary intentions, is that there is good reason to believe that the intention will be fulfilled (by being recognized). Generally, for an illocutionary act with a presumption, the truth of that presumption is necessary for the success of that act. With this rough notion of illocutionary presumption, we will be able to distinguish some of the other kinds of constatives partly in terms of what is presumed.

Concessives, retractives, assentives, dissentives, and *disputatives* all involve a presumption about the contextual relevance of the expressed belief. A concessive expresses a belief contrary to what S would like to believe or contrary to what he previously believed or avowed, whereas a retractive expresses that S no longer believes what he previously indicated he believed, but in both cases it is presumed that the question of S's belief has come up in the conversation or is otherwise directly relevant to the current stage of conversation. Assentives, dissentives, and disputatives all presume that a certain claim has been made by H or that someone's claim, not necessarily S's or H's, is under discussion. To assent that P is to express agreement with this claim, to dissent from it is to express disagreement, and to dispute it is to express the belief that there is reason not to believe that P.

Confirmatives express not only the speaker's belief that P but that he believes it as a result of some truth-seeking procedure, such as observation, investigation, or argument. Since the latter belief is also expressed, it is not a mere illocutionary presumption. *Responsives* are R-intended as replies to an inquiry by H. In responding that P, S expresses his belief that P and that he is so doing in answer to H. Obviously, in some contexts a responsive can be a dissentive or a disputative as well. *Suggestives* and *suppositives* that P are not expressions of belief that P. In suggesting (conjecturing, hypothesizing) that P, S expresses merely the belief that there is reason to believe that P, but not sufficient reason to believe it. And in supposing (assuming, postulating) that P, what S expresses is the belief that it is worth considering the consequences of P, irrespective of whether it is true that P. Here S is likely to have the perlocutionary intention that H is to expect S to take up a discussion of P or its consequences.

An analysis of constative verbs with specialized ranges of application, like "appraise," "testify," "recant," and "postulate," would specify what that range of application is and that the speaker presumes his utterance to fall within this range. Such an analysis would take into account the strength of the expressed attitude. Just as, among assertives, maintaining something expresses a stronger belief than alleging it, so among disputatives, to object to something expresses a stronger belief (regarding reasons for disbelieving the proposition in question) than does questioning something. There is a similar difference between the suggestives hypothesizing and conjecturing. The analyses for the central cases of each type would have to be modified slightly to reflect these differences.

For certain purposes, the subtypes we have given could be supplemented or subdivided further. No doubt additions could be made to our list of verbs for each type, though we suspect that most such verbs would be too specialized in scope to be of interest here. Finally, we should point out that some verbs occur under more than one heading. This does not necessarily mean that the types overlap, only that some verbs name more than one type. Nevertheless, there is such overlap. Most of the specialized types of constatives satisfy the definition of assertives, and responsives, for example, overlap with disputatives and with suggestives. This means not that our definitions or conceptions of these types of constatives are hazy, but that some illocutionary act tokens can be of more than one type, performed with the R-intention appropriate to each.

3.2. DIRECTIVES

Directives express the speaker's attitude toward some prospective action by the hearer. If this were all they expressed, they would be merely constatives with a restriction on propositional content (namely, that a prospective action be ascribed to the hearer). However, they also express the speaker's intention (desire, wish) that his utterance or the attitude it expresses be taken as (a) reason for the hearer to act. Rather than use Austin's term "exercitive," which seems somewhat restricted in scope, we have borrowed Searle's term "directive." It is both to the point and conveniently vague, being broad enough to cover the six kinds of acts that belong in this category.

Requestives: (ask, beg, beseech, implore, insist, invite, petition, plead, pray, request, solicit, summon, supplicate, tell, urge)
In uttering e, S requests H to A if S expresses:
i. the desire that H do A, and
ii. the intention that H do A because (at least partly) of S's desire.

Questions: (ask, inquire, interrogate, query, question, quiz)
In uttering e, S questions H as to whether or not P if S expresses:
i. the desire that H tell S whether or not P, and
ii. the intention that H tell S whether or not P because of S's desire.

Requirements: (bid, charge, command, demand, dictate, direct, enjoin, instruct, order, prescribe, require)
In uttering e, S requires H to A if S expresses:
i. the belief that his utterance, in virtue of his authority over H, constitutes sufficient reason for H to A, and
ii. the intention that H do A because of S's utterance.

Prohibitives: (enjoin, forbid, prohibit, proscribe, restrict)
In uttering e, S prohibits H from A-ing if S expresses:
i. the belief that his utterance, in virtue of his authority over H, constitutes sufficient reason for H not to A, and
ii. the intention that because of S's utterance H not do A.

Permissives: (agree to, allow, authorize, bless, consent to, dismiss, excuse, exempt, forgive, grant, license, pardon, release, sanction)
In uttering e, S permits H to A if S expresses:
i. the belief that his utterance, in virtue of his authority over H, entitles H to A, and
ii. the intention that H believe that S's utterance entitles him to A.

Advisories: (admonish, advise, caution, counsel, propose, recommend, suggest, urge, warn)
In uttering *e*, *S* advises *H* to *A* if *S* expresses:
i. the belief that there is (sufficient) reason for *H* to *A*, and
ii. the intention that *H* take *S*'s belief as (sufficient) reason for him to *A*.

Requestives express the speaker's desire that the hearer do something. Moreover, they express the speaker's intention (or, if it is clear that he doesn't expect compliance, his desire or wish) that the hearer take this expressed desire as reason (or part of his reason) to act. The corresponding perlocutionary intentions, as might be foreseen, are that *H* take *S* actually to have the desire and the intention he is expressing and that *H* perform the action requested of him. Verbs of requesting connote variation in strength of attitude expressed, as between "invite" and "insist" and between "ask" and "beg." The stronger ones convey a sense of earnestness or urgency. "Beseech" and "supplicate," among others, convey both an appeal to the hearer's sympathy and a special manner of performance. Some verbs of requesting are rather specialized in scope. "Summon" (or "invite" taken narrowly) refer to requests for the hearer's presence; "beg" and "solicit" apply to requests for contributions or favors.

Questions are special cases of requests, special in that what is requested is that the hearer provide the speaker with certain information. There are differences between questions, but not all of them are important for an illocutionary taxonomy. There are exam questions and rhetorical questions. "Interrogate" suggests duress in a way that "ask" does not. Finally, "quiz" and "query" do not quite fit our analysis, in that they cannot be used to report the content of a question but only its topic (*S* quizzed *H* about topology).

Requirements, such as ordering or dictating, should not be confused with requests, even strong ones. There is an important difference. In requesting, the speaker expresses his intention that the hearer take his (*S*'s) expressed desire as a reason to act; in requirements *S*'s expressed intention is that *H* take *S*'s utterance as a reason to act, indeed as sufficient reason to act. As a matter of fact, requirements do not necessarily involve the speaker's expressing any desire at all that the hearer act in a certain way. It might be quite clear that *S* couldn't care less. Instead, what *S* expresses is his belief that his utterance constitutes sufficient reason for *H* to perform the action. In expressing this belief and the corresponding intention, *S* is presuming that he has the authority over H (physical, psychological, or institutional) that gives such weight to his very utterances.

Prohibitives, such as forbidding or proscribing, are essentially requirements that the hearer not do a certain thing. To prohibit someone from smoking is to require him not to smoke. We list prohibitives separately because they take a distinct grammatical form and because there are a number of such verbs. We will let the entry for prohibitives speak for itself.

Permissives, like requirements and prohibitives, presume the speaker's authority. They express S's belief, and his intention that H believe, that S's utterance constitutes sufficient reason for H to feel free to do a certain action. The obvious reasons for issuing a permissive are either to grant a request for permission or to remove some antecedent restriction against the action in question. It would seem, therefore, that the speaker presumes either that such a request has been made or that such a restriction exists. It is not necessary but it is common, at least with noninstitutional permissives, that the speaker express that he does not wish, desire, or expect the hearer not to perform the action in question. But, as with requirements, it is not the speaker's expressed attitude but his utterance that is intended to figure in the hearer's reason. Some of the verbs of permitting are highly specialized, such as "bless," "dismiss" ('permit to leave'), "excuse" ('permit not to make restitution'), and "release" ('permit not to fulfill an obligation').

As for *advisories,* what the speaker expresses is not the desire that H do a certain action but the belief that doing it is a good idea, that it is in H's interest. S expresses also the intention that H take this belief of S's as a reason to act.[3] The corresponding perlocutionary intentions are that H take S to believe that S actually has the attitudes he is expressing and that H perform the action he is being advised to perform. (It is possible, of course, that S really does not care.) Advisories vary in strength of expressed belief. Compare suggesting with admonishing. Furthermore, some advisories imply a special reason that the recommended action is a good idea. In warning, for example, S presumes the presence of some likely source of danger or trouble for H.

3.3. COMMISSIVES

This is the one category of illocutionary acts for which Austin's original label has been retained universally. Commissives are acts of obligating oneself or of proposing to obligate oneself to do something specified in the propositional content, which may also specify conditions under which the deed is to be done or does not have to be done. In committing oneself to do A, one expresses the intention to do A and the belief that one's utterance commits one to doing it, at least under the conditions specified or mutually believed to be relevant. These conditions may include H's accepting one's proposal or commitment to do A or at least his not rejecting it (ordinarily, the absence of explicit rejection may be taken as—is mutually believed to count as—acceptance). In addition to expressing such intention and belief, the speaker expresses the intention that H take him to have this intention and belief. The corresponding perlocutionary intention is that H believe S has this intention and belief and that H himself believe that S is obligated to do A, at least if the required conditions are met.

We distinguish two main types of commissives, *promises* and *offers*. Promises are acts of obligating oneself; offers are proposals to obligate oneself. Under promising, we provide a sampling of special cases, including contracting and betting, three commissive/constative hybrids (swearing, guaranteeing, and surrendering), and one commissive/directive hybrid, inviting. The definitions are self-explanatory. As for offers, besides the general case we give but two special cases, volunteering and bidding.[4]

Promises: (promise, swear, vow)
In uttering e, S promises H to A if S expresses:
i. the belief that his utterance obligates him to A,
ii. the intention to A, and
iii. the intention that H believe that S's utterance obligates S to A and that S intends to A.

contract: S and H make mutually conditional promises; fulfillment of each is conditional on the fulfillment of the other.

bet: S promises to do something (for instance, pay a certain amount) if a certain event occurs, on condition that H promises to do a certain thing if a certain other event occurs.

swear that: S asserts (constative) that P and promises that he is telling the truth.

guarantee that: S affirms (constative) the quality of something, x, and promises to make repairs or restitution if x is relevantly defective.

guarantee x: S promises to make repairs or restitution if x is defective in some relevant respect.

surrender: S admits (constative) defeat and promises not to continue fighting.

invite: S requests (directive) H's presence and promises acceptance of his presence.

Offers: (offer, propose)
In uttering e, S offers A to H if S expresses:
i. the belief that S's utterance obligates him to A on condition that H indicates he wants S to A,
ii. the intention to A on condition that H indicates he wants S to A, and
iii. the intention that H believe that S's utterance obligates S to A and that S intends to A, on condition that H indicates he wants S to A.

volunteer: S offers his services.

bid: S offers to give something (in a certain amount) in exchange for something.

3.4. ACKNOWLEDGMENTS

Acknowledgments, as we call them, are the central cases of Austin's motley class of "behabitives." They express, perfunctorily if not genuinely, certain feelings toward the hearer. These feelings and their expression are appropriate to particular sorts of occasions. For example, greeting expresses pleasure at meeting or seeing someone, thanking expresses gratitude for having received something, apologizing expresses regret for having harmed or bothered the hearer, condoling expresses sympathy for H's having suffered some misfortune (not S's doing), and congratulating expresses gladness for H's having done or received something noteworthy. Commonly, but not necessarily, such an occasion, when it arises, is mutually recognized by S and H, and then it is not only appropriate but expected by H that S will issue the relevant acknowledgment.

Because acknowledgments are expected on particular occasions, they are often issued not so much to express a genuine feeling as to satisfy the social expectation that such a feeling be expressed. In our list of acknowledgments the disjunctive definitions reflect this fact.

Apologize:
In uttering e, S apologizes to H for D if S expresses:
i. regret for having done D to H, and
ii. the intention that H believe that S regrets having done D to H, or

i. the intention that his utterance satisfy the social expectation that one express regret for having done something regrettable like *D*, and

ii. the intention that *H* take *S*'s utterance as satisfying this expectation.

Condole: (commiserate, condole)
In uttering *e*, *S* condoles *H* for (misfortune) *D* if *S* expresses:

i. sympathy with *H*'s having (or suffering) *D*, and

ii. the intention that *H* believe that *S* sympathizes with *H*'s having *D*, or

i. the intention that his utterance satisfy the social expectation that one express sympathy for misfortunes like *D*, and

ii. the intention that *H* take *S*'s utterance as satisfying this expectation.

Congratulate: (compliment, congratulate, felicitate)
In uttering *e*, *S* congratulates *H* for *D* if *S* expresses:

i. gladness for *H*'s having *D*(-ed), and

ii. the intention that *H* believe that *S* is glad that *H* has *D*(-ed), or

i. the intention that his utterance satisfy the social expectation that one express gladness for good fortunes like *D*(-ing), and

ii. the intention that *H* take *S*'s utterance as satisfying this expectation.

Greet:
In uttering *e*, *S* greets *H* if *S* expresses:

i. pleasure at seeing (or meeting) *H*, and

ii. the intention that *H* believe that *S* is pleased to see (or meet) *H*, or

i. the intention that his utterance satisfy the social expectation that one express pleasure at seeing (or meeting) someone, and

ii. the intention that *H* take *S*'s utterance as satisfying this expectation.

Thank:
In uttering *e*, *S* thanks *H* for *D* if *S* expresses:

i. gratitude to *H* for *D*, and

ii. the intention that *H* believe that *S* is grateful to *H* for *D*, or

i. the intention that his utterance satisfy the social expectation that one express gratitude at being benefited, and

ii. the intention that *H* take *S*'s utterance as satisfying this expectation.
"No thanks": *S* thanks *H* for offering *D* and rejects the offer.

Bid: (bid, wish)
In uttering *e*, *S* bids *H* good (happy) *D* if *S* expresses:

i. the hope that *H*'s *D* will be good (happy), and

ii. the intention that H believe that S hopes that H's D will be good (happy), or

i. the intention that his utterance satisfy the social expectation that one express good hopes when the question of another's prospects arises, and

ii. the intention that H take S's utterance as satisfying this expectation.

Accept—acknowledge an acknowledgment:
In uttering e, S accepts H's acknowledgment if S expresses:
i. appreciation for H's acknowledgment, and
ii. the intention that H believe that S appreciates H's acknowledgment, or
i. the intention that his utterance satisfy the social expectation that one express appreciation of an acknowledgment, and
ii. the intention that H take S's utterance as satisfying this expectation.
"You're welcome": S accepts H's thanks.

Reject: (refuse, reject, spurn)
In uttering e, S rejects H's acknowledgment if S expresses:
i. lack of appreciation of H's acknowledgment,
ii. the intention that H believe that S fails to appreciate H's acknowledgment, and (perhaps also)
iii. the intention that his utterance violate the social expectation that one express appreciation of an acknowledgment, and
iv. the intention that H take S's utterance as violating this expectation.

When one apologizes to someone, either one expresses regret (for what one has done) or one expresses the intention that one's utterance satisfy the social expectation to express regret (without actually expressing regret). Perfunctory acknowledgments thus require the implicit cooperation of the hearer—they are issued, quite obviously to all concerned, routinely or as a formality, as when one apologizes for accidentally bumping someone.

Despite the fact that perfunctory acknowledgments do not express genuine feelings, in our society they are generally regarded as acts of courtesy. Indeed, when the acknowledgment is occasioned by something trivial or when the occasion warrants nothing more than a perfunctory acknowledgment, for the hearer to question the speaker's sincerity would be an act of gross discourtesy and social disruptiveness. On the other hand, there are occasions, owing to the seriousness of the matter or to the relation between the speaker and the hearer, when it is expected that genuine feelings be expressed. We won't pursue the sociology of acknowledgments.

In issuing an acknowledgment, the speaker presumes the existence of the occasion to which the acknowledgment is appropriate. For example, in thanking H for something, S presumes that he has received something from H, and in apologizing to H, S presumes that he has done something regrettable to H. His illocutionary act of acknowledging could not succeed—the hearer could not recognize his R-intention—unless this presumption were correct, or at least mutually believed. The existence of the relevant occasion is presumed, not asserted, by the speaker, and it is often unnecessary for him to mention the occasion explicitly: if someone gives you a cigarette, it is enough to say "Thank you." But if someone sends you a box of cigars, it is necessary to say, when you next see the donor, "Thanks for the fine cigars," or something to that effect. Condolences and congratulations generally require such a specification, because they are usually occasioned by some event removed from the current encounter of S and H.

In acknowledgments, the only hearer-directed intention expressed over and above the expressed feeling is that H believe that S has the expressed feeling. Hence the only perlocutionary intention associated with acknowledgments is that the hearer take the speaker to have the expressed feeling or, in perfunctory cases, to regard the utterance as satisfying the relevant social expectation. However, an acknowledgment may invite an acknowledgment in response, which might be construed as a perlocutionary effect if intended (it need not be, of course). Greetings and farewells are exchanged, thanks are accepted ("You're welcome"), congratulations and condolences are accepted with a "Thank you" or the like, and apologies may be accepted ("That's OK") or rejected ("Saying you're sorry isn't enough").

Similar to congratulations and condolences are biddings or (expressing) wishes, which may be negative, as in the case of curses. Strictly speaking, these may be only constatives (namely, to the effect that one has a certain wish), but in some cases biddings are called for and must then be classed as acknowledgments.

Pardoning, excusing, and forgiving may seem to be acknowledgments (asking to be pardoned, excused, or forgiven is clearly a request). However, though they may be related to acknowledgments, as when one forgives someone for something for which he apologized (or even excuses him from having to apologize), they seem to us to be permissives. They are acts of releasing a person from any obligation (or of refusing to acknowledge his putative obligation) incurred from doing something to the speaker. Thus, they permit him not to compensate the speaker for what he has done, or, where that is not at issue, they permit him not to feel responsible for what he has done.

3.5. FELICITY CONDITIONS

One taxonomic issue concerns the notion of felicity conditions introduced by Austin in his William James Lectures (1962). Many philosophers and linguists have adopted Austin's term, but their use of it has sometimes been rather less discriminating than his. The main problem has been failure to observe the distinction between conditions necessary (and sufficient) for the successful performance of an act, and the conditions necessary (and sufficient) for a completely nondefective or felicitous performance of the act. In most discussions of felicity conditions, those conditions necessary for the existence of an instance of the act are some unspecified subset of the conditions necessary for the nondefective performance of the act. For instance, Searle (1969) gives necessary and sufficient conditions for the (literal and direct) nondefective performance of various speech acts, yet the absence of only some of these conditions precludes the performance of the act. For the sake of clarity we will call conditions that are singly necessary and jointly sufficient for the performance of an act its *success conditions;* we will call those conditions that are not success conditions but are required for nondefectiveness *felicity conditions.* Is there any role for felicity conditions to play in a theory of speech acts? If there is, how would that role be filled in our theory?

When one looks at the literature on speech acts, there seem to be four different motivations for having felicity conditions in a speech act theory. First, Austin looked to the ways various acts can go wrong as a guide to what it takes for the act to go right (1962, Lecture II). Although he constructed a fairly elaborate taxonomy of "infelicities," his repeated reference to "conventional procedures" makes it pretty clear that his doctrine of infelicities is appropriate mainly for the "highly developed explicit performatives" associated with conventional, ritual, and ceremonial acts, which we discuss in chapter 6. Austin's doctrine has no obvious extension to communicative illocutionary acts.

A second motive for having felicity conditions comes from Searle (1965, 1969), who apparently includes felicity conditions among his necessary conditions because he is inclined to think that "we shall not be able to get a set of knock-down necessary and sufficient conditions that will exactly mirror the ordinary use of the word 'promise'. I am confining my discussion, therefore, to the center of the concept of promising and ignoring the fringe, borderline, and partially defective cases" (1965, 47). Still, it is not clear why adopting this strategy of first analyzing paradigm cases (then seeing the rest as deviations from the paradigm) should have the consequence that felicity conditions cannot be distinguished from success conditions. One could just pick central cases to give success conditions for. Of course this would involve some modifications of Searle's format for analyzing speech acts. Essential conditions and propositional content conditions always seem to be success conditions, and sincerity conditions always seem to be felicity conditions. Preparatory conditions (or parts thereof) go different ways for different acts. Thus, a preparatory condition for asserting (that it is not obvious to both S and H that H knows that p) is clearly a felicity condition, whereas part of the preparatory conditions on promising (that S believes H would prefer S's doing A to S's not doing A) is arguably necessary as a success condition to differentiate promising from threatening.

A third motive for felicity conditions has come to the fore recently in the discussion of indirect speech acts. There seem to be some generalizations over indirect speech acts that are best stated in terms of both success and felicity conditions of speech acts. We will return to this matter in chapter 4.

Finally, some authors have claimed (or suggested) that felicity conditions might be related to various grammatical phenomena. For instance, Heringer proposes that a variety of grammatical facts concerning "qualifying *if*-clauses," as he calls them, "can be explicated only by reference to the illocutionary acts performed by the utterances which contain them . . . the syntactic form of the *if*-clause is directly related to the intrinsic condition which it calls into question" (1972, 1). As it turns out, though, only some of the conditions are used in this way; in particular, they must be "conditions on the beliefs of the speaker performing the illocutionary act" (1972, 43). Any theory taking these beliefs into account can handle these facts if Heringer's can, and the discussion of qualifying *if*-clauses does not motivate a general theory of felicity conditions, at least not of the sort envisaged by Austin. The ways an act may be defective, in an unqualified use of "defective," may be limited only by one's imagination. Thus it is reasonable that only certain kinds of defect be singled out. But then some reason must be provided for why those particular kinds are theoretically significant. So far we have found no compelling reason for a general theory of felicity conditions and (assuming indirect speech acts will not provide such a reason) propose no such theory here.

3.6. INFELICITY AND OBVIOUS INSINCERITY

Our taxonomy distinguishes types of communicative illocutionary acts by the attitudes the speaker expresses in performing them: the speaker expresses a certain attitude toward the propositional content as well as the intention that the hearer have or form a corresponding propositional attitude. We have defined expressing an attitude as R-intending the hearer to take one's utterance as reason to believe that one has the attitude. The speaker's having the attitudes expressed is the mark of sincerity, but sincerity is not required for communicative success; nor is the hearer's believing the speaker has the attitudes expressed. Thus, a communicative illocutionary act can succeed even if the speaker is insincere and even if the hearer believes he is insincere. After all, in expressing certain attitudes the speaker is merely R-intending the hearer to take his utterance as *reason* to believe him to have those attitudes. So the speaker need not intend this reason to be sufficient, and the hearer need not take it to be sufficient. Generally, though, it is intended to be sufficient and is taken to be; generally it is sufficient. Even if the speaker does not have the attitudes he is expressing, there is no reason, most of the time, to think he does not have them. And even if there is reason to think he does not have them, there is likely to be no reason to think he does not R-intend one to think there is reason to believe he has them. We may not trust him, but he may not realize that.

But suppose that the speaker's insincerity is obviously obvious; that is, S and H mutually believe that S does not have one or another of the attitudes he is expressing. In the case of a statement, for example, it might be mutually believed that S does not believe what he is stating or that H inalterably disbelieves what S is stating. In the case of a request, it might be mutually believed that S really does not want H to perform the requested action or that H won't perform it no matter what S wants. Such cases as these raise certain questions for our taxonomy: (1) Does the speaker really express the attitudes it is mutually believed he does not have? (2) Is he really performing an illocutionary act of the sort (stating, requesting) that he would be performing if he weren't obviously insincere?

To take an example, suppose that S says to H that he (S) has not been drinking. However, S and H mutually believe that S has alcohol on his breath and that an empty Ripple bottle is lying at S's feet. Suppose that under these circumstances H cannot attribute to S the belief that he (S) has not been drinking or the intention that H believe that S has not been drinking.[5] It is obvious to H not only that S is lying but that S believes H believes S is lying. Assuming that H is right, does it follow (1) that S cannot be expressing the belief, and the intention that H believe, that S has not been drinking, and (2) that S cannot be stating that he has not been drinking? Notwithstanding the facts of the case, S's utterance is R-intended by S to be taken by H as reason to think that S believes, and intends H to believe, that he has not been drinking. Under the circumstances S cannot rationally R-intend his utterance to be *sufficient* reason for H to make these attributions, but that is not what our conception of expressing an attitude requires. By itself, S's utterance is, and can be R-intended to be taken to be, *a* reason, despite the fact that it can be overridden by mutual contextual beliefs to the contrary. Even when defeated, a reason is a reason. Accordingly, S can express a belief and an intention despite mutual beliefs to the contrary. By definition, then, he can state that he has not been drinking.

The case of obviously obvious insincerity does not present problems for our conception of expressing an attitude or for our taxonomy of illocutionary acts in terms of types of attitudes expressed. Indeed, the example couldn't have been described in the way it was unless it was a case of expressing a certain belief and a certain intention and of performing the illocutionary act of stating. Otherwise, how could it be described as a case of obviously obvious insincerity? After all, there had to be something for the speaker to be insincere about, namely, the attitudes he expressed. Equally, there had to be some illocutionary act that he was performing insincerely.[6]

In considering the case of obvious insincerity and its implications for our taxonomy of communicative illocutionary acts, one should keep in mind that all these acts are performed pursuant to the communicative presumption (CP) and that their identity is worked out by the hearer in accordance with the SAS. That is, the hearer must explain the speaker's utterance by identifying the intention with which it was issued, and this consists in identifying the expressed attitudes. Expressing an attitude is R-intending the hearer to take one's utterance as reason, not necessarily sufficient reason, to think that one has the attitude in question; therefore, in identifying the speaker's illocutionary intention, the hearer must consider whether the speaker is likely to have such an attitude. Before thinking S to be expressing attitudes that there is mutually believed reason to believe he does not have, H might rule out the possibility that the CP is inoperative, for example, that S is kidding.[7] In general, any reason to think that S does not have an attitude he appears to be expressing, especially if the reason is mutually believed, is a reason to think S is being nonliteral or that the CP is not in effect. However, there are other possibilities. For instance, to avoid admitting something or committing himself, S has good reason to express attitudes he does not have, despite its being obvious that he doesn't have them. His insincerity is transparent, and yet by his utterance he has provided H with a basis for determining precisely what S is being insincere about. The obviousness of S's insincerity does not prevent him from performing the illocutionary act of expressing attitudes he doesn't have. Rather, it prevents his utterance from providing (and being R-intended to provide) sufficient reason for H to think he has those attitudes. However, this does not mean his utterance provides no reason, for unless it provided some reason by being R-intended to, it would not be a case of obvious insincerity.

Obvious insincerity is not the only way in which S's utterance can fail to be R-intended to provide sufficient reason for the hearer to ascribe certain attitudes to the speaker. Another route is obvious superfluity, where it is already mutually believed what S's attitudes are, or where it is already mutually believed that, for example, H believes what S believes or will do what S wants him to do. Here the reasons that S's utterance would normally provide for attributing beliefs or intentions to S do not need to be provided. But that does not mean that they are not provided anyway. Of course, the hearer, in identifying the expressed attitudes, would need to figure out why the speaker is bothering to express them.

We have not attempted to enumerate the sorts of reasons a speaker might have for expressing attitudes he obviously does not have. We have pointed out only that he can successfully, however infelicitously, perform the communicative illocutionary acts of expressing such attitudes. Why a speaker should do that is the hearer's problem, a problem that can arise only if the speaker is actually expressing certain attitudes that he could not possibly have.

Chapter Four

Elaborating the Schema:
Illocutionary Acts

Having surveyed the kinds of communicative illocutionary acts, we will now refine the speech act schema by spelling out the ways in which illocutionary acts can be performed via the SAS. We will start with the most straightforward kind of case, the literal and direct act, then move to more complicated cases, elaborating the schema as we go and delineating its relation to other aspects of the communication situation.

4.1. LITERAL (AND DIRECT) ILLOCUTIONARY ACTS

If the suggestions made so far are correct, we should be able to select appropriate values for e, p, and so on, specify the mutual contextual beliefs, and instantiate the SAS with examples of various types of illocutionary acts, thereby characterizing their literal (and direct) performance. How does the SAS characterize the performance of literal (and direct) communicative illocutionary acts? Let's start with cases where the act is performed *directly* rather than by means of another illocutionary act (that is, indirectly). For convenience we repeat the presumptions introduced in chapter 1 which, together with MCBs, sanction various steps of the SAS.

Linguistic Presumption (LP): The mutual belief in the linguistic community C_L to the effect that:
i. the members of C_L share L, and
ii. whenever any member S utters any e in L to any other member H, H can identify what S is saying, given that H knows the meanings of e in L and is aware of appropriate background information.

Communicative Presumption (CP): The mutual belief in the linguistic community C_L to the effect that whenever a member S says something to another member H, S is doing so with some recognizable illocution-ary intent.

Presumption of Literalness (PL): The mutual belief in the linguistic community C_L to the effect that if in uttering e, S could (under the circumstances) be speaking literally, then S is speaking literally.

Then, S is F-ing that p if in the presence of some H, S utters some e in language L, intending, and expecting (pursuant to the LP, the CP, and the PL) H to recognize that he intends, H to infer (from the fact that S means ... by e and the fact that S is thereby saying that *(...p...)) that S is F-ing that p. That is, S intends, and expects H to recognize that he intends, H to reason as follows:

	Basis
L1. S is uttering e.	hearing S utter e
L2. S means ... by e.	L1, LP, MCBs
L3. S is saying that *(...p...).	L2, LP, MCBs
L4. S, if speaking literally, is F^*-ing that p.	L3, CP, MCBs
L5. S could be F^*-ing that p.	L4, MCBs
L6. S is F^*-ing that p.	L5, PL

Consider a particular case. Let e be the sentence "John will pay Sam back." H is to infer:

	Basis
L1. S is uttering e.	hearing S utter e
L2. S means 'John will repay Sam' by e.	L1, LP, MCBs
L3. S is saying that John will repay Sam.	L2, LP, MCBs
L4. S, if speaking literally, is constating (or ...) that John will repay Sam.	L3, CP, MCBs
L5. S could be speaking literally.	L4, MCBs
L6. (a) S is constating (or ...) that John will repay Sam.	L5, PL
(b) S is predicting that John will repay Sam.	L6(a), MCBs

Given that H has inferred L4 from L3, why does he infer L5, and how does he arrive at L6(b)?

First, on what basis does H suppose S could be speaking literally? That is, why does he infer L5? It would seem that the reasonableness of an expectation that one's intentions will be recognized depends on general coherence of belief as well as contextual and conversational appropriateness, as these are judged by the speaker and the hearer. Indeed, what we are working with are factors believed by the speaker to be believed by the hearer to be coherent or appropriate, and vice versa. The obvious problem is that what one person may be supposed to believe is coherent or appropriate can differ wildly from what another person may be supposed to believe. For instance, suppose S says something that if taken literally in L is outrageously false or inappropriate. Should H conclude that S does not mean by e what e means in L, that S is not speaking literally, or that S holds some outrageous belief (about the world at large or about the conversation in particular)?

We see no general way of deciding such a question. There would seem to be no limit on the things one person can suppose another to believe he believes—S can suppose H thinks S is a complete fool. The best we can hope for is solutions by cases. It depends on the case what is critical if S and H are to mutually believe that they share (1) similar idiolects, (2) similar general beliefs about the world, and (3) similar conceptions of the nature, stage, and direction of the current talk-exchange. We dealt with (1) in chapter 2, and because (2) is much too general to handle here, let us focus on issues surrounding (3).

Without a shared conception of the nature, stage, and direction of the talk-exchange, H could hardly tell whether S meant what he said. What is said may well be in and of itself perfectly reasonable but conversationally inappropriate if construed literally or as S's complete contribution to the talk-exchange at that point. In the course of a conversation on people's responsibilities to others, S might intone "No man is an island, you know." Had H been contending that no one has any connections with anyone else, S's remark could be interpreted as an objection, as well as a statement, to the effect that one is indeed affected by and responsible for others. It would be taken differently in a conversation concerning the analytical properties of "man." Yet in each case the sentence might well be meant literally, and it is not outrageously false (it is obviously true). What, then, makes a contribution conversationally appropriate?

Following Grice (1975) we assume that cooperative conversations are governed by certain maxims,[1] or as we prefer to call them because they are defeasible mutual contextual beliefs, *conversational presump-*

tions. When a person fails to fulfill one of them, *H* will take *S* as having spoken contextually inappropriately until or unless *H* finds a suitable explanation to the contrary.

In the course of a talk-exchange speaker and hearer presume that at any point in the talk-exchange,

Relevance (RE): The speaker's contribution is relevant to the talk-exchange at that point.

This is a very general and powerful presumption; it is also vague. Just what counts as being relevant? We do not have a general answer to this question,[2] but there are two major parameters of relevance—*force* and *content*. The following presumptions falling under (RE) pertain to force.

Sequencing (SE): The speaker's contribution is of an illocutionary type appropriate to that stage of the talk-exchange.

Sincerity (SI): The speaker's contribution to the talk-exchange is sincere—the speaker has the attitudes he expresses.

Examples of compliance with these presumptions are obvious. Ceteris paribus, questions are to be answered, requests and commitments acknowledged, greetings reciprocated, constatives concurred with (or dissented from, or elaborated upon), and so on. And all are to be done sincerely where sincerity is possible.[3]

Given that a certain type of illocutionary act is appropriate to the present stage of a talk-exchange, there are presumptions relevant to content. These fall into two major categories—quantity of information and quality of information. Like Grice, we can begin by formulating the presumptions for constatives:

Quantity (QT): The speaker's constative provides (or *S* assumes in constating) just the requisite amount of information—not too much, not too little.

Quality (QL):
i. The speaker attempts to make his constative true.
ii. The speaker has adequate evidence for what he constates (or assumes in constating).

Analogs of these presumptions exist for other types of speech acts. For directives, the presumptions are:

Quantity (QT): The speaker's directive provides (or *S* assumes in directing) requisite information for compliance.

Quality (QL):
i. The speaker attempts to make his directive such that compliance is possible. ("Don't ask for the Moon.")
ii. The speaker has reasons for what he directs (or assumes in directing).[4] ("Leave." "Why?" "I don't know.")

For commissives and for acknowledgments there seems to be no presumption for quantity, only for quality:

Quality (QL): The speaker commits himself only to something he believes he is able to do.

Quality (QL): The speaker acknowledges only that which he believes to have occurred.

Other presumptions concern not force or content but the manner of performance, the way what is said is in fact said. Following Grice (1975, 46) we will formulate them thus:

Manner (MA): The speaker speaks perspicuously, that is, *S:*
i. avoids ambiguity,
ii. avoids obscurity of expression,
iii. avoids unnecessary prolixity,
iv. is orderly.

Finally, there might be presumptions having nothing directly to do with relevance but, rather, with the speech act as a social act. Two dimensions that come to mind are politeness and morality. Because discussing these notions would take us far afield, we offer the following merely as first approximations:

Politeness (PO): The speaker (in speaking) behaves politely, that is, *S* is not offensive, abusive, rude, vulgar.[5]

Morality (MO): The speaker (in speaking) behaves morally, that is, *S:*
i. does not reveal information he ought not reveal,
ii. does not ask for information he shouldn't have,
iii. does not direct *H* to do/tell something *H* shouldn't do/tell,
iv. does not commit himself to do something for *H* that *H* does not want done.

These presumptions, from Quantity through Morality, need considerable refinement and supplementation (see Kempson 1975, chs. 7,8;
Harnish 1976b, 340–348). And there is the problem of how conflict
between presumptions is resolved. Nevertheless, we will press these
conversational presumptions into service in their present state.

We are now in a better position to give the notion of conversational
appropriateness some content. A speaker's contribution to the talk-
exchange is *conversationally appropriate* if and only if it accords with
those conversational presumptions in effect at that time. Then, other
things being equal, *H* will infer line L5 of the schema if he takes *S*'s
F*-ing to be conversationally appropriate.

Our second question about inferring literal illocutionary acts was
how *H* infers L6(b) from L6(a). This is the problem of determining
which of the possible illocutionary acts that *S* might be performing
literally is the one *S* actually is performing. How does *H* recognize *S*'s
specific illocutionary intent? If the CP is in effect, *S* will be presumed to
be speaking with recognizable illocutionary intent. If conversational
presumptions are in effect, *H* will conclude that *S* is speaking with the
illocutionary intent complying with them. In our original example, if it
is mutually believed that *S* can or will have no influence on John, then
S's saying that it will be the case that John repays Sam may be taken as
a prediction but not as a guarantee. If no one has claimed that John will
not repay Sam, then *S*'s remark will not be taken as a dissentive. In this
way, specific MCBs and the relevant conversational presumptions
interact with what has been said to lead *H* to *S*'s specific illocutionary
intent.

Three caveats: first, there is more to be said about how specific
illocutionary intent is identified, but, second, it should be realized that
often one speaks with no more specific illocutionary intent than, say,
just constating that something is (or will be) the case. Third, it is always
possible for *H*'s identification of that intent to be vague, inaccurate, or
just plain wrong. After all, he can follow the SAS without filling it in
correctly.

4.2. NONLITERAL ILLOCUTIONARY ACTS

In circumstances where it would not be reasonable to suppose that the
speaker is *F**-ing that *p* in saying that *(...*p*...), the hearer will seek
(and will be intended to seek) an alternative explanation for *S*'s utter-

ance. That is, *H* will suppose that some other illocutionary act is being performed which is not delimited by what *S* said and so is not being performed literally. If the CP is in effect, *H* must be reasonably expected to be able to recognize that *S* intends to be *F*-ing that *P*, and this requires some sort of recognizable connection between what *S* said and what *S* was intending to do. Accordingly, we can supplement the schema as developed in section 4.1 to handle direct but *nonliteral* utterances:

	Basis
L5′. *S* could not (under the circumstances) be *F**-ing that *p*.	L4, MCBs
L6′. Under the circumstances there is a certain recognizable relation *R* between saying that *(...p...) and some *F*-ing that *P*, such that *S* could be *F*-ing that *P*.	L3, L5′, CP
L7. *S* is *F*-ing that *P*.	L6′, MCBs

A nonliteral illocutionary act has three basic ingredients: what is said, what is done, and the (intended) relation between them. The schema assigns two important roles to the MCBs: in the first step they signal nonliterality; in the second step they guide *H*'s search for *S*'s nonliteral illocutionary intent.

What are some of the ways utterances and MCBs can help signal nonliteral acts? Although nonliterality can affect force as well as content, usually only content is affected. For instance, consider exaggeration, either understatement or overstatement (hyperbole). In understatement, one purports to claim what is in fact less, so to speak, than one intends to claim. Since understatements are true if what is intended to be communicated is true, recognition of *S*'s communicative intention cannot depend on saying something *S* obviously does not believe, and so they do not violate the conversational presumption of sincerity—one has told the truth.[6] Rather, one has not told the whole truth and so has violated the presumption of quantity, as in:

(1) a. Not bad! (Very good! Great!)
    b. It's OK. (Good!)
    c. He's getting by. (He's doing fine.)

d. I wasn't born yesterday. (I'm not that naive.)
e. Boys will be boys.
f. No man is an island.

In overstatement, one purports to claim what is in fact more than one intends to claim, as in:

(2) a. No one understands me. (Not enough people understand me.)
b. A pig wouldn't eat this food. (A person wouldn't eat it—if he had a choice.)
c. Her eyes opened as wide as saucers. (Her eyes opened very wide.)
d. I can't make a shot today. (I'm making very few.)

Since superlatives are a standard device for expressing extreme evaluations, many overstatements use superlatives:

(3) That was the worst food I've ever had. (It was very bad.)

Advertisers make systematic use of overstatement in slogans:

(4) a. Paul Newman *is* Jesse James. (Paul Newman plays the part convincingly, or with conviction.)
b. We do it all for you. (We look after your interests; you need do nothing.)
c. When you say "Bud," you've said it all. (all that needs to be said about beer)
d. If it's not Schlitz, it's not beer. (not the way beer should be)
e. The future is now. (You should prepare now for the future.)

In many of these cases there is some dimension toward one extreme of which the claim would fall if literal, but literally the claim is false and is contextually obviously so. Therefore, what the speaker is taken to be doing is some act falling closer to the midpoint of that dimension.

If exaggeration is carried all the way along the dimension that relates what is said to what is done, we get sarcasm, irony, and facetiousness. In these cases one means roughly the opposite of what one says:

(5) a. Boy, this food is terrific! (terrible)
b. That argument is a real winner. (loser)

Although these acts can be nonliteral, it might be that an ironic or sarcastic intonation contour signals one's intent. If so, such a contour might be considered a negation operator converting the sentence into one for performing the act literally—just as rising intonation can convert a declarative sentence into an interrogative.

Finally, there is the very difficult class of cases encompassed by the term *metaphor*. Some metaphors are dead ("The leg of the table"), others only moribund ("Are you a mouse or a man?" "Toss me some cheese and you'll find out"). Literary critics have developed a rich, though somewhat confusing, taxonomy of metaphors based largely on the type of connection between what is said and what is meant. For example, if the relation is part to whole it is called *synecdoche:*

(6) I've got three hands (workers) here to help.

If one thing bears a very close association to another, the expression is sometimes classified as *metonymy:*

(7) a. The White House (the president or staff) said so.
    b. The Crown (the monarch or staff) said so.
    c. I have read all of Chomsky (Chomsky's works).

It would be a mistake to assume that all nonliteral uses of language, or even just all metaphor, must be indicated by any single sort of cue or violation of presumptions. In our examples so far, nonliterality has been signaled in at least four ways:

Contradiction or anomaly: The future is now.
Conceptual truth: No man is an island.
Obvious factual falsehood: She's a gazelle.
Obvious factual truth: I wasn't born yesterday.

In the first two cases conceptual knowledge, plus context, is sufficient to trigger completion of the nonliteral strategy. In the remaining two cases H must identify what is being referred to, as well as some general (but nonessential) properties held true of these referents, in order to follow the nonliteral strategy. For example, H must suppose that "she" in "She's a gazelle" is being used to refer to a certain female person and that gazelles are graceful.

What sorts of relations to what is said can guide H to S's nonliteral intent? We have seen three in operation, roughly as follows:

(R1) *Sarcasm, Irony:* the opposite of what is said.
(R2) *Figure of speech:* a figurative or metaphorical connection.
(R3) *Exaggeration:* the next evaluation toward the midpoint of the relevant scale.

Does *H* just flounder around with R1–R3 in seeking *S*'s illocutionary intent, or are these relations ordered in some way? Interestingly, when two are used in a single sentence at the same time, the effects can be the same regardless of order. Consider a simple example. After a gourmet meal (mutually believed to be such) *S* utters "That was the worst dinner in my life." *H* could infer either (8) or (9) with the same result:

(8) a. That was the *best* dinner in *S*'s life. (by R1)
    b. That was a *very good* dinner. (from (8a) by R3)
(9) a. That was a *very bad* dinner. (by R3)
    b. That was a *very good* dinner. (from (9a) by R1)

The same can happen with some metaphors. Suppose that *S* utters "Hey, that's a hot car!" referring to a stock Edsel. *H* could infer (10) or (11):

(10) a. That is a *cold* car. (by R1)
     b. That is a *slow* car. (from (10a) by R2)
(11) a. That is a *fast* car. (by R2)
     b. That is a *slow* car. (from (11a) by R1)

Is there an example that uses R2 and R3? One can exaggerate a metaphor: *S* utters "She's a gazelle today," referring to someone who moves none too gracefully on the court, but is doing better today. *H* can infer:

(12) a. She is moving *most* gracefully today. (by R2)
     b. She is moving *very well* (better) today. (from (12a) by R3)

But these inferences cannot easily be reversed because *e* is already a metaphor before exaggeration. Is it possible to make a metaphor out of an exaggeration? Perhaps, but we have not found a plausible example.

If it is not plausible for R3 to apply before R2, the relations are indeed ordered as they are numbered, since R1 can always apply first, and R2 must come before R3. Thus *H* does *not* flounder around looking for *S*'s nonliteral illocutionary intent but rather has at least three interpretive substrategies, which are utilized (tested, rejected, used) in the order R1, R2, R3.[7] Though these relations may generate the metaphor-potential of various expressions, they do not select from the possibilities they generate. For instance R2 does not itself determine whether "Two hands showed up" is to be interpreted as 'two arms,' 'two pairs of arms,' or 'two workers.' To cut down these possibilities,

MCBs must be invoked for communication to succeed. If context is such that the sentence is understood as short for "Two hands showed up for work this morning," then H will infer (and be intended by S to infer) that two workers showed up. The same strategy can be applied to the example "She's a gazelle today." Gazelles have many distinctive properties, but only a few could reasonably be expected to be attributed to a tennis player (jumping ability, speed, grace) and in the context of utterance these will either be further reduced by the conversational presumptions (she has just jumped high for an overhead, and S may be presumed to be commenting on that event) or the exact interpretation will be left open. If left open, H will have only a general impression of what S is intending to convey.

4.3. INDIRECT ILLOCUTIONARY ACTS

Though speaking literally in F^*-ing that p by saying that $*(...p...)$, a person can be indirectly performing another illocutionary act as well, as illustrated by the utterances "The door is over there" and "My mouth is parched." In the first case, S can be requesting H to leave while stating that the door is over there; in the second, S can be requesting something to drink while informing H that his mouth is parched. We will use the label *indirect illocutionary act* for an illocutionary act that is performed subordinately to another (usually literal) illocutionary act. It is indirect in the sense that its success is tied to the success of the first act. That is, securing uptake requires H to identify the indirect act by way of identifying the first act.

This characterization of an indirect act is similar to that of Searle (1975a, 59–60) but differs from Searle's in covering nonliteral as well as literal cases. It differs substantially from the characterization made by some linguists. For them a disparity between the surface form of a sentence and the illocutionary act performed in its utterance is critical for the act's being indirect. For instance, Sadock (1974, 73) writes, "Based on this discrepancy between surface form and use, such sentences have been termed *indirect illocutions*" (see also Davison 1975, 143–144; Herringer 1972, ch. 3). On this use an illocutionary act performed in uttering e is indirect just in case the type of illocutionary act associated with the surface form of e is distinct from the type of act performed. Notice that these two kinds of characterization are importantly different. If a surface interrogative, say, is given the semantics of an imperative by some grammar, then on the linguistic characterization the request made by its utterance is *indirect*, but on our characterization it would be *direct*. In addition, the linguistic characterization would not represent as indirect an act of the same force but with different content from the act performed directly.

Let us supplement the basic SAS to cover *literally* based *indirect* acts:

		Basis
L7'.	S could not be merely F^*-ing that p.	L6, MCBs
L8.	There is some F-ing that P connected in a way identifiable under the circumstances to F^*-ing that p, such that in F^*-ing that p, S could also be F-ing that P.	L7', CP
L9.	S is F^*-ing that p and thereby F-ing that P.	L8, MCBs

Note that line L9 has S both F^*-ing that p and F-ing that P. Whereas the former is literal and direct, the latter can be either literal or nonliteral. In most cases the indirect act will be nonliteral, such as when one requests a drink by stating that one's mouth is parched. However, it is possible for the indirect act to be literal as well, though clear cases are hard to motivate. Consider the case of warning H that the bull is about to charge. Both warning (in this example) and stating are constative and so are L-compatible with e, and the propositional content is the same. Thus both acts are literal. To be indirect, and not just simultaneous, the warning must be performed by means of the stating. In this case it could be accomplished by way of an MCB that bulls are dangerous.

Not all indirect acts need be literally based. It is possible to speak indirectly by speaking nonliterally—for instance, sarcastically. A mother might say (sarcastically) to her son "I'm sure the cat likes having its tail pulled," intending to (a) directly and nonliterally state that S is sure that the cat does not like having its tail pulled,[8] and (b) indirectly request that H stop pulling the cat's tail. Accordingly, we extend the SAS to *nonliterally* based *indirect* acts:

Basis

L8'. *S* could not merely be *F*-ing
         that *P*.   L7, MCBs

L9'. There is some *F'*-ing that *Q*
         connected in a way identi-
         fiable under the circum-
         stances to *F*-ing that *P*,
         such that in *F*-ing that *P*, *S*
         could also be *F'*-ing that *Q*.   L8', CP

L10. *S* is *F*-ing that *P* and
         thereby *F'*-ing that *Q*.   L9', MCBs

Notice that with respect to indirect acts, whether literally or nonliterally based, the MCBs play two characteristic roles. First (at line L7' or
L8') they help determine that the direct illocutionary act cannot reasonably be taken to be the sole act being performed by *S* in his utterance. Then (at L8 or L9') the MCBs contribute to determining the
identity of the indirect act.

We have already seen how the conversational presumptions initiate
nonliteral strategies; how do they initiate indirect strategies? The main
cue in these cases involves the idea of *S*'s making an adequate contribution to the talk-exchange at that point. *H* is to reason that *S*'s
direct contribution to the talk-exchange cannot (pursuant to the conversational presumptions) be *S*'s total contribution at that point because it is inadequate in some recognizable respect. That is, it violates
some conversational presumption. Saying this, though, does not de-
lineate the contributions of these presumptions to the process leading
H to *S*'s indirect illocutionary intent.

What then is the process leading *H* from *S*'s direct to *S*'s indirect
illocutionary intent? What sorts of connections can *S* expect *H* to
utilize? Consider again some of the examples we have mentioned so
far:

(13) a. The door is over there. (used to request someone to leave)
       b. My mouth is parched. (used to request a drink)
       c. I'm sure the cat likes having its tail pulled. (used to request *H* to
          stop pulling the cat's tail)

To these cases we can add cases like the following:

(13) d. You're the boss. (used to agree to do what *H* says)
       e. I should never have done that. (used to apologize)

f. Did you bring any tennis balls? (used to inform *H* that *S* did not bring any)

g. It's getting late. (used to request *H* to hurry)

The schema at lines L8 or L9′ reflects the fact that the connection between the direct and indirect intent can be extremely context dependent, there being few substantive generalizations spanning all cases. This can be better appreciated after we investigate how the inference might go in some of the examples in (13).

(13a) Suppose *S* utters "The door is over there" to *H*, thereby stating that the door is over there. Then *H* may infer:

L7′. *S* could not be merely stating that the door is over there.
Basis: It is MB-ed that *S* and *H* are having a dispute and the location of the door is irrelevant to the discussion so far.

L8. There is some *F*-ing that *P* connected in a way identifiable under the circumstances to stating that the door is over there, such that in stating that the door is over there *S* could also be *F*-ing that *P*.
Basis: L7′, CP.

L9. *S* is stating that the door is over there and thereby requesting *H* to leave.
Basis: It is MB-ed that doors are customary means of leaving a room. *S*'s most obvious additional illocutionary intent under these circumstances (a dispute) is to request *H* to leave.

(13b) Suppose *S* utters "My mouth is parched" to *H*, thereby stating that *S*'s mouth is very dry. Then *H* may infer:

L7′. *S* could not be merely stating that *S*'s mouth is very dry.
Basis: It is MB-ed that *S* had earlier come in out of the sun, this was not the subject of previous conversation, and so it is irrelevant.

L8. There is some *F*-ing that *P* connected in a way identifiable under the circumstances to stating that one's mouth is very dry, such that in stating that his mouth is very dry *S* could also be *F*-ing that *P*.
Basis: L7′, CP.

L9. *S* is stating that *S*'s mouth is very dry and thereby requesting a drink.
Basis: It is MB-ed that people whose mouths are very dry are thirsty, that being thirsty is uncomfortable, and that drinking something relieves thirst. *S*'s most obvious additional illocutionary intent under the circumstances (*S*'s thirst) is to request a drink.

(13c) Suppose S utters "I'm sure the cat likes having its tail pulled" to H, thereby (nonliterally) claiming that S is sure that the cat does not like having its tail pulled. H may infer:

L8'. S could not be merely claiming that the cat does not like having its tail pulled.
Basis: It is MB-ed by S and H already that this is true, so S would violate the presumption of quantity.

L9'. There is some F^*-ing that Q connected in a way identifiable under the circumstances to claiming that the cat does not like having its tail pulled, such that in claiming that the cat does not like having its tail pulled S could also be F^*-ing that Q.
Basis: L8', CP.

L10. S is claiming that the cat does not like having its tail pulled and thereby requesting H to stop it.
Basis: It is MB-ed that H's pulling the cat's tail hurts the cat and that S cares about the cat. S's most obvious additional illocutionary intent under these circumstances is to request H to stop pulling the cat's tail.

(13d) Suppose S utters "You're the boss" to H, thereby asserting that H is the boss. H may infer:

L7'. S could not be merely asserting that H is the boss.
Basis: It is MB-ed by S and H that this is true, so S would violate the presumption of quantity.

L8. There is some F-ing that P connected in a way identifiable under the circumstances to asserting that H is the boss, such that in asserting that H is the boss S could also be F-ing that P.
Basis: L7', CP.

L9. S is claiming that H is the boss and thereby agreeing to do what H says.
Basis: It is MB-ed that H wants S to do A, that S is reluctant to do so, but that because of H's position of authority over S, S has to do A. S's most obvious additional illocutionary intent under these circumstances is to agree to do A.

(13e) Suppose S utters "I should never have done that" to H, thereby stating that S should never have done some specific act A. H may infer:

L7'. S could not be merely stating that S should never have done A.
Basis: It is MB-ed by S and H that A adversely affected H, that S

should not do such things, etc. So S would violate the presumption of quantity.

L8. There is some F-ing that P connected in a way identifiable under the circumstances to stating that one should never have done A, such that in stating that one should never have done A one could also be F-ing that P.

Basis: L7', CP.

L9. S is stating that S should never have done A and thereby apologizing for having done A.

Basis: It is MB-ed that people often regret doing things they believe they should not have done. S's most obvious additional illocutionary intent under these circumstances is to apologize for doing A.

(13f) Suppose S utters "Did you bring any tennis balls? to H, thereby asking H whether H brought any tennis balls. H may infer:

L7'. S could not be merely asking whether H brought any tennis balls.

Basis: It is MB-ed that it is S's turn to supply the balls, so a mere question would be irrelevant.

L8. There is some F-ing that P connected in a way identifiable under the circumstances to asking whether H brought any tennis balls, such that in asking whether H brought any tennis balls S could also be F-ing that P.

Basis: L7', CP.

L9. S is asking whether H brought any tennis balls and thereby claiming that he (S) did not bring any.

Basis: It is MB-ed that it is S's turn to supply the balls, so S would not need to ask unless he forgot. S's most obvious additional illocutionary intent under these circumstances is to claim that S did not bring any balls.

As these examples illustrate, there is a heterogeneous variety of connections between S's direct illocutionary intent and S's indirect illocutionary intent. However, some connections are more regular and systematic than others.

(14) a. I want you to move over. (used to request H to move over)

   b. I intend to be there. (used to promise to be there)

   c. I regret having done that. (used to apologize)

In these cases S directly states that he has an attitude which is expressed in the performance of the indirect act. That this connection is quite straightforward and recognizable may account for the systematic nature of these examples, as well as of the following:

(15) a. Are you going to put out the garbage? (used to request *H* to put out the garbage)
b. You won't come back here again. (used to order *H* not to return)

In these cases *S* directly expresses desire to be informed about, or belief in, the act indirectly requested.

(16) a. Ought you to smoke here? (used to request *H* to stop smoking)
b. You shouldn't smoke here. (used to request *H* to stop smoking)

In these cases *S* directly expresses either desire to be informed about, or belief in, a certain reason for *H*'s action. Such obvious connections as those illustrated in (14)–(16) can give rise to standardized illocutions, whereby segments of the SAS are short-circuited. This interesting phenomenon is explained in chapter 9.

4.4. THE ELABORATED SCHEMA

We can now pull together the elaborated version of the SAS that covers nonliteral and indirect, as well as literal and direct illocutionary acts. *S* is *F*-ing that *P* if in the presence of some *H*, *S* utters some *e* in some language *L* intending, and expecting (pursuant to the LP, the CP, and the PL) *H* to recognize that he intends, *H* to infer (from the fact that *S* means ... by *e* and the fact that *S* is thereby saying that *(...p...)) that *S* is *F*-ing that *P*. On occasion *S* may be also *F'*-ing that *Q*. That is, *S* intends, and expects *H* to recognize that *S* intends, *H* to reason thus:

	Basis
L1. *S* is uttering *e*.	hearing *S* utter *e*
L2. *S* means ... by *e*.	L1, LP, MCBs
L3. *S* is saying that *(...p...).	L2, LP, MCBs
L4. *S*, if speaking literally, is *F**-ing that *p*.	L3, CP, MCBs
Either (*direct literal*),	
L5. *S* could be *F**-ing that *p*.	L4, MCBs
L6. *S* is *F**-ing that *p*.	L5, PL

And possibly (*literally based indirect*),

L7'. S could not be merely
       F^*-ing that p.   L6, MCBs
L8.   There is some F-ing that p
       connected in a way identi-
       fiable under the circum-
       stances to F^*-ing that p,
       such that in F^*-ing that p, S
       could also be F-ing that P.   L7', CP
L9. S is F^*-ing that p and
       thereby F-ing that P.   L8, MCBs

Or (*direct nonliteral*),

L5'. S could not (under the
       circumstances) be F^*-ing
       that p.   L4, MCBs
L6'. Under the circumstances
       there is a certain recog-
       nizable relation R between
       saying that p and some
       F-ing that P, such that S
       could be F-ing that P.   L3, L5', CP
L7. S is F-ing that P.   L6', MCBs

And possibly (*nonliterally based indirect*),

L8'. S could not merely be F-ing
       that P.   L7, MCBs
L9'. There is some F'-ing that Q
       connected in a way identi-
       fiable under the circum-
       stances to F-ing that P,
       such that in F-ing that P, S
       could also be F'-ing that Q. L8', CP
L10. S is F-ing that P and
       thereby F'-ing that Q.   L9', MCBs

According to the elaborated schema, H's identification of an illocutionary act is the result of applying a selection of inference strategies to
the utterance (assuming H has inferred L1):

Locutionary Strategy (LS): Given L1, infer L2, L3, L4.

Direct Literal Strategy (DLS): Given L4 (from LS), infer L5, L6.

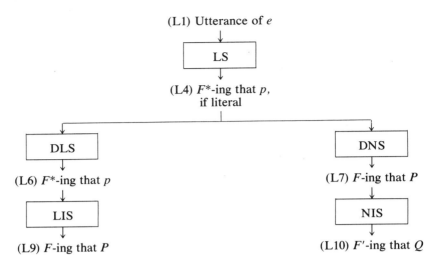

Figure 4.1 Organization of strategies

Literally-based Indirect Strategy (LIS): Given L6 (from DLS), infer L7', L8, L9.

Direct Nonliteral Strategy (DNS): Given L4 (from LS), infer L5', L6', L7.

Nonliterally-based Indirect Strategy (NIS): Given L7 (from DNS), infer L8', L9', L10.

All this is represented diagrammatically in figure 4.1.

We can now use an example presented earlier to show in more detail how to instantiate the SAS. Imagine the following situation: S has been working in the hot sun, H is in the kitchen, H asks S how the work is going, and S says that it is going fine and then adds "My mouth is parched." We will assume that these facts are among the MCBs held by S and H and that the LP, the CP, the PL, and the conversational presumptions are in effect. Then S intends (and expects H to recognize that S intends) H to reason thus:

Locutionary strategy:
L1. S is uttering "My mouth is parched."
L2. S means 'My mouth is very dry' by "My mouth is parched."
L3. S is saying that S's mouth is very dry.
L4. S, if speaking literally, is telling me (H) that S's mouth is very dry.

Literal strategy:

There is nothing (under the circumstances) incompatible with the supposition that S is telling me (H) that S's mouth is very dry. So

L5. S could be telling me (H) that S's mouth is very dry. So

L6. S is telling me (H) that S's mouth is very dry.

Literally-based indirect strategy:

(a) I (H) have not asked for or otherwise indicated in any way a desire for this information about S's mouth, nor has this come up in the conversation. So

(b) If L6 is all S is doing, S would be being irrelevant (violating presumption RE).

(c) But presumably S is being relevant. So

L7'. S could not be merely telling me (H) that S's mouth is very dry. So

L8. There is some further act connected in a way identifiable under the circumstances to S's telling me that his mouth is very dry, such that in telling me that his mouth is very dry, S could also be performing that act.

(a) One's mouth being very dry is usually symptomatic of thirst.

(b) Being thirsty is a state one wants to relieve by drinking something. So

(c) S desires a drink.

(d) S intends me (H) to infer (c).

(e) The obvious explanation for (d) is that S wants me to satisfy this desire, viz., by getting S a drink.

(f) S intends me (H) to infer (e).

(g) The obvious explanation for (f) is that S intends me (H) to get S a drink because S desires me (H) to. So

(h) S is expressing the desire that I (H) get S a drink and the intention that I (H) do so because S desires me to. So

L9. S is telling me (H) that S's mouth is very dry and is thereby asking me (H) to get S a drink.

This sort of inference operates in a wide variety of other examples, such as "Is your head cold, Private?" used to order someone to take off his hat, "I have the car tonight" used to offer to give someone a ride that night, and "That was a tough match" used to congratulate someone.

Do all indirect illocutionary acts involve such complex inferences? This question stems from two complementary considerations. First, certain types of expressions are especially suited to the indirect performance of certain types of illocutionary acts. Moreover, certain types of illocutionary acts are especially suited to being indirectly performed by the use of certain types of expressions. A good deal of linguistic literature, as well as philosophical literature prompted by it, has focused on these points. Sadock (1974), for instance, thinks that sentences like the following are ambiguous as to their force, with one meaning being interrogative, the other "idiomatically" imperative:

(17) a. Can you pass the salt? (Pass the salt!)
   b. Will you be quiet? (Be quiet!)
   c. Why not (don't you) shut up? (Shut up!)

Searle (1975a), on the other hand, thinks that these sentences are not ambiguous, but are "conventionally used" to request. We will postpone discussion of their positions (and of our alternative) until chapter 9, since almost everyone seems to agree that except for these special cases, most indirect acts should be analyzed inferentially and conversationally.

In summary, whether literal, nonliteral, or indirect, an illocutionary act must be such that if it is to be performed successfully and felicitously, the speaker can reasonably expect it to be identified by the hearer. This expectation is reasonable if it is based on what we have called mutual contextual beliefs, together with the various presumptions. What constitutes a reasonable expectation is complicated by the many sorts of inference routes that in different cases a hearer may be intended and expected to follow to arrive at the identity of the illocutionary act. We do not propose to catalog them here in any more detail than represented by the SAS, but whatever the exact route in a particular case, presumably (that is, by the CP) it must be such that the hearer can find it. Therefore, the utterance must be made with the intention that H can find the inference route, and part of what the hearer takes into account in trying to find the route is that the utterance is made with that intention.

Detailed as it is, the SAS does not represent the precise form of inference (to be) made by the hearer. Left open are the questions of just which mutual contextual beliefs are activated and of just how they enable the hearer to find the right candidate for the speaker's illocutionary intent (not that there is ever any guarantee of success). A complete account of the hearer's inference would require a systematic theory of saliency or obvious obviousness, a notion introduced by

Schelling (1960, ch. 3) in connection with coordination problems. To our knowledge no such theory has yet been developed. Until it has, the SAS can represent only the general pattern of the hearer's inference.

4.5. PERLOCUTIONARY ACTS

In section 1.7 we restricted perlocutionary acts to the intentional production of effects generated off of steps of the SAS, particularly off of illocutionary acts. In chapter 3 we noted the perlocutionary intentions correlated with the major types of illocutionary intents:

Constative: that H believe that P.

Directive: that H (intend to) do A.

Commissive: that H believe S intends to fulfill his obligation to do A.

Acknowledgment: that H believe S has the appropriate feeling.

In order to exclude irrelevant sorts of effects, such as neuron firings, we restrict perlocutionary acts to the (intentional) production of certain kinds of effects on H, namely, psychological states or intentional actions.

Unlike illocutionary intentions, perlocutionary intentions need not be recognized or intended to be recognized. They can be intended to be recognized, although in some cases (such as misleading or impressing someone) the hearer is intended *not* to recognize them. Not only can perlocutionary intentions be overt, they can be reflexive; but even when they are reflexive, they are not communicative in the way that illocutionary intentions are, for their fulfillment consists not in their recognition but in the production of some further effect.

The restrictions we have made on perlocutionary acts have at least two beneficial results. First, we can account for many of the differences (both well known and not so well known) between perlocutionary and illocutionary acts. Second, by restricting perlocutionary acts to (intended) effects generated off of steps of the SAS, the elaborated schema allows us to systematize some complicated and subtle perlocutionary actions and intents.

4.5.1. Perlocutions versus Illocutions

That perlocutionary effects are produced off of the SAS helps to explain why illocutionary acts are characteristically means to perlocutionary ends, and not vice versa. And that illocutionary intentions do, but perlocutionary intentions do not, need to be recognized to be fulfilled helps to explain why there should be illocutionary (performative) prefixes as in (18), but no perlocutionary prefixes as in (19).

(18) I (hereby) promise (order, state to, admit to, etc.) you that . . .
(19) *I (hereby) persuade (convince, surprise, etc.) you that . . .

Furthermore, because there are degrees of conviction, motivation, intention, and so on, perlocutionary intentions can have degrees of success in a way that illocutionary intentions cannot. *H* can be partially or completely convinced by *S*'s statement in a way that *S* cannot partially or completely make the statement. (Of course, *H* can be more or less accurate in his identification of the *contents* of *S*'s illocutionary intention.)

4.5.2. Perlocutions and the SAS

Every major step in the schema can give rise to some distinct perlocutionary effect and so be instrumental to the performance of some perlocutionary act. Not only does the schema enable us to identify these relationships systematically, it gains support from their very existence. It is hard to imagine how steps in the schema could have psychological effects without also having some psychological reality. Consider:

L1. By uttering "Don't wake up," *S* awakened *H*.
L2. In uttering "He cleaves to the principle" and meaning 'He adheres to the principle' by it, *S* impressed *H* with his vocabulary.
L3. By saying that religion is the opium of the people, *S* offended *H*.
L6. By predicting that Truman would win the election, *S* convinced *H* that he was clairvoyant.
L7. By (directly and nonliterally) stating that *H* could not have it both ways in uttering "You can't eat your cake and have it too," *S* reminded *H* that he usually remembered this proverb backwards.
L9. By (directly) demeaning *H*'s character and thereby (indirectly) challenging *H* to fight, *S* both irritated *H* and amused *H* with his pretension.

In addition to these sources of perlocutionary effect, there are some partially perlocutionary sources as well. First, *H*'s realization that *S* has a particular perlocutionary intention can itself give rise to a perlocutionary effect. For instance, the recognition of *S*'s intention to make H mad (in stating that P) can itself contribute to making H mad. Second, by F-ing that P, S may (intentionally) perform some perlocutionary act and, in virtue of doing that, intend to produce some further perlocutionary effect. For instance, in saying that the bull is about to charge, S might predict that the bull will charge. By predicting this, S may convince H that it will charge and by convincing H of this, S may frighten H enough to get H to move quickly out of danger. All of this could have been intended by S.

Chapter Five

The Status and Scope of the Speech Act Schema

Having elaborated the speech act schema we must now explain (1) its role in the analysis of linguistic communication, (2) the nature of the inferences it represents, (3) why such inferences can plausibly be attributed to people, and (4) what the schema leaves out.

The SAS represents the pattern of inference a hearer follows in identifying a speaker's illocutionary intent. We have claimed that linguistic communication essentially involves the speaker's issuing an utterance with an R-intention whose fulfillment consists in its recognition. Our analysis of linguistic communication does not require that this R-intention include the intention that the hearer make a detailed inference in exactly the form of the SAS. Such a requirement would preclude our concept of linguistic communication from applying to the utterances of everyday discourse. The SAS contains many steps as well as citations of mutual contextual beliefs and the several presumptions; to require the speaker to intend the hearer to make an inference of exactly the form of the SAS in every detail would be tantamount to attributing to the general public our theory of understanding communicative illocutionary acts, as encapsulated by the SAS. On the other hand, we cannot allow the speaker to have just any kind of intention as to how his illocutionary intent is to be recognized and his illocutionary act thereby identified. Without intending the hearer to follow the SAS in detail, the speaker must at least R-intend the hearer to identify his illocutionary intent on the basis of what he utters, in accordance with the linguistic presumption and the communicative presumption. That, we claim, is necessary and sufficient for attempted linguistic communication.[1]

If the full-blown SAS is not embodied in the (conceptual) analysis of linguistic communication, what is its status? If the SAS is not part and parcel of speakers' communicative intentions, it can represent only the pattern of inference hearers actually make in identifying speakers' intentions. The claim that it does so is an extremely strong empirical hypothesis, one for which we have provided little evidence, and so we must show why the SAS is at least a plausible model of the inferences that hearers actually make. Otherwise, what reason is there for taking it seriously? One possible response is that the SAS does not represent the inferences hearers actually make but constitutes *rational reconstruction* of such inferences.[2] Rather than weaken our claim for the SAS in this way, we hope to show that the SAS is much more realistic psychologically than it might seem, given its ostensible complexity.

5.1. THE SAS AND THE ANALYSIS OF LINGUISTIC COMMUNICATION

Our first task is to indicate the relation between the SAS and our analysis of linguistic communication. In our account, linguistic communication essentially involves issuing an utterance with an R-intention whose fulfillment consists in its recognition. Our taxonomy of communicative illocutionary acts (in chapter 3) catalogs what sorts of R-intentions are communicative. An R-intention whose fulfillment consists in its recognition is an expression of attitude; it is fulfilled if the hearer identifies that attitude in the way intended.

The analysis of linguistic communication does not require that the speaker's R-intention include all the details represented in the SAS about how his illocutionary intent is to be recognized. Then how should we construe a case in which the speaker intends the hearer to infer his intent in one specific way but the hearer identifies it (correctly) in some other way? It might be argued that the speaker has not performed a successful act of linguistic communication, even though the hearer does identify his illocutionary intent. The underlying assumption here is that if there is a discrepancy between the inference H makes and the inference he is intended to make—even if he manages to identify S's intent—then S has not succeeded in linguistically communicating his intent to H. To be problematic, presumably the discrepancy in question must be not just one of degree (the hearer following the SAS without being intended to follow its exact details) but one of outright conflict. Does such a conflict generate a counterexample to our analysis of linguistic communication?

Suppose S says to H "Dinner is ready," thereby indirectly requesting H to come to the table. S intends H to reason as follows:

1. *S* is uttering "Dinner is ready."
2. By "Dinner is ready" *S* means 'Dinner is ready.'
3. *S* is saying that dinner is ready.
4. *S* is stating that dinner is ready.
5. *S* is not merely stating that dinner is ready.
6. *H* is hungry.
7. *S* wants *H* (and is requesting *H*) to come to the table.

However, after step 5 *H* reasons differently:

6'. *S* gets upset whenever I show no interest in *S*'s cooking.
7. *S* wants me (and is requesting me) to come to the table.

This is a clear case where the hearer infers the speaker's illocutionary intent but not as he was intended to infer it. Is it therefore *not* a case of genuine communication, or is it a genuine case notwithstanding the discrepancy in how the illocutionary intent is identified? We are inclined to say that it is a case of successful requesting and that the discrepancy is not great enough to rule it out as linguistic communication. To be sure, there is an element of misunderstanding between *S* and *H,* but not about *S*'s illocutionary intent. *H* misunderstands *S*'s reason for having that intent and, derivatively, *H*'s reason for identifying it is different from the one *S* intended. Nevertheless, it seems to us that *S* has succeeded in expressing his desire that *H* come to the table and has thereby successfully performed the illocutionary act of requesting.

The discrepancy in this example concerns the relevant mutual contextual belief. Discrepancies regarding other inference elements in the SAS also can occur without vitiating successful linguistic communication and the performance of an illocutionary act. A speaker can intend to utter one thing, but utter another. He might utter "Foreman dealt Frazier a blushing crow." The hearer, if he recognizes this spoonerism, can correct for it and go on to make the intended inference. Similarly, with a malapropism the hearer can again make the appropriate adjustment.[3] Indeed a speaker, knowing that *H* misuses a certain word, can intentionally misuse it, relying on *H*'s mistaken belief about what the word means; *S* might use "enervated" to mean 'energetic,' thereby getting his misinformed audience to think that this is what he (*S*) thinks it means. This is an example of how there can be a discrepancy between the inference *S* intends *H* to make and the inference *H* thinks he is intended to make (and makes) without vitiating successful communication. Furthermore, in such a case the speaker intends the hearer's inference to contain a false step, namely, that "enervated" means 'energetic.'

In general, it seems to us that minor discrepancies between the inference intended and the inference made are compatible with successful linguistic communication, provided of course that the hearer does manage to identify the speaker's illocutionary intent. We do not see how to demonstrate this, though obviously if successful communication required perfect congruence between the inference intended and the inference made, successful communication would rarely take place. Nevertheless, there is a very difficult question that a thoroughgoing analysis would have to answer: what is the difference between a minor discrepancy and a discrepancy large enough to vitiate communication, even though the hearer does manage to identify the speaker's intent? Lacking a systematic account of this difference, we can still say that in everyday life minor discrepancies occur all the time without even being noticed, much less without disrupting communication.

Notice further that although successful communication requires that the hearer identify the speaker's illocutionary intent and recognize it as intended to be recognized, it does not require that the speaker and the hearer mutually believe that the hearer has identified the speaker's illocutionary intent. Even when communication has succeeded, it is possible for S to believe it has not succeeded (that H has misidentified S's illocutionary intent) or to believe that H believes it has not succeeded. For that matter, H might believe, quite mistakenly, that he has misidentified S's illocutionary intent. In practice, to the extent that the success of communication is verified at all by S and H (countless failures undoubtedly go unnoticed) verification is generally achieved not by repetition, direct inquiry, hearer paraphrase, and the like, but by a sense of coherence between the utterance in question and subsequent ones.

Although successful communication does not require verification or mutual belief, there seems to be (along with the communicative presumption) a presumption of understanding, of communicative success. Just as there is a presumption that the speaker's illocutionary intent be identifiable, so there is a presumption that the hearer has succeeded in identifying it. If there is no indication to the contrary (a request for repetition, paraphrase, or elaboration, or even a mere sign of bewilderment), it is assumed that successful communication has been achieved. In particular, if there is no expressed doubt by H (or by S) concerning success, the conversation proceeds normally. Moreover, if there is some discrepancy between the inference intended and the inference made, it is highly unlikely, assuming the hearer has correctly identified the speaker's illocutionary intent, that this discrepancy will become an issue.

We have seen that minor discrepancies do not vitiate linguistic communication. However, not just any hearer inference to the right illocutionary intent counts as successful communication. The hearer might totally misunderstand S and yet, quite coincidentally, identify S's illocutionary intent anyway. Surely that would not count as successful communication. But why not? We want to say that even when there are discrepancies of the sorts we have mentioned, still the hearer must make his inference on the basis of what the speaker utters (or intends to utter) and thereby on what the speaker says (or intends to say). Moreover, only if the communicative presumption applies to the context of utterance can the hearer reasonably take the speaker to have a certain illocutionary intent that he intends the hearer to recognize (on the basis of what is uttered). The presence of the CP, together with the LP, severely constrains the possible inferences the speaker can reasonably expect, and thus intend, the hearer to make and, correlatively, the possible inferences the hearer does make. The CP requires that the illocutionary intent be identifiable on the basis of what is uttered, and the CP is itself activated (if not activated already) by the very fact of utterance. When an utterance is made under one of the special circumstances in which the CP is suspended (recitation, elocution lesson, quotation), the speaker cannot reasonably expect the hearer even to seek, much less identify, some illocutionary intent, and the hearer has no reason to do so, unless there is some special indication.[4]

We suggest, then, that communication has succeeded just in case the hearer correctly identifies the speaker's illocutionary intent on the basis of what the speaker utters, under the supposition (normally justified by the CP) that this intent is intended to be recognized. It does not matter precisely how identification is made. It does not even matter that the speaker may intend the hearer to make a false step in his inference (and that the hearer makes it), or that the hearer may attribute an intention to the speaker by correcting for a slip of the tongue or a malapropism. Part of the reason that such discrepancies do not vitiate linguistic communication is that the existence of a communicative intention is determined independently of its identity. Its existence is determined in virtue of the communicative presumption—what is in question for the hearer when the CP is in effect is not the existence but the identity of the speaker's communicative intention.[5] However, an account is needed of just how big a discrepancy (and of what sorts) is compatible with successful linguistic communication.

5.2. THE EXPLANATORY VALUE OF THE SAS

The speech act schema represents, we claim, the pattern of inference hearers usually make in identifying speakers' communicative intentions. This pattern of inference is complex, and to attribute it to people in ordinary communication situations is to impute to them complex cognitive abilities that are exercised whenever they are addressed. (We have not attributed to speakers the intention that hearers identify communicative intentions precisely in accordance with the SAS.)

In attributing this complex pattern of inference to people in their role as hearers, we are offering a psychological description (or at least the form of one) of what goes on in everyday communication. In the next section we endeavor to show that this description is psychologically realistic (we cannot prove that it actually applies). For the moment, we wish to show what explanatory value it has, assuming it to be genuinely applicable to the inferences that hearers make. Its explanatory value, we suggest, is twofold. (1) From the point of view of the hearer, to go through an inference in the pattern of the SAS is in effect to provide himself with an explanation of the speaker's utterance: to explain S's utterance is to identify the intention with which it is issued. (2) From the standpoint of psychological explanation, the organization of ingredients in the SAS provides a framework in terms of which the ability of hearers to identify speakers' illocutionary intents can be described and ultimately explained.

What sort of explanation does the hearer seek of the speaker's utterance? The utterance is the act of uttering a certain sentence with a certain meaning, and the hearer's identification of it (up to ambiguity) involves nothing more than the exercise of the hearer's linguistic competence. However, he seeks also to identify the locutionary and the illocutionary act performed by the speaker in his utterance, and this involves ascribing intentions to the speaker, in particular, the intention to be performing a certain illocutionary act (by way of performing a certain locutionary act). To identify the intended illocutionary act is to explain the utterance. The sort of explanation involved here is just what we use whenever we explain what somebody is doing by citing the intention with which he is doing it.[6]

For psychology the organization of ingredients in the SAS provides a framework in terms of which the abilities and performances of speaker-hearers can be described in detail. Of course, the SAS does not cover everything involved. There is the further problem for cognitive (and social) psychology of determining how social norms, mutual contextual beliefs, and other beliefs about the social situation enter into concrete communicative intentions and inferences. Moreover, the SAS abstracts from the ongoing nature of verbal interchange. Sentences are produced one after another, often in fits and starts, with each speaker-hearer cognitively engaged not only in the production or perception of strings of words but in the social interchange of the conversation itself, as well as in private cognitive activity, which is not only unexpressed but may even be irrelevant to the social situation. Producing a sentence to express one's illocutionary intent requires selecting what to express and finding the words to express it, all the while thinking on what the conversation is about.

We have offered the SAS as representing inferences the hearer has to make to identify the speaker's illocutionary intent. If hearers generally do identify speakers' illocutionary intents in this way, it may be argued that the SAS does indeed represent the form of inference hearers make. However, this line of argument may seem suspect. In particular, what is the force of saying that hearers *have* to make such inferences in order to identify illocutionary intents? Any inference that results in a correct (or even justifiable) identification will do as far as identifying the illocutionary intent is concerned, but that is not what we want. We want an inference form that yields justified identifications, one that does so using information available to hearers in ordinary communication situations. Our claim is that the SAS represents just such an inference pattern. To claim further that it represents inferences hearers actually make requires further claims: (a) that hearers cannot make justified inferences without using such information, (b) that no other pattern of inference using just that information leads to justified identifications, and (c) that hearers' identifications are, at least generally, justified. If these claims can be established, it follows that hearers generally do make inferences in the form of the SAS. Otherwise, there would be no explaining hearers' general success. We consider psychological data relevant to these claims in chapter 11.

Here we should make clear just what we are claiming for the SAS and what we are not claiming. On the one hand, we are claiming that the SAS represents both the search procedure and the justification used by the hearer in identifying the speaker's illocutionary intent. These are not normally distinguished for a very simple reason: that the hearer arrives at a plausible candidate for the identity of the intent is, and is taken to be, good reason to believe it to be the correct one. On the other hand, although the step-by-step character of the SAS represents the natural way of organizing, linearly, the abundance of information available to and relied on by the hearer, we are *not* claiming that the process of inference is necessarily sequential in nature. When S's intention isn't transparent and the inference made automatically, H may have to go through a trial-and-error process of toying with different interpretations compatible with both S's utterance and with what he (H) believes about S and S's likely intentions under the circumstances. Though operating on the overarching assumption, the CP, that S's intention can be recognized and is expected to be, H may still need some imagination to work it out. He may have to go back and reinterpret what S said, by changing references or the operative senses of ambiguous terms. He may decide that S is speaking nonliterally, or he may conclude that he didn't hear S correctly and try to recall S's exact words. H may have trouble arriving at a determination of force and content that are compatible, for one reading of the content may suggest one way to take the utterance, another another. In practice, of course, H can ask S to repeat himself or to restate what he said.

5.3. ON THE PSYCHOLOGICAL REALITY OF THE SAS

To suppose that the SAS represents the pattern of inference that hearers make in identifying communicative intentions is to make a rather strong assumption about the human cognitive abilities involved in communication. We cannot demonstrate that people normally do make inferences represented by the SAS, but we will attempt at least to show that this supposition is empirically plausible. We suggest that inferences according to the SAS are no more complex than all sorts of other inferences people commonly make. Moreover, we argue that communicative inferences must follow the pattern of the SAS if they are to be rational at all—and we assume they are. Then in section 5.4 we discuss those aspects of the SAS that rest on an assumption that the role of the presumptions and of mutual contextual beliefs in communication is no different from the role of mutual beliefs in social phenomena generally. Our overall goal is to show that the SAS imputes nothing to people, either cognitively or socially, that is not reasonable to attribute to them in other contexts than communicative ones. In other words, we suggest that the cognitive and social aspects of communication are but special cases of much more general phenomena in cognitive and social psychology.

One thing we are assuming is that people can and do perform complex mental operations very rapidly, generally unaware of the details of what they are doing. This assumption may be objectionable to those who reject the idea of mental operations altogether or to those enthusiasts of introspection who believe that every mental state is subject to its possessor's awareness. We know of no general way to appease dogged behaviorists on the one hand or die-hard Cartesians on the other and can only challenge them to account for people's ability to identify communicative intentions without appealing to such complex cognitive processes as those we are assuming to take place. We believe that there is nothing unusual about the complexity of the inferences we attribute to hearers. Equally complex operations seem to be involved in such processes as perceptual identification, motor coordination, and problem solving. Of course, it makes little sense to make quantitative comparisons of this sort, hence there is little content to the claim that communicative inference is no more complicated than, say, listening to music or playing tennis. We are in no position to say what any of these abilities involves; on the other hand, we see no reason to deny that a detailed scientific account of communicative inference should be of the same order as that of other human cognitive abilities. In particular, our cognitive assumption is no more extravagant than that made by many contemporary linguists and psycholinguists that aspects of the grammar of a language reflect certain highly complex cognitive abilities involved in the perception and production of sentences.

Let us turn to the details of the SAS. An inference in the pattern of the SAS is not deductive but what might be called an inference to a plausible explanation, namely, of the speaker's utterance.[7] In general, one good explanation is enough. The inference is abetted by the presumptions, which license the belief that there is some communicative intention identifiable from what is uttered and relevant mutual contextual beliefs. The latter provide the basis for determining what that intention is. The pattern of the SAS plays the dual role of representing both H's procedure for identifying S's communicative intention and H's justification for thinking he has identified it. The very fact that an intention has been picked out is usually sufficient to justify the claim that the speaker has it. However, the SAS gives no detail, at least in the case of nonliteral and indirect acts of communication, about the specific strategy the hearer uses to identify a particular communicative intent. It gives no indication of how certain mutual beliefs are activated or otherwise picked out as relevant, much less how the correct identification is made. And yet people do it somehow. So there is even more to hearers' inferences than what is represented in the SAS.

It would be preposterous to claim that hearers ordinarily[8] go through the SAS explicitly, consciously proceeding from one step to the next. Were this the rule, we would not be so hard put to specify the sorts of mutual contextual beliefs that enter into illocutionary inferences, or to spell out the search strategies that exploit them. But we should not be too skeptical about the existence and unconscious use of mutual beliefs and search strategies. Think of the comparably complex and inexplicit processes (whatever they may be like in detail) involved in such cognitive operations as perceptual identification, motor coordination, and social behavior. Our empirical thinking in general is rife with generalizations and inference principles that we are not conscious of when we use them, if we are conscious of them at all. It would take us well beyond present-day cognitive psychology to speculate on the details of any of this. Instead, we merely suggest that complex, inexplicit operations are commonplace, that most of our everyday practical thinking involves much more than meets the introspective eye. Whatever these processes are, whatever activates them, whatever principles or strategies are involved, they work and work well. Almost all such inference is implicit. We cannot merely by introspection formulate in any detail the principles we use, and it is extremely difficult to reflect on the patterns of one's own past inferences to ascertain what principles or strategies they embody. Nevertheless, they seem to possess the same order of differentiation and articulateness that linguistic performance possesses, and cannot be regarded as being less complex or governed by rules (principles, strategies) of lesser complexity. That we cannot readily identify all their ingredients attests to their complexity and subtlety, not to their nonexistence or blatant simplicity.

5.4. THE SAS AND SOCIAL PSYCHOLOGY

We have suggested that there is nothing inordinate about the cognitive complexity of the pattern of inference in the SAS. Such inference involves the activation of mutual contextual beliefs and the application of the presumptions, which are themselves mutual beliefs. We claim that there is nothing extraordinary in the supposition that communication situations involve such mutual beliefs. Indeed, as argued in the appendix, social situations in general are governed by mutual beliefs of various sorts. There it is also proposed that basic sociological concepts, such as rules, roles, and groups, can be analyzed in terms of certain mutual beliefs. Here we would like merely to give some indication of how social situations have certain features describable in terms of mutual belief, features shared by communicative and noncommunicative situations. Our hope is to show that from the standpoint of social psychology there is nothing special in kind about the nature of communicative situations and the fact that they involve mutual beliefs. We will not pretend to have offered a theory of the social psychological side of linguistic communication. As with the cognitive psychological side, we seek merely to make the attribution of inferences in the fashion of the SAS empirically plausible.

In virtually every interpersonal situation, a person can and does classify the situation and the persons present as being of certain sorts. If he is at a ball game, he is aware of that fact and he classifies those present as players, managers, coaches, umpires, spectators, ushers, and vendors. There are not only rules of the game proper, but rules governing spectator, vendor, and usher behavior. Certain subsituations are defined as selling, seating, or applauding situations. How a person is categorized has much to do with what he is to do when. The rules governing behavior in the various subsituations that arise are by and large mutually believed by those present, so that almost everyone not only knows what to do and what not to do when, but has reason to believe that almost everyone else has like knowledge regarding himself. What is more, each has reason to attribute this knowledge of everyone else's knowledge to everyone else. In short, the various rules applying to types of persons and types of situations are mutually recognized. Of course, there may also be more specialized rules, not mutually recognized by all concerned, that pertain to such matters as how a player should wear his socks or how a hot dog vendor should apply mustard.

We suggest that every interpersonal situation, ranging from casual (or intimate) two-person encounters to elaborate ceremonies and complex institutional activities involve mutually recognized rules that apply to persons and types of situations. What is especially germane to our subject is that part and parcel of the existence and sustenance of such rules are people's expectations, both descriptive and normative, about one another's behavior in various situations that arise in everyday life. Not only do people expect one another to act in certain mutually recognized ways, as determined (at least in part) by mutually recognized rules governing mutually recognized types of persons and types of situations, they expect others to expect them to act in these ways.

None of this excludes the possibility of either individual differences in social behavior (generally social rules do not specify all that is to be done, but impose general requirements that may leave open many options) or individual violations of the rules. The point is merely that social situations are invariably, though to different degrees, constrained by mutually recognized rules and that people have expectations, recognize expectations, make judgments, and acknowledge judgments concerning each other's behavior. In particular, they judge others' behavior, and assume that others judge their behavior, in terms of these rules, and regard compliance with or violation of them as intentional. Indeed, not only is this behavior intentional and regarded as such by others, at least to some extent it is intended to be regarded as intentional. Not that people always explicitly formulate intentions about how others are to construe their behavior, though this happens fairly often. But given their awareness of the situation and the persons in it and their recognition of the rules that govern it, and given the mutuality of this awareness and this recognition, people's behavior vis-à-vis the rules cannot but be expected to be regarded by one another as intentional. Awareness of the situation invokes the rules; recognition of the rules activates the expectations.

It does not follow that social behavior, though generally intentional and expected to be recognized as such, is communicative, but it comes close. Social behavior is not necessarily communicative because people need not intend that others make inferences on the basis of their behavior (much less expect to be recognized as intending it). However, it is perfectly possible and hardly unusual for social behavior to be communicative. Rule violations, if committed with recognizable R-intentions, can communicate the agent's contempt for society, his disrespect for those present, or even his acknowledgment that the rules can be relaxed. Or a person can obey the rules in such a way that he communicates his contempt for them or for those present. So communication in the course of obeying or violating social rules is quite possible. Needless to say, nonlinguistic communication in the course of social interaction need not be based on obeying or violating social rules. We do not propose to catalog the variety of such acts of communication, but we do believe they involve R-intentions and recognition thereof. Of course, the linguistic and the communicative presumptions are not relevant. In general, a piece of social behavior is communicative if it has some feature that is R-intended to be recognized and to serve as a basis for recognizing the agent's intent. Since (generally) no CP is involved, that feature must call attention to the fact that the behavior is communicative, that is, that it is R-intended to serve as a basis for explaining the behavior by identifying the agent's intent. After all, communication, whether linguistic or otherwise, is the upshot of behavior exhibited with the intention that relevant observers ("addressees") explain it by attributing a certain (R-) intention to the agent.

Lack of linguistic knowledge and of social knowledge generally makes it not only impossible to know what to do and not to do when, but impossible to form communicative intentions or recognize others' intentions. This is obvious to anyone who has experienced a radically unfamiliar or alien social situation. Moreover, we are able to identify people who lack this knowledge. Indeed, part of our knowledge is of how to categorize those who lack it: as foreigners, morons, or children. Finally, there are those who seem not just ignorant of but oblivious to social rules and expectations. It is no wonder that communication to and from them is especially difficult and frustrating.

Much more could be said about the cognitive aspects of language and of nonlinguistic social behavior. We have tried merely to indicate that there is nothing unusual or unrealistic about the attributions to people made implicitly in the SAS. We have suggested only that nonlinguistic communication is an everyday affair and that it involves complex beliefs, intentions, and inferences. It may be somewhat less complex than linguistic communication, but only because of the complexity of language itself and of the resultant richness and variety of linguistic acts.

5.5. COLLATERAL ACTS AND SOCIAL MOVES

We have so far given the SAS center stage in the discussion of talk-exchanges, mainly because linguistic communication is one of the primary purposes of such exchanges and, if we are right, the SAS is central to linguistic communication. But not all linguistic acts are performed via the SAS. In this section we survey noncommunicative linguistic acts and classify the intentions with which they are performed. Moreover, inasmuch as talk-exchanges are social as well as linguistic events, we think it useful to mention some of the ways a talk-exchange may be advanced, as well as the conditions necessary to sustain it.

5.5.1. Collateral Acts

An assortment of conversational acts can be performed in conjunction with or in lieu of illocutionary acts. Let us call these collateral acts. Like the perlocutionary intentions discussed in chapter 4, the intentions behind these acts may or may not be intended to be recognized. In some cases the intention can be fulfilled only if it is *not* recognized; in other cases the intention is an R-intention and thus cannot be fulfilled without being recognized. We might call the first sort *covert* acts and the second *overt*. And some collateral acts involve intentions whose fulfillment is independent of their recognition; these are neither covert nor overt in the senses just defined.

Collateral acts that exploit the communicative presumption in one way or another are necessarily *overt*, since to succeed the hearer must recognize this exploitation. Kidding, storytelling, joking, punning, mimicking, and reciting are essentially overt collateral acts at least when the addressee is among those who are intended to appreciate the act. Of course, you can kid or mimic someone without intending him to recognize it.

To *kid* someone is, roughly, to R-intend to say something without meaning it. Suppose, in a romantic situation, S says to H, who is affectionately tickling her toes but with nearly excruciating results, "If you don't stop that, I'll tell my mother to stay home." H's mother-in-law has been invited for dinner, you see, but considering the mutual contextual belief that H is not excited about this prospect, S intends it to be obvious to H that she does not mean what she is saying, that she is not making a threat. Besides, it is mutually believed that S has a low tickling tolerance, so there is no reason for H to think that S intends to be informing him of anything. Rather, S is simply kidding—she does not mean what she says and she R-intends H to recognize that. When she really wants H to stop tickling her, she will withdraw her feet.

If a speaker states that he is about to *tell a story* or a *joke*, he has thereby suspended the communicative presumption explicitly, R-intending his audience to recognize the sequel for what he is stating it to be. But suppose there is no explicit indication that the CP is being suspended, so that the audience has to recognize the utterance as a story or a joke. S R-intends H to do this, expecting H to realize that S's utterance is not a genuine illocutionary act. That is, what S is saying cannot be taken, either literally or figuratively, directly or indirectly, as expressing any attitude on the part of S, including the belief that his utterance is an expression of an attitude (it is not necessary to the successful telling of a story or a joke that one be taken as believing or intending it to be edifying or amusing). S R-intends H to take his utterance to be simply a presentation of something fictive; presumably this intention is fulfilled because of the content of S's utterance. S is exploiting the CP by violating it to the extent that he is not performing an identifiable illocutionary act but not to the extent that what he is doing is not identifiable. The content makes it identifiable as a story or joke. Of course, the story or the joke may itself require the audience to make certain inferences, but these reflect the intentions of the originator of the lines. In general, it is irrelevant whether the originator happens to be the speaker.

Puns are a special case of jokes for two reasons. For one thing, they exploit linguistic relationships, be they phonetic, semantic, or even syntactic. Moreover, unlike jokes, puns generally occur within regular discourse. Suppose after finishing his sausage S says to his luncheon companion at the Dusseldorf Deli "That was the worst thing I could have done for my liver." He may not have meant what he said, but only that the liverwurst tasted terrible enough to make him sick, at least figuratively speaking. As for the pun, his R-intention is that his companion recognize the phonetic connection between "worst . . . liver" and "liverwurst." Not that a pun must be intended to be recognized. In any case, especially with a pun like this one, there is always the out, usually disingenuous, "No pun intended." A known punster, however, may rely on his reputation to produce plays on words that would be undetectable but for the presumption that he makes them at all costs. Indeed, a punster can exploit his own reputation (and that of puns generally) by producing puns so trite, trivial, or otherwise outrageous that his R-intention can only be (one hopes) to produce a pun that is amusing precisely because it is bad. This is verbal high camp.

Then there is the overt collateral act of *mimicking*. When a person imitates someone else's manner of speaking, assuming he has not announced he is going to mimic, he R-intends the audience to recognize his intent by means of the similarity between how he says whatever he says and how the person in question characteristically speaks. Even when the content of the utterance is relevant, as when Nixon imitators would begin by saying, "Let me make one thing perfectly clear," the speaker need not mean anything or intend to be performing any illocutionary act, though he does have an R-intention; in this case the intention includes that H recognize that what S is saying is what the person imitated typically says.

Finally, for the overt act of *reciting* (a poem), as well as for acts like quoting and play acting or rehearsing, the context is normally such, either in virtue of some prefatory remark or of the situation itself, that no one takes the CP to be operative. In these contexts it is mutually believed by all concerned that the lines of a poem or play are being uttered. Still, it is a matter of R-intention, however transparent, that this is what is going on.

Certain collateral acts are not necessarily either covert or overt. It is indifferent to their success whether the intention with which they are performed is recognized. This is true of many perlocutionary acts as well, but the collateral acts to be examined here are not perlocutionary in the strict sense of the term.

In *circumlocution* the speaker compromises the presumption of manner in order to avoid the offense to the hearer or the embarrassment to himself that explicit language would engender. Instead of saying "It's about time you got here," one might say to a tardy guest "We were beginning to worry about you." Both utterances acknowledge the guest's late arrival, but only the second does so tactfully.

Changing the subject is a common collateral act with a range of possible purposes. One may change the subject to avoid revealing a secret, to keep from committing oneself on something, to avoid excessive dwelling on a subject painful to oneself or to the hearer, to confuse the hearer, to test the hearer's interest or persistence, or simply to liven up the conversation. The speaker may have an R-intention, namely, to implicate by violating the presumption of relevance his reason for changing the subject, but his intention need not be recognized to be fulfilled. Whether the hearer cooperates depends on more than his recognition of the speaker's intention to change the subject.

And there is the phenomenon of *small talk,* conversation whose primary purpose is to ease the awkwardness of silence. Here the unexpressed intention is to fill the air and pass the time with a minimum of discomfort. This does not imply that the speakers' illocutionary intentions in saying whatever they say are insincere, though the exchange may lack the importance they are cooperatively pretending it has—you do not have to care to be sincere. The main thing is that everyone recognizes, perhaps recognizing that others recognize, the vacuum-abhorring nature of the conversation, but no one is willing to be explicit about this recognition for fear of embarrassing himself or insulting the others.

The social management of embarrassment is a topic for social psychology; we will only point out a general feature of it. There are many things that when mentioned are embarrassing, to either the speaker or the hearer, even though they are obvious to both: an unsightly facial blemish, a nervous tic, a foul odor, a faux pas. By keeping touchy topics verbally concealed, people cooperate to protect their social selves from one another. Any utterance that focuses attention on something else is collaterally the act of covering up a source of embarrassment. The intention to do so may be intended not to be recognized, but it need not be so intended.

The examples just mentioned are special cases of a pervasive social phenomenon, the *verbal taboo,* a rule against mentioning a certain thing. Something need not itself be taboo for mentioning it to be. For example, there seems to be a taboo against mentioning certain features of social relationships. In a doctor-patient relationship the ground rules may permit the doctor to touch, and prohibit the patient from preventing him from touching, the patient's private parts. Despite the lack of personal familiarity between the two, this physical contact is regarded as perfectly proper—most patients are not overly embarrassed by it, and most doctors do not feel that they are intruding. Nevertheless, there seems to be a social dictate against mentioning the nature of this situation; to do so would be embarrassing. Similarly, when people of unequal social or professional position have occasion to interact, even though the inequality is mutually recognized as the superior exercises his rights and enjoys his privileges over his inferior, it would be socially awkward for either to mention the inequality of the situation. Not only would that be an act of disrespect, it would threaten, or be perceived to threaten, the social structure in which this relationship obtains. As in the cases of cooperative coverup, in an utterance issued with the collateral intention of avoiding mention of and diverting attention from a verbal taboo, the intention need not be covert to be fulfilled. Verbal taboo does not prevent the unmentionable item from being an object of awareness, but it protects all concerned from having any responsibility for making the awareness explicit, much less mutual.

Motives of politeness, respect, and self-protection figure in a variety of collateral acts. Social grace may require speaking in a certain style, evidenced by using certain forms of words and certain modes of pronunciation and inflection. Forms of address can be carefully chosen, and the do's and don'ts of social propriety can be carefully observed. To some extent the motive of social propriety may be evident from a person's illocutionary intentions, but largely one's intention to be and

to appear proper is collateral to the performance of particular illocutionary acts. This intention, whether recognized or not, is fulfilled more
in the how than in the what of one's utterances and other acts of social
exchange. The intention to be or appear proper (or improper, offensive,
cool, hip, sophisticated, powerful, important) cannot be an R-intention,
although one may wish to communicate that one has knowledge of how
to be proper (or whatever) and utter something with an R-intention to
this effect. But the intention to be or to appear proper cannot be overt
and, if it is to be fulfilled, may even have to be covert. For in some
circles part of what being proper involves is not having to make an
effort, hence not having to intend, to be proper.

Covert collateral acts are performed with intentions that are intended
not to be recognized. Generally, these are acts of manipulation, including such devious acts as innuendo, deliberate ambiguity, and
"sneaky presupposition." Whereas indirect illocutionary acts are not
explicit and yet are performed with R-intentions, covert collateral acts
succeed (the intention with which they are performed is fulfilled) only if
their intent is not recognized, or at least not recognized as intended to
be recognized. The idea is to get someone to think you think something
and thereby to get him to think it without recognizing that that's what
you want him to do. Whereas an indirect act is performed with an
intention that can be reasonably expected to be recognized (on the
basis of the utterance and the context), so that the speaker cannot, if
challenged, plausibly deny that he intended the hearer to infer his intention, the key to innuendo is deniability. One can make a veiled
suggestion that someone is a foreign agent by saying "Sparsky didn't
look the least chagrined when Krasny told him that Azevedo's Portu-
guese cover had been blown." If this sentence is uttered in the course
of a matter-of-fact account of an observed conversation between
Sparsky and Krasny, both of them on the same side as the speaker and
his audience, the inference that Sparsky is a traitor is not going to be
drawn on the basis of recognizing an R-intention. The speaker knew
this in choosing his words and bears no responsibility for the inference
he covertly intends to be drawn.

Deniability is preserved also in what Ann Weiser (1974) calls "deliberate ambiguity." If Boy says to Girl, "Are you doing anything tonight?" he protects himself from the embarrassment of rejection by
intending his utterance to be taken merely as a question if her answer is
"Yes" and as an invitation if it is "No." Assuming the hearer does not
recognize the speaker's intention to be ambiguous, the speaker has

direct control over how the utterance will be taken, given the response. If the hearer does recognize his intention, she can determine how the utterance has to be taken, by saying such things as "Yes, but I'm free tomorrow night" or "No, I'd rather stay home and read tonight." In a later article Weiser (1975) calls the move of taking the ambiguity one way rather than the other "selection by reply."[9]

In deliberate ambiguity clearly the speaker does not have an R-intention that his utterance be taken in one of two ways. Rather, since his deliberate ambiguity is covert, he has a simple intention that the hearer take him to have one of two possible R-intentions, which one to be determined by the subsequent course of conversation. Weiser (1974) emphasizes illocutionary ambiguity in her discussion of devices for managing socially tricky situations, but semantic ambiguity can work equally well, as in "I'd like to see more of you" uttered under suitable circumstances. Of course, deliberate ambiguity need not be covert, but then its motive is not self-protection but titillation, as "I'd like to see more of you" would be if uttered with rising intonation and eyebrows in the manner of Groucho Marx. Double entendre is semantic ambiguity that is intended to be recognized, as when S, admiring H's gilded coathangers, says "I'd love to hang up your clothes for you," which can be taken as both an offer and an invitation.

Another kind of covert collateral act is what Hutchinson (1971) speaks of as "sneaking new information into presuppositions." For example, one might say "Fortunately, the CIA is no longer involved in political assassinations" in order to avoid asserting explicitly that the CIA used to be so involved and thereby to make it more difficult for the hearer to challenge this proposition. To cover for the possibility of error or refutation, instead of making a bald assertion one might ask a question like "Did you know that there are abstract performatives?" intending to agree with the hearer whether he says "Of course I know that!" or "Whad'ya mean—are there unicorns?" In the latter case the speaker is prepared to cancel the implication that he believes in abstract performatives by saying "I only wanted to see whether you've fallen for that line." Generally speaking, whatever the speaker's reason for slipping something into a presupposition, whether it is to avoid committing himself, to protect himself against being challenged, or to be verbally economical, his intention is most effective if it can be covert. But even if he expects the hearer to recognize his intention, still he has succeeded in putting the onus on the hearer to question the presupposition or admit ignorance of it.

No doubt there are other kinds of collateral acts, be they overt, covert, or neither. Our object has been merely to give some common examples of each of the three types.

5.5.2. Conversational and Social Moves

A conversational situation is a social situation. Certain sorts of speech acts are essentially concerned with the course or direction of the social situation. Some of the acts listed in our taxonomy of illocutionary acts, such as responsives and acknowledgments, are of this sort, but situationally oriented acts are not limited to illocutionary acts. There are two general kinds of such acts, those that presuppose certain specific features of the social/conversational situation and those that directly affect these features. Acts of the first kind help *sustain* the social/conversational situation by keeping it within mutually expected bounds, either by being appropriate to a given stage of the exchange or by carrying the exchange to the next stage that is mutually expected. Acts of the second kind do not sustain but *restructure* the situation. Their purpose is to change the terms or the course of the exchange, and their success requires cooperation or at least lack of opposition from the hearer.

Both kinds of acts invoke certain mutual beliefs about the nature of the situation. If the mutual belief invoked is intended by the speaker to be invoked and intended to be recognized as so intended, the situationally oriented act is overt—the speaker cannot but expect the hearer to refer to this mutual belief in identifying his illocutionary intent; thus the illocutionary intent is identified in terms of the invoked mutual belief, and so the act expressing one's intention to sustain or to alter the situation is an illocutionary act. However, since more than uptake is required for this intention to be fulfilled, the act of actually sustaining or of altering the situation is perlocutionary. Perhaps a few examples will clarify these remarks.

Grice (1975) has suggested that "talk-exchanges" are governed by a cooperative principle under which fall various conversational presumptions (he calls them maxims). They must be mutually recognized if they are to apply to a given conversational/social situation, and can thus be viewed as rules (see section 7.1). They are fairly general in their application, although, as Grice notes, his maxims have to be generalized to cover exchanges whose purpose is not merely conveying information. Particular social situations are governed by whatever rules the participants mutually believe to govern them—not that there is always agreement on what they are. To the extent that there is less than mutual agreement, the situation is ill defined and one or both (all) of the participants may be unsure of what to expect from the other or unclear about what the other expects of him. What social psychologists sometimes call "role negotiation" may occur here if the participants take measures to clarify the situation and their places in it.

The rules that govern a situation, assuming they are mutually recognized, may be determined by the generic character of the situation as belonging to a certain institutional procedure. In this case the primary determinant of what the situation is (the rules of the institution) are mutually recognized among the members at large. The personal relationship of the participants may thus be incidental, and their relative institutional positions may be the decisive factor. Even when an encounter is of a more personal nature, with considerable intimate knowledge between the participants, it cannot be assumed that the rules governing the encounter are idiosyncratic to that relationship. The participants may still categorize each other in socially recognized terms and mutually define the situation as being essentially, say, a student/teacher situation, governed by socially recognized rules. However, insofar as the participants have developed a relationship of relatively long standing, it is likely that they have developed a certain mutual personal understanding, including an understanding about what is required or permissible in various recurrent situations that they have learned to classify in certain ways: as a neighborly visit, a coffee break, or a lovemaking scene.

However a situation is defined and whatever the source of the rules that govern it, by and large there is at any given moment a mutual awareness of how the situation is proceeding and what sorts of acts are appropriate to its furtherance. For example, a neighborly visit has to be initiated somehow—the visiting neighbor does not (usually) just walk in the door, sit down, and start talking. Each party is likely to have a certain view of why visits are made (say for idle conversation), how they should be initiated, what is a good reason for refusing a visit, and how frequent, long, and involved visits should be. So the visitor, after the exchange of greetings, might (especially if he is not invited in immediately) ask the host if he's busy at the moment. After he enters, he may presume to sit down, perhaps wherever he likes, or it may be mutually expected that the host ask him to sit down. Clearly, what is mutually understood affects how a given act will be taken. If it is usual for the host to ask the visitor to sit down, sitting without being asked might be regarded as presumptuous or offensive. Indeed, it might be regarded as being intended to be regarded as such. On the other hand, the visitor might so presume in order to make the relationship less formal. Tactfully, he might say as he sits "I hope you don't mind," inviting his host to say "Of course not" and thereby making future permissions to be seated unnecessary. If this becomes the established state of affairs, then for the host on some future occasion to ask the visitor to sit down suggests a preference for less intimacy and more formality. Analogous patterns emerge regarding such aspects of a visit as taking off one's coat, serving (or helping oneself to) refreshments, turning on the TV, and so on. Finally, there is the matter of terminating the visit. Neither party is likely to say he's bored with the conversation or would rather just be alone, but either can mention a real or plausible commitment or obligation that justifies taking leave. Then things can end as they began, on mutually agreeable terms.

Conversational situations are never just conversational. They are governed by social rules as well as conversational rules. Insofar as these are mutually recognized—whether institutionally imposed, determined by the sorts of persons involved, or personally imposed and reflective of the individuals involved—they provide guidelines within which acts (linguistic and otherwise) are performed and perceived. Compliance with the rules, unless it is unexpected, provokes no special attention and invites no special inference. However, violation does more than raise eyebrows. It calls attention to itself and invites inference as to why it occurs. Perhaps the point of it is civil disobedience: violating a rule in order to call attention to the rule and change it. More common, though, are violations designed not to change rules but to change the nature of a situation. The person objects not to certain rules governing certain situations but to a particular situation's being of the sort to which a certain set of rules applies. He seeks to change the situation to one with different rules.

What counts as relevant to a conversation depends on its mutually accepted purpose or direction. But this can change—or be changed— during the course of a conversation. There are rules that determine acceptable ways in which the course of social situations can be changed. A person might want to change the subject abruptly in midstream; perhaps he is bored with it, perhaps it is getting too touchy for him. Although it may be socially proper to change the subject without giving reasons for so doing, sometimes reasons are required, as when the subject is of obvious interest and importance to the other person. On the other hand, it is socially improper to say that one is bored and at least awkward to say the subject is getting too touchy—saying so would only make it touchier. So one must find an acceptable way of changing the subject without conveying one's real reason. Fortunately, it is possible to change the subject without one's intent being recognized and without its being recognized as one's intent. A possibly ploy is simply to change it, perhaps with an innocent-sounding "Oh, by the way, did you know that . . . ?" One relies on the likelihood that even if the other recognizes that the subject is being changed intentionally and even if he is thereby piqued at this, he won't accuse one of willfully changing it. Such accusations are themselves not socially acceptable, especially if they aren't backed up. And unless one repeatedly changes the same subject, one can always plead innocent, denying any vicious intentions. Another move, not without its irony, is to use a disclaimer like, "I don't mean to change the subject, but did you know that . . . ?" Here the person changes the subject explicitly and intentionally, at the same time paying obeisance to the right, which he is in the process of violating, of the other that he stick to the subject. Moreover, he puts the onus on the other to call him to task for what he is doing.

Most of the time changing the subject is perfectly acceptable. Most conversations are not all that regimented and subjects are dropped right and left in the normal course of events. Nevertheless, some discretion is required. Questions should be answered (or be allowed to be answered), points should be allowed to be completed, and civil attention should be paid. But all this is not so much a matter of relevance as politeness.

The countermove to changing the subject is to change it right back, perhaps after giving the changer the benefit of the doubt (maybe his mind was just wandering). This can be done bluntly and without any explanation or by using such words as "Getting back to what we were talking about," "Before I forget what we were discussing . . . ," or "Anyway, as I was saying . . ." This can be done tactfully, of course, but if persistence is required, it may not be appreciated. However, the changer of the subject bears the onus of having to change it again or of finding a suitable way to accuse the other of obnoxiously pursuing a tiresome topic.

Other Gricean maxims (presumptions) can be overridden by social rules. For example, the presumption of quality might require telling the truth but propriety might demand a white lie. The presumption of quantity might require considerable detail (perhaps required also by the presumption of quality), and yet going into those details might be boorish or just plain boring to participants in the conversation. The presumption of manner might be overridden by various social considerations; for example, it might be necessary to be ambiguous (Weiser 1974) in order to provide the hearer with options that, if not taken up, one has not openly committed oneself to—as in "Are you doing anything tonight?" Again, one might have to violate the presumption of orderliness if, for example, the situation is so informal that any attempt at order would seem inappropriate. In general conversational situations are not merely conversational, and conversational presumptions can be overridden not just by each other but by social rules.

Conversational scenarios, even when not multilayered and emotionally charged, are governed not simply by (strictly) conversational presumptions. Conversations are social encounters, encounters that have to be initiated, furthered, and terminated; sometimes they can be prolonged, sometimes they must be abbreviated. Although many linguistic devices are suitable for affecting the course of a conversation, the rules governing their use are not limited to purely conversational presumptions. There may be rules, depending on the nature of the situation, governing who can start a conversation—in some situations the rule may be that one speak only when spoken to. The same point applies to terminating conversations. Authority relationships may determine not only who can start and end a conversation but who directs it and how. Even in casual exchanges between equals, there are principles of propriety and a catalog of offenses that are to be avoided in initiating, directing, or terminating a conversation. These are not exclusively conversational in nature and indeed may conflict with strictly conversational presumptions.

Chapter Six   Conventional
                                 Illocutionary Acts

The speech act schema and the pattern of analysis for communicative illocutionary acts do not apply to conventional illocutionary acts. A different story is needed for them. Seeing why they do not fit the SAS will help one appreciate the explanatory value of the SAS for communicative acts. We will see just how conventions take the place of R-intentions in determining that utterances count as performances of particular kinds of acts. Whereas a communicative intention is fulfilled by means of recognition of that intention, a conventional intention is fulfilled by means of satisfying a convention.

Conventional illocutionary acts include such diverse acts as voting, resigning, arresting, acquitting, marrying, christening, dedicating, and abolishing. Despite their diversity, they fall into two general categories, *effectives* and *verdictives,* both of which affect institutional states of affairs.

6.1. CONVENTIONS

The idea of conventionality is quite broad; our conception of convention captures, and is meant to capture, but one part of it. For us conventions are *counts-as* rules and nothing else. When we talk about conventional illocutionary acts, we will be referring to what makes utterances count as acts of certain sorts. Conventional illocutionary acts need not be ritualistic, artificial, formal, fashionable, orthodox, or anything else that might fall under the broad notion of conventionality. We hope that once mentioned, these ideas won't be confused with what we mean by *convention.* Confusion is possible not only because the term *conventional* applies to so much, but also because these different aspects of conventionality often go together. Our notion of convention is not to be confused with any of the conceptions of rules that have been bandied about in the philosophy of language (such as semantic rules and constitutive rules) nor with social rules, practices, or norms.

As we understand them, conventions are not, or are not necessarily, what people expect one another to do in certain situations. Rather, they are actions which, *if* done in certain situations, count as doing something else. In other words, a convention is a mutually recognized means for doing something, counting as such only because mutually recognized, perhaps by having been agreed upon. Conventions of this sort occur, for example, in the game of bridge: the Blackwood convention and the Stayman convention, for instance. Bridge conventions are conventional means, within the rules of bidding, for requesting or conveying information. Similarly money is a conventional means of exchange. And it is a commonplace, however unexplicated, that language is a system of conventional means for communicating. The explication that we offer spells out the ingredients essential to the existence of a convention, namely, by virtue of mutual belief (MB) in a community or group (G) an act of a certain sort (A) counts as doing such and such (D) in a certain sort of recurrent situation or context (C):

Convention: A (in C) is a convention for D-ing in G if and only if:
i. it is MB-ed in G that whenever a member of G does A in C, he is D-ing, and
ii. A in C counts as D-ing only because it is MB-ed in G to count as such.

The second condition is necessary to exclude cases of mutually recognized habitual action, like the act of trying to get warm by putting on a coat. Thus, to A conventionally counts as D-ing not just for happening to be, but *because* it is mutually regarded as D-ing. Specification of the type of situation is essential: shaking hands is a way of greeting in one situation, a way of bidding farewell in another, a way of congratulating in a third, and a way of sealing an agreement in still another. In general, only in certain circumstances do certain kinds of acts count as baptizing someone, stealing a base, saluting an officer, calling a meeting to order (using a gavel), or signaling a touchback.

Before applying our definition (which is intended as an explication of but one sense of *convention*) to illocutionary acts, we wish to make two general observations. First, there can be rules requiring the performance of a conventional action such as saluting, paying taxes, or toasting someone. Where such rules exist, they must be clearly distinguished from the conventions defining the actions they require.[1] Second, the notion of convention, defined for our purposes over types of acts, can be extended to types of persons, situations, and objects: being a spouse or a judge requires having some mutually recognized feature that may include having performed some conventional act (like vowing) or having been the subject of such an act (like being appointed). Analogously, a situation's being a trial, a debate, or a wedding is a matter of convention, and the same goes for a thing's being a uniform, a stoplight, or a crucifix.

Communicative illocutionary acts succeed by means of recognition of intention, whereas conventional ones succeed by satisfying a convention. Utterances are the A's in the definition of convention, and what they count as (the D's) depends on the conventions they fall under. In some cases the convention requires a specific form of words, in other cases not. For example, a voice vote must be cast with an "aye" or a "nay," and a verdict must be brought in with the words "guilty" or "not guilty." An oath of office or a marriage ceremony requires specified sentences to be pronounced by the participants. We may call conventional illocutionary acts of this sort *locution-specific*. In other cases, what must be uttered is identified by the meaning of what is said, not by the specific form of words. It does not matter whether a boss fires an employee by saying "You're fired" or "You are hereby relieved of your duties and their attendant remunerations."

For an utterance to be a conventional illocutionary act, not only must it be the utterance of what the convention requires (the specified words, or words with the specified meanings), it must be issued by the right person under the right circumstances. Not just any utterance of "guilty" counts as finding a person (defendant) guilty. It must be said by the judge (or the foreman of the jury) at the appropriate stage of the judicial proceedings. Thus, where it says in our definition of convention "whenever a member of G does A in C," it should be understood that the specification of C may include a requirement on who the agent is. This could also be included under the specification of A, but for convenience in discussing conventional illocutionary acts we will let values of A be of the form "says that $*(...p...)$" or "utters e," in the case of locution-specific acts.

6.2. EFFECTIVES AND VERDICTIVES

Conventional illocutionary acts come in two categories, effectives and verdictives.[2] *Effectives* effect changes in institutional states of affairs;

they are necessarily conventional inasmuch as they achieve their effects only because mutually believed to do so. Only thus is a student graduated, a bill vetoed, or a site consecrated. *Verdictives* are judgments that by convention have official, binding import in the context of the institution in which they occur. Thus, to call a runner out, to find a defendant guilty, or to assess a piece of property is not just to make a judgment; given the position and attendant authority of an umpire, a judge, or a tax assessor, it is also to make it the case, if only so far as the relevant institution is concerned, that what is judged to be so is so in fact.

Generally speaking, conventional illocutionary acts, whether effective or verdictive, are endemic to particular institutions. In most instances they affect the institutional status of persons or things. In other cases they create institutional rights and obligations. In still others they further or are otherwise part of some institutional practice, process, or procedure. We will not attempt an exhaustive enumeration of such acts. That may well be a futile effort, considering the variety of institutions there are. Things would get out of hand if we were to include conventional acts performed in writing—for starters, think of the number of forms there are in bureaucracies, forms for reporting, billing, requisitioning, applying, notifying, and on and on. Our sampler will be restricted to fairly familiar acts designated by simple verbs. Generally they are effectives; verdictives will be marked with a "V." It should be kept in mind that many of these acts can be, and in some institutions must be, performed nonverbally. Sometimes words accompany the nonverbal action, as with christening a ship.

A great many conventional illocutionary acts affect the institutional position or social status of a person. He may be admitted into an institution or a position in it by being hired, appointed, nominated, elected, promoted, naturalized, or ordained; he may be removed by being fired, suspended, demoted, expelled, or banned. He himself can enlist, apply, join, or accept membership, and resign, abdicate, retire, or take a leave of absence. Formal or ceremonial acts can make such a change of position official, as in installing, inaugurating, graduating, confirming, and administering or taking an oath of office. With respect to the criminal law, one is arrested, indicted, convicted or acquitted (V), sentenced, pardoned, paroled, or reprieved. One can be certified (V) as to competence in a field, social pedigree, or sanity. Finally, one can be disqualified (V), blacklisted, censured, or, for that matter, cleared (V).

The institutional status of objects is affected by a variety of different acts. As to ownership, things can be bought, sold, borrowed, lent, traded, donated, conferred, awarded, bequeathed, bid for, put up for sale, accepted, or rejected. Property can be appropriated, expropriated, repossessed, surrendered, or deeded. Items can be consigned, supplied, received, designated (for some purpose), or relegated (say, to the junk heap). Uniforms, emblems, flowers, and colors can be adopted as official symbols. Special institutional status is conferred when something is dedicated, consecrated, or enshrined. For that matter, people can be canonized, memorialized, inducted (into a hall of fame), or knighted. These honorific acts are not verdictive, although they are predicated on highly positive evaluations. Essentially verdictive are acts of appraising, assessing, grading, ranking, and estimating the value of something.

Then there are institutional permissions, prohibitions, and requirements, which create or remove rights or obligations, perhaps by imposing or abolishing rules. Kinds of acts can be sanctioned, licensed, exempted, prohibited, legalized, or banned. Particular acts can be permitted, authorized, enjoined, assigned, delegated, commissioned, commanded, countermanded, or excused. Rules and permissions themselves can be adopted, decreed, repealed, revoked, abolished, or rescinded. And states of affairs, such as emergencies and holidays, in which certain rules or permissions apply, can be declared, proclaimed, or declared over.

It would be a virtually endless task to enumerate the types of conventional acts that are part of or further the procedures of such diverse institutions as hospitals, schools, government agencies, factories, churches, and clubs. Take just the familiar and standardized case of parliamentary situations. Motions can be introduced, seconded, voted on, or vetoed. Points can be raised, objected to, ruled on (V), adjudicated (V), or overruled (V). People can seek recognition and be recognized, and meetings can be called to order, recessed, or adjourned.

A special case of conventional act involves symbolizing or categorizing, linguistically or otherwise. There are acts of naming, abbreviating, coding, classifying (information), labeling (products), and such ritualized acts as baptizing, christening, and dubbing.

Finally, institutions themselves can be subject to conventional action. They can be legalized, banned, exempted (as from a law), admitted (to an association). Indeed, they must be founded or organized in the first place, and can be dissolved or disbanded. Acts of founding an institution require the formation of mutual beliefs among the founding members; when an institution is disbanded, there is a general mutual belief among the remaining members that the rules and expectations that make up the mutual beliefs within the institution will dissolve.

6.3. CONVENTIONAL ILLOCUTIONARY ACTS AND INSTITUTIONAL FACTS

Effectives produce or alter institutional states of affairs. Since they are mere utterances, this essential feature may make them seem ontologically problematic and invites the question, How are effectives possible? Verdictives are determinations of fact, natural or institutional, which have official consequence. Subsequent institutional activity proceeds as if what has been officially determined to be so is in fact the case. As an aid to understanding both sorts of acts, we will formulate a distinction between natural and institutional facts and thereby explain why effectives and verdictives must be conventional.

6.3.1. Effectives

Effectives are utterances that, when issued by the right person under the right circumstances, make it the case that such and such. This is a matter not of causality but of mutual belief. An utterance counts as an act of a certain sort in virtue of being mutually believed to be an act of that sort. Only thus does it count as an act of resigning, bidding, vetoing, seconding, exempting, or bequeathing, as the case may be. However, as is evident from a case-by-case analysis of what these acts essentially involve, to mark such an act with an effective verb is just shorthand for describing it as fact-producing. Resigning just is removing oneself from a position, vetoing just is nullifying a piece of legislation, exempting just is making an exception to a rule, and so on. Of course, not every kind of institutional fact-changing act is designated by a simple verb, but every effective verb can be paraphrased in institutional fact-changing terms. Since to perform an effective just is to issue an utterance (in a situation) which is mutually believed to be such that a certain institutional state of affairs is thereby produced, if there is anything mysterious about effectives, it would seem that they are no more mysterious than the institutional states of affairs they produce.

What are institutional facts? As argued in the appendix, they are intersubjective in character, constituted by mutual belief. We might define them quasi-inductively: an institutional fact is (1) anything that is the case in virtue of being mutually believed in some collectivity or (2) anything that follows from one or more institutional facts.[3] For example, the existence of some obscure law is a matter of institutional fact whether or not anyone has heard of it, much less whether everyone mutually believes in its existence. However, it is mutually believed that there is a legislature which enacts laws (perhaps as provided for by the mutually recognized constitution) and that its members are determined by election. So the obscure law exists in virtue of meeting certain mutually recognized conditions, namely, being passed by the duly constituted legislature (perhaps also being signed by the executive).[4]

In general, given the basic institutional fact of the existence of the institution itself, institutional facts concern positions, rights, responsibilities, and obligations of persons, as well as the actions that people take and the conventional effects of these actions. Within a particular institution there may be a structure of diverse official positions whose occupancy is determined by certain recognized procedures. There will be rights and responsibilities associated with each position, as well as rules imposing obligations on everyone. The rules may specify rewards for exemplary performance or punishments for deficient performance. Included or implied by the rules specifying rights and responsibilities of particular positions are power relations between positions, rules that specify who can (or must) do what to whom and who must tolerate what from whom (see the appendix). If the institution is organized toward certain ends, presumably it will have a set of policies and procedures for furthering those ends. These procedures may be extremely complex, requiring a huge number of coordinated actions by many people in diverse positions. Furthermore, there are institutional facts about these procedures, such as how far along a certain procedure has progressed (in the legislative process, on the production line) and the current state of some proposal or production.[5]

To mention the main matters of institutional fact is but to scratch the surface of social metaphysics. We have answered our question about the possibility of effectives only by subsuming it under the larger question of the possibility of institutional facts. No one will be content with the answer that institutional facts are possible because of mutual belief, because there is still plenty of room for puzzlement about how facts can exist in virtue of being mutually believed. At any rate (to pass the metaphysical buck) effectives exploit conventions (one sort of institutional fact) that count utterances, because of what is uttered or said, as producers of institutional facts. Descriptions of conventions make reference to persons and situations, and these involve specifying the institutional positions of the speaker and others and the relations between them, as well as institutional facts (such as stages of a process or procedure) that define the situation. So conventions are not separable from the framework of institutional facts that effectives, by falling under conventions, elaborate and help sustain.

6.3.2. Verdictives

Whereas effectives produce facts, verdictives are merely determinations of fact. They have official and binding consequence, however, and what they determine to be so is the case, as far as the institution is concerned. Since what is determined may be a matter of natural rather than institutional fact, we cannot say that verdictives make it the case that such and such, only that they make it *as if* it were the case in the sense that it is a fact *for* the institution in question. There is nothing metaphysically mysterious about these as-if facts. Their status is epistemological, not ontological. To say that verdictives produce as-if facts means, from a practical point of view, that as far as further institutional processes and procedures are concerned, what has been determined to be so is then acted upon as if it were so.

Verdictives are commonly determinations of natural fact. They settle such questions as who killed Jones, whether Smith was tagged, and whether Johnson signed his name to a certain document. Since such natural facts are describable in institutional terms (that someone murdered Jones, that Smith was tagged out, and that Johnson forfeited his rights), verdictives are determinations of institutional fact as well. In some cases, institutional fact, rather than natural fact, is directly at issue. For example, there may be no dispute about what Brown did to Jones, the only questions being whether he acted in his capacity as officer of the law and whether he did so rightfully. In general, verdictives serve the institutional purpose of settling issues in order that institutional activity can carry on, proceeding from what has been determined to be the case.

A verdictive would be merely a constative if it had no institutional import of the sort described. However, verdictives do have this import and can have it only in virtue of being mutually believed to have it. In short, they must be conventional. Utterances that in other contexts would be taken as mere constatives count, depending on the case, as findings, rulings, certifications, etc., only because they are issued by the right person in the right situation (right, as conventionally determined).

It turns out, then, that effectives and verdictives must be conventional. They are utterances that satisfy certain descriptions couched in institutional terms, at least when the meaning of the conventional verb is unpacked. As such, they are acts of either creating institutional facts or of officially determining there to be certain facts, whether institutional or natural. Either way, these utterances count for what they are only in virtue of being mutually believed to so count; thus they must be conventional.

6.4. PERFORMING CONVENTIONAL ILLOCUTIONARY ACTS

Both communicative and conventional illocutionary acts are utterances issued with the intention that the utterance count as an act of a certain sort. The means are different in the two cases, intention by means of recognition of intention in one case and intention by convention in the other. Nevertheless, they have in common the feature that the speaker's utterance, his saying that *(...p...) by uttering e (or simply his uttering e, in locution-specific cases), counts as F-ing that P only under certain circumstances and never merely because of what e means. A theory of illocutionary acts must explain how such utterances count, when issued with certain intentions under certain circumstances, as performances of illocutionary acts of certain sorts.

On our account communicative illocutionary acts are acts of expressing attitudes. To express an attitude is to R-intend the hearer to take one's utterance as reason to think one has that attitude. For this intention to be fulfilled, the hearer must identify it on the basis of what is said together with mutual contextual beliefs, given the application of the linguistic and the communicative presumptions. Whereas the LP and the CP are general mutual beliefs within the linguistic community, the mutual contextual beliefs are between the speaker and the hearer in particular. Only because these mutual contextual beliefs are activated (perhaps by the utterance itself) can the hearer identify, and can the speaker reasonably expect him to identify, the speaker's illocutionary intent. Only thus can the illocutionary act succeed.

On the other hand, in the case of conventional illocutionary acts, a given utterance counts as an act of a certain sort just in case what is said (or uttered, in some instances) and the conditions of utterance meet the specifications of the relevant convention. The convention is a matter of general mutual belief in the community or group involved. No R-intention is required for performing a conventional illocutionary act, and the speech act schema is inoperative. Instead, the speaker simply intends that his utterance count as an act of a certain sort merely in virtue of falling under the relevant convention. Now his intention in this case is not to express a certain attitude but to affect institutional affairs; his intention is fulfilled if his utterance meets the required specifications. Insofar as those present must reckon that these specifications have indeed been met, the only relevant contextual belief mutual among those present in particular, as opposed to the community or group at large, is that the utterance and the conditions of utterance meet these specifications. In most cases it should be clear to all concerned whether or not these specifications are met.

Conventional illocutionary acts are not essentially communicative and do not require R-intentions. Indeed, as Strawson notes (1964, 456), there may be no particular persons to whom such utterances are directed: uptake is not so much their point as their verification. The hearer's role, even when he is the addressee rather than a mere onlooker, is to recognize that the utterance falls under a certain convention and only incidentally to recognize that it is issued with a certain communicative intention (if any). Although the speaker's intention is not essentially audience-directed and although no communicative presumption is involved in conventional illocutionary acts, the speaker's intention is nonetheless overt. As a member of the group or community in which the convention obtains, he may be presumed to know this convention and hence to intend his utterance to fall under it. Indeed, he may expect and thus intend to be so presumed, but such an intention is inessential to the success of his primary intention to be performing a certain conventional illocutionary act.

In drawing a sharp distinction between conventional and communicative illocutionary acts, we do not mean to imply that both sorts of acts can't be performed in the same breath. Quite the contrary, one and the same utterance can count as an act of both sorts. If a policeman says to a person "You're under arrest," he is both arresting the person and telling him (indirectly) that he has violated the law. It is common for utterances to be both conventional and communicative illocutionary acts; when a speaker performs a conventional act, he is likely to have a reason for doing it, and he may very well R-intend the hearer to infer what that reason is. This common occurrence does not vitiate the distinction between the two types of acts, because they are issued with different sorts of intentions and succeed in different sorts of ways.

Conventional illocutionary acts are identified by the speaker's utterance and the conditions of utterance, with R-intentions unnecessary and the SAS inoperative. It would seem, therefore, that they cannot be performed nonliterally. For example, it seems that to fire someone the speaker must say something that means 'You're fired.' But suppose he says "George, remember that gold watch you've always wanted? Guess what! Now you're getting it." Is this an indirect act of firing? We're inclined to say that it is not, but instead an indirect way of telling George that he's fired (or involuntarily retired). In general, conventional illocutionary acts must be performed literally, since the conventions that govern them specify what must be *said,* not meant. However, in locution-specific cases, it is irrelevant whether or not the utterance is literal. All that matters is that the right words be uttered.

For a conventional illocutionary act to be successful, either by changing an institutional state of affairs or by being an official determination of fact, the speaker's utterance and the conditions of utterance must meet the specifications of the relevant convention. However, that it meets these specifications is itself something that must be determined, so when there is a question whether a certain act was performed and thereby whether a certain institutional change took place, the speaker is not the sole judge. Hearers, perhaps positionally privileged ones, may be consulted to verify that a certain utterance was genuinely issued and that the circumstances were of the right sort. If there is a dispute on this question subsequent to the time of utterance, special procedures may be required to determine whether or not a certain conventional illocutionary act had been duly performed.

One issue that may arise when it becomes necessary to determine whether a certain act has been performed is the speaker's intention to be performing that act. In some cases it does not matter, as with bidding in the game of bridge. In general, however, the speaker is presumed to be intending to be performing the act that his utterance counts as the performance of under the circumstances. Although it is possible to find someone guilty while intending to acquit him (one might not correct onself after having omitted the word "not") or to resign jokingly (the boss seizes an opportunity of not having to fire an employee when the latter jokingly says "I quit"), generally, as institutional rules may provide, the act is nullified if it is shown not to have been performed intentionally.

Finally, conventional illocutionary acts, though resulting in institutional change, are not necessarily final. These changes can be reversed, the act that effected them rescinded. In the case of verdictives, the judgment of the umpire or the court may be challenged or appealed. The umpire can, conceivably, change his mind, and the judge can be overruled by a court of appeals. Whether created by effectives or determined by verdictives, institutional facts live by mutual belief and die by mutual belief.

Chapter Seven

Communication and Convention

Effectives and verdictives are fundamentally different from communicative illocutionary acts. They are implemented not by recognition of intention but by convention. This is possible—and necessary—because effectives and verdictives essentially affect institutional states of affairs and are only incidentally communicative. Now we have not shown explicitly that communicative illocutionary acts are not conventional. Austin held that all illocutionary acts are conventional, but unfortunately, he did not specify what he meant by "conventional." The closest he ever came was when he said that the use of a sentence with a certain illocutionary force "may be said to be conventional in the sense that at least it could be made explicit by the performative formula" (1962, 103). This strangely qualified remark makes it evident that whatever Austin meant by conventionality, it was something quite different from what we mean; it suggests that there is some special sense in which explicit performative utterances are conventional. We contend that communicative illocutionary acts are not conventional, in our sense. We cannot show that they are not conventional in every sense, however bizarre, but we argue that Austin's sense is no sense of "conventional." Indeed, we argue that explicit performative utterances are not conventional at all and that their special character can be accounted for via the notion of illocutionary standardization. Finally, we indicate one way in which all utterances are conventional—as locutionary acts.

7.1. RULES AND CONVENTIONS

In order to evaluate claims to the effect that the use of language is rule-governed behavior or that it is conventional, it is imperative that the notions of rules and of conventions be distinguished. On our conception conventions are not what people expect one another to do in specified situations. Rather, they are actions that, if performed in certain situations, count as doing something else. This was reflected in our definition, repeated here.

Convention: A (in C) is a convention for D-ing in G if and only if:
i. it is MB in G that whenever a member of G does A in C, he is D-ing, and
ii. A in C counts as D-ing only because it is MB in G to count as such.

Rules, on the other hand, are socially expected forms of behavior. Several types of rules are distinguished in the appendix, but for our purposes it is enough to mention what they have in common. Indeed, we will restrict ourselves to the central sort of case.

It is ambiguous to say that a rule is a socially expected form of behavior. This can mean either that it is expected in a group G that people will do A when C arises or that it is regarded in G that people should do A when C arises. Our conception of rules reflects both the anticipatory and the normative aspects of social expectations.

Rule: A (in C) is a rule in G if and only if:
i. the members of G do A in C,
ii. it is MB in G that (i), and
iii. it is MB in G that the members of G should do A in C.

Clause (i) has it that A is actually done, but this condition can be relaxed to cover less central cases. It is difficult to imagine a situation where clause (ii) could be true for long unless (i) were generally true. On the other hand, (iii) could and often does obtain without (i) and (ii) holding. A type of action that satisfies (i) alone is a *statistical regularity;* one that satisfies both (i) and (ii) is a *social regularity;* and one that satisfies (iii) is a *social standard.* The appendix may be consulted for further explanation and for an argument justifying the requirement of mutual belief in G, rather than merely shared belief.

Having distinguished rules from conventions, we can now make several observations about rules and their application to illocutionary acts. First, it should be plain that not every rule-governed act is conventional and not every conventional act is rule-governed. Workers might be required not to smoke, but there is nothing conventional about not smoking. On the other hand, raising one's hand in a classroom conventionally counts as an act of seeking recognition for purposes of speak-

ing, but there is no rule requiring one to raise one's hand; if there is a
relevant rule here at all, it is that one should not speak out of turn and
not use other means than the designated one of getting attention (such
as jumping up and down or banging on the table). Although rules and
conventions are distinct, an action can be both rule-governed and conventional. It might be a rule that spectators rise when the judge enters
the courtroom, and it is a convention that rising when the judge enters
counts as a show of respect. With the distinction between rules and
conventions in mind, we may say that rules can be observed or violated, whereas conventions can be merely applied or misapplied. Rules
specify things to be done, conventions ways of doing things. Clearly,
then, not every act performed in the context of an institutional practice
or procedure is conventional.

7.2. WHY COMMUNICATIVE ILLOCUTIONARY ACTS ARE NOT CONVENTIONAL

Why are only effectives and verdictives conventional? To answer this
question we will run through the four categories of communicative
illocutionary acts and show why each cannot be conventional (except
in the irrelevant sense of being performed through conventional means,
that is, linguistically). It may seem especially plausible to regard commissives and acknowledgments as conventional. After all, commissives
create obligations, and acknowledgments are part of social rituals.
However, these facts do not make them conventional.

In arguing that only effectives and verdictives are conventional, we
imply that none of the other four categories of illocutionary acts over-
laps either of these two categories. Yet of the effective and verdictive
verbs listed in section 6.2, some have appeared before in other categories. For example, the verdictive "certify" was listed as a constative
(in particular, a confirmative), and the effective "bid" was included
under commissives. However, just as verbs like "inform" and "order"
cut across the illocutionary/perlocutionary distinction and verbs like
"tell" and "suggest" cut across communicative categories (being both
constative and directive), so certain verbs bridge the communicative/
conventional gap. We cannot expect ordinary usage to be sensitive to
every philosophical or other theoretical distinction, and so it should
come as no surprise that the same verb can name both a communicative
and a conventional illocutionary act type. Nothing in our formulation
of the distinction between the two kinds of acts precludes the possibil-

ity that one and the same utterance can be both. Although we argued that conventional acts don't require R-intentions, surely they can be, and indeed often are, issued with R-intentions: when a boss fires someone, he may be also telling the employee what he thinks of his performance.

Now in considering whether communicative illocutionary acts can be conventional, we must not trivialize the issue by arguing that since communicative intentions are R-intentions and conventional intentions are not, communicative acts can't be conventional. The issue is whether the kinds of illocutionary effects produced communicatively can also be produced conventionally. Communicative effects could be achieved conventionally if certain conventions and rules existed. For example, there could be a rule that people are never to speak nonliterally or indirectly. Indeed, they could be required always to use the explicit performative formulas "I state," "I request," and so on. No inference along the lines of the speech act schema would then be required to identify the illocutionary act being performed. The performative verb would make the force (type of act) explicit, and the rest would make the propositional content explicit. Finally, there would be a convention stipulating that whenever someone says that he F-s that p, his utterance counts as F-ing that p. Given a rule requiring sincerity, an utterance would thereby obligate the speaker to have just those attitudes that he would be expressing in communicatively F-ing that p. Thus, in saying that he F-s that p, S would intend conventionally, rather than by means of recognition of intention, his utterance to be reason for H to think S has those attitudes. In this way, anyone could express his attitudes conventionally.[1] Whether a person actually has the attitudes he expresses would be another matter.

We have conceded that communicative illocutionary acts could be performed conventionally if certain conventions existed. However, as things are, can they be conventional? We will consider the four categories of communicative illocutionary acts individually.

Constatives
Ignoring the differences between the various types of constatives, we may say, speaking generally, that they consist in expressing a certain belief together with the intention that the hearer believe likewise. As things are, this cannot be a matter of convention. Of course there are conventional means for constating, such as using performatives like "I report" and "I dispute," but it does not follow that using these means

counts ipso facto as expressing a belief (and the corresponding intention). The hearer might have good reason to think that the speaker is not being serious or literal in his utterance and conclude that no belief is being expressed. Even using conventional means for constating, the speaker must have the requisite R-intention, which is to be recognized not only by what is said but also by supposing that the speaker is being serious and literal in his utterance. Thus, conventions such as we have, as opposed to those imagined, cannot supplant R-intentions in determining the identity of constative utterances.

Directives

Similar reasoning applies to directives. In general (considering the various types), directives express the speaker's intention that the hearer act because of S's desire or S's utterance itself. S succeeds communicatively if H recognizes this intention. Even if standardly directive forms of words are used, such as the imperative mood or directive performatives, S may not have the requisite intention. As in the case of constatives, there is no guarantee that S is being serious and literal in his utterance and H may have good reason to think that he is not. So what is uttered and what is said do not suffice to make an utterance directive.

Although effectives like licensing and prohibiting create rights or obligations, it should not be thought that directives do likewise, at least as illocutionary acts. At best, they create mutual beliefs between S and H about rights or obligations, and it is a moral question whether (or when) they create rights and obligations. Even directives like authorizations and commands, which typically are issued within the framework of some institution, create (institutional) rights and obligations only if there are rules to that effect, for example, that people should do what they are rightfully ordered to do. That such utterances are intra-institutional does not make them conventional.

A wide range of institution-bound acts have the appearance of directives, acts such as legislating, licensing, and exempting. In some cases, like ordering, prohibiting, and authorizing, they may even be marked by directive verbs. They seem to have the force of directives inasmuch as they require, prohibit, or permit certain types of action. However, although they are directives in appearance, they are effectives in fact. In particular, they are rule-making (or rule-unmaking) acts: they make it the case in an institution or group that a certain action must be done, must not be done, or may be done, whether by members in general or by some specific category. Obviously, acts of legislating make laws, which are a kind of rule, and legalizing something formerly prohibited or rescinding legislation is to dissolve a rule. Acts of licensing and exempting are not rule-making acts, for they apply to particular persons and are, indeed, acts of permitting. Nevertheless, they have the effect of removing a person from the scope of a rule that prohibits a certain form of action, thereby changing his institutional status from someone to whom the rule applies to someone to whom it does not. Therefore, unlike communicative permissives these acts do not merely provide a reason for the person to feel free to do something, they put him in the position of being free to do it.

Commissives

Commissives are acts of undertaking obligations, but to undertake an obligation is not automatically to create one, even if S uses a performative like "I promise." S's utterance may express his belief that an obligation is thereby created, but that does not make the belief true even if H shares the belief and it is mutual. That S is obligated to fulfill his commitment is a moral question not answerable by the theory of illocutionary acts. Of course, in institutional contexts it makes clear sense to speak of obligations (which may or may not be moral) that exist in the institution as a matter of mutual belief. For commissives issued in institutional contexts to *create* institutional obligations, there must be institutional rules to the effect that one should honor one's commitments, but this does not make them conventional. However, formalized acts like taking an oath or signing a document are genuinely conventional. These acts count not merely as undertaking an (institutional) obligation but as creating one, and that they count as such is a matter of convention, independent of any R-intention S may have.

Acknowledgments

In considering whether acknowledgments are conventional, we must be especially careful not to be confused by the ambiguity of the term *conventional*. Clearly such acts as greeting, thanking, and apologizing observe social convention in some sense of the term. They are part of everyday social rituals, they are expected on certain occasions, and they can be performed with an air of perfunctory formality. But none of this makes them conventional in the sense of falling under *counts-as* rules. If they were conventional in this, the relevant sense, they would succeed not in virtue of H's recognizing S's R-intention but by falling under a convention.

One reason that acknowledgments might seem to be conventional (in the required sense), and not merely expected acts of social propriety (an irrelevant sense), is built right into our definitions of them. Each definition is disjunctive, and the second disjunct is of the form "S expresses the intention that his utterance satisfy the social expectation … and the intention that H take S's utterance as satisfying this expectation." Acknowledgments that satisfy this disjunct are the perfunctory, neither sincere nor insincere, gestures of everyday civility. The social expectation referred to reflects a social rule to the effect that one issue an acknowledgment when circumstances call for it. That acknowledgments satisfy such rules does not make them conventional. Even if the speaker is not expressing any feeling, as he would be if his utterance satisfied the first disjunct of the definition of acknowledgments, that it satisfies the second disjunct is still a matter of R-intention. The obvious insincerity of a perfunctory acknowledgment doesn't mean it isn't issued with an R-intention, namely, that the utterance satisfy a social expectation.

Another feature of acknowledgments that makes them seem conventional is that a distinctive locution, often of just one word, is associated with each type: "Thank you," "Congratulations," "Hello." Does this mean that they are conventional, indeed locution-specific? Although each such form has a specific illocutionary use as a matter of linguistic convention (of meaning), still these forms can be used nonliterally or unseriously. Thus, an R-intention is required if an utterance of any of these forms of words is to be a genuine acknowledgment.[2]

The upshot of this argument is that in the absence of such conventions as those in the fanciful situation described at the outset, communicative intentions must be R-intentions—conventional intentions are no substitute. This is apparent from our analyses of the four categories of communicative illocutionary acts. In each instance the speaker expresses certain attitudes, sometimes rather complex but always as a matter of R-intention. In the hypothetical situation in which there are rules and conventions to give hearers reason so to take speakers' utterances, R-intentions would be unnecessary. However, people could speak only literally and people would be presumed to have the attitudes they conventionally expressed. As things are, on the other hand, the only conventional illocutionary acts are effectives and verdictives: uptake is not so much their point as their verification. That a conventional illocutionary act counts as an act of a certain sort is not a matter of

R-intention but of what convention it falls under. Thus, although in practice a given utterance can be both communicative and conventional and the same verb can designate acts of both sorts, the difference between the two, in theory, is clear and distinct.

7.3. CONSTITUTIVE RULES AND COMMUNICATION

In our view an utterance counts as a communicative illocutionary act of a certain sort as a matter of R-intention not convention. Successful communication consists in the hearer's recognition of that intention by way of an inference in the pattern of the SAS.

A rival view, which has gained considerable currency, is Searle's (1969) theory of illocutionary acts based on the notion of *constitutive rules*. Although only a detailed discussion would do full justice to the theory, we wish to suggest that the underlying difficulty with this approach is that (a) Searle has given us insufficient reason to believe that there are rules constituting types of communicative illocutionary acts and (b) even if there were such rules, the most they could explain would be the literal (and direct) performance of the illocutionary acts with which they are associated.

Searle introduces the notion of constitutive rules not by definition but by description and example. "Constitutive rules do not merely regulate, they create or define new forms of behavior" (p. 33), such as playing football or chess. To create the possibility of new forms of behavior, constitutive rules take the form: *X* counts as *Y* in context *C* (p. 35). This is essentially the form of what we call *conventions*. Since Searle nowhere gives an explicit definition or a set of necessary and sufficient conditions for the existence of a constitutive rule, as far as we can tell, our notion of convention is congruent with Searle's notion of constitutive rules (at least those that take the counts-as form[3]).

How does Searle connect constitutive rules with illocutionary acts? He writes, "The procedure which I shall follow is to state a set of necessary and sufficient conditions for the performance of particular kinds of speech acts and then extract from those conditions sets of semantic rules for the use of the linguistic devices which mark the utterances as speech acts of those kinds" (p. 22). Notice that Searle refers to the relevant constitutive rules as *semantic rules;* yet nowhere does he give us reason to suppose that semantic rules, at least as construed by linguists, qualify as constitutive rules (perhaps only those that "create" illocutionary acts so qualify). More serious is his failure to explain why it should be that to "extract from those conditions sets of semantic rules" will give us the slightest reason to believe in the existence of these rules. Indeed Searle does not explicitly say how the rules and conditions are related. Given other things he says, it is natural to suppose Searle holds the following:

Rule-Condition Connection (R-C):
If R are the rules for promising and C are the conditions for promising, then in uttering e, S obeys R iff in uttering e, S satisfies C. (We use e (for expression) instead of Searle's symbol T.)

Searle then (1969, 54–61) turns to the analysis of promising as his "initial quarry." But he does not really deal with promising per se, only with *nondefectively promising in literally uttering a sentence e to a hearer H*. We will see that this qualification makes a difference. Searle presents nine singly necessary and jointly sufficient conditions for promising (pp. 57–61), which we label and group as follows (phrasing and all but the last two labels are Searle's):

(a) *Input-output conditions:*
  1. Normal input and output conditions obtain.
(b) *Propositional content conditions:*
  2. S expresses the proposition that p.
  3. In expressing that p, S predicates a future act A of S.
(c) *Preparatory conditions:*
  4. H would prefer S's doing A to his not doing A, and S believes H would prefer his doing A to his not doing A.
  5. It is not obvious to both S and H that S will do A in the normal course of events.
(d) *Sincerity condition:*
  6. S intends to do A.
(e) *Essential condition:*
  7. S intends that the utterance of e will place him under an obligation to do A.
(f) *Grice condition:*
  8. S intends (i-1) to produce in H the knowledge (K) that the utterance of e is to count as placing S under an obligation to do A. S intends to produce K by means of the recognition of i-1, and he intends i-1 to be recognized in virtue of (by means of) H's knowledge of the meaning of e.

(g) *Literal condition:*

 9. The semantical rules of the dialect spoken by S and H are such that e is correctly and sincerely uttered if and only if conditions 1–8 obtain.

From these conditions Searle (p. 63) extracts the following rules for the *indicator of illocutionary force*, in this case Pr for promising (phrasing and labels are Searle's):

R(b) *Propositional content rule:*

Rule 1. Pr is to be uttered only in the context of a sentence (or larger stretch of discourse) e, the utterance of which predicates some future act A of the speaker S.

R(c) *Preparatory rules:*

Rule 2. Pr is to be uttered only if the hearer H would prefer S's doing A to his not doing A, and S believes H would prefer S's doing A to his not doing A.

Rule 3. Pr is to be uttered only if it is not obvious to both S and H that S will do A in the normal course of events.

R(d) *Sincerity rule:*

Rule 4. Pr is to be uttered only if S intends to do A.

R(e) *Essential rule:*

Rule 5. The utterance of Pr counts as the undertaking of an obligation to do A.

Clearly these rules do not accord with R-C. One could utter e in accordance with these rules and not literally and nondefectively promise. What are missing are rule analogs to conditions (a), (f), and (g). In saying that these conditions "apply generally to all kinds of normal illocutionary acts and are not peculiar to promising" (p. 62), Searle seems to suggest that there are some general rules that, if followed, will guarantee that these conditions are met. But this remark and suggestion seem false.

 The literal condition (g) is not necessary for the performance of illocutionary acts. The one-word sentence "Yes" can be literally uttered in the making of a promise, yet it is not governed by semantic rules that guarantee that conditions (a)–(f) obtain. Indeed, the only sort of sentence that might satisfy condition (g) is an unambiguous[4] explicit performative, whose meaning determines and exhausts its force. Besides artificially restricting his analysis and making it much less interesting, Searle makes his analysis easily falsifiable, since these restrictions are not built into the sentence e in the analysandum.

The general problem is how to write rules that accord with R-C. What happens when one actually tries to formulate them as analogs of the conditions that they are to guarantee the satisfaction of? First, corresponding to conditions (a), (f), and (g) we would have the rules:

R(a) *Input-output rule: Pr* is to be uttered by S (to H) only if normal input and output conditions obtain.

R(f) *Grice rule: Pr* is to be uttered by S (to H) only if condition (f) obtains.

R(g) *Literal rule: Pr* is to be uttered by S (to H) only if the semantic rules of the dialect spoken by S and H are such that Pr is correctly and sincerely uttered iff conditions (a)–(f) obtain.

Recall that R(g) must (in accordance with R-C) guarantee that condition (g) is satisfied if R(g) is followed, and that R(g) is a *semantic* rule governing e (containing Pr). There is a problem here with R(g). It will be satisfied if the semantic rules of the dialect are such that conditions (a)–(f) are satisfied. But of course these conditions will be satisfied if rules R(a)–R(f) are satisfied. So R(g) is redundant.

The trouble is that Searle has gone too far in formulating as condition (g) what he takes to be the noncontingent relation between what e means and what S meant in uttering it. It is not necessary for literally and nondefectively promising in uttering e that the semantic rules of e be such that e is correctly uttered iff one is thereby promising (ambiguity and synonymy seem to falsify this in each direction[5]); therefore, why not drop R(g) and let R(f) carry the weight? Presumably because R(f) does not yet rule out nonliteral utterances of e (like sarcasm or metaphor). But why should literalness be a part of the analysis of promising? Surely there are less radical ways of stating what is true in the observation that one can't mean just anything by uttering just anything under any conditions.[6] A more natural and general approach would be to define the notion of promising in uttering a sentence e and then define a special case where the utterance of e with its full conventional force is *sufficient* for promising.

The fundamental problem for Searle's account of illocutionary acts in terms of constitutive rules, apart from the question of the existence of these rules (those tied specifically to illocutionary acts), is how to specify the rules in such a way as to allow for nonliteral or indirect

performances of illocutionary acts. The reason for this is that the rules
for a given type of illocutionary act are presented as rules for using the
associated illocutionary force indicating device. Thus, for example, the
rules for promising are presented as rules for using Pr. Obviously, Pr
does not need to occur in a nonliteral or indirect promise, and thus the
constitutive rules for promising cannot be invoked to explain promises
made nonliterally or indirectly.

Our intention/inference approach to communicative illocutionary
acts provides enough room between meaning and illocutionary force to
handle nonliteral and indirect, as well as literal, performances of illocutionary acts. Whereas Searle uses his conditions for performing illocutionary acts to attempt to extract constitutive rules, for us they are
nothing more than conditions for reasonably expecting one's communicative illocutionary intentions to be recognized, namely, in accordance
with the SAS. Satisfaction of the input-output conditions enables the
hearer to identify the utterance act. Satisfaction of the propositional
content and the preparatory conditions (S's predicating, literally or
otherwise, a future act of S that is mutually believed H would prefer
and S would not otherwise do) enables H to delimit the types of illocutionary acts that could be performed in S's utterance. And satisfaction
of the essential condition enables H to identify just what that illocutionary act is. For us the sincerity condition need not be met for the act
to succeed communicatively, and the Grice and the literal conditions
are inapplicable to our formulation.

7.4. PERFORMATIVES AND CONVENTION

We noted at the beginning of this chapter that Austin held that *all*
illocutionary acts are conventional but that he neglected to explain
what he meant by "conventional." An illocutionary act is, he says, "an
act done as conforming to a convention" (1962, 105) and "is constituted
not by intention or by fact, essentially, but by convention (which is, of
course, a fact)" (p. 127). The only clue to what he actually meant by
"conventional" is his bewildering remark that the illocutionary force of
an utterance "may be said to be conventional in the sense that at least it
could be made explicit by the performative formula" (p. 103). However, as Strawson observes (1964a, 445), there seems to be no such
sense of "being conventional," and "if this is a sense of anything to the
purpose, it is a sense of 'being *capable* of being conventional'." This
suggests that explicit performatives *are* conventional.

Strawson seems to hold this view. He categorically denies that all illocutionary acts are conventional: "Some illocutionary acts are conventional; others are not" (p. 445). Indeed, it was Strawson who, later in this paper, introduced the idea that the nonconventional acts are performed with reflexive (Gricean) intentions. Why does he think that explicit performatives are conventional? Whereas communicative illocutionary acts in general are issued with an intention to produce a certain response "by means of recognition on the part of the audience to produce that response, this recognition to serve as part of the reason that the audience has for its response" (p. 450), the "peculiar logical character" of performatives is "to *make explicit* the type of communication intention with which the speaker speaks, the type of force which the utterance has" (p. 451). Apparently, Strawson thinks that if the form of words makes explicit the illocutionary force, no reflexive intention is necessary or need be ascribed by the hearer to the speaker. Instead, it can be read off of what is said, that is, "illocutionary force is exhausted by meaning" (p. 456).

Our reply to this view should come as no surprise. Even where the speaker is being not only literal but fully explicit about the force of his utterance (as when he uses the explicit performative formula) still he must R-intend to be taken as speaking literally and explicitly and must be so taken. Meaning never exhausts illocutionary force, even when the speaker is doing precisely what he says he is doing and nothing else. The meaning may fully specify what in fact the speaker is doing, but it does not determine that this is what he is doing. Thus, just as with literal illocutionary acts in general, an inference in the pattern of the SAS is required even for explicit performative utterances. And the speaker must R-intend the hearer to make such an inference. We will leave our reply to Austin and Strawson as it stands until we take up the subject of illocutionary acts and linguistic devices in chapter 10.

7.5. WHY LOCUTIONARY ACTS ARE NOT FULLY CONVENTIONAL

Communicative illocutionary acts are not conventional qua illocutionary acts. Yet there seems to be an important, though obvious, respect in which *all* utterances in a language are conventional. It is worth spelling out in what respects utterances are and are not conventional.

Strawson (1964a, 442), in examining Austin's view that all illocutionary acts are conventional, contrasts this with the uncontroversial view that "we must refer . . . to linguistic conventions to determine what *locutionary* act has been performed in the making of an utterance, to determine what the *meaning* of the utterance is." Schiffer (1972, 155) describes utterance types as "conventional means for communicating." Without saying just what conventional means are,[7] he does indicate that they take the form "if one does X, then such-and-such will be the case" and that this is a matter of mutual knowledge (his analog to our notion of mutual belief). Since this parallels our notion of conventional action, we can use that notion to state to what extent an utterance in a language is conventional qua locutionary act.

It is natural to think of language as conventional in the sense that the meaning of its words is conventional. In our terms, what words mean is what we mutually believe them to mean. To be sure, no one knows what every word means, so allowances must be made for words not in the common parlance, such as technical terms. Even then at least it is mutually believed in the linguistic community that such terms mean whatever the relevant experts mean by them. In any case, there are thousands of words in the core vocabulary of the vernacular, and virtually everyone shares the mutual beliefs about their meanings.

People's (conscious) knowledge of the principles that determine how words (or *formatives*) combine to form determinately meaningful sentences is less explicit than their knowledge of the vocabulary. Members of the general public are not linguists or grammarians, but they do employ the linguistic presumption: that they share the language they use and that sentences as well as words mean more or less the same for all. They do not have explicit mutual beliefs about every particular sentence but, given the LP, it is at least the case that whenever someone utters a sentence to someone else, they mutually believe that the sentence e means such and such. Although it is a matter of convention that e means ..., uttering e conventionally counts as saying that *(...p...) only when the meaning of e determines what S says (provided S is *saying* something in uttering e).

Since locutionary acts are conventional only in this way, what a speaker says, as opposed to what he does in saying it, is a matter of R-intention only as regards resolving ambiguity and determining indeterminate references. Just as a conventional illocutionary act is something for the hearer to identify on the basis of his knowledge of the relevant convention, so a locutionary act, insofar as it is determined by what the utterance e means, is identified on the basis of H's knowledge of the language. Up to ambiguity, H does not have to figure out what S

means by e by inferring that S has certain intentions. So whereas S can deny that he has the illocutionary intent H attributes to him—by saying he was not serious or was not speaking literally—S has no deniability regarding what he says, at least as delimited by the meaning of e. One can admit to a malapropism or plead slip of the tongue, but this only shows that one can mean (to say) one thing and say another. To understand what a speaker is doing in uttering something, it is of course relevant to know that his utterance was intentional. Nevertheless, given what was uttered, the identity of what was said is not a matter of intention—it is determined, except for ambiguity and indefinite reference, by linguistic convention. These two factors keep most locutionary acts from being fully conventional.

Part Two   **Issues**

Chapter Eight

Locutionary Acts: Philosophical and Linguistic Issues

In part I we often used notions of meaning and occasionally notions of presupposition and implication without saying very much about them. We said enough for the purposes of the speech act schema, but then the schema is designed to reflect ordinary patterns of inference by normal hearers in response to speakers speaking normally. For this purpose we could not stray very far from ordinary concepts, because the normal speaker is neither a philosopher nor a linguist and so no philosophical nor linguistic analysis should be imputed to him.[1] Philosophers and linguists, though, *can* raise certain conceptual and linguistic questions about lines in (and aspects of) the schema.

Our first topic will be linguistic meaning. When we say that an expression has a certain meaning, what are we specifying and how is it to be specified? More fundamentally, what is it for an expression to have meaning? Then there is the topic of speaker meaning, of what a speaker means by an expression. For our purposes the concept of operative meaning, as explained in chapter 2, will suffice, although Grice and Schiffer have introduced further notions of what a speaker means. While operative meaning, together with reference, determines what is said, it seems relevant also to what is presupposed and to what is implied. Various notions of presupposition (semantic as well as pragmatic) have been proposed, and Grice has offered a systematic account of implication. Our general concern will be not only to unravel these notions, but also to ascertain their place in our overall account of linguistic communication. We will argue that some of these notions are already incorporated in our account, while others are theoretically superfluous. The reader should be warned that to keep the length of this chapter within reasonable bounds, we must assume some familiarity with the cited literature.

8.1. LINGUISTIC MEANING

In general the linguistic meaning of an expression is simply the meaning or meanings of that expression in some linguistic system. This rough characterization can be clarified in a number of ways, in particular, by saying more about the format for specifying linguistic meaning and the conditions for correctly attributing linguistic meaning.

At L2 of the SAS H identifies the operative meaning of e, so H must be able to represent that reading of e to himself. To do this H must have some system of (semantic) representation for specifying meaning. What it is, what it looks like, we don't know, though not from lack of suggestions. The literature contains proposals concerning the nature of semantic representation ranging from (1) the language L itself (Evans and McDowell 1976, Introduction), through (2) a regimented and augmented version of L (Harman 1973; Davidson 1967, 1970), (3) an intensional logic (Lewis 1969, 1970; Montague 1974), (4) special systems of conceptual notation (Katz 1972; Bierwisch 1970), to (5) a language of thought (Fodor 1975; Miller and Johnson-Laird 1976). Even if we rule out some of these as psychologically implausible (for example, present intensional logics—see Partee 1977), the options are still widely diverse.

We reject view (1), according to which the semantics of sentences in L can be represented to H by those very sentences of L, simply because of the ambiguity (syntactic or lexical) of most sentences. Operative meaning specifications identify the result of contextual disambiguation and so cannot themselves be ambiguous. Although it is possible that for every n-way ambiguous sentence of English there are n unambiguous English sentences each of which means just the same thing as one reading of the original sentence, we think it most unlikely. And we know of no evidence that hearers actually come up with such sentences to represent operative meaning. Concerning view (2), some regimented form of L, with no syntactic or lexical ambiguity,[2] avoids the problems raised by ambiguity, but it renders hopelessly mysterious how a person could ever learn the language in the first place or translate between languages. This is no conclusive objection, for maybe these are indeed mysteries. But we would prefer to trade them in for other problems, such as motivating the special systems of (4), or for other mysteries, such as the nature of a language of thought (5).

Many systems of semantic representation are compatible with the schema, which demands only psychological plausibility and nonambiguity in specifications of meaning. In philosophy currently the most popular approach is Davidson's (1970) project of giving a truth-definition for a natural language, but we know of no way (and suspect there is none) to make it psychologically applicable. In linguistics and psychology the most popular approach seems to be decompositional, along the lines of Katz (1972), Bierwisch (1970), and most versions of generative semantics. In the spirit of our approach to communication in general, we will tentatively endorse a more inferential perspective on semantics, but first let us give some reasons for suspecting the decompositional approach.

8.1.1. Decompositional Theories

We consider a semantic theory to be *decompositional* just in case it represents the meaning of a syntactically (or morphologically) unstructured item as being composed of more than one semantic element, that is, the semantic representation is complex. The classical statement of such a semantics was Katz and Fodor (1963). The theory has undergone substantial revision and elaboration, becoming considerably more sophisticated (see Katz 1972, 1977c, or Bierwisch 1970) while retaining its decompositional character. The same is true of its once-bruited alternative, *generative semantics*. On each of these theories a word like "bachelor" or "chase" or "kill" is represented as having internal semantic structure in the sense that parts of the semantic representation of each of these words can appear in the semantic representation of other words and so represent the same semantic contribution to the meaning of those words. Put another way, a decompositional semantics extends *compositionality* to the internal structure of lexical items. In effect the claim is that much the same representational machinery in semantics can be used for syntactically structured and unstructured expressions alike. Behind this claim is the idea that it is somewhat an historical accident which semantic representations (or meanings) become associated with a single word in a language and which ones get associated with compound words or phrases. For instance, English has the phrases "to intentionally kill oneself" and "to commit suicide," but no single word to express this notion. According to a decompositional semantics, this peculiarity should be viewed as only an historical accident, on a par with the fact that English has the single word "thumb" whereas Japanese uses the equivalent of "mother finger."

The common goals of semantic theories, at least in linguistics (see

Janet Fodor 1977), are to attribute to each well-formed expression in the language the correct range of semantic properties (meaningful, meaningless, redundant, analytic, contradictory, ambiguous, and so on) and relations (entails, contradicts, is synonymous with, is similar in meaning to, presupposes, and so on), though one need not subscribe to all these goals. A decompositional semantics usually is combined with a pair of additional claims to the effect that (i) the representation of the semantics of an expression *defines* the expression (gives necessary and sufficient conditions for its correct application) and (ii) the attribution of the range of semantic properties and relations to an expression is *mediated* by the representation of its meaning either as given in the definition (for syntactically/morphologically unstructured lexical items and idioms) or as the result of compositional operations on such definitions. Thus, on a semantics like Katz's the meaning, or meanings, of a sentence such as "He is a bachelor" would be represented in the theory by a formula f (or set of formulas) in the system of semantic representation such that f is the result of general principles of composition applying to the definitions of the constituent words and their grammatical relations, whereby f forms the basis for attributing the sentence's semantic properties and relations. And f does this by means of a system of formal theoretical definitions. For instance, being *meaningful* (as opposed to meaningless) might be defined as having a semantic representation in the theory, *ambiguity* can be defined in terms of receiving multiple semantic representations, *synonymy* in terms of receiving the same semantic representation(s) in the theory, and so on. Such definitions are theoretical in that they are stated within the vocabulary of the theory; they are formal in the sense that the correctness of their application to cases can be determined by inspecting the form or shape of the semantic representation.

Although we will return to these notions later, what we have said is sufficient to see how one might motivate decompositional semantics. Probably the central form of linguistic argument in favor of lexical decomposition is simplicity of predictions concerning various semantic properties and relations.[3] Just as transformational rules capture generalizations missed by phrase structure grammars (Chomsky 1957; Akmajian and Heny 1975, ch. 3), so it could be claimed that systems of semantics without decomposition fail to reflect certain generalizations concerning semantic properties and relations (see Akmajian, Demers, and Harnish 1979, ch. 11).

The price of such theoretical elegance is a concomitant strengthening of constraints on the adequacy of a semantic description of a particular language. Decomposition demands definitions of all meaningful words, definitions yielding necessary and sufficient conditions of correct application, as well as formal identity of synonyms and nonidentity of nonsynonyms. Some theorists have found such constraints highly desirable in principle but too strong in fact (see Fodor, Bever, and Garrett 1975, 209–214; Fodor, Fodor, and Garrett 1975, sec. 3; J. D. Fodor 1977, ch. 5.1, 5.6; J. A. Fodor 1975, 147–156). The counterargument proceeds in three stages.

First, the decompositional theory is softened up by arguing that decomposition and theoretical definition are not sufficient machinery to make *all* relevant semantic predictions. For instance, to predict that "is a male mother" is contradictory, one needs a way of inferring that if something expresses FEMALE, then it expresses NOT-MALE, so that the representation of "is a male mother" could be shown to comprise MALE(x) & NOT-MALE(x) and so be contradictory. To accommodate such facts, Katz (1966, 1972) and others (Bierwisch 1970) incorporate into the semantic component a set of *redundancy rules*, which mark the first piece of semantic machinery supplementing the devices of decomposition and theoretical definitions.

The second stage is to claim that the general requirement of formulating decompositional definitions is too strong. Some relations cannot be plausibly accounted for in these terms, for instance, the relations between:

(1) necessary: not possible not
    some x is: not every x is not
    p and q: not (not-p or not-q)

If it is proposed that the right side define the left side, then what does one do with their duals, which have equal claim to definitional status?

(2) possible: not necessary not
    every x is: not some x is not
    p or q: not (not-p and not-q)

Furthermore, sometimes only necessary conditions seem to be possible:

(3) green: COLORED

To get a sufficient condition one would have to fill in the ellipsis, but what could so define "green" and not entail COLORED?

(4) COLORED & ... : green

In other cases what are offered as definitions are plausibly only necessary conditions:

(5) kill: CAUSE (BECOME (NOT-ALIVE))

Finally, there are types of expressions such as proper names, natural kind terms, various particles, and perhaps performative verbs which might not have necessary conditions of the sort required by decompositional theories. (See J. Katz 1975, 1977a,b,c, and references therein for discussion of these kinds of cases and objections.)

The third stage of the case against compositionality is to argue that a semantic theory could be a mixture of redundancy (or inference) rules and decompositional definitions. So far the main complaint against mixed theories has been that they provide no principled reason for making a semantic prediction on the basis of decomposition as opposed to inference (see Fodor, Fodor, and Garrett 1975, 522). However, there is no reason at present to suppose a decompositionalist could not come up with such a principle or principles (see G. Lakoff 1970, sec. 7). But if principles could be found for drawing such a distinction, is it the sort of distinction one wants? What is the difference, semantically, between being necessitated by the inference rules

(6) father → MALE,
    green → COLORED,

and being necessitated by the dictionary definitions,

(7) father: MALE & ...,
    green: COLORED & ...?

If there is no difference in the semantic property being predicted, should there be a difference in the semantic machinery that predicts it? On the other hand, if a principle cannot be found for allocating predictions to lexical definitions rather than inference rules, a mixed theory would be unacceptable. But since the demand for decomposition is sometimes too strong, inference rules would be the preferable single piece of machinery to use (supplemented by definitions of semantic properties and relations that any theory needs). Can an inferential theory be worked out? The matter is currently under dispute and much remains to be done, but we can sketch the outlines of such an alternative and say how it fits the SAS.

8.1.2. Inferential Theories

One of the main attractions of an inferential theory for practicing semanticists is the modesty of its ambitions. Instead of seeking definitions as the basis for semantic description, it seeks entailments, and these are generally easier to come by than synonyms. Such a semantics has the virtue of making us preach what we practice. In the (rare?) cases where one finds fairly uncontroversial sufficient as well as necessary conditions, the inference-rules approach posits a two-way inference. *Synonymy* would be defined perhaps as 'mutual inferability,' *contradiction* as 'entailing F and not-F,' and so on. Before attempting to assess the range of semantic properties and relations that could plausibly be covered by a theory of this sort, we should see what the specific advantages of this approach might be.[4]

Fodor (1975) sees at least three (nonpsychological) advantages to inference rules over lexical decomposition. If a theory contains just inference rules (and theoretical definitions), then, first, it would not "posit a sharp distinction between the logical and nonlogical vocabulary . . . the logical behavior of 'bachelor' is not, on this view, treated fundamentally differently from the logical behavior of 'and' . . . the entailments they engender are determined by the inference rules under which they fall" (1975, 150). Second, although definition is a symmetrical relation, entailment is not, and "there is no reason why, on the present account, analyticity must rest upon symmetrical relations. Some rules of inference go one way, other rules of inference go both ways. There is nothing special about the latter" (1975, 152). Finally, theories having both decomposition and inference seem to "posit an unwarranted distinction in kind between formulae true by virtue of definitions and certain other kinds of 'analyticity'" (1975, 148). In fact, mixed theories fail to provide "principled grounds for claiming that the two relations [of definition and entailment] have anything in common at all" (1975, 149).

Although these may be advantages, they are not decisive. The second argument is simply an endorsement of inferential semantics, and it is not all that clear what the first and third considerations amount to. Why are these distinctions unwarranted? Fodor does not say. It is

tempting to try to strengthen the point by arguing that homogeneity of
the entailment relation (or the univocality of "analyticity") requires a
single underlying mechanism to account for the pertinent semantic
facts. But such a move is in danger of proving too much. Applied to
ambiguity, it would establish the conclusion that a grammar should not
make use of different devices such as lexical entries, rewrite rules, and
transformations to account for lexical, surface, and underlying ambiguities—surely a conclusion not warranted on any independent grounds.

Since one of the best ways of refuting a theory is providing a superior
alternative, we can ask what a semantic theory that used inference
rules as the basic semantic device would look like. According to Fodor,
Bever, and Garrett (1974, 184) it would have to contain (1) a set of
semantic representations (equivalent to a language), (2) a set of rules of
assignment which assign semantic representations to sentences, and (3)
a set of inference rules applying mechanically to the semantic representations to determine entailments. Since the inference rules apply
to semantic representations, these representations must be rich enough
to determine (via the inference rules) all entailments of the expression
assigned that representation. It is thus appropriate to call such a representation the *logical form* of that sentence (in this system). The set of
entailments can be called the *logical force* of the sentence. Semantics,
in this conception, has as one of its basic tasks the specification of the
logical force of every expression in the language having such force.

What does the system of semantic representations look like? What
are the rules of assignment? What are the rules of inference? These are
matters for empirical investigation, but they are also partly matters for
decision. For instance, one must decide whether one's semantics is also
to be interpreted psychologically as an account of what a person is
intending to communicate when using a sentence literally. If one demands psychological reality of one's semantic machinery, the constraints on it are increased appreciably (see chapter 11; also Fodor
1975; Harnish 1977c). Apart from questions of psychological reality,
what can be said about the nature of the inference rules? Since in the
Fodor, Bever, and Garrett (1975) account, inference rules are defined
over semantic representations, the exact nature of these inference rules
cannot be determined independently of the investigation into the nature
of semantic representation. But because it is plausible to believe that
the result of applying one inference rule can be in the domain of application of a different rule, such rules of inference seem to determine
sets of pairs of semantic representations, $\langle F_1, F_2 \rangle$, each pair having the

characteristic that the sentence expressing F_1 entails (on that reading) the sentence expressing F_2. If the theory is to be finite (or finitely representable) it will not do for rules of inference to *be* such pairs: there is a potential infinity of them. Inference rules must therefore collect together classes of semantic representations. Traditionally this is done in terms of crucial logical words that occur, in the sentences to be represented. Sentences of the grammatical form "S and S" are represented by a wff of the form "... & ____"; sentences of the form "S or S" are represented with a wff of the form "... v ____"; and so on. An inference rule defined over such representations might have the form:[5]

(8) From a wff of the form "... & ____" infer a wff of the form "..." and infer a wff of the form "____."

The logical force of a sentence would be determined by applying the relevant inference rules to its semantic representation.

Having gone this far down the road from decomposition in accounting for entailments, one might wonder whether there is reason for retaining a level of semantic representation at all. Why not just have rules legitimating inferences from one sentence (under a description) to others? What else is needed in a semantics in which the basic semantic notion to be captured is entailment? Two considerations in favor of semantic representations come to mind. First, a semantic representation can function as an object of understanding, belief, confirmation, and so on, and an account of understanding a sentence, belief, and so on, can plausibly be given in terms of recovering or computing this representation (see Fodor, Bever, and Garrett 1975, 374–384; J. A. Fodor 1975). Since questions about the nature of a representation system functioning in this capacity will be taken up in chapter 11, we will not pursue this issue here.

Second, the existence of a semantic representation allows us to make sense of the recurrent observation that grammatical form is misleading as to logical form; without logical forms it might be thought difficult to explain such disparities. Philosophers who make the observation rarely say exactly how grammatical form is misleading as to logical form. Strawson, however, has made such an attempt:

We might reasonably say that the verbal form of a statement was (at least potentially) misleading as to its logical form in the following circumstances: (1) the sentence used to make it has a certain verbal pattern in common with a great many other sentences; (2) most, or a great number, of the statements made are analogous to one another in a certain formal respect; (3) the statement in question is not analogous to these statements in that formal respect. (1952, 51)

There is something importantly right here, despite the obscurities. We will assume that sentences have a logical form and will adapt Strawson's remarks to that end.

The grammatical form of *s* is misleading if it makes *s* appear to have particular logical form F that it does not really have.[6] That is,

1. *s* has the grammatical form T;
2. *s* appears, in virtue of its grammatical form T, to have the logical form F;
3. *s* does not have the logical form F.

More needs to be said about the phrase "appears in virtue of." Taking a clue from Strawson that most, or a great many, sentences with grammatical form T have the logical form F, then grammatical misleadingness comes to this:

1. *s* has a grammatical form T;
2. Most, or a great many, sentences with the grammatical form of *s* have the logical form F;
3. *s* does not have the logical form F.

According to this account (potential) misleadingness is the result of (potential) overgeneralization.

Philosophers who subscribe to the doctrine of logical form seem to take a rather traditional view of grammar and grammatical form. However, since contemporary grammars reconstruct the traditional notion of grammatical structure in terms of phrase-markers, to say of a sentence that it has a particular grammatical form T_i is just to say that an optimal grammar would assign some particular phrase-marker to that sentence. Thus,

The grammatical form of a sentence s is misleading as to its logical form iff:
i. *s* is assigned the phrase-marker PM_i by some (correct) grammar,
ii. Most, or at least a great many, sentences assigned the phrase-marker PM_i have the logical form F_i,
iii. *s* does not have the logical form F_i.

So far our explication of the misleadingness of grammatical form has utilized the notion of a semantic or logical representation. Can we make

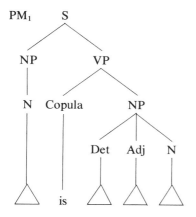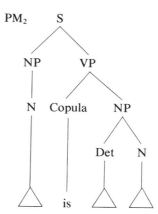

Figure 8.1

sense of the notion of misleadingness without appealing to some formal system? We can, and something closer to such an explication of misleadingness lies behind many of the traditional examples of how grammatical form is misleading as to logical form. Let $s_1, s_2, \ldots, s_m$, be a nonredundant enumeration of all and only the sentences of the natural language L under consideration. Let $PM_1, PM_2, \ldots, PM_n$, be a nonredundant enumeration of all and only the phrase-markers for the sentences of that language. This can be done with a phrase structure grammar. As Chomsky remarks, "The natural mechanism for generating Phrase-markers . . . is a system of rewriting rules" (1965, 66). Then let $PM_k[s]$ be the equivalence class of sentences that have the phrase-marker PM_k assigned to s. Finally, suppose there to be an enumeration of *grammatical inference rules*, $R_{h,i}^1, R_{j,k}^2, \ldots, R_{l,m}^n$, each of the form,

(9) $R_{y,z}^n$: From a sentence assigned the phrase-marker PM_y *infer a sentence assigned the phrase-marker* PM_z.

For example, consider the phrase-markers in figure 8.1, which would probably occur in an enumeration of the phrase-markers of English. And consider the grammatical inference rule,

(10) $R_{1,2}^n$: From a sentence of the form PM_1 infer a sentence of the form PM_2—identical branches on both trees to receive the same words.

For instance, from "John is a strong boy" infer "John is a boy." We can now say what it is for a sentence, in virtue of its grammatical form, to be misleading as to its logical form:

The grammatical form of a sentence s is (at least potentially) *misleading as to its logical form* iff:

i. s is assigned the phrase-marker PM_i by a correct grammar,

ii. There is a grammatical inference rule $R^n_{i,j}$ that is valid for most or a great number of $PM_i[s]$,

iii. $R^n_{i,j}$ is not valid for s.

By this definition, the two phrase-markers in figure 8-1, and inference rule (10), we get the result that the sentence "John is a converted heathen" is misleading as to logical form, since one cannot infer that John is a heathen (one can infer that he was one).

These two characterizations of how grammatical form is misleading as to logical form have the virtue of bringing out some further aspects of the notion and doctrine of logical form. For instance, they can be used to explicate, and motivate the study of, ideal languages and can be shown to explicate a wide variety of classical examples of ways in which grammatical form is misleading as to logical form (see Harnish 1972, ch. 1). If this is a sound approach, traditional wisdom on logical form need not rule out a purely inferential account of semantics. The notion of the misleadingness of grammatical form can be explicated without invoking forms to compare. To speak of the logical form of a sentence is, on this view, just an odd (and misleading) way of speaking of a particular kind of description of a sentence (like describing a sentence as being of the form NP + VP); it is not another object to be described.

Thus, the possibility remains that inference rules are a main, perhaps the main, device in a semantic theory after theoretical definition. Inference rules would be a part of the apparatus used by a hearer in the interpretation of a speaker's remarks. What the rules are and how notions like synonymy and analyticity might be defined in terms of them are matters of future research. This conclusion still leaves at least one question unanswered: with no lexical decomposition (beyond definitional abbreviation) what does *meaning specification* amount to? Fodor (1975) has argued that the vocabulary of the language of thought is roughly equivalent (in size) to that of a natural language, and that it is the system of unambiguous, psychologically real semantic representation. This hypothesis is compatible with the absence of decomposition, but doesn't the hypothesis still require a distinct system of semantic representation? Fodor (1975) argues that it does, but perhaps something weaker will do (see Harnish 1977b). It could be that many sentences in the language of thought are regimented forms of the language one speaks, with entailment (or translation) principles connecting them with nonlinguistic modes of representation. This hypothesis would allow for the possibility of learning a language in which one eventually thinks and would not necessitate a system of semantic representation independent of the vocabulary (and syntax) already required in a grammar. Of course we have not explained the nature of such representation, linguistic or nonlinguistic, but explaining it can be considered a problem for future research (see Rosenberg 1974). In any event its outcome does not effect the SAS.

Finally, theories of semantic representation usually contain, implicitly or explicitly, definitions of the semantic properties and relations predicted to apply to the expressions they cover. Thus, synonymy (on a reading) might be defined as sharing a semantic representation. How would such a theory define meaningful (as opposed to meaningless) expressions? A typical definition would run as follows:

(11) Expression e has a meaning (is *meaningful*) if and only if grammar
     G assigns e some semantic representation.

This will not do as a general definition of being meaningful, for the obvious reason that the grammar G might be wrong about e. If grammar G failed to assign "It is raining" a semantic representation, it would not follow that the sentence is not meaningful (is meaningless) but only that grammar G is wrong.[7] And when a grammar assigns a semantic representation to an expression, thereby indicating that the expression means something (whatever the representation represents), it does not say what this pairing amounts to. Formally, the pairing of sound and meaning in a grammar could record all sorts of things. Thus, definition (11) cannot be used as evidence for the existence of a level of semantic representation.

We saw in section 2.2 that L1(a) in the SAS requires representing that e means ... (as well as perhaps ____) in L. In this section we have been looking at issues surrounding the problem of what kind of semantic representation should replace the ellipses. We have given some reasons for preferring an inferential approach to a decompositional one, quite apart from its being more consonant with the SAS.

8.2. SPEAKER MEANING

So far, we have tried to avoid using the term *speaker meaning* (as opposed to "expression meaning" or "sentence meaning") for two important reasons. First, a number of distinct things go by the label "speaker meaning" and we have not yet sorted these out. That will be our first task here. Second, as we will show, there is no reason to suppose there to be a single, stable, pretheoretic notion of speaker meaning capable of bearing the theoretical weight put upon it in many analyses.

8.2.1. Varieties of Speaker Meaning

At least five different things can be meant when it is said that somebody means something. (1) When we say that somebody meant what he said, we may mean that he is serious or sincere about it. Or (2) we may mean that he is speaking literally: "S said that p and meant it" is ambiguous between the seriousness and the literalness of S's utterance, depending on whether emphasis is on "meant." Generally, when a person is speaking literally, he is also speaking seriously, but it is possible to be literal without being serious ("I was just kidding"), just as it is possible to be serious without being literal ("Not until Hell freezes over"). However, we probably would not say that S meant what he *said* if he was speaking seriously but not literally.

(3) In a third use, "means" has the sense 'intending': in saying something a person may mean (intend) to be doing such-and-such. This may be an illocutionary act, or a perlocutionary act, or even some collateral act.[8] (4) Then there is operative meaning, as used in line L2 of the SAS, which specifies how a speaker is using an expression (word, phrase, or sentence). Such a specification is of the form: S meant ... by e. This use is to be contrasted with (5) the notion of speaker meaning proper, as given by: In uttering e, S meant that p—which Grice (1957, 1969) introduced.[9]

It is important to distinguish these five uses of "means" lest we fall into hopeless confusion in trying to understand what it is for a person to mean something by an utterance ("utterance" itself suffers from act/object and type/token ambiguity). Confusing uses (4) and (5) collapses an essential distinction in the theory of speaker meaning. Frye, in an important article (1973) concerned with such distinctions, herself fails to distinguish (4) and (5), or perhaps singles out (4) while ignoring (5). She is explicit about use (3), and points out that Searle confuses (3) and (4) when he says of his essential condition on promising that it "captures our amended Gricean analysis of what it is for the speaker to mean to make a promise" (1965, 237). Searle's revised Gricean analysis

(1969, 49–50) is explicitly of "the different concept [from Grice's meaning$_{nn}$] of saying something and meaning it," which Searle glosses as our use (2), meaning literally what one says.[10]

It might seem that uses (3) and (5) are coextensive: that to mean (3) to be performing some illocutionary act $F(p)$ is to mean (5) that p. For example, it might be thought that—except for illocutionary acts that lack propositional content (utterance of "Hello"), which are hardly candidates for meaning (5) anything—"means" is equivalent to "intends to be performing some illocutionary act," that is, that "means" (5) falls under "means" (3). The trouble is that there seems to be no way of filling in the blank in: S means that p—that is, in specifying p for certain sorts of illocutionary acts *with* propositional content. There is no problem with constatives and directives (these correspond to Grice's (1969) indicative and imperative cases). However, it is not clear what S means when issuing an acknowledgment, even one that ostensibly has propositional content like "Congratulations on getting promoted" or "Thanks for the wonderful time." One way out, for which there are independent reasons, is to deny that these really have propositional content. But still there is the case of commissives. Is there something of the form, "that p," which S means (5) when he promises to return? If S meant merely that he would return, his utterance would not be distinguished, as far as meaning (5) is concerned, from making a prediction or from merely expressing an intention that he would return. On the other hand, it is not clear that S meant (5) that he promised that he would return, even if he meant (1), (2), or (3) that he promised.

8.2.2. A Critique of Speaker Meaning

Let us now examine the notion of speaker meaning proper, that is, meaning (5). Illocutionary acts are performed either with R-intentions or with intentions implemented by illocutionary conventions, C-intentions. Clearly those acts with only C-intentions are not cases of speaker meaning, since speaker meaning requires R-intentions not C-intentions. Conventional illocutionary acts have as their primary illocutionary point the changing or as-if changing of institutional states of affairs, and insofar as they involve uptake, uptake is more verificatory than constitutive of success (see section 6.3.2). Even restricting speaker meaning to communicative illocutionary acts, for reasons mentioned at the end of section 8.2.1, we should further restrict the present discussion to constatives and directives, corresponding to Grice's indicative and imperative acts of meaning, respectively, and to Schiffer's cases of "meaning that p" and of "meaning that A is to Ψ."

The most glaring question about the notion of speaker meaning is whether there really is a sense of the term "meaning" that corresponds to just the idea of "attempted communication in the sense which Grice seeks to elucidate" (Strawson 1964a, 447). It is possible, one starts surmising after surveying the literature, that the endless parade of counterexamples to successive analyses designed to accommodate previous counterexamples betokens a spurious notion. This sentiment is intensified when one examines details of successively more refined analyses: more and more subtle intentions are ascribed to speakers, and the ability to recognize such subtler and subtler intentions is ascribed to hearers, not to mention S's ability to ascribe this ability to H and H's ability to ascribe the attribution of this ability to S, and on and on. Intentions are proliferated ad infinitum, but allegedly harmlessly. Alternatively, what is required is mutual knowledge, with an allegedly harmless infinite regress condition, of a single, but awesomely complex, intention (given by Schiffer 1972, 63). One wonders, simply, just what these proposed analyses are analyses of.

The difficulties become evident when one considers Schiffer's objections to, first, the alleged *sufficiency* and, second, the alleged *necessity* of Grice's analysans. Objections of the first sort give rise to the addition of more and more intentions to the analysans (later replaced by Schiffer's mutual knowledge condition). The second sort pertain to the necessity of Grice's "by means of recognition of intention" condition and to the specification of the intended response by the hearer. Roughly speaking, considerations of the first sort raise the question of how much it takes to mean something; considerations of the second sort concern what one is doing when meaning something.

Schiffer's objections to the alleged *sufficiency* of Grice's analysans involve raising a counterexample to the analysans and to successive modifications incorporating further intentions inspired by previous counterexamples. And, says Schiffer (1972, 26), "What makes each of the examples . . . a counter-example is that S intends to deceive [H] in one way or another," namely, as to one or another of S's intentions. The general pattern of successive modification is, indeed, that each additional intention be that H recognize some previous intention of S's. Before arriving at his replacement of the iterated intentions with the mutual knowledge condition, Schiffer notes Grice's efforts to deal with the regress either by a condition that instead of adding more and more intentions simply requires that no deceptive intentions be present or by claiming that there is a de facto limit on the number of intentions that can realistically appear on the list: a limit to the subtlety of human intellect. Although Schiffer's mutual knowledge condition is a substantial improvement on Grice's iterated intention conditions, nevertheless its point is still to preclude "counter-examples based on deception . . . what precludes these cases from being instances of [speaker] meaning is that S does not utter e expecting that if the intentions with which he uttered e are satisfied, [H] will recognize that S meant something by uttering e" (Schiffer 1972, 41).

A curious fact about these various attempts to define speaker meaning by ruling out more and more subtle cases of deception is that simple deception is not precluded at all. By simple deception we have in mind cases where S means that p but doesn't believe that p and where S means that H is to Ψ but doesn't want H to Ψ. Simple deception, or insincerity, does not involve S's having any *intentions* that H is not to recognize, only that S have a certain belief or desire that H is not to recognize. On the one hand, it seems clear that any analysans permitting S to deceive (simply) cannot be an analysans of meaning, at least not if meaning implies sincerity. However, it might be argued that meaning permits insincerity—we are not talking about meaning in the sense of "saying something and meaning it," as Searle (1969, 49), for example, seems to think—but meaning in the sense of communicating, irrespective of whether one believes what one is communicating. But if simple deception is allowed, why should meaning preclude any of the more subtle forms of deception that involve hidden intentions? Besides, if these cases, as given in the various counterexamples, aren't cases of meaning, what are they cases of? It seems that each successive refinement of the analysans of meaning widens the gap between clear cases of nonmeaning, ruled out by Grice's original analysis, and clear cases of meaning, as provided by the analysans in question. What, again, are we to call these intermediate cases?

Schiffer's objections to the alleged *necessity* of Grice's analysans concern two things, first, Grice's "by means of recognition of intention" requirement, and second, the "production of belief or action (intention)" requirement. The first need not concern us here, for it simply points out the excessive narrowness of Grice's requirement, which Schiffer broadens to a "by means of recognition of connection" requirement, as we might call it, between the utterance and the intended response. Only in some cases of speaker meaning does the relation that H is to recognize between e and the intended response have to be the relation of being intended by S to be recognized by H as related.

However, the production of belief or action requirement is much too strong, and hardly necessary, even if qualified by the activated belief or intention stipulation. The reason is simple: for S to succeed in meaning something, H must understand what S means and nothing more. Understanding what S means does not require, if S means that p, for H to believe that p, or if S means that H is to Ψ, for H to Ψ or intend to. Therefore, this requirement is too strong. Searle is quite right when he charges Grice with conflating illocutionary and perlocutionary effects (1969, 46), and the charge applies to Schiffer as well. An adequate account of meaning and speech acts must distinguish the two types of effects, even if, in general, no illocutionary act is performed without an intended perlocutionary effect.[11]

Finally, if Schiffer's (1972, 63) analysis were correct, his mutual knowledge condition would be incompatible with the requirement of apparent sincerity. If the analysis implies that S is sincere and also requires that S's primary intention be recognized on the basis of mutually known conclusive evidence (and mutually known to be conclusive evidence), it would seem to follow that S cannot mean something while being insincere, even if his insincerity is not recognized and H believes S is sincere. For if S is insincere (and, presumably, knows it), he cannot consistently believe, as required by the mutual knowledge condition, that the obtainment of E, as realized by his utterance of e, is conclusive evidence that he uttered e with the primary intention that there be some reason for which H responds (as S's utterance of e is supposed to cause H to respond). For from S's point of view, there can be no such reason. Hence S cannot even have that primary intention. Instead, his primary intention is, inter alia, to provide H with a bad reason for his response. And surely the badness of this reason cannot be mutually known if it is still to serve as a reason for H's response. What seems to be the contradiction immersed in Schiffer's analysis is that meaning does require sincerity after all, even though it should not, since the sense of meaning that implies sincerity is not the one in question, speaker meaning.

8.3. PRESUPPOSITION

In this section we examine the variously drawn contrast between what is *said* and what is *presupposed*. We suggest that presuppositional facts can be handled in terms of independently motivated notions from the SAS.

In the past decade the notion of presupposition has been applied to a multifarious collection of phenomena: necessary conditions for truth-valuation (Lakoff 1972, V), felicity conditions of speech acts (Fillmore 1971), shared information (Jackendoff 1972), and conditions necessary for an utterance to be meaningful (Muraki 1972). Though widely utilized, presupposition has been rarely scrutinized in linguistics (see Kempson 1975; Wilson 1975; Katz and Langendoen 1976). One might well suspect its popularity is due primarily to its adaptability. Such wanton adaptability can rob the notion of most of its predictive and explanatory value.[12] It is not our ambition to untangle the various conceptions (and misconceptions) of presupposition. Rather, we want to locate the relevant phenomena in our theory and see whether they pose any problem for the SAS, as regards either what it covers or what it omits. To this end we will discuss the two main species of presupposition (as we understand it), each of which contrasts with what is said, entailed, and implied. These are semantic and pragmatic presupposition.

8.3.1. Semantic Presupposition

The central feature of semantic presupposition, as introduced by Frege (1892)[13] and revived by Strawson (1950, 1952),[14] is that the presuppositions of a statement made in uttering a sentence (the SMU of a sentence) are *referential conditions* that must be satisfied for the SMU of the sentence to be either true or false. Thus, Frege contended that the SMU of the sentence (13a) does not include but presupposes (13b)[15] —

(13) a. Kepler died in misery.
    b. Kepler exists.

—because he also held that (14),

(14) Kepler did not die in misery.

is used to make the contradictory statement of (13a), and that the SMU of (14) presupposes that Kepler exists (13b), and so bears the same relation to (13b) as (13a) does. In other words, the SMU of a sentence and the SMU of its contradictory have the same presupposition.

Strawson's extension of the presuppositional data beyond Frege's was fairly conservative. Like Frege he includes sentences with singular definite descriptions, and so the SMU of (15a) is said to presuppose that (15b):

(15) a. The present King of France is bald.

b. There is only one present King of France.

But Strawson (1952, 173–179) also counts quantified plural referring expressions as carrying presuppositions,[16] so that the SMU of (16a) presupposes that (16b):

(16) a. All John's children are asleep.

b. John has children.

Thus the original core conception of presupposition had the following characteristics:

Presupposition:
(a) The presuppositions of the SMU of a sentence *s* concern conditions of reference on the truth-valuation of the SMU of *s*.
(b) The SMU of a sentence *s* and its contradictory not-*s* have the same presuppositions.[17]

If we assume that certain conditions are satisfied if a statement expressing such satisfaction is true, then we can add a third characteristic:

(c) The truth of the presupposition of SMU of *s* is guaranteed (*necessitated*) by:
i. the truth of the SMU of *s*, and
ii. the falsity of the SMU of *s*.
iii. If its presuppositions are not true, the SMU of *s* has no truth value.

The classical conception of (statement) presupposition held that the SMU of sentences such as (13a)–(15a) presuppose (13b)–(15b) respectively; and that the relation of presupposition has characteristics (a)–(c).

As thus characterized, how would semantic presupposition be represented in the speech act schema? Should presupposition be included in the meaning specification of a sentence whose SMU has a presupposition? One could bifurcate semantic representations into two parts, one specifying what is being presupposed and one specifying the remainder (see Katz 1977c, ch. 3). However, (operative) meaning contributes to what is said (see chapter 2), so if presupposition is a part of sentence meaning but not a part of what is said, the schema must be supplemented with a procedure for selecting only nonpresuppositional aspects of meaning as contributing to what is said. Since this complication of the schema would not be necessary if there were no semantic presupposition, it is worth inquiring whether there really is such a phenomenon as semantic presupposition. We think not, though here we cannot fully document our reasons.

First, considered purely as linguistic judgments, the data are not really as clear as usually thought. Fluent speakers show considerable variation when asked to judge whether the SMU of a sentence is false or neither true nor false, when the putative presupposition fails. And even if tests were devised which showed stable responses to sentences like (13a)–(15a), there seem to be clearly related sentences whose statements speakers judge not to have presuppositions of the relevant sort. For instance, the SMU of (17a) does not presuppose that (17b)—

(17) a. Pegasus was ridden by Gene Autry.

b. Pegasus exists.

—because knowing that (17b) is false, speakers judge that (17a) is simply false. The same goes for (18b) and (18a) and for (19b) and (19a):

(18) a. The present King of France sold you a vacuum cleaner.

b. There is just one present King of France.

(19) a. All of John's children came for dinner.

b. John has children.

Why is it the case that the SMUs of (17a)–(19a) are judged as nonpresuppositional? We do not know for sure, but notice that these sentences are all overtly *relational,* and the verbs are all transitive, whereas the original (13a)–(16a) are purely *predicative* (in surface form). Perhaps when a putative object is claimed to bear some relation to something else, it counts toward the falsity of that claim that the object does not exist.

Even if there were stable judgments about such sentences and a presuppositional theory could account for them, we could still ask whether a presuppositional theory is the best account of these judgments. Deciding which is the best theory involves settling questions of overall explanatory power and simplicity. Since such a theory would have to account for the full range of relevant data, it would have to deal with the presuppositions of compound sentences as well, as in Karttunen (1973). However, recent work by Kempson (1975), Wilson (1975), and Boer and Lycan (1976) suggest that what has been called "semantic presupposition" is better viewed as a special case of entailment, plus *pragmatic presupposition* (but see Katz 1977c). Entailment is a semantic relation already utilized in our discussion of the locutionary act portion of the schema. Thus, if the notion of pragmatic presupposition relevant for the explanation of semantic presupposition can be explicated in terms of concepts already developed in the schema, the phenomenon of semantic presupposition will be accounted for without complicating the basic structure and conceptual resources of the schema. What, then, is the relevant notion of pragmatic presupposition that can, in conjunction with entailment, help account for the facts commonly thought to be cases of semantic presupposition?

8.3.2. Pragmatic Presupposition

There appear to be three main kinds of pragmatic phenomena labeled "presupposition" in the literature. For neutrality we label them with numbers. In each case the (b) sentence is thought to be a pragmatic presupposition of the (a) sentence.

(Pragmatic) Presupposition$_1$

One conception of presupposition is that it concerns speaker's assumptions (beliefs) about the speech context. As Lakoff writes, "Natural language is used for communication in a context, and every time a speaker uses a sentence of his language . . . he is making certain assumptions about that context" (1970, 175). As examples of such phenomena we find factives and aspectuals:

(20) a. Sam realizes that Irv is a Martian.
     b. Irv is a Martian.
(21) a. Sam does not realize that Irv is a Martian.
     b. Irv is a Martian.
(22) a. Sam has stopped beating his wife.
     b. Sam was beating his wife.
(23) a. Sam has not stopped beating his wife.
     b. Sam was beating his wife.

(Pragmatic) Presupposition$_2$

Another notion of (pragmatic) presupposition is that the (pragmatic) presuppositions of a sentence are those conditions that have to be satisfied in order for the intended speech act to be felicitous and appropriate in the circumstances. Keenan writes:

In general I want to consider that the presuppositions of a sentence are those conditions that the world must meet in order for the sentence to make literal sense . . . Now how many sentences require that certain culturally defined conditions or contexts be satisfied in order for an utterance of a sentence to be understood . . . these conditions are naturally called presuppositions of the sentence . . . An utterance of a sentence pragmatically presupposes that its context is appropriate. (1971, 45, 49)

Fillmore puts the matter another way:

By the presuppositional aspects of a speech communication situation, I mean those conditions which must be satisfied in order for a particular illocutionary act to be effectively performed in saying particular sentences. (1971, 276)

As examples of such phenomena we are given the following:

(24) a. John accused Harry of writing the letter.
    b. There was something blameworthy about writing the letter. (Fillmore 1971)
(25) a. John criticized Harry for writing the letter.
    b. Harry wrote the letter. (Fillmore 1971)
(26) a. Tu es dégoûtant.
    b. The addressee is an animal or child, socially inferior to the speaker, or personally intimate with the speaker. (Keenan 1971)[18]

(Pragmatic) Presupposition$_3$

A third notion of (pragmatic) presupposition is that of shared (or background) information: "We will use . . . 'presupposition of a sentence' to denote the information in the sentence that is assumed by the speaker to be shared by him and the hearer" (Jackendoff 1972, 230). As Bates puts it, "Presupposing is the act of using a sentence to make a comment about some information assumed to be shared or verifiable by speaker and listener" (1976, 25). As examples of such phenomena we are given:

(27) a. Was it Margaret that Paul married?
   b. Paul married someone.
(28) a. Betty remembered to take her medicine.
   b. Betty was supposed to take her medicine.
(29) a. That Sioux Indian he befriended represented the Chief.
   b. He had befriended a Sioux Indian.
(30) a. He befriended that Sioux Indian who represented the Chief.
   b. Some Sioux Indian represented the Chief.

These three notions of pragmatic presupposition are loosely related. Presupposition₁ and presupposition₃ overlap in that if p is assumed by the speaker to be shared, it must be assumed by the speaker and so be a case of presupposition₁. Likewise, if a certain condition is necessary for the successful and felicitous performance of an illocutionary act, then in general that condition must be believed by the speaker to obtain and so be a special case of presupposition₁. The main problem with presupposition₁ is that it is too inflationary with respect to contexts. If someone presupposes₁ that Irv is a Martian (that is, from the planet Mars), then the belief that this is true is a belief about context—so Mars is a part of the context. If, on the other hand, one adopts an entailment analysis of factives and aspectuals, then presupposition₁ (in the positive case) is an entailment and belief in the presupposition₁ is a consequence of the presumption of sincerity. This leaves presupposition₂ and presupposition₃ to account for.

Presupposition₂ seems to amount to success and felicity conditions on speech acts, no more, no less (see section 2.5). As such it is a part of the general theory of speech acts and does not require any modification of our theory. How about presupposition₃? Pretty clearly for us, background assumptions made by S are simply assumptions made by S as to what is currently a mutual belief.[19] By accounting for the data supporting the notion of semantic presupposition in terms of entailment together with these conceptions of pragmatic presupposition, we need not modify the SAS to handle presupposition: we can do without semantic presupposition since the phenomena of pragmatic presupposition are handled by independently motivated (and independently labeled) aspects of the schema. For this reason we avoid the term *pragmatic presupposition* except when discussing the views of others.

In summary, sentences like (a) and (b) in (31) and (32) have been said to presuppose the (c) sentences, where this has been explicated either as *necessitation* of or as belief in their truth.

(31) a. John realizes that his car has been stolen.
   b. John doesn't realize that his car has been stolen.
   c. John's car has been stolen.
(32) a. John has stopped playing tennis.
   b. John hasn't stopped playing tennis.
   c. John was playing tennis.

We account for the necessitation of (c) by (a) in terms of bidirectional entailment:

(33) i. x realizes that p iff:
   ii. x believes that p & p.
(34) i. x has stopped ϕ-ing iff:
   ii. x was ϕ-ing & x is not now ϕ-ing.

And if the presumption of sincerity is observed, the speaker implies that he believes that p, and that x was Ψ-ing.

   But how are we to account for the presupposition on the negative (b) sentences? Entailment plus the presumption of sincerity will not do because the negative sentences do not entail the presupposed (c) sentences, for the semantics of the negatives are disjunctive:

(35) i. x does not realize that p iff:
   ii. $\sim x$ believes that p v $\sim p$.
(36) i. x has not stopped ϕ-ing iff:
   ii. $\sim x$ was ϕ-ing v x is now ϕ-ing.

The clue to our answer is noticing a similarity between the semantics of the positive sentences and the way one normally understands their (internal) negations. The negatives give the understanding:[20]

(35') i. x does not realize that p:
   ii. $\sim x$ believes that p & p.
(36') i. x has not stopped ϕ-ing.
   ii. x was ϕ-ing & x is now ϕ-ing.

Suppose that p or that x was ϕ-ing is assumed by the speaker to be mutually believed. Borrowing a formal device from Grice (1967, ch. 4), we can bracket off these clauses:

(37) x realizes that p: x believes that p [& p].
(38) x has stopped ϕ-ing: [x was ϕ-ing &] x is not now ϕ-ing.

Given that bracketed material is assigned the status of a mutual belief, it will be resistant to negation—the brackets tend to restrict the scope of such an operator. The result of negating (37) and (38) without penetrating the brackets (and thus violating its common ground status) is the following:

(39) x does not realize that p: $\sim x$ believes that p [& p].
(40) x has not stopped ϕ-ing: [x was ϕ-ing &] x is now ϕ-ing.

Notice that these are just the normal understandings we earlier recorded in (35′) and (36′). We can now accommodate two facts. First, the negative factives and aspectuals are understood in such a way that the semantic presuppositions are accepted as true by the speaker. Second, one can always explicitly deny the bracketed material, and still speak truly:

(41) x does not realize that p because $\sim p$.
(42) x has not stopped ϕ-ing because x never started ϕ-ing.[21]

These can be true in virtue of the *disjunctive* semantics of the clause before "because":

(41′) ($\sim x$ believes that p v $\sim p$), because $\sim p$.
(42′) ($\sim x$ was ϕ-ing v x is now ϕ-ing), because $\sim x$ was ϕ-ing.

The bracketing device is encouraging, but still there are some questions to be answered about it. For instance, how does material get assigned to or marked as common ground? We propose that it comes in two steps. First, expressions have a certain bracketing for internal linguistic reasons or by historical accident. Then, there is a rule[22] of language use to the effect that,

Bracketing (Br): S is to utter e containing bracketed [q] in saying that *(...p...) just in case S believes that q is mutually believed by S and H.

S is not to utter a sentence with a factive or aspectual predicate unless he takes it to be common ground that [q], other things being equal. Of course context (linguistic and nonlinguistic) can force negation into the bracketed material, and so brackets are defeasible. This is the result we want.

How does an element get bracketed in the first place? Sometimes there are semantic reasons. In (43) both (a) and (b) presuppose (c):

(43) a. John has finished practicing.
      b. John has not finished practicing.
      c. John started practicing.

If the semantics of (43a) and (43b) are

(43′) a. x started ϕ-ing & x completed ϕ-ing,
      b. $\sim x$ started ϕ-ing $\vee$ $\sim x$ completed ϕ-ing,

then the bracketing of (43a) has to be as in (44) because the second clause entails the first.

(44) [x started ϕ-ing &] x completed ϕ-ing.

This rules out the other possible bracketing, represented in (45),

(45) x started ϕ-ing [& x completed ϕ-ing]

because the result of negating (45) and not penetrating the brackets would result in the self-contradictory (46):[23]

(46) $\sim x$ started ϕ-ing [& x completed ϕ-ing].

Thus there is internal semantic reason for the bracketing to be as we have postulated it. With "stop," however, there is no such semantic dependency in its analysis, so this cannot be the explanation of why its bracketing is indicated in (40). Notice, though, that the element assigned common ground status is time-indexed for the past, and that does make it more suitable as something already believed (assumed to be mutually believed). But with "realize" neither of these expression-internal reasons can be used to account for its bracketing—there is no entailment nor temporal asymmetry between conjuncts. Perhaps it is an historical accident that the truth clause and not the belief clause is bracketed, though we suspect not. The same bracketing pattern occurs in a variety of other cases, as we will see.

Finally, why should there be such a device as bracketing at all? What might its status and role in communication be? Assume that many conversations are governed by the presumptions of not being overly ambiguous and nonspecific. Negative factives, on the standard analysis, have the form of disjoined negations. If the speaker meant to communicate such a disjunction, he would be flouting the presumption, for without bracketing the denial would still be unspecific, ambiguous, or indeterminate. The bracketing device (in the negative cases) reduces ambiguity and increases specificity, since the negative operator goes to just one condition.

What is the status of this bracketing device? Is it a part of the language, a conventional device that serves a purpose like the one sketched above? Or is it just a principle of interpretation based on conversation or discourse? To us the latter seems more plausible; the bracketing reflects normal expectations about what a speaker intends to communicate. These expectations are based mainly on previous experience with the point or topic of such remarks in the past. If these experiences were to change, expectations would change and so in many cases the bracketing would change. This account has the virtue of meshing in an obvious way with our earlier justification for the device, and it also meshes with the fact that in certain circumstances, context can force a change in bracketing. In a context in which it is obvious that x believes that p ($x\mathrm{B}p$), the negative factive will not be interpreted as the denial of $x\mathrm{B}p$. The general principle seems to be:

Operator Scope (O): If C is a condition in the analysis of an expression e, and C is contextually satisfied, then the operator is taken as going to the next most deeply embedded condition consistent with what is meant and with the context.

Thus, if the context is such that it is clear that $x\mathrm{B}p$, then the principle (O) predicts that the negative factive will be taken as a denial that p.

With some reservations we suggest that this proposal can be extended in three directions: to other operators besides negation, to other factives besides "realize," and to nonfactives (see Harnish 1976b, 374–376, for discussion of complexities of individual cases).

Other Operators: It seems that, at least in an unbiased context, sentences containing the following operators would be taken primarily as remarks about belief:

possibly: Possibly x realizes that p. (possibly $x\mathrm{B}p...$)

unlikely: It's unlikely that x realizes that p. (unlikely that $x\mathrm{B}p...$)

uncertain: It's uncertain that x realizes that p. (uncertain that $x\mathrm{B}p...$)

must: x must realize that p. (x *must* $\mathrm{B}p...$)

finally: Finally x realizes that p. (finally $x\mathrm{B}p...$)

Other Factives: The same sort of analysis and bracketing seems to work with other factives like "recognize," "remember," "be aware," "admit," and "know." For instance, if we suppose the following to be roughly correct,

(47) x is aware that p iff $x \mathrm{B} p$ [& p]

then the denial of (47) has just the force we take it to have—as the denial that x believes that p. The same seems to hold for one common propositional use of "recognize." And if we suppose "admit" to have an analysis something like

(48) x admits that p iff x states that p [& p],

then the negative factive, "x didn't admit that p," comes out right, as primarily a denial that x stated (or would state) that p. Perhaps other cases could be handed as these are.

Other Nonfactives: As a final application we reanalyze some of Fillmore's verbs of judging (1971, 188–189), though we do not claim (nor does Fillmore) that these analyses are adequate as they stand:

(49) x accused y of ϕ-ing iff x stated that y ϕ-ed [& x believes y's ϕ-ing is blameworthy].
(50) x criticized y for ϕ-ing iff x stated that ϕ-ing is blameworthy [& x believes y ϕ-ed].
(51) x blamed y for ϕ-ing iff x stated that y ϕ-ed [& x believes y's ϕ-ing is blameworthy].

This is only a sample of the possible range of phenomena susceptible to a bracketing analysis.[24] A classical case like definite descriptions is a further example and can be handled similarly.

We conclude from this glimpse at presupposition, both semantic and pragmatic, that the SAS does not need to be elaborated just to accommodate presuppositional data. So-called presuppositional facts can and should be analyzed in terms of independently motivated notions from the schema.

8.4. IMPLICATURE

We need to contrast what is *said* not only with what is presupposed but also with what is *implied*. In an important series of papers, published and unpublished, Grice has been developing a theory of the relationships among an expression, its meaning, the speaker's meaning, and the implications of the utterance. The relevant categories are indicated by the tree in figure 8.2.[25] One convenient way of investigating Grice's theory is by tracking down the implicature branches of the tree.

In a number of places (1961, 444; 1967; 1968, 225), Grice has attempted to draw, both pretheoretically and theoretically, a distinction

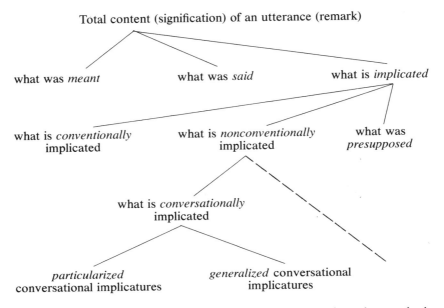

Figure 8.2 Relationships among an expression, its meaning, the speaker's meaning, and the implications of an utterance

between what someone *stated* or *said* on an occasion, and what was *implied* or *implicated*.[26] To our knowledge, he has not attempted to formulate necessary and jointly sufficient conditions for implicating nor to give a general procedure for identifying, on an occasion, what has been implicated.[27] Rather, he has been concerned mainly with sorting out different kinds of implicature and analyzing their modes of operation. Grice distinguishes three major kinds of implicature: *conventional* implicature, *conversational* implicature, and *presupposition*. He has little to say about the first type, and we have taken up the last category already; we will therefore look only at his views on the second type, conversational implicature.

In contrast with conventional implicatures (which turn on the meanings of the words used) there is a class of implicatures that turn not only on what a person says but also on principles governing discourse. Grice's theory is the latest, and most sophisticated, in a line of attempts to account for what has been called *contextual* or *pragmatic* implication (for a survey of earlier efforts, see Hungerland 1960). Grice's account applies to discourse governed by the *cooperative principle:*[28]

Cooperative Principle (CooP): "Make your conversational contribution such as is required, at the stage at which it occurs, by the accepted purpose or direction of the talk-exchange in which you are engaged" (Grice 1975, 45).

Under this principle come the maxims[29] of quantity, quality, relation (relevance),[30] and manner. The first three pertain to *what is said*, the fourth to *how what is said is said*.[31] These maxims are essentially imperatival versions of the conversational presumptions of quantity, quality, relevance, and manner respectively, which we have formulated in section 4.1.

According to Grice, there are many different ways for participants in a talk-exchange to fail to observe a maxim. Since Grice has no one term for this, we adopt the neutral term *infringement* for any failure to fulfill a maxim (or the CooP). Saying that A infringed a certain maxim means simply that he failed to fulfill it. This use commits us to nothing regarding the way the maxim was not fulfilled or the consequences of not fulfilling it. Of the four ways Grice discusses, only three of them give rise to implicatures.[32]

First, one may *opt out* by indicating plainly that he is unwilling to cooperate ("I cannot say anything more"). This seems to be the only infringement that does not give rise to implicature.

Second, one may quietly and unostentatiously *violate* a maxim. In violating a maxim one is likely to mislead. Grice does not say very much about this as a way of infringing a maxim distinct from the next two. In fact, sometimes he uses *violate* in the general way we have reserved for *infringe*. Opting out is logically distinct from violating. That is, if *S* opts out of a maxim, he does not infringe it "quietly and unostentatiously" and thereby violate it. Conversely, if *S* violates a maxim, he has not indicated plainly that he is "unwilling to cooperate" and so is opting out.

Third, one may be faced with a *clash* between one maxim and another. In this case a maxim may be infringed, but its infringement is explained by supposing it to conflict with another maxim. Consider Grice's example. Suppose A is planning an itinerary with B for a holiday in France. Both know that A wants to visit his friend C.

(52) A: Where does C live?
     B: Somewhere in the south of France.
     Gloss: (a) B is not opting out. (b) B has infringed the maxim of

quantity (say as much as necessary). (c) Observation (b) can be explained only by supposing that B is aware that to be more informative would be to infringe the maxim of quality (have evidence for what you say). (d) So B implicates that he does not know which town C lives in.

It is in the nature of the clash that under the circumstances the speaker cannot fulfill both of the maxims in question at once. However, Grice does not claim that any particular maxim must override any other. In this case, the maxim of quality overrides the maxim of quantity. Notice also that Grice claims that the supposition in (c) is the only one that could explain (b), but he does not spell out why.

Let us view this clash from both speaker's and hearer's standpoints. From the speaker's point of view, under the circumstances S must infringe either the maxim of quantity or the maxim of quality and so he must make a choice between giving not enough information and giving groundless information. If the speaker does not opt out of the maxim of quality (by saying "I do not know exactly"), the hearer is faced with an infringement he can explain (or explain away) by positing a clash and supposing the speaker opted for fulfilling the maxim of quality. This suggests that there is an ordering or weighting of the maxims that can be explained as follows. If it can be assumed that the speaker S is observing at least CooP, then S will pick quality over quantity if only because truly groundless information has at least as good a chance of being wrong as right, and as such would probably not be helpful, thereby violating CooP.

On the hearer's side, there seems to be a corresponding metaprinciple at work, the *principle of charity:*

Principle of Charity (PC): Other things being equal, construe the speaker's remark so as to violate as few maxims as possible.

However, since some maxims may be more highly weighted than others, we need a weighted principle of charity (for pairs of maxims):

Weighted Principle of Charity (WPC): Other things being equal, construe the speaker's remark so that it is consistent with the maxim of higher weight. Or, if the speaker has infringed one or other of a pair of maxims, other things being equal, assume that he has infringed the lowest valued maxim.

Using WPC it is possible to reconstruct Grice's gloss in more detail and to tighten the appeal to explanations (see Harnish 1976c, 344).

Fourth, the speaker may *flout* a maxim—he may blatantly fail to fulfill it. *S* exploits a maxim when he flouts it, with the consequence that *H* must reconcile *S*'s saying what he said with the supposition that *S* is obeying the conversational maxims and the cooperative principle. With this in mind we can now characterize conversational implicature more precisely.

Conversational Implicature: S conversationally implicates that *q* to *H* iff:

i. *S* implicates that *q* to *H*.

ii. *H* presumes that *S* is observing the conversational maxims (or CooP) when *S* says that *p* to *H*.

iii. If *S*'s saying that *p* is *S*'s total contribution to the conversation at that point, then *S*'s saying (only) that *p* is not consistent with the presumption that *S* is observing the conversational maxims (or CooP).

iv. Only on the supposition that *S* thinks that *q*, is *S*'s saying that *p* consistent with the presumption that *S* is observing the conversational maxims (or CooP).

v. *S* thinks (and expects *H* to think that *S* thinks) that it is within the competence of *H* to work out or grasp intuitively that iv.

Since it is a necessary condition for something to be a conversational implicature that it at least be capable of being worked out, we can schematize *H*'s working out in terms of this definition (Grice (1975, 70) mentions all but (2).):

1. *S* said that *p*.

2. If *S*'s saying that *p* is his total contribution to the conversation at this point, his saying only this is not consistent with the presumption that *S* is observing the conversational maxims (or CooP).

3. There is no reason to suppose that *S* is not observing the conversational maxims (or CooP).

4. Only if *S* thinks that *q*, is *S*'s saying that *p* consistent with the presumption that *S* is observing the conversational maxims (or CooP).

5. *S* knows that I can figure out 4.

6. *S* has done nothing to block my thinking that *q*.

7. Therefore *S* intends me to think that *q*.

8. So *S* has implicated that *q*.

Notice that the implicature (that *q*) has been achieved by virtue of special features of the context, and very much in the pattern of the SAS.[33] This sort of conversational implicature Grice calls *particularized* conversational implicatures. As he says (1975, 56), "There is no room for the idea that an implicature of this sort is *normally* carried by saying that *p*."

Grice coins the category of *generalized* conversational implicatures for cases where saying that *p* would normally carry such and such an implicature. As examples of generalized conversational implicatures, he gives the following:

(53) a. "*x* is meeting a woman this evening" implicates "the woman is not his sister, mother, wife, or close platonic friend."
 b. "*x* went into a house yesterday and found a tortoise inside the front door" implicates "the house was not his own."

Grice claims that sometimes, as with "I've been sitting in a car all morning," there is no such implicature. It is an interesting question why not, since there is an implicature in "*x* climbed into a car yesterday and found a tortoise behind the seat."[34]

Grice concludes (1975, 57–58) that a conversational implicature possesses certain features. (1) Since observance of the conversational maxims is a necessary condition for calculating a conversational implicature, a generalized conversational implicature can be canceled by either explicitly or contextually opting out. (2) Since calculation of a conversational implicature requires determination only of (i) contextual information, (ii) background information, and (iii) what is said, but not the manner in which it is said, then any way of saying what is said is likely to have the same conversational implicature. Since a generalized conversational implicature is fairly insensitive to context and background information, it should have a high degree of nondetachability. (3) Since calculation of the conversational implicature requires prior knowledge of what is said, the conversational implicature is not a part of the meaning or force of what is said. (4) Since what is said may be true and what is conversationally implicated false, the implicature is not carried by what is said, but only by "the saying of what is said or by 'putting it that way'."[35] And (5) in many cases the conversational implicature is a disjunction.

All of Grice's examples, we might add, are clear cases of indirect constatives.

8.4.1. Some Issues Concerning Conversational Implicature

Grice's account of the various conversational data was a significant advance, in both rigor and insight, over previous accounts. However, it raises a number of issues needing further work, among which are the following two. First, there is a problem with the mechanisms that are supposed to generate conversational implicatures. Recall that Grice distinguished four ways in which a maxim could be infringed: by opting out, by violation, by clash, and by flouting. At times Grice seems to reserve the title *conversational implicature* for those aroused by flouting a maxim. For instance, he writes "The presence of a conversational implicature must be capable of being worked out; for even if it can in fact be intuitively grasped, unless the intuition is replaceable by an argument, this implicature will not count as a *conversational* implicature; it will be a *conventional* implicature" (1975, 50).

When one turns back to the working out schema, it seems that such a working out is sufficient for flouting, since step 2 requires a maxim to be infringed and step 5 requires H to suppose that S thinks H is aware of this in making the inference to the implication that q. Thus, a conversational implicature must at least be capable of being produced by flouting a maxim. At other times Grice writes as if to be conversational an implicature need depend merely on the supposition that some relevant maxim (or maxims) be in effect. For instance, Grice (1975, 51) offers the following dialogue as an example of B's implicating that Smith has a girlfriend in New York:

(54) A: Smith doesn't seem to have a girlfriend these days.
     B. He has been paying a lot of visits to New York lately.

Part of the problem here is Grice's use of the notion of an implicature being capable of being worked out. It seems that implicatures produced by means of violation, clash, and flouting are all capable of being worked out, but with flouting, the implicature is intended or intended to be recognized as intended.[36] Since it is plausible to suppose that all implicatures involve infringement or apparent infringement of some maxim, we propose that the term *conversational implicature* be reserved for this latter kind of case where H's inference that q is intended to be recognized as intended.[37] When the inference to the implicatum q results simply from H's concluding (or intuiting) that S's believing q is required to preserve conformity to the maxims, we can call this *implicature* simpliciter. Distinguishing these cases has the benefit that complex inferences involving flouting a maxim need not be sought to explain every case of implicature. (See Kempson 1975, ch. 8, for examples, and Harnish 1976b for further discussion.)

A second problem area is *generalized implicature,* where "I broke a "finger" is said to imply that the finger was the speaker's (attached). Although Grice is inclined to think of these as conversational implicatures, it is not clear that such cases involve infringement of a maxim. But if no maxim is infringed there is nothing to work out, in which case by definition they would not count as (conversational) implicatures. On the other hand, they are not conventional implicatures either, since the implicatum is cancelable: "I broke a finger from my finger collection." Is there an alternative to the choice between conversational and conventional implicature that might plausibly describe these cases? We suggest that these are simply immediate, plausible (or precedented) inferences by *H* from what *S* has said. If this is correct then all of the phenomena Grice has discussed under the rubric of (nonconventional) implicature can be subsumed under some aspect of the SAS.

8.5. CONCLUSION

We have contrasted what is *said* in the utterance of an expression with the notions of what is *meant* (both in the language and by the speaker), with what is *presupposed* (both by the expression uttered and by the speaker), and finally with what is *implied*. Our purpose was twofold: to separate (and untangle) a number of distinct concepts and to relate each of them to the speech act schema.

In order to specify, at line L2 of the schema, the operative meaning of the expression uttered, we had to specify some type of linguistic meaning (language, dialect, or idiolect). In accordance with the inferential nature of the SAS we tentatively endorsed an inferential account of meaning specification. However, an adequate conception of meaning specification does not automatically yield an adequate theory of meaning attribution, inasmuch as it leaves open the answer to the question of what it is for an expression *e* to mean ....[38] The notions of semantic and pragmatic presupposition have been applied in the literature to a wide variety of phenomena. However, we found that the facts supporting semantic and pragmatic presupposition are better accounted for, respectively, by the (already needed) notions of entailment and mutual contextual belief. Finally, we showed how the information presupposed by the inferences underlying Grice's conversational implicatures is already represented by aspects of the SAS. Indeed, all of Grice's examples are cases of indirect constatives. We conclude from this survey that the theory presented in part I provides a framework that will support most, if not all, of the major concepts in the study of locutionary acts and their relations to linguistic communication.

Chapter Nine

Indirect Acts and Illocutionary Standardization

According to the speech act schema, all illocutionary acts but conventional ones are performed with R-intentions and succeed only if those intentions are recognized. Even literal illocutionary acts involve R-intentions, contrary to the view that illocutionary force is part of conventional meaning. According to that view, no distinction is to be drawn between locutionary acts and literal illocutionary acts. Although we allow for illocutionary force potential, as evidenced by our notions of L-compatibility and F-determinacy, we maintain that for any utterance to be a communicative illocutionary act, it must be issued with an R-intention. Except for conventional cases, no utterance can count as an illocutionary act solely in virtue of what is uttered. The speaker can always fail to have an illocutionary intent or can be speaking nonliterally or indirectly. Therefore, the meaning of what is uttered can at most determine the identity of whatever literal illocutionary act is being performed, if any. It cannot determine *that* any such act is being performed.

Having recapitulated this basic feature of our position, we can pose the problem of illocutionary standardization. Certain indirect illocutionary acts do not seem to fit the SAS. These involve the use of certain standardized sentence forms, such as the following:

(1) Can you pass the salt?
(2) You might consider dropping out.
(3) I must ask you to leave.
(4) I want to thank you for coming.

Although each can be used literally, (1) as a question and the others as constatives, they are forms of sentences standardly used for acts of requesting, advising, demanding, and thanking, respectively. Because their use is standardized, the hearer can determine the speaker's illocutionary intent just as immediately as if a literal illocutionary act were being performed. The process of inference spelled out in the SAS is short-circuited: instead of having to rule out the literal intent as primary and infer S's indirect intent, H can identify the indirect intent without having to search for it. Standardized indirect acts are like literal acts in that the identity of the speaker's illocutionary intent is the first candidate to be arrived at in the process of inference. Therein lies the problem. Is the standardization of the use of such sentence forms a matter of meaning, in which case they must be regarded as systematically ambiguous? Or is standardization a matter of linguistic convention somehow distinct from meaning? Perhaps it is neither. We find the first alternative unattractive and will argue that it multiplies meanings beyond necessity. As for the second, we will argue that illocutionary standardization is not a case of convention, although it comes close.

9.1. THE AMBIGUITY THESIS

The ambiguity thesis is the view that sentences standardly used indirectly have additional meanings. On this view the standardized use of such sentences is not indirect after all, but literal and direct. If ambiguous, these sentences have two meanings which delimit two literal uses. For example, sentence (1) could be used literally either as a question or as a request. Since it has the surface form (interrogative) of a question, we will designate its use as a question as its *direct* use and its use as a request its *indirect* use. The diachronic vision (Sadock 1974, 98) behind the ambiguity thesis is that sentences like (1) were not always ambiguous and originally could be used literally and directly only as questions. With the standardization of their indirect use as requests they came to have a second literal meaning; in this way their secondary literal use was preceded historically by a pattern of indirect departure from their basic literal use.

There are two kinds of arguments for the ambiguity thesis, psychological and linguistic. The psychological argument appeals to the introspective immediacy of the inference to the secondary illocutionary intent; the linguistic argument appeals to various paraphrastic and distributional phenomena.

The primary claim underlying the *psychological* argument is that the second meaning of sentences like (1) is not computed via the basic meaning. We seem to identify the indirect intent of an utterance of

(1) as we would the direct intent in contexts where that is more natural. For example, if (1) "Can you pass the salt?" is uttered at the dinner table, it would normally be taken as a request for the salt, whereas if it were uttered by a physical therapist to a patient recovering from polio, it could be taken as a question. The indirect use is more common than the direct use, but the psychological argument for the ambiguity thesis does not depend on the indirect use being predominant. Indeed, in some cases it is not, as in "Do you have any weapons?"

The psychological argument comports well with the introspective consideration that the basic meaning of these standardized locutions does not flash across one's mind in contexts where the indirect use is the obvious one. So not only is the indirect illocutionary intent not inferred from the direct one, the direct one does not even enter into the determination of the indirect intent (or if it does, one is not aware of it). Conscious disambiguation is no more necessary here than with sentences like "He put his money in the bank" and "He jumped into the water from the bank"—it is difficult (though hardly impossible) to imagine circumstances in which either of these sentences would have to be consciously disambiguated with respect to the word "bank."

Since sentences like (1)–(4) do not have the superficial form of sentences usually used to make requests, and so on, a proponent of the ambiguity thesis would concede that if such a sentence did not have its purported second meaning, its indirect intent would have to be inferred from its direct intent. However, since the indirect use is standardized (in virtue of an alleged second meaning), no such inference is necessary or actually made. If the psychological argument for the ambiguity thesis is correct, the apparent absence of inference (and of any intention that such an inference be made) can be accounted for only by supposing that the sentences in question are ambiguous. To parry this argument we must either demonstrate the psychological reality of the process of inference (and of the appropriate speaker intention), even though it is not conscious, or we must accept the claimed psychological facts put forth in support of the argument but show that they can be accommodated without positing second meanings. When we present our account of illocutionary standardization in section 9.3, we will take the latter course.

The primary claim underlying the *linguistic* arguments is that the ambiguity thesis is to be incorporated in an adequate theory of a certain range of linguistic phenomena. Sadock (1974, chs. 4–6) systematically tries to work out such a position. He presents half a dozen arguments against any theory that claims all cases are inferential in the way that "My mouth is parched" or "It's really getting late" are. Some of Sadock's arguments boil down to simplicity arguments—an inferential theory will be more complicated than an ambiguity theory (or require duplication of machinery) (1974, 79–82). Other arguments concern language change (pp. 91–93) and language comparisons (pp. 93–94). The remaining arguments (pp. 82–83, 88–91) present challenging evidence in favor of noninferential theories.

Sadock does not want to handle all cases of illocutionary standardization in terms of force-ambiguity. But which ones? Without tests to distinguish cases the theory would collapse into vacuity, claiming that only those cases that can be treated as ambiguous are ambiguous. To avoid this problem, Sadock (ch. 5) offers three sorts of test for the existence of an idiomatic reading and thus ambiguity: cooccurrence restrictions, paraphrasability, and transformational accessibility. Consider "Spill the beans": *as an idiom* (a) it will not take nominal or verbal modifiers freely ("He (*clumsily) spilled the (*green) beans"); (b) it resists paraphrase by substitution (*"He spilled the legumes"); and (c) it does not undergo a number of transformations—certain reductions, for example (*"Ernest spilled the beans and Max the chickpeas"). Sadock then applies these sorts of tests to sentences like:

(5) a. Can/can't/could you VP?
    b. Will/won't/would you VP?

He comes to the conclusion that "we perceive, as speakers of English that ["Will you close the door?"]—despite its surface form—*is* a request on one reading—in other words, that it is actually ambiguous between a request sense and a question sense" (1974, 108). That is to say, these are speech act idioms.[1]

Sadock then extends his theory from these whimperatives (as he calls them) to various other cases of "force-ambiguity" (ch. 6). Although some of the theoretical conclusions he draws are questionable (see Harnish 1978), some of the data he adduces do need explaining. Sadock deals with six kinds of cases:

1. *Whimperatives:* Can you VP?
   Indirect force: (I request you to) VP![2]
   Tag-imperatives (fractured whimperatives): VP, will you?
   Indirect force: same as for whimperatives.
2. *Impositives:*
   (a) Why don't you/we VP?

(b) Shouldn't you/we VP?

(c) How(s) about VP-ing?

Indirect force: (I suggest that you/we) VP.

3. *Queclaratives:* Does anyone VP anymore?

Indirect force: (I declare that) no one VPs anymore.

4. *Pseudo-imperatives:*

(a) Seek and ye shall find.

Indirect force of a generic statement: Anyone who seeks will find.

(b) Move and I'll shoot; Move or I'll shoot.

Indirect force of a threat: If you move, I'll shoot; If you don't move I'll shoot.

(c) Eat your vegetables and I'll give you dessert.

Indirect force of an offer: If you eat vegetables, I'll give you dessert.

5. *Requestions:* Columbus discovered America in?

Indirect force of a disinterested request for someone to say the right answer.

6. *Tag questions:*

(a) John likes beans, doesn't he?[3]

Force (indirect?) of a reported assumption plus a question.

(b) John likes beans, doesn't he![4]

Force (indirect?) of a statement plus request for confirmation.

Since opponents of the ambiguity thesis (Searle 1975a, for instance) have concentrated on interrogatives and declaratives used as directives, classes 1 and 2 constitute the main common data base. How good is the case that sentences of forms such as (6) are ambiguous between a question reading and another reading?

(6) a. Can you VP? (request for action)

  b. Why don't you VP? (suggestion)

9.1.1. Whimperatives

(7) $\left.\begin{array}{l} \text{Will} \\ \text{Can} \\ \text{*Shall} \\ \text{*May} \end{array}\right\}$ $\left\{\begin{array}{l} \text{subjunctive} \\ \text{negative} \end{array}\right\}$ you VP?

The proposal is that sentences having a surface structure like (7) come via "whimperative formation" from a semantic structure like that in figure 9.1, which is also thought to underlie imperatives. The obvious way to argue for deriving surface structures of form (7) from such

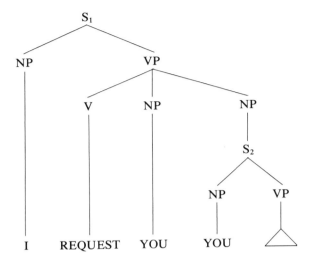

Figure 9.1 Semantic structure underlying (7)

semantic structures is to find evidence that these sentences (in their indirect use) behave as imperatives. Another strategy is to find evidence that these sentences (or transforms thereof) do *not* (in their indirect use) behave as interrogatives used to question. Sadock offers three main sorts of evidence in favor of the ambiguity thesis.

First, there are considerations about the distribution of words like "please" and "kindly." In particular, "please" seems to occur preverbally and without a pause just when the verb denotes a requested action (pp. 104, 124).

(8) a. Please close the door!
   b. Passengers will please not lean out the windows!
   c. I (*please) enjoy (*please) playing tennis.
   d. When will you (*please) keep score?

Whimperatives of the form (7) conform to the generalization in (9):

(9) Will/won't/would ⎫
                      ⎬ you please VP?
    Can/can't/could ⎭

Furthermore, if we posit an optional rule that moves "please" from preverbal to postsentential position, we can account for the following analogs of (8a)–(8d):

(8') a. Close the door, please!
    b. Passengers will not lean out the windows, please!

c. *I enjoy playing tennis, please.
d. *When will you keep score, please?[5]

On this version of the ambiguity theory, the verb denoting the action requested will be in VP_2 of S_2 in figure 9.1, and so is "formally" locatable. Thus, the data (8) and (8') provide some support for deriving sentences of form (7) from structures like that in figure 9.1.

Second, only the tagged ("fractured") forms of (7) are grammatical with "please" either preverbally or postsententially:

(7')

(Please) VP, $\left\{\begin{array}{c} \text{will} \\ \text{can} \\ \text{*shall} \\ \text{*may} \end{array}\right\}$ $\left\{\begin{array}{c} \text{subjunctive} \\ \text{negative} \end{array}\right\}$ you, (please)

A rule relating (7) to (7') would account for these facts, but notice that if (7') is a request, then unless the transformation changes meaning, (7) must have a request reading as well. What evidence is there that sentences of form (7') are requests and not questions? They do not behave like questions in at least four respects. Consider the following (from Sadock 1974, 112):

(10) a.   When will you wash the car, *or don't you know?*
     b. *Wash the car, will you, *or don't you know?*
(11) a.   When will you wash the car, *by any chance?*
     b. *Wash the car, *by any chance,* will you?
(12) a.   *Tell me,* when will you wash the car?
     b. *Tell me,* wash the car, will you?
(13) a.   When will you wash the car, and when will you do the dishes?
     b. *When will you wash the car, *and I'll do the dishes.*
     c.   Wash the car, will you, *and I'll do the dishes.*

In cases (10)–(12) some type of expression that cooccurs with clear cases of interrogatives used to question does not cooccur with fractured whimperatives. In case (13) only a question can be conjoined to a question, but a nonquestion can be conjoined to a fractured whimperative. Thus, fractured whimperatives do not behave like interrogatives used to question; since they clearly can be used to request (action), if sentences of form (7') come from (7) and transformations do not change meaning, then (10)–(13) constitute evidence for deriving sentences of form (7) from structures like that in figure 9.1.

Although these data support the ambiguity thesis, there are problems. For instance, one can conjoin a nonquestion to a question if the nonquestion relates to the question in some way:

(13') b. When will you wash the car, and $\begin{cases} \text{be careful how you answer.} \\ \text{I want to know quickly.} \end{cases}$

Just how this restriction might be stated formally is another problem for this proposal.

Third, certain expressions cooccur with (or in) clear cases of imperatives but do not cooccur with (or in) interrogatives (pp. 104–105):

(14) a. Wash the car, someone!
  b. *When will you wash the car, someone?[6]
  c. Will you wash the car, someone?
(15) a. Buzz off!
  b. *When will you buzz off?[7]
  c. Will you buzz off!
(16) a. Since I haven't finished these exams, (please) start dinner!
  b. *Since I haven't finished these exams, (please) when will you start dinner?
  c. Since I haven't finished these exams, will you start dinner?

In each case, the vocative "someone," the idiomatic imperative, and the reason adverbial whimperatives are behaving like imperatives and not like questions. But can the ambiguity theorist really explain all of these (putative) facts? For instance, the connection between the reason adverbial and the underlying REQUEST is fairly indirect; it provides a reason for requesting only because we take into account the act being requested as well as general background information to the effect that it is hard to grade exams and cook dinner simultaneously:

(16') c. ?Since I'm chewing gum, will you start dinner?

Sentences like (8)–(16) provide some, though not overwhelming, evidence for the ambiguity thesis as regards whimperatives. At least these sentences constitute interesting data that should be explained, or explained away.

9.1.2. Impositives[8]

Sadock (p. 118) proposes that sentences having surface structures as in (17) come, on one reading, from semantic structures like that in figure 9.2.

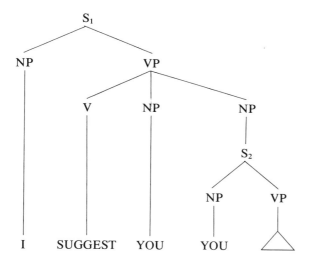

Figure 9.2 Semantic structure underlying (17)

(17) a. Why don't you VP?
    b. Shouldn't you VP?

Furthermore, if we supposed that surface structures like (18)[9] can be derived from (17) by a version of fracturing—

(18) a. VP, why don't you?
    b. VP, shouldn't you?

—and that forms like (19) can be derived from (17a) by you+tense deletion—

(19) Why not VP?

—we could account for the similarity in meaning and force among these sentences as well as for a variety of syntactic facts, such as that sentences like (19) take only second-person reflexives, as in (20):

(20) Why not wash $\left\{ \begin{array}{l} \text{yourself} \\ \text{yourselves} \\ \text{*himself} \\ \text{*myself} \\ \text{*themselves} \end{array} \right\}$?

(It seems to us that "Why not wash ourselves?" is acceptable too.) Is there any evidence that these impositives are (semantically) suggestions (pp. 119–120) and neither questions (pp. 114–115) nor whimperatives (p. 116)? Evidence that they are suggestions is very weak and that they are neither questions nor whimperatives is only a bit stronger.

Impositives are suggestions. First, it is claimed that with suggestions it is the case both that one can assent with "OK" ("Sure," "Alright," "You bet," and so on)[10] and that one must refuse with "No" ("Nope," "Nah") *plus a reason for refusing* if one is to be accommodating (raise no conversational animosities):

(21) A: Let's go to the movies tonight!
     B: OK.
     B':   No, I have to study.
     B'': *No.

The same is true of impositives:

(22) A: Why don't you go to the movies? (Shouldn't you go to the movies?)
     B: OK. (But *Yes.)
     B':   No, I have to study.
     B'': *No.

Unfortunately, the line between these cases and clearly imperatival cases is very delicate:

(23) A: Go to a movie tonight!
     B: OK.
     B':   No, I have to study.
     B'': ?No.

Second, Sadock (1974, 120) notes that suggestions can take the post-sentential tag "OK?" as do whimpositives (but *not* "shouldn't" impositives):

(24) a. Let's go to the movies tonight, OK?
     b. Why don't we go to the movies tonight, OK?
     c. *Shouldn't we go to the movies tonight, OK?

What Sadock does not note is that this seems to be true of imperatives as well:

(24) d. Go to the movies, OK?

Impositives are not whimperatives (nor imperatives). First, impositives do and whimperatives do not take an inclusive first-person plural subject:[11]

(25) a. Why don't we go to the movies?
     b. Won't you/*we go to the movies?

Moreover, these impositives cannot be fractured:

(26) *Go to the movies, why don't we?

Second, impositives resist preverbal "please":

(27) ?Why don't you please go to the movies?

Finally, impositives may require slightly different negative responses than whimperatives (the data are tricky):

(28) a. A: Would (could, etc.) you move over a little?
       B: I can't, . . .
       B: No, I can't, . . .
     b. A: Why don't you move over a little?
       B: I can't, . . .
       B: ??No, I can't, . . .

Impositives are not questions. First, questions take questioning of their epistemic felicity conditions, but impositives do not:

(29) When (at what time) are you going to the movies, or don't you know?
(30) *Why don't you (please) go to the movies, or don't you know?

Second, impositives can, and questions cannot, take a nonquestion conjunct unrelated to the first question:

(31) Why don't you go to the movies, and I will too.
(32) *When (at what time) are you going to the movies, and I will too.

Thus there does exist *some* distributional evidence for treating whimperatives and impositives as having an underlying structure distinct in illocutionary type from their surface structure. Even if the case for the ambiguity thesis is not particularly strong, at least it represents an effort to explain these data. An adequate alternative must explain them better.

9.2. THE CONVENTIONALITY THESIS

Although the ambiguity thesis does account for the indirect uses of sentences like (1a)–(1d), a viable alternative to it would have the virtue of not multiplying meanings beyond necessity. Of course, if the psychological and the linguistic arguments for it were sound, the thesis would not be guilty of multiplying meanings beyond *necessity*—the arguments would necessitate the multiplication.[12] These arguments are not conclusive, but we should not reject the ambiguity thesis unless we can produce a viable alternative. One possibility is that the indirect use relies on *illocutionary conventions*. We will call this the *conventionality thesis*.

Being able to produce and to perceive standardized illocutions seems to be part of a speaker's linguistic knowledge. Even if it is not knowledge of the meaning of sentences of certain forms, it is knowledge about their use. On the conventionality thesis this is knowledge that the utterance of a sentence of a certain form literally used to perform one sort of illocutionary act *counts as* the performance of some other sort of illocutionary act.[13] On this view a speaker's knowledge of illocutionary conventions is not part of his linguistic competence proper, and need not be captured in a descriptively adequate grammar, although one could, as a matter of terminological preference, include such knowledge as part of linguistic competence. Whether or not one does, on the conventionality thesis the existence of illocutionary conventions accounts for the fact that standardized illocutionary acts can be performed in the indirect but immediately identifiable way that they are. Since these conventions involve mutual belief that certain sorts of utterances count as certain sorts of illocutionary acts, speakers and hearers can omit the intermediate steps in the SAS for indirect acts. These conventions serve to bypass the inference, and its conclusion is reached without further ado. As Searle (1975a, 73) says, the hearer "simply hears it as a request." It is clear, then, how the conventionality thesis could use introspective evidence for its position and so circumvent the psychological argument for the ambiguity thesis.

Linguistic considerations provide evidence against the ambiguity thesis as well as positive evidence for the conventionality thesis.

9.2.1. Against the Ambiguity Thesis

Evidence that whimperatives and impositives function as questions in addition to functioning as requests or suggestions is evidence against ambiguity,[14] as is evidence that their indirect force is not idiomatic.

Whimperatives
There is some evidence that whimperatives (in their indirect use) func-

tion like interrogatives (in their direct use). (See Green 1975, 109–114, 137–138; Sadock 1974, 113.)

In the first place, conversationally felicitous responses to whimperatives pattern like responses to interrogatives, not like responses to imperatives, in that whimperatives require a verbal response whether or not they are complied with, imperatives only if they are not:

(33) A: Do you have the ability to pass the salt?
     A': Can you pass the salt?
     B: *salt-passing
(34) A: Pass the salt!
     B: (optional: Sure) salt-passing

Furthermore, "Yes" without a title or vocative ("Yes, sir," "Yes, ma'am") is a bit odd as a response to an imperative, though "OK," "Sure," and so on, are all right.

(35) A: Pass the salt!
     B: ?Yes.

Second, Sadock (p. 113) has noted that directives can be reported using "ask" and "tell," but questions prefer "ask" and imperatives prefer "tell":

(36) A: When are you going to VP?
     B: S asked H when . . .
     B': *S told H when . . .
(37) A: Take out the garbage!
     B: S told H to take out the garbage.
     B': *S asked H to take out the garbage.

Whimperatives appear to pattern with questions:

(38) A: Can you VP?
     B: S asked H to VP.
     B': *S told H to VP.

One complication is that "ask" and "tell" appear to be sensitive not just to the form of the directive, but to its politeness:

(39) A: Please VP.
     B: S asked H to VP.
(40) A: Shut up, will you? Will you shut up!
     B: S told H to shut up.

If this is right, it suggests that one should explain (36) and (37) not directly in terms of the form of A, but in terms of the politeness of the form. Imperatives may be a less polite form, ceteris paribus, than interrogatives and this may be what is reflected by the distribution of "ask" and "tell." Since politeness is such a tricky notion, we do not put much weight on this observation.

In sum, the data suggest that whimperatives pattern in part like questions, in requiring verbal responses, and in part like imperatives, in requiring action for compliance. The conventionality thesis, which has them being both, is better able to accommodate such facts than the ambiguity thesis is.

There is evidence that whimperatives do not function as idioms (Searle, 1975a, 68–69). First, they can be answered like questions:

(41) A: Could you be quiet?
     B: I could, but I won't.

Such dialogues seem "smart-alecky" (Green 1975); this is true of whimperatives in a way that it is not true of answers to (mere) questions. But that does not tell against whimperatives functioning *at least as* questions. In fact, there is a specific reason why such responses are smart-alecky: when it is obvious to S that H realizes that S in questioning is also requesting action, H's responding appropriately to just the direct illocutionary intent is seen as linguistically defensible ("You asked me if I could") but socially uncooperative. Following the letter but not the spirit of an utterance is just the sort of thing we deem smart-alecky. Rather than detracting from the conventionalist's case, Green's observation enhances it.

Another consideration is that word-for-word translation often produces expressions with the same indirect speech act potential (see Searle 1975a, 68):

(42) a. Could you give me the salt?
     b. Pourriez-vous me donner le sel?

This is not the case with most idioms:

(43) a. How are you? *Comment êtes-vous?
     b. Ça va? *It goes?

Sadock (p. 90) observes that, within English, whimperatives resist paraphrase, preserving indirect speech act potential:

(44) a. Can you please VP?
    b. *Are you able to please VP?
(45) a. Will you please VP?
    b. *Are you going to please VP?

It is just this that suggests that special illocutionary conventions might be operative. We will return to this point after discussing impositives.

Impositives
There is similar evidence that impositives also function (in part) as questions and not as direct suggestions. Impositives (like whimperatives) allow for a literal and direct question response:

(46) a. A: Why don't you VP?
      B: Because I am tired.
    b. A: I suggest you VP.
      B: *Because I am tired.

Again, these are smart-alecky, and the reason is the same as before—only part of the speaker's communicative intent has been cooperated with.

9.2.2. For the Conventionality Thesis

Do proponents of the conventionality thesis have data to support their claim as well as explanations for the evidence supporting the ambiguity thesis? If we turn to Searle (1975a)—the most sophisticated articulation of this position so far—we find the theory wanting. Searle notes just two of the various types of syntactic data that support the ambiguity thesis. First, he observes that "please" can occur postsententially with certain nonimperative surface forms such as

(47) a. I want you to stop making that noise, please. (p. 68)
    b. Could (can) you lend me a dollar, please? (pp. 68, 75)

but not with other forms:

(48) a. *Do you desire to do A, please? (p. 75)
    b. *Are you able to do A, please? (p. 75)

Second, Searle notes that "Why not . . .?" impositives with a second-person direct object require a reflexive ("Why not wash (*you) yourself?") just like imperatives ("Wash (*you) yourself!") and unlike other interrogatives ("Why won't he wash (*yourself) you?") and declaratives ("He will wash (*yourself) you"). How does Searle account for these facts? He offers no account of the reflexive-impositive data (p. 78).

As for the "please" data, Searle rightly says that "please" "explicitly and literally marks the primary illocutionary point of the utterance as directive" (p. 68). But what is it to mark the point as directive? It is not clear whether "please" is itself a directive force-indicating device or whether it merely cooccurs with something that is. In either case, why are (48a, b) so bad? Searle's answer (p. 76) is in two stages. He claims first:

Certain forms will tend to become conventionally established as the standard idiomatic forms for indirect speech acts. While keeping their literal meanings they will acquire conventional uses . . . there can be conventions of usage that are not meaning conventions.

Second, he claims that conversations are governed by the maxim:

Speak idiomatically unless there is some special reason not to.

How do these observations add up to an explanation of the "please" data? In Searle's words,

In order to be a plausible candidate at all for use as an indirect speech act, a sentence has to be idiomatic. But within the class of idiomatic sentences, some forms tend to become entrenched as conventional devices for indirect speech acts. In the case of directives, in which politeness is the chief motivation for the indirect forms, certain forms are conventionally used as polite requests. (p. 77)

It is not clear to us how these observations explain the data. Part of the problem is the obscurity of the notions of *speaking idiomatically* (which is not to amount to speaking with idioms), and *conventions of use* (which are not conventions of meaning). We suspect that with regard to the first point Searle probably means the maxim to read "speak colloquially" rather than "speak idiomatically." Surely no maxim of conversation dictates that one should say (49a) instead of (49b):

(49) a. Joan's old man kicked the bucket.
     b. Joan's husband died.

However, "speak colloquially" is almost as empty as "speak idiomatically" is obscure (if it has nothing to do with using idioms). To speak colloquially is just to speak as people speak, rather than as they write. Such a maxim can have little utility in explaining the "please" data.

As for the second point, it is not clear what Searle takes conventions of use to be, as opposed to conventions of meaning. If by conventions he means something like customs, the explanation of the data would presumably reduce to this:

1. It is customary to request by using certain declarative and interrogative forms (if not using an imperative).
2. Conversations are governed by the maxim "Speak colloquially": speak as people normally speak unless there are reasons to the contrary.
3. Postsentential and preverbal "please" indicates that the speaker is intending to request.
4. It is not customary to request using sentences of form (48) (without "please"), but it is customary to request with (47).
5. So (48a,b) are odd, but (47a,b) are not.

By this account the oddity of (48) reduces to a statistical fact about the frequency of requests, but surely the oddity does not consist in this. Nor is it clear exactly how it follows that (48a, b) are odd. To get an explanation out of 1–4 we need an account of what it is customary to request with. Given such an account, how would we explain these judgments of oddity by fluent speakers? What is the connection between a statistical fact about usage and these psychological states of speakers? There is no stated connection and so no explanation. Even if Searle could work up an explanation of these judgments, he could still not account for the following distributional facts concerning "please":

(50) a. How old (*please) are you, (please)?
     b. Are you (*please) able to do A, (please)?
     c. Can you (please) do A, (please)?

Since taking conventions to be customs does not seem to explain the facts, let us try construing *conventions* as we did in section 6.1. Are there conventions of use in this interpretation? They would take the following form, if we let T range over *sentence forms* (such as "Can you . . . ," "Will you . . ."):

Illocutionary Convention (IC): There is an (illocutionary) convention in group G for F-ing in uttering (a sentence of form) T (in context C) if and only if:

i. It is MB-ed in G that whenever a member of G utters T in C, he is F-ing, and

ii. Uttering T in C counts as F-ing only because it is MB-ed in G to count as such.

An example of one such sentence type is (1), repeated here:

(1) Can you pass the salt?

To utter (1) is to ask whether the hearer is able to pass the salt. Suppose the situation is one in which to utter (1) with merely its literally determined force (to ask the hearer whether he can pass the salt) violates the presumption of relevance (RE) and thereby the communicative presumption (CP). Then if there is a convention to the effect that to utter a sentence of the form "Can you . . . ?" counts as a request, the speaker might expect to achieve his illocutionary intent.[15] But are there such illocutionary conventions? We think not.

Utterances of the locutions in question can count as the performance of the specified type of illocutionary act without being mutually believed to count as such. In accordance with the SAS, the hearer can identify the speaker's illocutionary intent without recognizing any convention or participating in the mutual belief falling under it. Relying on the communicative presumption, he can make the inference in the usual manner. Thus, satisfaction of clause (ii) of the definition of illocutionary conventions (IC) is not necessary for the performance of the illocutionary act of F-ing in C when one utters a sentence like (1).

Finally, there seems to be a prima facie conflict between the psychological argument and the linguistic argument for the conventionality thesis. Recall that psychologically the hearer "just hears it as a request"—he understands just one act to have been performed. Yet Searle also wants to subscribe to the "putative facts" he numbers as 7 and 8 (1975a, 69–70):

[Fact 7] In cases where these sentences [like "Can you pass the salt?"] are uttered as requests, they still have their literal meaning and are uttered with and as having that literal meaning.

[Fact 8] It is a consequence of fact 7 that when one of these sentences is uttered with the primary illocutionary point of a directive, the literal illocutionary act is also performed.

These facts suggest that two acts are being performed. The conventionality thesis cannot have it both ways. The problem is exacerbated by the way Searle sets up the problem of indirect speech acts: "How is it possible for the speaker to say one thing and mean that but also to mean something else . . . how is it possible for the hearer to understand the indirect speech act when the sentence he hears and understands means something else?" (1975a, 60) On the one hand, if in performing *indirect* illocutionary acts the speaker means (and intends it to be recognized that he means) to be speaking *directly* as well, then the hearer cannot understand the speaker and just hear it as a request. If, on the other hand, there were conventions of use that would allow the speaker to perform the indirect act conventionally and so allow it to be heard as a request only, then it does not conform to putative facts 7 and 8, nor to the statement of the problem in the first place. It would no longer be an indirect act, by Searle's own definition.

One way out of this dilemma would be to make a sharper division between those cases governed by some additional conventions of use (where such conventions need to be explicated in some as yet unknown way) and those cases that are not. Although Searle distinguishes between the forms (51a) and (51b) with respect to conventions of use, he does not distinguish between (51b) and (51c) in this regard:

(51) a. Is it the case that you presently are capable of VP-ing?
     b. Can you VP?
     c. Are you able to VP?

If one supposes that conventions of use govern (51b) only, then one could say that in such a case one hears it as a request in virtue of these conventions. However, one would still have to deny putative facts 7 and 8 for these cases, and these conventions of use would have to be stated in such a way as to allow for the explanation of the relevant linguistic data. Clearly the work has just begun for the conventionality thesis.

9.2.3. Ambiguity versus Conventionality

The main strength of the ambiguity thesis is that it has outlined how certain syntactic relationships might be formalized. However, it has not yet produced an account of most of the syntactic data adduced in its own support—no actual derivations using antecedently motivated rules are given. Of course, anyone familiar with how a transformational grammar accounts for various linguistic facts might be tempted to suppose that explaining these facts will just be more of the same. But that is a mistake for two reasons. First, rules that seem plausible in isolation can generate serious problems when one attempts to make them work together.[16] Second, much of the data involve sentence-final co-occurrence restrictions of *force* (having little to do with traditional transformations) which are susceptible to alternative explanations in terms of speech acts. After all, there is no reason to suppose every oddity induced by putting words together must be explained as a grammatical oddity. The main weakness of the ambiguity thesis (in its present form) is its failure to show how, in general, indirect acts are related to direct acts. This would involve, in part, a theory of speech acts rich enough to support generalizations concerning alternative ways of performing illocutionary acts, where the expressions used do not (or need not) bear any derivational relation to each other.

The main strength of the conventionality thesis is that it is a part of an interesting theory of speech acts, a theory that contains generalizations relating indirect to direct acts. Its main weakness is the implausibility of illocutionary conventions and of how they could account for the lin-guistic facts. A wide variety of relations between sentences and illocu-tionary acts can constitute their indirect illocutionary act potential. Clearly some are figured out conversationally, at least the first time they are encountered. As remarked in section 4.3, these seem to fall neatly under the SAS. Other cases seem to be moderately plausible cases of speech act idioms: Searle (1975a) offers "How about . . . ?" used to suggest or recommend. In this and similar cases the force is learned in the way that other idiomatic meanings are learned, as a unit. In between these two extremes lie the problematic cases like "Can you pass the salt?" which have dominated the literature. We think these are cases of standardized force, and we turn now to our account of them.

9.3. THE STANDARDIZATION THESIS

Although it is a mistake to think of illocutionary standardization as a matter of convention, the conventionality thesis is on the right track. Without multiplying meanings, it meets the psychological argument for the ambiguity thesis by providing a picture of how the SAS might be short-circuited: the mutual beliefs that constitute illocutionary con-ventions enable the hearer to infer the speaker's indirect intent im-mediately, without going through the usual working-out process. Fortunately, it is possible to formulate a concept of illocutionary stan-dardization that does not require illocutionary conventions, even though it does involve mutual beliefs that short-circuit the SAS.

In rejecting the conventionality thesis, we saw that clause (ii) of the definition of illocutionary conventions (IC) is unnecessary for the effectiveness of a standardized illocution. The reason is that the illocution would be effective even if not standardized, since the hearer could, if necessary, infer the speaker's illocutionary intent from what is uttered and the relevant mutual contextual beliefs, as with any indirect illocutionary act. Indeed, it is assumed on all sides that these standardized illocutions become standardized through use over time. Only by accumulating precedent for indirect use do such sentences come to be standardized, and their being standardized consists in whatever it takes for the SAS to be short-circuited. What this amounts to is the satisfaction of clause (i) of IC. Putting these observations together, we offer the following preliminary definition of *illocutionary standardization:*[17]

Illocutionary Standardization (1): *T* is standardly used to *F* in *G* if and only if:
i. It is MB-ed in *G* that whenever a member of *G* utters *T* in contexts in which it would violate the CP to utter *T* with (merely) its literally determined force (*F**-ing), his illocutionary intent is to *F*, and
ii. The mutual belief in (i) is (nonvacuously) true.

Without the stipulation in (ii) that the mutual belief in (i) be true, it would not be the case that *T* is in fact standardly used to *F*, even if it is mutually believed to be so used. Of course, it is highly unlikely that such a mutual belief could arise without being true. The "in contexts" stipulation indicates that the situation is just the sort in which the utterance of *T*, if *T* were not standardized, would be readily identifiable as having the illocutionary intent of *F*-ing. Thus, if sentence (1) "Can you pass the salt?" were not standardized as a request, then in a context where the hearer could not reasonably attribute to the speaker the illocutionary intent of asking him if he has the ability to pass the salt he might be able to infer (following the SAS) that the speaker is requesting him to pass the salt. The point of the definition is to capture what short-circuits the SAS: the utterance and the context activate the mutual belief that the speaker and the hearer share, so that the speaker can reasonably intend, and the hearer can recognize him as intending, to be *F*-ing. The intermediate steps of the SAS are thereby skipped.

It might be objected that our formulation of the nature of illocutionary standardization is psychologically implausible—that people do not in fact have the mutual belief mentioned in our definition. Indeed, they do not individually believe, much less mutually believe, that whenever certain sentences are uttered in contexts where their having (merely) their literally determined force would violate the CP, they are used with some other illocutionary intent. The objection, then, is that such a belief would require that people have certain theoretical concepts that they do not seem to have, such as the concept of literally determined force and the concept of the communicative presumption.

We can concede the point of the psychological objection and reformulate the definition of illocutionary standardization in a psychologically more realistic way:

Illocutionary Standardization (2): *T* is standardly used to *F* in *G* if and only if:
i. Whenever a member of *G* utters *T* in contexts in which it would violate the CP to utter *T* with (merely) its literally determined force, it is MB-ed between *S* and *H* that *S*'s illocutionary intent in uttering *T* is to *F*, and
ii. Whenever a member of *G* utters *T* in such contexts, his illocutionary intent is to *F*.

This formulation places the objectionable material outside the scope of the mutual belief. Instead, the relevant context is specified and the mutual belief that obtains therein is a contextual mutual belief between *S* and *H* rather than a standing mutual belief in *G*. Unfortunately, it is not clear how this MB in (i) comes into existence in the context, nor what its status is. Also (ii) seems too strong. We could opt for a standing mutual belief in (i), namely:

i. It is MB-ed in *G* that whenever a member of *G* utters *T*, his illocutionary intent is to *F*.

But this mutual belief would be patently false. However, considering that the sentences with illocutionary standardization are not ordinarily used with their literally determined force, perhaps there is a weaker mutual belief, replacing "whenever" by "generally," which would be true:

i. It is MB-ed in *G* that generally when a member of *G* utters *T*, his illocutionary intent is to *F*.

What we need to do now is to formulate the clause that contextually activates this standing MB. Accordingly, we offer the following as our definition of illocutionary standardization:

Illocutionary Standardization (IS): T is standardly used to F in G if and only if:

i. It is MB-ed in G that generally when a member of G utters T, his illocutionary intent is to F, and

ii. Generally when a member of G utters T in a context in which it would violate the CP to utter T with (merely) its literally determined force, his illocutionary intent is to F.[18]

This definition has the virtue of realistically ascribing a true mutual belief to people, while at the same time specifying the conditions in which the sentences in question have their standardized indirect use. It is clear that if members of G have merely the mutual belief specified in clause (i), this mutual belief will be activated whenever T is uttered, thereby short-circuiting the SAS. The inference using what is mutually believed is generally made in the appropriate contexts, since T is generally uttered only in such contexts. Therefore, S can reasonably intend H to make, and H can reasonably make, a correct inference to S's illocutionary intent.

9.4. INFELICITY AND STANDARDIZED INDIRECTION

A consideration seeming to favor the ambiguity thesis is that most standardized illocutions appear not to be used with their literally determined force at all.[19] In using "Can you pass the salt?" as a request, one does not seem to be asking the hearer if he is able to pass the salt. Presumably it is mutually believed that the hearer has this ability; therefore the speaker has no reason to inquire about the matter. Indeed, in contexts where the hearer's ability is genuinely at issue, a literal question about that ability is usually not taken or intended as an indirect request. But where the hearer's ability is not at issue, it would seem that in saying "Can you pass the salt?" the speaker is not inquiring about the hearer's ability at all, and therefore that he is not *indirectly* requesting the hearer to pass the salt, contrary to what our account of standardization requires.

However, an illocutionary act can be performed, and an attitude can be expressed, despite obvious insincerity on the part of the speaker.[20] In particular, one can ask a question even if it is mutually believed that one does not want to know the answer and does not intend the hearer to provide one: S can still express this desire and this intention and thereby ask H a question. We are suggesting, then, that an utterance of

"Can you pass the salt?" as a request is literally an act of asking a question, albeit with obvious insincerity. Indeed, S relies on H's recognition of his (S's) obvious insincerity to convey his indirect request, since otherwise, under the circumstances, there would be no identifiable reason for his utterance.

It is often remarked that the point of requesting indirectly is politeness. Given the social supposition that it is impolite to impose on people and in particular to tell them to do things, to request indirectly is to "ask without asking," or to ask without explicitly asking—that is, by doing something else and letting the request be implied. One is asking, of course, but in such a way that one gives the appearance, albeit transparent, of not asking. Instead, one gives the appearance of posing a question. The reason that a so-called whimperative works as a request is that the obviously insincere question it involves makes reference to the desired action by H, or at least to some obvious precondition for it, thereby enabling H to identify the attitudes whose expression makes the utterance a request. In this way whimperatives bring up the issue of H's action without explicitly telling H to perform it.

Let us consider the illocutionary intents—the expressed attitudes—of various standardized forms, keeping in mind that one means for performing an indirect illocutionary act is to perform a direct one with obvious insincerity, so that the hearer is induced to seek some other expressed attitude that could be genuinely attributed to the speaker.

9.4.1. Can, Could

Utterances of sentences of the form "Can you A?" are literal questions about the hearer's ability to A and indirect requests that he A.[21] Such an utterance is obviously insincere as a question if S obviously knows the answer (and is not, for instance, testing H) or if it is obvious that S is not interested in the answer per se.

Utterances of sentences of the form "You can A" can also be used as requests for H to A. Such an utterance is literally a statement, but where it is obvious that S and H know that H can A or where it is obvious that S and H are not interested in whether H can A, H can infer that the utterance is intended as a request.[22] There is nothing insincere about S's statement, but in the circumstances it is obvious that there is not sufficient reason for S to be making merely the statement. Obvious insincerity is only one way in which a literal utterance can be (R-intended to be) taken indirectly. Obvious pointlessness is another.

What is true of "can" applies also to "could," as in the forms "Could you *A?*" and "You could *A*." Although "could" in these contexts is taken by some (Searle 1975a; Green 1972) as the subjunctive form of "can" (in other contexts it is the past tense of "can"), we see no reason to dispute Webster's construal of it as a polite form of the present tense of "can." After all, if "could" is really a subjunctive in these sentence forms, what are the suppressed conditions? Besides, as Searle and Green both note, supplying a condition detracts from the indirect requestive force: "Could you be a little more quiet if I asked you to?" To support our interpretation, we note that the simple present "could" can be used to make a literal statement, without there being an expressed or suppressed condition: "You could solve that problem easily."

As Searle points out, forms like "Are you able to *A?*" and "You are able to *A*" are not standardly used as indirect requests, and he suggests the reason is that they are not as idiomatic as the other forms. Since we have rejected Searle's maxim of idiomaticity, we offer a different explanation. Comparing "Are you able to pass the salt?" with "Can you pass the salt?" it seems that the use of "able" somehow focuses the hearer's attention on the question (or statement) of his ability, rather than on the action itself.

9.4.2. Will, Would

An utterance of a sentence of the form "Will you *A?*" is a literal question, but under the circumstances in which such a question is used as an indirect request, were no request being made, the answer to this question would be negative. However, if *H* were to take the utterance merely as a literal question and respond "No, what made you think I was going to *A?*" clearly he would have failed to see the point of the utterance as an indirect request. This point is (R-intended) to be inferred from the fact that it was obvious that *H* was not about to *A*. Similarly, the negative form "Won't you *A?*" is used as an indirect request when it is expected that *H* won't *A* and recognized that for informational purposes the question needn't be asked.

As with "could" we do not construe "would" in the contexts "Would you *A?*" and "Wouldn't you *A?*" as the subjunctive form of "will." On that interpretation there is again the problem of finding the suppressed condition and the fact that if it is supplied ("Would you leave if I asked you to?''), the utterance doesn't have the force of a request. We suggest that "would" in the contexts here is a simple present tense verb of willingness, just as it is in "I wouldn't do that myself." Accordingly, to ask about H's willingness to A is, when the answer is obviously negative, a literal question intended as an indirect request.

9.4.3. Must, Ought, Should

When H is A-ing, questions of the form, "Must/ought/should you A?" are standardly used as requests for H *not* to (continue to) A. The answer to these literal questions is obviously negative, so if there is to be a reasonably attributable intent to such an utterance, it must be to request H not to A any further. The same point applies, mutatis mutandis, to negative literal questions of the form "Mustn't/oughtn't/shouldn't you A?"[23]

Statements of the form "You must/ought/should A" are literal statements indicating that there is a strong reason for H to A. In contexts where it is obvious that this reason is S's desire, it may be inferred that S is requesting H to A. Statements of S's desire ("I want you to A," "I'd like you to A") function as indirect requests by actually specifying one such reason.

9.5. STANDARDIZATION AND PARAGRAMMATIC FACTS

In the standardization thesis, the requestive use of certain interrogative forms short-circuits the SAS, the hearer identifying the speaker's requestive illocutionary intent without having to identify the literal intent of questioning. He does this by relying on the precedent for the form's being used requestively. This precedent and the hearer's unthinking reliance on it depend on the form's being specifiable in some syntactically determinate way, and it must be such that the connection between the literal force/content and the indirect force/content is simple and systematic. Then both the existence and the identity of the indirect illocutionary intent can be immediately inferred by the hearer.

The standardization thesis does justice to the psychological facts without assigning additional meanings to the forms in question. However, there are also linguistic facts (or seeming facts) to account for, and Sadock (1974) relies on such facts in developing his version of the ambiguity thesis. One such fact is the preverbal occurrence of "please" in interrogative forms like (52) and (53) when used as requests.

(52) Can you please pass the salt?
(53) Will you please pass the salt?

Without "please" these sentences can be used as questions; with "please" they can be used only as requests. To account for this fact, as well as to account for the requestive use of such sentences (with or without "please"), Sadock supposes that they have an underlying imperative form and that they are only interrogative on the surface. On this supposition it is easy to see why the "please" can occur pre-verbally, just as in imperative sentences.

The acceptability of "please" in these contexts presents a problem for the standardization thesis. If (52) and (53) without "please" are unambiguously interrogatives, how can "please" acceptably occur in them? We suggest that sentences like (52) and (53) in which "please" occurs, are not fully grammatical, although their recurrent use makes them seem perfectly acceptable;[24] they are not grammatical interrogatives and cannot be used as literal questions. Although "please" can be paraphrased as "if you please," "if it pleases you," "be so good/kind as to," or in some such way—any of these paraphrases seems plausible to us—it can occur only in sentences used to make requests (or commands) not in sentences used to ask questions or to make statements. For example, it seems that (54) and (55) are clearly not grammatical.[25]

(54) *Why do you please pass the salt?
(55) *You never please pass the salt.

So it appears that (52) and (53) are grammatical only if used as requests, but this suggests that without "please" they have two literal readings, one interrogative and one imperative. To avoid this consequence while allowing that "please" can be used, in the relevant sense, only to make requests (or commands), we propose that (52) and (53) are not grammatical sentences and should not be generated by a grammar of English. Instead, they are examples of the phenomenon of syntactic liberty (see section 10.4), ungrammatical but usable sentences that are perfectly acceptable to fluent speakers.

Of course, it would be arbitrary to construe sentences like (52) and (53) as ungrammatical if there were no motivation independent of saving one's theory (the standardization thesis) against the opposition (the ambiguity thesis). It is no argument to say that since the "please" phenomena can be fit into grammar only if the ambiguity thesis is true, the "please" phenomena cannot be fit into grammar. Instead of begging the question, we wish to show how difficult it is to fit the "please" phenomena into grammar, because of the problem of describing these phenomena in grammatical terms.

The occurrence of "please" is unproblematic in imperative forms such as (56) and (57).

(56) Please pass the salt.
(57) Pass the salt, please.

For these cases the grammar can simply restrict the occurrence of "please" to imperatival contexts. Sentences like (58) and (59) might seem odd, but they are grammatical:

(58) Please shut up.
(59) Clean the latrine, please.

They are odd because of our attitudes toward what is requested or how it is requested (compare "He's such a nice little boy" with "He's such a nice little bastard"—both grammatical), but there is no reason to deny that they are grammatical.

Problems arise when we try to give a grammatical specification of when "please" can occur in interrogative forms, for it appears that reference to the speaker's intentions is necessary, and it is anything but clear how a grammar can represent information of this sort. To be sure, the ambiguity thesis provides for a reading of certain interrogative sentences as whimperatives (as of underlying imperatival form), so it could be said that no modification need be made in the restriction of "please" to imperatival contexts. An independent story might be needed of just which superficially interrogative sentences are the ones that have this underlying form and can therefore take "please," but assuming that can be given, there is no special problem about the occurrence of "please." However, there is another problem. Sentences like (60) and (61) can be used as requests,

(60) Can you reach the salt?
(61) Will you pass a mailbox?

but if "please" is inserted, as in (60') and (61'),

(60') Can you please reach the salt?
(61') Will you please pass a mailbox?

the ambiguity thesis and its account of "please" in grammatical terms would require that (60') be taken as an imperative used to request the hearer to reach the salt, not pass it, and (61') as an imperative used to request the hearer to pass a mailbox not to post the speaker's mail. Of course, a proponent of the ambiguity thesis would say that as requests to pass the salt and to post one's mail (60') and (61') are not grammatical at all, but then the problem is how the information that the sentences are so used is to be represented in the grammar. A further problem for the ambiguity thesis is how to block the interpretations of (60') and (61') as imperatives used respectively to request the hearer to reach the salt and to pass a mailbox.

"Please" can occur preverbally or postsententially in sentences like (62) and postsententially in sentences like (63).

(62) I'd like you to please pass the mustard (please).
(63) I'd like some mustard, please.

It would be preposterous to claim that sentences like these, when used to make requests, have an underlying imperative form. After all, when used to make requests, they do so by way of making statements about the speaker's preference. Whatever plausibility there is to the claim that whimperatives are not used to ask questions but only to make requests (hence their imperative reading) is totally lacking in the claim that (62) and (63) are only superficially indicative.[26]

An interesting fact, even if the ambiguity thesis can't explain it, is that "please" can occur in these sentences when they are used to make requests, even though it couldn't occur if they were used merely to make statements. A diehard ambiguity theorist might propose that they have two underlying forms, one merely declarative and one both declarative and imperative. But even if this claim could be made intelligible, there would still be the problem of accounting for (63), in which the hearer's requested action is not even mentioned. Perhaps this problem could be solved by proposing that the underlying form of (63) contains a verb designating that action ("giving," "passing," "spreading," "cutting"?).

To deal with the "please" phenomena, such as the occurrence of "please" in (52), (53), (62), and (63), the standardization thesis must recognize that "please" cannot occur unless the sentence is used to make a request. If without "please" these sentences are used merely to ask questions or to make statements, the insertion of "please" makes no sense and seems to us just plain ungrammatical. Since we claim that when used indirectly, these sentence forms are also being used literally, we are committed to the view that with "please" they are ungrammatical, though perfectly acceptable. We construe "please" in these contexts (unlike in superficial imperatives) as an illocutionary modifier and claim that it occurs paragrammatically, as do illocutionary modifiers in general. That is, "please" modifies what the speaker is doing (indirectly) not what he is saying.[27]

We do not yet have an explanation of just when "please" can occur and when it cannot. We could indulge in a bit of hand-waving and say that since certain forms have become standardly used nonliterally as requests, they have come to be able to take "please" just as if they could be used to make literal requests. This is hardly an explanation. However, we do believe that "please" phenomena, just like other phenomena of illocutionary modification, exemplify a special kind of linguistic fact, which we dub *paragrammatical* only to indicate that it cannot be accommodated in grammars as we know them. Along with special cases of illocutionary standardization, illocutionary modifiers are one of the topics of the next chapter.

Chapter Ten   **Standardization and**
                               Illocutionary Devices

What linguistic devices have standardized uses for indirectly performing illocutionary acts? And what connections are there between particular linguistic devices and the various illocutionary acts they are
used to perform? We begin with the case of simple performatives,
perhaps the clearest case in which linguistic material and illocutionary
force are intimately connected.[1]

10.1. PERFORMATIVES AS CONSTATIVES

Austin held (1962, 5) that performative utterances "do not 'describe' or
'report' or constate anything at all, are not 'true or false.'" Rather, they
are, or are part of, the doing of an action. Because the sentence uttered
in a performative utterance is grammatically declarative, Austin's
doctrine once seemed paradoxical. It has lost its air of paradox as philosophers have become more cognizant of the distinction between
sentences and statements and realize, thanks in part to Austin, that not
all sentences are used to make statements. Nevertheless, we wish to
argue that the negative side of Austin's doctrine—that performative
utterances do not constate, are not true or false—is mistaken. Since we
accept the positive side—that they are, or are part of, the doing of an
action—our position is that performative utterances (other than conventionalized ones) are both doings and statings. Thus, they comprise
two illocutionary acts. To utter a performative sentence is to do what
one is stating one is doing; indeed that is what makes the statement
true.
    An (explicit) performative is the utterance of a sentence with main
verb in the first-person singular, simple present indicative active,[2] this
verb being the name of the kind of illocutionary act one would ordinar-

ily be performing in uttering that sentence (call such a verb a *performative verb*). For example, typical utterances of "I order you to leave," "I promise you a job," and "I apologize for the delay" are order, promise, and apology, respectively.[3] Such utterances appear to be of a form which, with nonperformative verbs, can be used to make true or false statements, statements to the effect that the speaker is in the state named by the verb, such as "I see the light" or "I hate spinach."[4] Indeed, the use of a sentence with a performative verb not in the first-person singular, simple present indicative active would ordinarily be to make a true or false statement: "I ordered him to leave," "(By signing this) I am promising you a job," and "He apologizes for the delay." Austin (1962, 63) hopes vainly that this asymmetry will distinguish performative from other verbs.

Austin held that despite their declarative grammatical form, performative utterances are not statements,[5] are not true or false. Rather, the job of the performative formula is that of "making explicit (which is not the same thing as stating or describing) what precise action it is that is being performed by the issuing of the utterance" (1962, 61). And to use that formula is to perform an act of the sort named by the performative verb. This seems to be Austin's reason for thinking that performatives (not counting explicit constatives like "I state") are not constative. That is, in uttering a performative sentence, performing an act of the sort named by the verb is incompatible with one's also stating thereby that one is performing such an act. But why cannot one both perform an act and in the same breath state that one is performing it? Why should the use of certain verbs in a performative utterance be any less a statement than the use of the same verbs in nonperformative utterances, just because this use is also something other than a statement? These rhetorical questions require an explanation of how it is possible to do both, but first let us examine several arguments that doing both is impossible.

The following three arguments, which seem to reflect Austin's thinking on the matter (he gave no explicit argument), are totally inconclusive because all they show is that a performative utterance is not merely a statement, not that it is not a statement at all. They seem to assume that an order, for example, is not a statement just because it is also something else.

First, *(nonconstative) performative utterances are neither true nor false. Therefore, they are not statements.* This argument (Austin 1962,

12ff) is clearly question-begging. As orders per se (or as promises, apologies, and so on) performative utterances are neither true nor false. But if they are also statements, then as statements they are true or false. Indeed, if true, they are true in virtue of being made.

Second, *someone who utters to A "I order you to leave" would not be said to have stated that he was ordering A to leave.* Even if he would not be said to have stated that he was ordering . . . , it does not follow that he did not state that he was ordering A to leave. In fact, he would not be said *merely* to have stated that he was ordering A to leave. And that he would be said to have ordered A to leave does not imply that he was not stating that he was ordering A to leave.

Third, *someone who utters "I order you to leave" does not intend to convey information, namely, that he is ordering A to leave; he intends to be thereby ordering A to leave.* He could very well be intending and doing both. Indeed, we suggest that he succeeds in ordering A to leave precisely by virtue of stating that he is ordering A to leave. To be sure, conveying this information was not his primary intention, but insofar as it was necessary to the fulfillment of his primary intention, it too was intended.

A much subtler argument is offered by Schiffer (1972, 104–110) to show that performatives are not used constatively. He holds that a verb used performatively has the same meaning as when used merely descriptively, and that explicit performatives are constative, as he puts it, in their logical form or conventional force. However, he argues ingeniously, they are uttered with "something slightly less than their full conventional force" (p. 109). It is not clear just what this means, but the argument for it is clear enough. Schiffer shares with Austin the view that the performative formula makes explicit the full illocutionary force of one's utterance. If this force includes being constative—what Schiffer calls the "full conventional force"—an infinite regress is supposed to result. Take the utterance, "I order you to leave." If its full illocutionary force includes being a statement, its full illocutionary force is not being made explicit—only its being an order is made explicit. The speaker could make explicit the fact that he is making a statement by uttering "I state that I order you to leave." But on the view that this utterance was, like the previous one, made with *its* full conventional force, he would have been stating that he stated that he ordered. Thus, he would have still not made explicit the full illocutionary force of his utterance. Further attempts to make explicit the full illocutionary force would always leave more to be made explicit, ad infinitum.[6] From this Schiffer concludes that if the full illocutionary force of a performative includes being constative, its full force cannot be made explicit. But since (he assumes) the performative formula does make the full force explicit, it follows that the full force does not include being constative. On the other hand, linguistic considerations—essentially that a performative sentence has no special grammatical feature and that the performative verb (or the sentence as a whole) has no special meaning—indicate that being constative is part of the full conventional force of performatives. Hence a performative is uttered "with something slightly less than its full conventional force."

The trouble with Schiffer's argument[7] is his acceptance of Austin's view that performatives make explicit the full illocutionary force of the utterance. If the utterance is both an order and a statement, then its full force is not made explicit by "I order." But that it is an order is made explicit, and that, of course, is the point of using the performative formula.

On a related point Austin held, without argument, that although using the performative formula makes explicit the precise action performed by the utterance, making it explicit is not to state what it is or to describe it. Granted, there are many ways to make things explicit other than to state what they are or to describe them. For example, I can make explicit my gratitude to someone by praising him ("You're so kind"), by saying "You didn't have to do that," or by returning the favor.[8] But why isn't the use of the performative formula a statement of what I am doing, as when I say "I thank you"? After all, in general it is possible to perform several actions in one fell swoop, so why should the utterance of "I thank you" not be both a giving of thanks and a stating that I am so doing? To be sure, the first is my primary intention, but its fulfillment is abetted by my secondary intention of making the first explicit.

We hold that the efficacy of the performative formula is not a consequence of the meaning of the performative verbs. Imagine a state of affairs in which speakers of English did not make performative utterances in using sentences like "I order you . . ." or "I warn you . . ." but used them merely to make statements. If such statements could be made truly and sincerely, something other than the utterance itself would have to constitute the order or the warning. This could be the utterance of another sentence or some gesture from a "vocabulary" of performative gestures. Then the statement "I order . . ." would be regarded as false if not accompanied by the utterance of an appropriate sentence or by the appropriate gesture. This method might be inefficient compared to ours, but there is no reason (except on a hard meaning-is-use line) to hold that for these speakers words like "order" and "warn" would differ in meaning from what they mean for us. After all, they call orders or warnings the same things we do, except for the utterances of sentences that for us, but not for them, are performatives. Surely for us "order" in "I order" means the same as it does in other constructions.[9] Moreover, since they use the same sentences we do but without performative effect, no special grammatical feature can account for that effect.

As a matter of fact, we have a device other than the performative to make illocutionary force explicit. An explication can follow the utterance: "Leave; and that's an order." "I will come; and that's a promise." Here the acts of doing and stating are kept distinct. A speaker issues an order, and then states that he has done so, thereby making explicit what he has done. Using the performative formula is to do both at once, we suggest, and that we have this convenient formula at our disposal is not due to the meaning of the performative verbs.

Why then is "I order you to leave" an order, whereas "It is the case that I order you to leave" and "I state that I order you to leave" are not orders? The latter two utterances are mere statements, true or false depending on whether or not the speaker gives the addressee an order at approximately the time of utterance, by performing or having just performed some other act, verbal or otherwise, such as forcefully pointing to the door. They can be true only if there is something other than themselves to be about. Now suppose that an utterance of "I order you to leave" is a statement. Suppose, moreover, that the speaker is performing no other act that could even remotely be construed as giving an order. In this event, either the speaker is mistaken or he must be doing something that counts as an order, and the only candidate for this is his utterance. It itself is the only thing for it to be about. That is, as a statement, the utterance is about itself, as an order. There is nothing paradoxical about this, despite the utterance's self-reference. After all, its self-reference can be made explicit by using the word "hereby," as in "I hereby order you to leave." What "hereby" adds to the original is something like this: "In uttering this sentence, I order you to leave."[10] The speaker thereby makes explicit not only the force of his utterance (that it's an order) but the vehicle of that force, namely, the utterance itself.[11]

So far we have rejected known reasons for denying that performative utterances are statements too; we haved denied that the efficacy of performatives is a matter of meaning; and we have suggested, with the help of the "hereby" argument, that taking a performative utterance as a statement may explain why it is a performative as well. We have not yet explained why an utterance like "I order you to leave" is a performative. To do this is not to explain historically how or why there came to be the performative practice, but to show what has to be the case for such an utterance to count as an order.

The communicative presumption among users of a language is that when they say something, what they are doing in saying it is determinable by their audience. Because this is a matter of mutual belief, the speaker can reasonably intend the hearer to take him as intending his act to be determinable, and it is on this basis, together with the utterance itself and the circumstances surrounding it, that the hearer determines what that act is. The speaker succeeds insofar as this determination is made correctly. In the case of performative utterances, even those without the use of "hereby," normally the hearer could reason, and could be intended to reason, as follows:

1. He is saying "I order you to leave."
2. He is stating that he is ordering me to leave.
3. If his statement is true, then he must be ordering me to leave.
4. If he is ordering me to leave, it must be his utterance that constitutes the order. (What else could it be?)
5. Presumably, he is speaking the truth.
6. Therefore, in stating that he is ordering me to leave he is ordering me to leave.

This reasoning is artificially elaborate—or needlessly explicit—but that is only because there is ample precedent for it. The performative practice short-circuits the steps of this inference pattern, both as intended by the speaker and as carried through by the hearer. Still, the success of the performative would be vitiated if any of the steps in the inference were blocked. Explicit performative utterances are indirect illocutionary acts.[12] The hearer's intended inference, warranted by the communicative presumption, is compressed by precedent. The explicit performative formula is standardized for the indirect performance of the illocutionary act named by the performative verb.

10.1.1. Locutionary Performatives

It has not been previously observed that there is a class of performative verbs that are not illocutionary but locutionary. These verbs of saying are performative in that sentences in which they occur in the first-person present can be true of their very utterance, as in the case of (1) and (2),

(1) I repeat that there will be no fooling around.
(2) I close by saying that, hard as it is, this problem can be solved.

Among the locutionary performatives are "say," "utter," "comment," "mention," "note," "remark," "repeat," "add," "begin," "continue," "close," "list," "enumerate," "formulate," and "reformulate." Locutionary performative utterances are true just in case what the speaker says in issuing them is what he predicates of himself. Unlike communicative illocutionary performatives, no R-intention is required of the speaker nor need be recognized by the hearer. Unlike conventional illocutionary acts no special nonlinguistic convention is involved. That the speaker is mentioning something, repeating himself, or listing items depends merely on what he says and is identifiable thereby. Of course, the speaker will also be performing, in issuing a locutionary performative, some illocutionary act, and this will fit the SAS like any other. We will say nothing further about locutionary performatives, but it is well to note that not every performative verb is an illocutionary verb.

10.2. EMBEDDED AND HEDGED PERFORMATIVES

In his reply to Ross (1970), Fraser (1971, 2) noted apparent counter-examples to the claim that the performative verb must be the highest verb in surface structure:

(3) I regret that I must inform you of your dismissal.
(4) I am pleased to be able to offer you the job.
(5) I would like to congratulate you.

Since on our view performativity is indirect even in explicit performative utterances, these sorts of sentences offer no special problems for our account. Embedding increases the inferential load on the hearer, but there is no difference in kind between performative utterances with unembedded and those with embedded performative verbs. Sadock (1974, 55–61) has in effect argued against the indirectness of these cases, and Fraser (1975) has gone on to investigate sentences like these in some detail under the label of *hedged performatives*.

10.2.1. Embedded Performatives

Sadock (pp. 56–61) gives four arguments that are supposed to cast doubt on the view that illocutionary acts performed by uttering sentences like (3)–(5) are performed indirectly.

First, suppose that Mr. Frambes has received a letter from his insurance company beginning,

(6) a. We regret to inform you that your policy is canceled.

After having an accident he takes the company to court, claiming that the company simply expressed a certain negative psychological state—regret at informing. Sadock concludes "Who wins? Pretty obviously, the insurance company does" (p. 56). Maybe so, but why does this count against the indirect hypothesis? Surely the law does not require that the policy holder be informed by a direct rather than indirect illocutionary act.

Second, Sadock notes that one can report the act performed using (6a) with sentences like (6b), but sentences like (6c), (6d), and (6e) are misleading, incomplete, or ungrammatical:

(6) b. Mutual of Hoboken informed Mr. Frambes of the cancellation of his policy.
   c. Mutual of Hoboken canceled Frambes's policy.
   d. Mutual of Hoboken expressed their regret about informing Frambes of the cancellation.
   e. *Mutual of Hoboken regretted to inform Frambes of the cancellation of his policy.

Sadock concludes that "It would seem that the underlying clause whose main verb is *inform* is, after all, a performative clause" (p. 57). And if this is right, the act would be for Sadock literal and direct, not indirect. There are some objections to this argument. There is a grammatical version of (6e):

(6) e'. Mutual of Hoboken regretted informing Frambes of the cancellation of his policy.

More seriously, Sadock's reasoning would rule out the report of indirect illocutionary acts by the use of any performative verb. But surely one can report that someone requested a drink in uttering "My mouth is parched," although there is no underlying imperative or verb of requesting.

Third, Sadock notes that (6a) will take "hereby" as in (6f):

(6) f. We regret to inform you that your policy is hereby canceled.

Apparently this is supposed to count for the directness and literality of the act, but Sadock does not say why, and we have already offered a different account of "hereby" (see section 10.1).

Fourth and finally, Sadock claims that verbs like "regret" "require that their complements have all the salient properties of explicit performatives" (p. 59). For us, of course, this may well be true and still not preclude the possibility of indirection in the utterance of (6a). Again, we are given no argument to the contrary.

We conclude that these arguments cast little if any doubt on the view that such acts as illustrated above can be indirect.

10.2.2. Hedged Performatives

Fraser (1975) has discussed the interesting case of utterances that differ from simple performative utterances in that the performative verb is preceded by a modal like "must," "can," "will," "would," "might," "should," or a semimodal such as "have to." Such utterances seem to have the illocutionary force of the act named by the performative verb used, as illustrated by typical utterances of sentences like (7)–(10), which Fraser calls *hedged performatives:*

(7) I must ask you to leave.
(8) I can promise you I'll be home.
(9) I want to thank you for the Beaujolais.
(10) I would suggest you try some.

Fraser is concerned both to account for their illocutionary force in terms of certain conversational principles, and to account for cases ("weak performatives") that do not have the force of the act named by the performative verb, such as "I must forbid you from cutting off your right arm." Fraser seems to assume (he says nothing explicitly) that simple performatives do not pose the same explanatory problem as hedged performatives. Since he indicates nothing to the contrary, presumably he thinks that simple performatives are literal and direct illocutionary acts and therefore that they have their illocutionary force solely in virtue of literal sentence meaning.[13] We have argued that simple performatives are indirect and that literally they are constatives; we take the same position on hedged performatives. Nevertheless, hedged performatives do contain modals, whose distinctive functions need to be explained.

Consider Fraser's approach to cases involving the modal "must." He proceeds on the assumption that utterances of sentences like (7) are statements that the speaker has a certain obligation (he does not mention that it may be otherwise necessary that he do something)—in this example, to ask the hearer to leave. The question is why such an utterance counts as the performance of the act the speaker says he is obligated to do. Fraser (1975) posits three principles:

Principle of Obligation Fulfillment. Given nothing to suggest the contrary, whenever someone has an obligation to perform some action, one can infer that he will perform that action.

Principle of Unspecified Time. Given nothing to suggest the contrary, whenever the time of an action is left unspecified, one can infer that the agent is expected to perform the action at the earliest chance.

Principle of Efficiency. Given nothing to suggest the contrary, whenever a further utterance would be redundant, one can infer that the speaker need not make the utterance but that he will operate as if he had made it and will expect the hearer to operate similarly.

Fraser does not discuss the epistemological or conversational status of these principles. To sanction the intended inference, though, they need to be mutual beliefs between speaker and hearer.

The first principle (obligation fulfillment) is weak by itself, but in conjunction with the second (unspecified time) it may be inferred that the speaker of (7) will, at the earliest chance, ask the hearer to leave. The third principle (efficiency) is needed to account for the fact that the utterance of (7) is in itself the fulfillment of the obligation that the speaker is ascribing to himself. However, the formulation of this principle makes it unclear how and why the utterance of (7) constitutes an act of asking the hearer to leave. If anything, it suggests that no such act need be performed once the effect of that would-be act has been achieved. However, matters are made worse by the use of the word "redundant." It is redundant for a speaker who says "I must ask you to leave" to ask the hearer to leave only if he has indeed asked the hearer to leave, or if his utterance at least has the effect (expresses the illocutionary intent) of asking the hearer to leave. Perhaps these problems with the principle of efficiency can be removed if we follow the spirit of one of Grice's (1975) maxims of manner, "Be brief." Grice means brevity in saying what one has to say, but allowance could also be made for illocutionary brevity. A maxim to this effect would take the form, "Don't go on to perform an illocutionary act directly when its intent can be inferred from the utterance you have just (or already) made." If such a maxim applies to ordinary conversational situations, then the speaker of (7) need not explicitly request the hearer to leave, provided the intent to make such a request can be inferred from the utterance of (7). Obviously our maxim of illocutionary brevity tells us nothing about when indirect illocutionary intents can be so inferred.

Recall that one of the basic ideas underlying the speech act schema is the implication of the communicative presumption that there is a recognizable sufficient reason (explanation) for the speaker's utterance. If there is no apparent sufficient reason for an utterance to be taken literally, the hearer must search for a nonliteral or indirect interpretation of the utterance for which there is sufficient reason of utterance. The operant principle would take the form "Don't issue an utterance for which (taken literally) there is insufficient recognizable reason unless you have some further (or other) illocutionary intent that can be inferred." This still does not tell us how the inference is to be drawn, but surely it must be based, as the SAS requires, on the content of the utterance and on the mutual contextual beliefs that obtain between the speaker and the hearer. How would the inference run in the case of (7)? As usual, the inference is one that S intends H to make partly on the basis of recognizing S's intention that he make it. For the sake of simplicity, we will omit the steps preceding the literal illocutionary act.

1. S is stating that he must ask me to leave.
2. S's stating that he must ask implies that he is reluctant[14] to do so.
3. S's having to ask me to leave is a reason for so doing.
4. S's stating that he has this reason is reason to think that he intends to ask me to leave.
5. S is not explicitly asking me to leave.
6. In stating that he must ask me to leave, S intends thereby to be asking me to leave.
7. S is asking me to leave.

Why do only certain utterances of the form "I must V . . . ," where V is a performative verb, count as acts of V-ing? Fraser argues quite plausibly that when the speaker does not want to avoid responsibility for V-ing (because he is not reluctant) as with typical utterances of (11) and (12), the utterance is not clearly an act of V-ing (Fraser calls it "weakly performative"):

(11) I must congratulate you on winning.
(12) I must welcome you home.

There is no point in stating that you must do what you don't mind doing, hence no reason to use the hedged performative with "must." Indeed, not only is there no reason, the utterance will not be taken as an act of V-ing if the hearer does not think V-ing is a sort of act S should be reluctant to do. Thus, if you arrive home and you are greeted with an utterance of (12), you are likely to expect either a reluctant welcoming sequel or no welcome at all. If anything, then, when "must" precedes the performative verb, the speaker can be taken as expressing his reluctance to V. The utterance counts as an act of V-ing that p only if it is the sort of act that people in general are reluctant to do or if it is mutually believed between S and H that S is reluctant to do it. Notice that the question of the speaker's reluctance figures in the inference H is intended to make as to S's illocutionary intent. For this reason, the inference is blocked if H has reason to believe, and to believe that S believes he believes, that S is not reluctant to V.

We will not review Fraser's account of the other main kinds of hedged performatives. In each case he posits certain conversational principles that are supposed to account for the force of the utterance. Unfortunately, he fails to justify these principles, although he represents many of them as being akin to Grice's principles. That of course does not mean they are, and even if they are, that does not make them true. He does not discuss their conversational or epistemological status. Some are formulated as inference principles of the form "Given such-and-such, one can infer so-and-so." But what validates such principles? What makes them applicable to particular conversational situations? On our view they have to be mutually believed to be applicable; otherwise they could not figure in intended hearer inferences. Since Fraser himself disavows (1975, note 6) any claim to finality in his formulation, we will not quibble about details. Rather, we have tried to show in the case of "must" that there is no need to appeal, either as theorists or as speaker-hearers, to such principles. The communicative presumption is quite sufficient to account for hedged performatives in that it requires the hearer to search for a sufficient reason for the speaker's utterance. Just as in the case of "must," the other kinds of hedged performatives can be understood in terms of recurrent patterns of inference to sufficient reasons for utterance.

Therefore we might suggest a general maxim to cover all the kinds of hedged performatives, whose exploitation follows Grice's pattern of conversational implicature:

Maxim of Sufficient Reason: Make your utterance such that there is identifiably sufficient reason for its issuance.

Grice's maxims do not govern illocutionary acts generally, only acts of constating. He intimates that they can be generalized and we suggest the maxim of sufficient reason as one such. Indeed it is central because in effect it requires the speaker to utilize the communicative presumption in making his utterance. In the case of hedged performatives, and for indirect illocutionary acts generally, this maxim is utilized in just the way that Grice's are for conversational implicature: the speaker intends his utterance to be taken literally as a certain illocutionary act, identifiable on the basis of what is said, and it will be viewed by the hearer as being issued with sufficient reason only on the assumption that there is some other illocutionary act being performed in the process. That is just what happens in the case of hedged performatives.

For hedged performatives, like standardized indirect acts generally, there is ample precedent for the inference the hearer is intended to make; consequently the SAS is short-circuited. What distinguishes direct performatives and hedged performatives from illocutionary standardization generally is that the illocutionary verb explicitly occurs in the utterance. Thus the hearer's search procedure, even if such utterances lacked precedent, would be simple and short. In reviewing the other main cases of hedged performatives, we will give brief versions of the inference required in accordance with the maxim of sufficient reason.

According to Fraser, hedged performatives with "can" generally require some adverbial like "now," "finally," or "at last" to count as the sort of illocutionary act named by the performative verb:

(13) I can now admit that I did it.

Such an adverbial is not necessary, however, as shown by example (8), repeated here:

(8) I can promise you I'll be home.

Whether or not the sentence includes temporal specifiers like "now," it must have sufficient reason for being uttered. We agree with Fraser (except that he needlessly posits a "principle of expressed ability" to account for it) that the hearer is to think, "The speaker wouldn't have told me this unless he intended to do it." Instead of invoking Fraser's principle of efficiency to account for the fact that the utterance itself is the execution of that intention, we can say that the only identifiable sufficient reason for the utterance is that it be the execution of that intention, as indeed a hearer would recognize by reasoning (invoking the maxim of sufficient reason) roughly as follows:[15]

(13) a. He is stating that he can now admit that he did it.
     b. He wouldn't so state unless he intended to.
     c. If he intends to admit that he did it, he will.
     d. No (additional) utterance to that effect is forthcoming.
     e. Therefore, in stating that he can, he is admitting that he did it.

One question not to be overlooked is why, at least in some instances, replacement of the modal with a periphrastic version takes away the indirect illocutionary effect. Compare the following two sentences:

(14) I can promise you I won't squeal.
(15) I am able to promise you I won't squeal.

An utterance of (15), unlike (14), would not normally be taken as a (hedged) promise but simply as an assertion of the speaker's ability. Not only that, it would imply (at least if so taken), contrary to the analog of (13b), that the speaker does *not* intend to make such a promise. However, the same effect is achieved by an utterance of (14) in which "can" is stressed:

(14') I cán promise you I won't squeal (but that doesn't mean I will promise).

Fraser rightly points out that both the stressed and the periphrastic version call attention to the assertion of ability (the direct illocutionary act), but he mistakenly concludes that they suggest that there is some reason to doubt the speaker's ability. Rather, they implicate that S is not willing to, and is not going to, do what he says he can do.[16]

The pattern of inference suggested for "can" cases is applicable to cases of "will"/"shall"/"am going to"/"intend to," except that step (b), where the speaker's intention is inferred, is omitted since what the speaker is stating is that he intends to do something. Otherwise, these cases require no special comment: if no further utterance is forthcoming, the speaker is doing what he states he intends to do. Notice that adverbs like "now" and "hereby" can be inserted in such sentences as (16), just as with simple performatives.

(16) I will $\left\{ \begin{array}{c} \text{now} \\ \text{hereby} \end{array} \right\}$ propose going home.

We are not suggesting that "will" in this context is a present auxiliary verb rather than a future one, but we do suggest that the speaker's reference to the time of his forthcoming proposal does not extend beyond the time of completion of his utterance.

Cases involving "want to"/"wish to"/"would like to" have a rather special feature. Fraser points out that sentences like (17) are taken as requests for permission, or, we may add, for cooperation.

(17) I want to ask you a question.

Since utterances of such sentences are literally statements of what the speaker wants, they are indirect requests. Therefore, utterances like (18) would be doubly indirect.

(18) I want to ask you if you've seen *Jaws*.

For Fraser such an utterance is literally a statement, indirectly a request (for permission), and indirectly a question. Now Fraser posits a principle of permission seeking to account for the inference from the request to the performance of the requested act, in this case a question. Aside from our usual problems with his principles, we suggest that the indirect question works directly off the literal statement of want, not off the indirect request. Thus, the pattern of inference is the same as with "will" and other statements of intention. Indeed it seems that no indirect request at all is being made, because the utterance has the force of a question just because it is presumed by the speaker that no permission is necessary for such a question.

The hedged performatives with "would"/"might"/"should" are interesting because grammatically they seem to be consequents of subjunctive conditionals without any expressed antecedent. A sentence like (19) might be construed as an elliptical version of a conditional, with an antecedent like "If you were to ask my opinion."

(19) I would suggest a shot of Irish whiskey.

Fraser claims further that there is no need for any conversational principles to interpret such examples and that they can be interpreted as if the "would" were absent: according to Fraser, the illocutionary force (in the case of (19), as a suggestion) cannot be denied by the speaker. Unfortunately, he does not state whether the result of denial is a contradiction or an ungrammaticality. We are not sure what to claim here. Consider the cancellation of (19) as in (19').

(19') I would suggest a shot of Irish whiskey, but I won't.

Without the antecedent made explicit, it is not clear what the point of an utterance of (19') could be. (For that matter, it is not clear what the point would be with an explicit antecedent but without an explanation—say, that the speaker is out of Irish whiskey.) In any case, we see an inadequacy with this account as it stands. What grammatical reason is there that the suppressed antecedent must be something like "If you wanted my opinion"? If the suppressed antecedent were "If I approved of alcohol," the utterance of (19) would not count as a suggestion (to someone suffering from a sore throat), but this is not a grammatical fact. So it appears that reference to conversational principles is needed here after all.

At the end of his paper, Fraser mentions but does not discuss cases like (20) and (21) and doubly hedged performatives like (22) and (23).

(20) I am happy to inform you that you're accepted.
(21) I hasten to add that I didn't see her either.
(22) I will have to request that you leave at once.
(23) I should now be able to assure you that this will work.

He suggests that further conversational principles are needed for these. Our position, as should be clear, is that no special conversational principles are needed to account for the performativity of any of these cases. Indeed hedged performatives are not fundamentally different from simple performatives. In both cases the hearer merely has to identify a sufficient reason for the speaker's utterance. Considering the occurrence in the sentence uttered of the verb designating the very type of act being performed (as well as precedent for such performances—see 9.3) it is no surprise that the identification can be made.

Finally, Fraser claims that for each kind of hedged performative only certain sorts of illocutionary verbs work performatively with the modal (or other expression) in question. The following, for example, are clearly not acts of the sort named by the performative verb.

(24) I must invite you to stay.
(25) I can (now) ask you to go.
(26) I will order you to sit down.

However, it is not the verb itself but the verb together with its complement that determines whether an utterance of a sentence in normal circumstances has the illocutionary force designated by the verb. The following examples, with the same verbs as in (24)–(26), seem to have that illocutionary force:

(27) I must invite you to another one of those horrible parties at the boss's house.
(28) I can (now) ask you to turn up the radio—the kids are asleep finally.
(29) I will order you never to come back until I tell you to.

In each case the hedged form has the illocutionary force named by the verb because the utterance meets the conditions that hedged performatives of that sort meet. Hedged performatives with "must" are acts that the speaker is reluctant to do. Those with "can" imply that the conditions were not right previously but are now. Those with "will" imply that the speaker was not previously willing or that a certain condition is assumed under which he is willing. And so on for other cases.

The point is that performativity, simple or hedged, is not a question of semantics. The only question about the acceptability of a performative utterance is whether there is reason for it—identifiable reason. Contrary to some of the literature, there is no need to posit such a thing as a performative reading of sentences used performatively, that is, to perform an act (indirectly in our view) of the sort named by the performative verb. When such a sentence is so used on a given occasion, no special reading is required to explain that use. The explanation is pragmatic, not semantic.

10.3. ILLOCUTIONARY ADVERBIALS

Many locutions can be used to comment upon the illocutionary intent behind the utterance of the very sentences in which they occur. Consider the following:

(30) Frankly, you bore me.
(31) If I may say so, this conversation is getting tedious.
(32) By the way, I couldn't find your underwear.

(33) Speaking of linguistics, did you know that procedural semantics is a notational variant of Fortran?

(34) If you're so smart, who is the voice of Bugs Bunny?

(35) On the other hand, he who hesitates is lost.

(36) Moreover, we have no bananas.

(37) Since you'll find out anyway, your wife is carrying on with the butler.

Each of these sentences appears to be a perfectly grammatical and fully meaningful English sentence, and yet the prefatory adverbial is not used to modify the main clause of the sentence (it may not even contribute to the locutionary act). Rather it is used to characterize, in one way or another, the *utterance* of the main clause. In (30) "frankly" describes *S*'s act of stating that *H* bores *S*. "By the way" in (32) indicates the digressive character of the utterance to follow. "On the other hand" in (35) and "moreover" in (36) indicate, respectively, that what follows contradicts or supplements something said previously. In (37) the prefatory clause "Since you'll find out anyway" supplies part of a reason for making the ensuing statement; obviously it provides no reason for believing what is stated. In the case of (34) the prefatory clause provides a reason for the addressee to answer the question that follows.

There are many types of *illocutionary adverbials,* as we call them. What is important about them is not their variety, interesting as it is, but the issues they raise regarding the relation of linguistic theory to language use. As illustrated by our discussion of illocutionary standardization and of performativity, we maintain that there is a place where linguistics leaves off and the theory of illocutionary acts takes over. The only concessions we have made to the use-is-meaning view, shared by many generative semanticists and speech-act semanticists, is to allow that the type of saying, as determined by the grammatical sentence type (declarative, imperative, or interrogative) delimits literal illocutionary force potential and that there is a semantic connection between the meaning of indexicals and how people use them to refer. Apart from these concessions, we have enforced a strong use/meaning dichotomy. However, it seems that the existence of utterance adverbials collapses this dichotomy and that a linguistic account of sentences involving them must make reference to the use of those sentences.

The higher performative analysis is an approach to the problem of illocutionary adverbials which identifies use and meaning. For example, on this theory (31) becomes (31P), with embedded performative.

(31P) If I may say so, *I say that* this conversation is getting tedious.

And (34) becomes (34P):

(34P) If you're so smart, *I request that you tell me* who is the voice of Bugs Bunny?

In both cases the performative analysis provides a syntactic place for the if-clause, in which the semantic role of that clause is straightforward. Can this sort of analysis be motivated for the rest of (38)–(45) We will look briefly at some representative suggestions by Schreiber (1972) and Sadock (1974) concerning such cases. First we will compare some manner adverbs ("frankly," "truthfully") with some sentence adverbs ("fortunately," "clearly") and argue that their distribution does not support a performative explanation (though it may be consistent with one). Instead we offer an *illocutionary* explanation of the data. We then generalize our position to expositive and reason adverbials such as "If I may say so" and "Speaking of Jones."

10.3.1. Manner Adverbs

Consider Schreiber's (1972) application of the performative analysis to manner adverbs, a special case of illocutionary adverbials illustrated by (30) and by (38) and (39):

(38) Truthfully, you lied to me.
(39) Truthfully, did you lie to me?

After arguing that manner adverbs like "truthfully" and "frankly" differ syntactically from sentence adverbs like "fortunately" and "clearly" (clauses in which the former occur, unlike those in which the latter occur, cannot be embedded in predicate complement constructions[17]), Schreiber supports the performative analysis by suggesting that it accounts for the fact that in (38) the speaker is predicating truthfulness of himself, whereas in (39) truthfulness is predicated of the addressee. Indeed on the performative analysis this asymmetry is exposed neatly when (38) and (39) are derived from, respectively, (38P) and (39P):

(38P) *I tell you* truthfully that you lied to me.
(39P) *I request that you tell me* truthfully whether you lied to me.[18]

It is evident that in each case a syntactic place is provided for "truthfully" to modify just what it is supposed to modify.

Greenbaum (1969, 84) noted that sentence adverbs like "fortunately" and "clearly" do not occur freely in sentence-initial position in questions.

(40) *Fortunately, did you lie to me?
(41) *Clearly, did you lie to me?

Sadock (1974, 34) has converted this sort of observation into the following argument for the presence of an abstract (higher) performative verb:

1. Sentence adverbs (such as "fortunately") do not occur with imperative sentences: *"Fortunately, leave the room!"
2. Sentence adverbs "begin life as the subject clauses of predicates that express adverbial ideas."
3. A verb of ordering demands that "its indirect object and the subject of its complement clause be coreferent[ial]."
4. Conclusion: "An imperative with a sentence adverb would have to stem from a structure such as [figure 10.1] which does not meet the condition on semantic well-formedness, since NP_i, which refers to an individual, cannot be coreferent[ial] with NP_k, which is a proposition."

This argument cannot be accepted as it stands because the generalization in 3 mentions indirect object position (NP_v), while the conclusion mentions subject position (NP_i), a problem that can be easily remedied by changing NP_i to NP_v in the conclusion on the plausible assumption that NP_v too must refer to a person or at least a nonproposition. But even with this modification the argument does not motivate the conclusion, since no argument is given for why the adverb cannot come from a higher predicate, as in figure 10.2. As Sadock says, "it has been supposed that adverbs in general are reduced versions of higher clauses" (p. 34).

That the argument for an abstract performative verb is consistent with the data doesn't make it sound. Compare (42) and (43) with (38), "Truthfully, you lied to me."

(42) Fortunately, you lied to me.
(43) Clearly, you lied to me.

In these two cases the sentence adverb modifies the sentence "you lied to me," whereas in (38) "truthfully" modifies, so to speak, the illocutionary act of uttering that sentence or, as the abstract performative

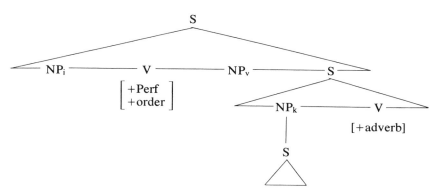

Figure 10.1

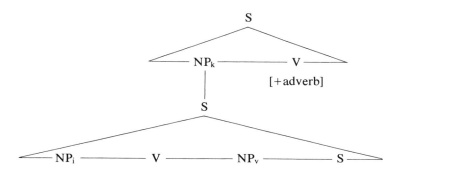

Figure 10.2

proposal would have it, "truthfully" modifies the deep performative clause.[19] But why does "truthfully" not modify "you lied to me"? Not only does it obviously modify the main clause in (44) and (45)—

(44) Truthfully, you answered the question.
(45) Truthfully, you conveyed how you felt.

—but the only reason it seems not to modify the main clause in (38) is that a contradiction would result, as is evident if "truthfully" is postponed, as in (38').

(38') You lied to me truthfully.

But surely this does not mean that (38') is not a literal paraphrase of (38). We see no reason to deny that it is. The question is whether (38) has two literal readings or only one, the one paraphrased by (38′) and syntactically like (42) and (43). If there are two, then (38) is syntactically ambiguous. However, this supposition seems to require the higher performative analysis, and we have just seen its difficulty in handling the data. Therefore the other option is worth examining. It requires the assumption that the use of manner adverbs like "truthfully" as illocutionary modifiers is nonliteral. Since this phenomenon is general in scope, it looks like a case of illocutionary standardization, analogous to the cases of explicit and of hedged performatives.

A grammatical form is a case of illocutionary standardization if there is ample precedent for using it to perform an illocutionary act of a certain type. Illocutionary standardization is not a matter of linguistic fact, at least in the narrow sense of being established by a linguistic rule. On our view standardization short-circuits the SAS by by-passing the steps involved in determining the literal illocutionary act. Indeed, in some cases we will now consider there is no literal illocutionary act to be identified, for the sentence uttered makes no sense literally. It is grammatical, however, from a purely syntactic standpoint, and a standardized form of inference is R-intended to be made to determine the speaker's illocutionary intent. In the case of (38), "Truthfully, you lied to me," the sentence uttered makes sense literally, but the presumption of sincerity invites H to find an alternative interpretation of the utterance, which would be literally rendered as "I tell you truthfully that you lied to me," the nearest plausible candidate for what the speaker could have meant. This account is no mere notational variant of the performative analysis: the locus of explanation is not in the grammar but in the social psychology of the situation. A theory of linguistic performance might have to account for the inference made, but this does not make it a matter of grammar.

Where the presumption of literalness is overridden, the hearer relies on the presumption of sincerity in searching for a nonliteral intention. For example, the manner adverbs we have considered cannot be plausibly construed as modifying the verb of the sentence uttered and in some cases they cannot even be sensibly so construed. In either event, the strategy is to take the preposed adverb as modifying the utterance of the sentence. There is no more a priori reason to assume this to be impossible than there is to posit gratuitous constructions like higher performatives. Pretheoretically, it is intuitively plausible to regard these manner adverbs, as well as the other sorts of adverbials in examples (31)–(37), as illocutionary modifiers, but the theoretical question is how to deal with this intuition linguistically. The performative analysis takes the bull by the horns and posits a linguistic form for the illocutionary act modified. Our approach, on the other hand, denies that illocutionary acts so modified are fully literal, much less that they have linguistic forms. They have literal correlates, the utterance of precisely those sentences occurring in performative paraphrases, but no higher performatives are posited in the sentences actually uttered.

Our argument for denying that sentences with preposed manner adverbs have literal meanings of the sort assumed by the performative analysis can be summarized as follows. Manner adverbs can be straightforward sentence adverbs, like "clearly" or "unfortunately." However, when they function as illocutionary modifiers, they cannot be taken literally as sentence adverbs because such an interpretation is nonsensical. Relying on the presumption of sincerity, together with the overarching communicative presumption, the hearer takes, as he is intended to take, the uttered sentence as lexical shorthand for what would be said explicitly using the full performative form. There is no reason to assume or postulate that that form underlies the sentence actually uttered.

To deny that sentences like (30) and (38) with manner adverbs contain higher performative verbs requires us to deny that they are grammatical. Intuitively, such sentences seem grammatical, and yet we are denying that they are. Our theoretical justification is that there is nothing in the sentence for the manner adverb to modify. (Of course, a proponent of the higher performative approach disagrees—but only by inventing something for the adverb to modify.) Our proposal is indeed controversial, but as we argue in section 10.4, a wide variety of expressions, extending far beyond those even seemingly amenable to the higher performative approach, can and commonly do serve a conversational purpose without being grammatical. Usability is not grammaticality, and acquiring a use does not turn the ill-formed into the well-formed.

10.3.2. Generalizing the Argument

The pattern of argument for manner adverbs can be generalized to cover all sorts of illocutionary adverbials, including those illustrated in examples (31)–(37). If anything, the argument is more compelling in these cases, because the alternative, the higher performative approach, requires greater theoretical contortions and is supported by fewer data than for manner adverbs.

The performative approach is relatively plausible for case (31); at least the performative paraphrase is easy to formulate.

(31) If I may say so, this conversation is getting tedious.
(31P) If I may say so, *I say that* this conversation is getting tedious.

Taken literally, (31) contains an inappropriate juxtaposition of antecedent and consequent, although it is not clear that this inappropriateness is linguistic—the conditional just seems absurdly false and the literal utterance of it pointless. To argue that (31) is derived from (31P) it must be argued either that this literal interpretation is based on a false grammatical reading of (31) or that it is based on a genuine but irrelevant reading, in which case (31) is held to be syntactically ambiguous. The first alternative makes the absurdity of the conditional a matter of grammar when obviously it is not, because a hypothetical case, however wild, could be constructed in which the conditional is true and its utterance appropriate: suppose that S is permitted to speak only when conversational tedium sets in. The latter alternative has the onus of showing just how and when an interpretation of form (31P) is required. And if the performative analysis requires higher performatives under both interpretations, then it has the onus of explaining when sentences like (31) are to be read as (31P) and when they are to be read as (31P′):

(31P′) *I say that,* if I may say so, this conversation is getting tedious.

This would correspond to what we have been calling the literal interpretation, and if it seems less than acceptable, try the two performative readings of (46):

(46)   If I may continue, this conversation won't get tedious.
(46P) If I may continue, *I say that* this conversation won't get tedious.
(46P′) *I say that,* if I may continue, this conversation won't get tedious.

How, on the performative analysis, can performative deletion be freely allowed regardless of where the higher performative is located in the complex sentence?

The adverbial in (32) seems clearly not to be a sentence adverb.

(32) By the way, I couldn't find your underwear.

However, clearly it is in (32′), which seems to be a more natural paraphrase of (32) than (32P).

(32′) By the way, *I might mention that* I couldn't find your underwear.
(32P) By the way, *I say that* I couldn't find your underwear.

On the performative analysis, is "by the way" a sentence adverb only if an explicit performative occurs in the sentence and otherwise a modifier of the deeper performative? After all, a sentence like (32′) is derived, on the performative analysis, from (32′P):

(32′P) By the way, *I say that I might mention* that I couldn't find your underwear.

Again it seems that a nonliteral reading of (32), in accordance with an inference parallel to those required in the previous cases, is sufficient to account for the illocutionary force of its utterance.

   With the possible exception of (37) the remaining examples do not lend themselves to straightforward performative paraphrases at all. Consider, for example, (33):

(33) Speaking of linguistics, did you know that . . . ?
(33P) Speaking of linguistics, I ask you did you know that . . .

The performative paraphrase (33P) really doesn't do justice to (33) because the dangling phrase "speaking of linguistics" describes not the speaker's subsequent utterance but the subject matter of the stage of the conversation at which the utterance occurs. Roughly, the force of this phrase is to give a hedged assurance that what follows is relevant to the conversation, that is, it is but it isn't.

   We might use the term *conversational paraphrase* to designate a sentence whose literal utterance has the same force as an utterance of a sentence like those under consideration. Unlike the performative paraphrase, which supposedly corresponds to a deeper level of linguistic representation, conversational paraphrases can take a variety of forms. The only constraint is that they be readily identifiable so that *S* can reasonably expect *H* to identify his illocutionary intent pursuant to the communicative presumption. The case of (34) brings this out clearly.

(34) If you're so smart, who is the voice of Bugs Bunny?

In order to identify the connection between the two clauses of this sentence, it is necessary to supply several suppressed steps. A performative paraphrase won't do the trick. Instead, the sequence looks something as follows:

(34) a. If you're so smart (as smart as you say/think/suggest you are), you know and can therefore tell me who is the voice of Bugs Bunny.
b. To see if you can tell me . . . , I'll ask you.

Conversational paraphrases can be provided analogously for the remaining cases of (35)–(37).

Once we recognize that not every conversationally usable sentence must have a literal linguistic representation, or at least one that makes literal sense, and that the requirement of conversational paraphrasability suffices instead, we can forgo the wild-goose chase for deeper structures from which to derive, by deletion, otherwise anomalous sentences. Our approach is to regard such sentences as not used literally, in some cases as not even having literal meanings. However, they are not sheer nonsense but readily decipherable ways of saying succinctly what could be said literally only in a cumbersome way. They are readily decipherable because they are standardized in their illocutionary force. We have argued that this is not a matter of meaning, and we have openly admitted that to take this position is to assume a fairly clear-cut distinction between what is ungrammatical and what is otherwise unacceptable. These distinctions impose clear limits on both the power and the scope of linguistic explanation. But then linguistics cannot do everything. We shall now see that leaving room for extra-grammatical phenomena relieves linguistic theory of having to explain the conversational role of other syntactic liberties and lexical omissions besides those involved in illocutionary adverbials.

10.4. SYNTACTIC LIBERTIES

In linguistics as elsewhere there are few if any pure data. The data that a theory has to explain, or at least accommodate, must be described somehow, and how the data are described reflects at least low-level theoretical commitments. Moreover, when a theory is constructed with an eye to the data, the interests of simplicity and generality inevitably require throwing out some of the data, not by ignoring them but by explaining them away, either in terms of the theory in question or in terms of some already accepted theory of phenomena that the recalcitrant data fall under. When it comes to the point where residually stubborn data are excluded just to sustain the theory in question, it is time to look for another theory.

Among other things, the object of a grammar of a language is to describe a fluent speaker's intuitions of grammaticality. Ideally, every string of words in a language is clearly and consistently judged by fluent speakers to be either grammatical or ungrammatical, and those judged grammatical constitute the set of sentences generated by an adequate grammar of the language. In practice the grammatical/ungrammatical distinction as reflected by speakers' intuitions is not clear-cut. Speakers may be unsure in some cases; even when sure, they may disagree among themselves; they may find some sentences relatively more grammatical than others; and in different cases they may give different reasons for judging sentences ungrammatical. A working grammarian must take all this into account. If he retains the objective of producing a grammar that generates just those sentences judged grammatical, he is forced to throw out certain data and idealize those that remain. Or he may opt for degrees of grammaticality and perhaps for kinds of relative ungrammaticality. In this way he minimizes the unsalvageable data, but if his theory is adequate, it will be at the expense of simplicity. Whichever tack he takes he cannot avoid (either in fact or in effect) putting words in the mouths of his respondents, since he has to indicate to them the kind of judgment he wants them to make, namely, of grammaticality or ungrammaticality.

What does all this have to do with a theory of speech acts? Sentences and illocutionary acts do not correlate at all neatly. The semantics of a language cannot coherently be based on correlating grammatical sentences with illocutionary act types, since allowance must be made for nonliteral and indirect illocutionary acts. Here we wish to point out something further: an utterance does not have to be grammatical to have been produced with an identifiable illocutionary intent. Instead of uttering a grammatical sentence a speaker can produce a word, a phrase, or a dependent clause and thereby successfully perform an illocutionary act. For that matter, he can utter an ungrammatical sentence that expresses his illocutionary intent. We maintain that any theory is misguided which attempts to treat as grammatical (and to assign semantic representations to) every locution that can be uttered with an identifiable illocutionary intent. Even for those locutions that native speakers judge to be in some sense acceptable, a theory of the language must not automatically construe them as grammatical.[20] Even if significant generalizations can be made about such diverse classes of locutions as occur in sportscasts, commercials, pop lyrics, and on traffic signs, medicine bottles, and cereal boxes, we think it a serious theoretical mistake to regard as necessarily grammatical those locutions that fall under such generalizations (see Sadock 1974, 139ff). Equally mistaken is requiring a theory of a language to single out all those locutions, grammatical or not, that can be used to perform illocutionary acts. Not only is a theory of grammaticality not a theory of usability (if that is relevant to acceptability) but we believe there is no hope at present for a theory of usability. Thus we maintain that linguistic competence in the sense of knowledge of a language (assuming that this is what the theory of a language captures) does not exhaust competence at *using* expressions in a language. Chomsky remarks,

Use of language involves cognitive systems beyond grammatical and pragmatic competence. The theory of performance, then, will attempt to develop models incorporating grammar and other cognitive structures, as well as an account of the physical and social conditions of language use that are ignored in the abstraction to grammar. (1977, 3)

Consider some examples of ungrammatical locutions whose utterance is a readily identifiable illocutionary act.

(47) a. Close cover before striking.
   b. No smoking
   c. The Steelers going for a field goal
   d. Lucerne two-ten low-fat milk
   e. Slippery when wet
   f. Two nonstudents, please

None of these locutions is a grammatical English sentence. Example (47a) comes close to the sentence "Close the cover before striking the match," and (47c) comes closer to being a sentence, needing only an "are" before "going"; (47b) can be interpreted as "Smoking is not permitted here," (47d) as "This carton contains Lucerne two-ten low-fat milk," (47e) as "This road is slippery when wet," and (47f) as "I would like tickets for two nonstudents." Although the examples are to different degrees ungrammatical, at least by traditional standards, it is no trick to decipher the illocutionary point of their use. The communicative presumption is not waived merely by the utterance of an ungrammatical locution. If there is a likely candidate for the illocutionary intent of such an utterance, one may infer, barring any reason to the contrary, that that candidate is the intent. To be sure, there are precedents for such utterances—some are even standardized—but that does not make them grammatical. Rather, it makes their illocutionary intents especially easy to identify.

These examples illustrate how speakers can use ungrammatical sentences or even nonsentences with identifiable illocutionary intents. To use a locution thus is to take what we call a *syntactic liberty*. A great deal of ordinary language use involves syntactic liberties, everything from answers to questions to newspaper headlines and telegrams. We do not intend to cover the subject in any great detail, but we should give some indication of how this phenomenon fits into the speech act schema. The problem is that if the locution uttered is not a grammatical sentence or not a sentence at all, it has either no meaning or not enough meaning to make an utterance of it a locutionary act of the form, saying that *(...p...); so the SAS is blocked at the level of saying. But there is a solution. Consider slips of the tongue (or mispronunciation). If S accidentally utters something other than what he intends to utter, H may be able to figure out what S meant to say. If S utters "Did you hear about the First Lady's girl bladder operation?" presumably he meant to ask about her gall bladder operation, and H makes the appropriate inference. H makes a similar inference in deciphering malapropisms, where S uses a word to mean something that some similar-sounding word means, like "resemble" for "resent" in "I resemble that remark." The same thing occurs in the case of syntactic liberties, except there is nothing unintentional about the locution used. H, assuming the CP to be in effect, is able to figure out what S means by what he utters, perhaps by associating a grammatical sentence with the locution uttered.[21] Perhaps what one does, using strategies developed through experience, is ascertain *(...p...) directly, without the mediation of a grammatical sentence. In any event, our point is that the SAS can be easily stretched to accommodate whatever goes on—we offer no detailed account—when illocutionary acts are successfully performed with the use of ungrammatical sentences or nonsentences.

Another kind of syntactic liberty is worth mentioning.[22] In these cases a grammatical sentence is used, but what the speaker means by it is not what the sentence means, at least not exactly. Examples (48) and (49) illustrate, respectively, what we will call *scope shifting* and *lexical omission*.

(48) Walter only watches the news.
(49) The Steelers don't look tired, they are tired.

Normally (48) is used to say that Walter watches only the news, but literally S says that Walter does nothing else but watch the news (or if "watches" is stressed, that Walter does nothing else with the news but watch it). Words like "only," "just," "also," and "even" exhibit scope shifting. In (49) it is literally denied that the Steelers look tired, but what a speaker of (49) means to say is that the Steelers don't *merely* look tired, they are tired. Other examples of lexical omission include "or" for "or else" and "and" for "and then." To think sentences like (48) and (49) mean what their users intend them to mean as well as what they literally mean but are not intended to mean is to multiply meanings beyond necessity.

Our general policy is not to take as a matter of meaning whatever can be construed as a matter of communicative intention or inference. Thus a locution that violates grammatical rules need not be regarded as grammatical just because it can be used with identifiable illocutionary intent. Similarly, we need not attribute additional meanings to sentences that are standardly used nonliterally, at least in ways like those involving scope shifting or lexical omission (obviously, we do not want to rule out sentential idioms like "That's water under the bridge"). We believe that the interests of theoretical simplicity are better served by dividing the labor between a narrowly conceived grammar of a language and a pragmatic account of the use of sentences and other locutions.[23] Although generalizations can undoubtedly be made about the various types of syntactic liberty (restrictions on scope shifting, for instance), we see no reason to regard them as facts about linguistic competence rather than as facts about standardized linguistic performance. We have said little about how these phenomena take place, that is, about how speakers and hearers produce and perceive locutions other than grammatical sentences (and grammatical sentences used other than in their strictly grammatical way) with identifiable illocutionary intents. Whatever the explanation ultimately looks like, it must account for the fact that people do say and do understand remarks like the following descriptions of automobile accidents by drivers:[24]

(50) a. The other man altered his mind, so I had to run over him.

b. A pedestrian hit me and went under the car.

c. I badly misjudged a woman crossing the street.

d. I blew my hooter (horn) but it would not work because it had been stolen.

e. Coming home I drove into the wrong house and collided with a tree that I haven't got.

f. I thought the side window was down but it was up . . . as I found when I put my head through it.

g. My car had to turn sharper than necessary owing to an invisible lorry.

Chapter Eleven

The Speech Act Schema and Psychology

In our introduction we mentioned a venerable conception of linguistic communication that dates back at least to John Locke. Linguistic communication is viewed as a process whereby a speaker encodes a message into a signal from which a hearer decodes the message. As far as it goes this picture is probably correct, but it idealizes linguistic communication in various important respects.[1] The utterance is taken to be unambiguous and no mechanisms for contextual (linguistic or nonlinguistic) disambiguation are required. The speaker is presumed to be speaking literally, not ironically or sarcastically, and so is taken to mean just what he says. The reference and force of the utterance are taken as uniquely determined by the meaning (or message). The speaker is assumed to be speaking directly and not indirectly. As part I showed, theoretical devices must be added to this idealized conception if we are to account for the full variety of linguistic communication represented in the SAS; when this is done the process will have the general structure represented in figure 11.1.

However, if construed as representing the actual process of linguistic communication, the model is seriously defective in failing to reflect the parallel or simultaneous nature of much of the information processing. Clearly, different levels of processing are going on simultaneously as we speak or hear a sentence from "left to right" (see Marslen-Wilson 1975). At the very least, while a hearer is determining the meaning and reference of some earlier part of an incoming sentence, he is also determining the syntax of some later part and the phonetics of some still later part. However, the model does depict the overall direction of information flow, and even though constituents of e may proceed through the steps at different times, we will use this diagram as a starting point for our investigation.

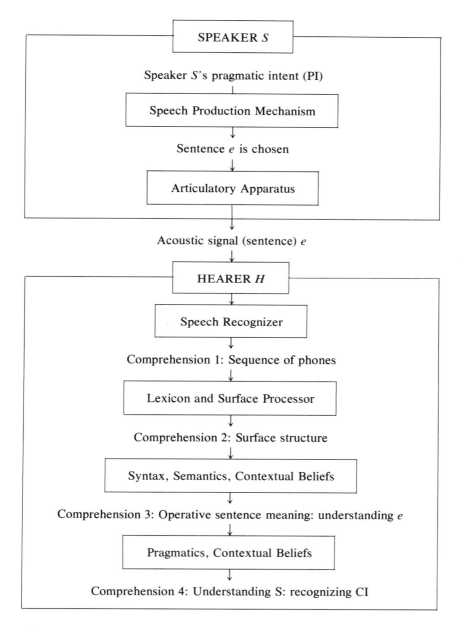

Figure 11.1 Some stages of information flow in linguistic communication

Semantic and pragmatic information enter at two prominent points: (a) at the beginning of the speech production phase, and (b) at the end of the speech comprehension phase. Although much more work has been done on comprehension than on production, some interesting preliminary findings about production are worth considering.

11.1. PRODUCTION

The most interesting proposal to date for a model of speech production comes, we feel, from the work of Fodor, Bever, and Garrett (1974) and Fodor (1975). Their proposal has three central features. First, speech production is taken to be a special case of considered action and as such falls under any plausible psychological model for considered action. It is proposed, second, that the best general model for considered action is decision-theoretic and, third, that the performance of such speech acts involves translating pragmatic intentions, formulated in a language of thought, into sound sequences.

Issues surrounding the existence and nature of a language of thought are highly controversial;[2] we will assume only that pragmatic intentions are formulated in *some* system of representation.[3] Given this assumption, we will consider the ideas that speech production is a species of *considered action* and that speech production (speech acts) involves a *translation* of a pragmatic intention into a signal.

Fodor, Bever, and Garrett (1974, 375) offer the following schematic model of relevant information processing underlying ideal[4] cases of speech production:

(1) A variety of candidate messages are formulated in mentalese . . . (2) The speaker attempts to predict the consequences of communicating one or another of the candidate messages . . . (3) The utility of bringing about these various [effects] is [calculated] and compared . . . (4) A best candidate is chosen. (5) [This message is translated into the] sentence which best expresses [it]. (6) The sentence is uttered.

This model is an idealization in two ways, according to Fodor, Bever, and Garrett. First, steps (2)–(4) are not always present in that we do not always consider the consequences of what we communicate nor do we consider a variety of possible messages. Second, we do not always choose the best way of saying something, so step (5) is not always present. However, we sometimes do consider how to phrase what we want to communicate, and there is no obvious reason why we should not take this process to be of the same kind as the process marked by steps (2)–(4). Thus step (5), when present, could have internal structure like the following:

(a) The message is translated into a variety of sentences.
(b) The consequences of uttering each of them are calculated and compared.
(c) The best sentence for achieving S's pragmatic intent is chosen.

Two serious idealizations still remain unnoted. One is that our pragmatic intention often comprises more/less than communicating some message to H. Sometimes we have perlocutionary intentions as well (see section 4.5), and sometimes we are intending to perform some conventional speech act (see chapter 6). In either case S's pragmatic intention will not be (just) to communicate some message in uttering the chosen sentence. When S does intend (just) to communicate some message, the relation between that communicative intent and the chosen sentence is rarely one of translation, even though from S's point of view disambiguation is not a problem: there is reference to be fixed and illocutionary force to be delimited (see chapter 2). The closest approximation to a translation of a given communicative intent would be an "eternal" sentence (see Quine 1960, sec. 40) containing an explicit performative prefix, and we rarely speak in this fashion. The relation between the communicative intent (the message) and the meaning of the chosen sentence is closer to compatibility (discussed in chapter 2) than to translation. For nonliteral illocutionary acts, clearly the relation between the communicative intent and the meaning of the sentence uttered will be less direct than with literal utterances. In short, if we are correct in part I, this schematic model of a speech producer will more and more approximate the outlines of the elaborated SAS presented in chapter 4, and so the speaker's pragmatic intention will, depending on the case, comprise various aspects of the SAS.

A second remaining idealization concerns the determination of the pragmatic intention (PI).[5] Since a speaker's PI can include a number of subintentions (in particular, intentions to perform utterance, locutionary, illocutionary, and perlocutionary acts), part of what goes into determining a speaker's PI will be such familiar things as mutual contextual beliefs, beliefs about H's beliefs, beliefs (and desires) about the social and physical context, and S's beliefs and desires concerning the nature and direction of the discourse. If these and the previous remarks are correct, our schematic speech production model should have the following minimal structure:[6]

Speech Production Model (SP):

1. Speaker S has a variety of beliefs and desires concerning such factors as:
   - (a) the nature and direction of the discourse,
   - (b) the social and physical context of the utterance,
   - (c) H's beliefs in general, H's beliefs pertinent to S's impending remark in particular, and whatever mutual contextual beliefs H shares with S.

2. On the basis of 1, S forms a variety of pragmatic intents $PI_1, \ldots, PI_n$, which may include subintentions:
   - (a) to utter something (utterance intent),
   - (b) to say something (locutionary intent), and so
   - (c) to refer to something (referential intent),
   - (d) to perform some illocutionary act(s) of a communicative or conventional sort (communicative intent, conventional intent),
   - (e) to perform these acts literally, nonliterally, directly, or indirectly,
   - (f) to have various effects on the hearer H (perlocutionary intent).

3. S attempts to predict the consequences of fulfilling these various intents.

4. The utility of each is assessed.

5. A particular pragmatic intent PI_i is formed.

6. A variety of expressions $e_1, \ldots, e_n$ are constructed, each compatible with PI_i.

7. S attempts to predict the consequences, for fulfilling S's pragmatic intent PI_i, of uttering each expression.

8. The expression e_i judged most likely to succeed in fulfilling PI_i is chosen.

9. Expression e_i is uttered.

We are not aware of any experimental work directly relevant to steps 1–5. However, there do seem to be data relevant to parts of steps 6–9.

First, the work of Tannenbaum and Williams (1968) and Osgood (1971) suggest that there are regular connections between the form of the chosen expression e_i and aspects of the speaker's pragmatic intent; thus it is pertinent to steps 7 and 8. Tannenbaum and Williams gave subjects a paragraph to read concerning some topic such as (1) trains, (2) cars, or (3) something else. The subjects were then given a picture of, for instance, a train hitting a car, with an A (for active) or a P (for passive) written in one corner. Subjects were then asked to produce the active sentence "The train is hitting the car" or the passive sentence

"The car is being hit by the train," depending on which letter occurred in the picture. The resulting latencies to completion had the structure:

A: (1) < (3) < (2)
P: (2) < (3) < (1)

If the topic of the paragraph was referred to by a certain NP, subjects were best able to continue mentioning that topic with sentences having that NP in surface subject position, even if a passive sentence (which is longer) was required to get it there. Osgood (1971) illustrated a similar tendency among subjects asked to describe a short skit in simple sentences. As an object became the focus of attention, NPs referring to that object tended to occur in surface subject position.[7]

Second, there is a body of data relevant to aspects of the process underlying step 6. If the view of linguistic communication embodied in the SAS is right, knowledge of the language plays a major role in enabling H to recognize S's communicative intention. Fodor (1975, 106) proposes that this knowledge be explicated in terms of shared linguistic conventions:

One might think of the conventions of the language as a sort of cookbook which tells us, for any C that can be communicated by an expression of the language, "if you want to communicate C, produce an utterance (or inscription) which satisfies the descriptions $D_1, D_2, \ldots D_n$" where specimens Ds might be syntactic, morphological, and phonological representations of the utterance. The converse remarks hold for the hearer: To know the conventions of a language is at least to know that an utterance which satisfies $D_1, D_2, \ldots D_n$ also standardly satisfies the description "produced with the intention to communicate C."

This suggests (Fodor 1975, 109) that it is with these descriptions $D_1, \ldots D_n$ that contact is made with a grammar of the language:

A generative grammar of L specifies (some or all of) the descriptions that a token must satisfy if it is to conform to the linguistic conventions of L. To put the same point slightly differently, it specifies, for each M, the descriptions (morphological, phonological, syntactic, etc.) that a token must satisfy if it is to belong to that sentence type which expresses M in L.

Given that messages (contents of a communicative intention) are rarely identical to the meaning of the sentence uttered, is there evidence that any of the linguistic levels between message and signal (semantic representation, deep structure, surface structure) are or are not computed

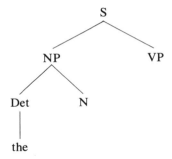

Figure 11.2 A partially developed clause, constructed top to bottom and left to right

during the process of speech production, and if they are, what might the nature of the operations underlying their computation be? According to Fodor, Bever, and Garrett (1974, 434) there are considerable data in favor of the view that surface structures are one such level and that the process of constructing a surface phrase marker is from top to bottom, left to right, and clause by clause, thus yielding structures in memory having the form of the tree in figure 11.2.[8] Though these results are psychologically interesting in their own right, they shed little light on the semantic and pragmatic aspects of speech production. As Fodor, Bever, and Garrett (p. 397) remark, "Both the conceptual and empirical issues in the most interesting areas of the production problem are largely unsolved." The picture does not change much in a recent survey by Clark and Clark (1977, 248): "It is fairly clear what considerations speakers must pay attention to, but it is far from clear what mental processes are involved or how the final decision is arrived at. The study of sentence planning has barely begun." Since it is the semantic and pragmatic aspects of speech we are primarily interested in, we turn to the body of literature surrounding speech perception and comprehension, where there seem to be fewer methodological problems and firmer results.[9]

11.2. COMPREHENSION

Speech comprehension can be divided into four steps, as represented in figure 11.1. Phonological ability and lexical knowledge take the hearer from step 1 to step 2, and semantics (along with syntax and contextual beliefs) mediates steps 2 and 3. We will focus on steps 3 and 4, which are mediated by knowledge of language use in conjunction with beliefs about context. In order to understand this stage, it is useful to break steps 3 and 4 down into several substeps.

To reach step 3, H must settle on the operative reading of the expression; to do this he must first assign the right syntactic description, then assign the right meanings to the lexical items, and finally assign the right meaning to the sentence. Given that the syntactic aspects of the processor can assign enough of a syntactic description to get the rest going, the process of speech comprehension then resolves into two major subproblems. We call this the *operative meaning* stage of comprehension:

3. *Operative meaning stage:*
   (a) Determine the operative lexical reading(s) of expression e.
   (b) Determine the operative sentential meaning(s) of expression e.

In order to reach step 4, H must infer the speaker's communicative intention, *CI*. This process resolves into two stages, the *propositional content* stage and the *illocutionary force* stage, each comprising major subproblems:

4. *Propositional content stage:*
   (a) Determine the intended referents.
   (b) Determine the propositional content.

   Illocutionary force stage:
   (c) Determine what direct (literal or nonliteral) illocutionary intention S had in uttering e.
   (d) Determine what indirect illocutionary intention S had in uttering e.
   (e) Determine S's communicative intention, CI, on the basis of 4(c) and 4(d).

A hearer who manages to get from 3(a) to 4(e) has in effect completed his side of the process of linguistic communication. To better understand this process we examine the psychological details of these stages.

Since we process a sentence in real time from "left to right" (speaking metaphorically, as if of written English), and since we start processing almost immediately, it is probable that we process almost all of this information in parallel. That is, syntactic analysis may be influenced by semantic analysis and semantic analysis by pragmatic analysis—which may in turn be influenced by prior syntactic analysis. So we should not view these steps as strictly ordered, either for the sentence as a whole or for its constituents. Rather, the ordering reflects general information flow and the necessity of discussing components one at a time.

11.2.1. Operative Meaning Stage

Step 3(a) involves determining the intended readings of the minimal functioning constituents of the expression. Step 3(b) involves integrating these into a reading for the whole sentence and determining its intended reading. Clearly this is, in real time, a highly interactive parallel process, from which these steps are an abstraction. Another dimension of abstraction is away from syntax. Semantic processing can serve to assist in syntactic processing and vice versa. Nevertheless, in discussing the lexical level we will try to discuss problems in the semantic representation of lexical items independently of syntactic details other than clause boundaries.

Let us assume that words are the minimal semantic units involved in speech comprehension. Then the hearer goes through two substages: he must represent the potential meanings of each word and determine its operative meaning.

Lexical Representation during Comprehension
We said in section 8.1 that there were some considerations in favor of replacing lexical definitions with inference rules in an empirically adequate semantics. We left aside the question of whether such definitional processes were part of the comprehension process. We now turn to some of the relevant psychological data.

Fodor, Fodor, and Garrett (1975) present both intuitive and experimental evidence against the hypothesis that lexical decomposition is usually involved in comprehension. On the intuitive side, the hypothesis predicts that the more elaborate the definition, other things being equal, the more complex and difficult the comprehension process should be. In particular, when the definition of one word is a proper part of the definition of another word, there should be asymmetry in the difficulty of comprehending them. Yet pairs like the following do not seem to exhibit noticeable asymmetries:[10]

(1) a. x is unmarried: x is a bachelor
   b. x chases y: x catches y

On the experimental side, Fodor, Fodor, and Garrett report an experiment in which subjects were required to evaluate the validity of different arguments such as:

(2) a. If practically all of the men in the room are *not married,* then few of the men in the room have wives.
b. If practically all of the men in the room are *bachelors,* then few of the men in the room have wives.

Each of the arguments contained either a quantifier ("all," "few") or an explicitly negative (free) morpheme ("not") together with one of the following sorts of negative elements: (EN) another explicitly negative free morpheme; (MN) a morphological negative, "in-," "un-," "im-"; (IN) an implicitly negative morpheme, "doubt," "deny"; or (PDN) a pure definitional negative, "bachelor," "kill." The importance of PDNs is that they contain negation at the semantic level but have no syntactic reflexes of negation. If semantic representations are decompositional and computed during comprehension, there should be no significant difference between the reaction times to a correct evaluation of arguments containing PDNs, such as (2b), and times for the evaluation of the others, such as (2a). Since it is fairly well established that when negatives interact with quantifiers or other negatives, latencies are lengthened, this experiment can be seen as testing for the presence of a negative element in the comprehension of a word like "bachelor."

According to Fodor, Fodor, and Garrett, arguments containing PDNs (2b) were significantly easier than paired arguments with ENs (2a). In addition, the difference in reaction times between ENs and PDNs was significantly greater than the difference in times between either ENs and MNs or ENs and INs (though figures were not given). That is, EN $-$ PDN $>$ EN $-$ MN, and EN $-$ PDN $>$ EN $-$ IN. Fodor, Fodor, and Garrett conclude: "We take this result to suggest strongly that PDNs do not act as though they contain a negative element in their linguistic representation; and therefore, that PDNs are not semantically analyzed at any level of linguistic representation" (p. 522).

This experiment is hard to evaluate in the absence of more details (see Katz 1977b), but two considerations would have to be ruled out before we could accept it as a strong case. First, it was also found that subjects performed the same for MNs and INs, and this might argue for decomposition of these items.[11] Second, a decompositionalist might claim that the results show only that decomposition during comprehen-

Figure 11.3 Two-stage model of sentence comprehension

sion did not reach negation. For example, the relevant decomposition of "bachelor" might simply be (Def) bachelor: ADULT & MALE & SINGLE. If such a theory were supplemented by the inference rule SINGLE → NOT-MARRIED, which was optional in the process of comprehension, then the experiment would prove nothing.[12]

Another consideration Fodor, Fodor, and Garrett cite in favor of inference rules over lexical decomposition is comprehension time (p. 526). If words like "bachelor" and "kill" are not decomposed during the process of understanding, then "bachelor" is the minimal meaning-contributing (or meaning-representing) unit—or its translation in the comprehension language is (see Fodor 1975, 150–152). In that case the vocabulary of the representation would approximate that of the language itself. This means that comprehension could, semantically speaking, be direct and quick since the process of drawing inferences could be separated out as a distinct stage (see figure 11.3). As Fodor (1975, 151) comments, "the operations of the sentence understander are on-line operations. We understand an utterance when we hear it. But the operations of the logic may take any amount of time at all." Is quickness a virtue? Marslen-Wilson (1973) reports the results of an experiment involving the restoration of disrupted words during a sentence shadowing task. In the course of arguing for a parallel processor with high interaction between phonological, morphological, syntactic, and semantic information processing, Marslen-Wilson notes that good shadowers working at 250 msec can be seen to be affected by semantic information; indeed, at a shadowing latency of 250 msec, they began to repeat the target-words when only the first syllable could have been heard.

The model diagrammed in figure 11.3 suggests that sentences receive a quick semantic representation, that quickness here is a virtue. But then we must ask what exactly *are* these semantic representations (or formulas in mentalese) if understanding "bachelor" need not involve inferring that the referent is male or adult or unmarried? What does understanding "bachelor" amount to if it has nothing to do with these other notions? Perhaps one could say that the semantic representation does no more than represent the property of being a bachelor and that what constitutes that property is inferred. Then, of course, we need an account of *properties* as well as an account of *representation* which explains understanding, and we are a long way from this (but see Field 1978).

Ambiguity

On hearing an expression, sometimes we are aware that it is ambiguous—we may even have each meaning in mind. At other times we are not aware of the ambiguity; either we do not know one of the meanings or one of them fails to come to mind. An adequate theory of comprehension must account for both kinds of cases.

A variety of psychological work has been done on three sources of ambiguity:

Lexical: I found a bat.
Surface structure: It was in a little bat house.
Underlying structure: He had the bat stolen.

There is some evidence (see MacKay and Bever 1967; MacKay 1966) that when ambiguity is perceived, lexical ambiguity is perceived quickest, then surface ambiguity, and finally underlying ambiguity. In MacKay (1966) subjects were visually given sentence fragments containing these types of ambiguity, separately and jointly, and asked to complete the sentences by saying the entire sentence out loud. The time for completion was recorded and the subjects were asked whether they had noticed the ambiguity. If they had, their responses were put aside. The results are as indicated in figures 11.4 and 11.5. Clearly something different is going on in each of these cases. MacKay (1973) has suggested that lexical and surface ambiguities are processed (by some finite state device) in short-term memory, but that underlying ambiguities must await transfer to long-term memory before they can be processed. However, this division (apparently) conflicts with the presently most plausible account of disambiguation, the *clausal-closure* theory discussed in the next section. On that theory, clauses are processed in short-term memory, then recoded for long-term memory. But this computation in short-term memory requires deep structure projections, and so does processing transformational information. If both theories were correct, there would, contrary to fact, be no such thing as underlying ambiguity, since by MacKay's account such computation must await long-term transfer whereas by the clausal-closure theory

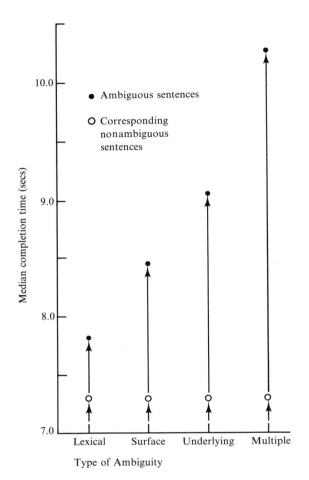

Figure 11.4 The median completion time for multiple ambiguous sentence fragments for the three types of ambiguous sentence fragments and for their corresponding nonambiguous fragments. (From MacKay 1966)

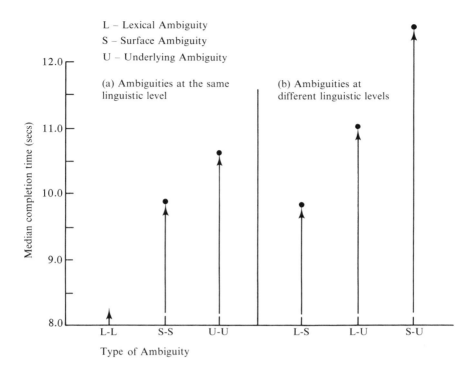

Figure 11.5 The median completion time for the six types of multiple ambiguous sentence fragments, with ambiguities at (a) the same linguistic level and at (b) different linguistic levels. (From MacKay 1966)

what goes to long-term memory has been unambiguously recoded. It is not clear at present how to reconcile the findings supporting each of these theories, but the evidence supporting MacKay's account is sometimes weak.[13]

Disambiguation
What goes on when we hear an ambiguous expression which, though we know on reflection to be ambiguous, we do not at the time perceive to be ambiguous? And, what happens when we perceive an ambiguity but immediately pick one meaning as the operative intended one? Is the former process like the latter, only unconscious?

One of the more promising hypotheses concerning the general constraints on disambiguation (Garrett 1970; Lackner and Garrett 1973; Bever, Garrett, and Hurtig 1973) postulates three information processing stages:

Clausal-closure Hypothesis:

Stage 1: *H* computes clause-internal ambiguities.

Stage 2: At the end of a clause, *H* picks one meaning for the whole clause and continues.

Stage 3: If that meaning turns out to be inappropriate, *H* goes back to stages 1 and 2.

There is evidence for each of these stages.

Stage 1. In a dichotic listening task Lackner and Garrett (1973) presented subjects with an ambiguous sentence such as (3) in one ear.

(3) The spy put out the torch as our signal to attack.

To the subject's other ear they presented (at a 5- to 10-db lower intensity level) either a *neutral* context sentence or a disambiguating (or *biasing*) context sentence such as (4).

(4) The spy extinguished the torch in the window.

Subjects were instructed to attend to what they heard in the ear presented with the ambiguous sentence and to begin paraphrasing it before the sentence ended. Even though after the experiment subjects could not give any information about the material in the unattended ear, Lackner and Garrett found (pp. 365–366) that the unattended biasing sentences significantly affected the choice of paraphrase. They argue from their data (p. 370) that some linguistic analysis of the unattended sentence is taking place, since occasionally the biasing sentence, to exert its effect, had to be analyzed beyond the lexical level to the phrase level, as in the following examples:

(5) The sailors liked the port at night. (ambiguous)
(6) The sailors liked to be in port at night. (biasing)
(7) Visiting relatives can be a bore. (ambiguous)
(8) I hate relatives who visit often. (biasing)

They conclude that while a subject is listening to an ambiguous sentence and determining its meaning "both readings are in some sense available to him. If this were not the case, it would have been impossible to bias the interpretation of the ambiguous sentence" (p. 367). Although this may be true, the occurrence of any of several different processes is compatible with their claim. As they note (p. 361), the subject can compute all the options for the sentence when an ambiguity is encountered or he can postpone assignment until context can be used to determine the appropriate reading. Lackner and Garrett (p. 371) prefer the multiple ambiguity hypothesis because it can explain the effect of context on disambiguation and because a parallel processing strategy can help explain why there should be differences in processing difficulty between ambiguous and unambiguous sentences. Probably most would agree that these are not overwhelming considerations in favor of parallel processing of ambiguities, but in the absence of a clear alternative, it should be given the nod (see also Holmes, Arwas, and Garrett 1977).

Stage 2. Evidence in favor of stage 2 comes from Bever, Garrett, and Hurtig (1973). On their view the clause is a primary perceptual unit whose elements perceptual operations map directly onto underlying structures. When a clause boundary is reached, its contents are re-coded in a fairly abstract form, outside of immediate memory, leaving immediate storage free for the next clause. Ambiguities are computed during the projection onto underlying structures, but at the point of clausal recoding, one projection is selected and the rest are dropped. Bever, Garrett, and Hurtig have various kinds of support for this the-ory. One kind of support arises from a reanalysis of the data in MacKay (1966). In this reanalysis they grouped MacKay's sentences into two classes: those, like (9), that could be complete clauses at the underlying levels and those, like (10), that could not be:

(9) Although I knew the new position had advantages . . .

(10) After her injury that summer she couldn't bear . . .

MacKay's data showed no effects of ambiguity for sentences of the first type, but effects were found in sentences of the second type. On Bever, Garrett, and Hurtig's theory these results follow from the fact that just before a clause boundary is the time of maximum processing load and hence of the potential effects of such a load, whereas after a clause boundary one reading has been selected and there is little processing effect.

To test this idea further Bever, Garrett, and Hurtig (1973, experiment 2) had subjects complete ambiguous incomplete sentences such as the following. Notice that some of the incomplete sentences had complete internal clauses and others did not.

(11) a. After taking the right turn at the
     b. After taking the right turn at the intersection
     c. After taking the right turn at the intersection I

d. After taking the left turn at the
e. After taking the left turn at the intersection
f. After taking the left turn at the intersection I

Clearly the effects of ambiguity on the second class (those with incomplete internal clauses) should have been considerably greater than
on the first. The results are curious in that only effects of underlying
ambiguity were significant, so the theory is supported only to that
extent. Bever, Garrett, and Hurtig propose that the classification of
ambiguities usually given is not based on the perceptually most salient
characteristics. Perhaps ambiguities should be classified in terms of the
perceptual independence of the operations recovering underlying relations. They suggest that "it is the perceptual independence of interpretations that governs behavioral differences in response to ambiguities"
(p. 285). If the operations required at a given level are quite different
from one another, computational difficulty goes up before clause
boundaries.

Support for this idea, as well as further support for stages 1 and 2,
comes from another experiment (experiment 1) reported by Bever,
Garrett, and Hurtig (1973), in which they presented subjects with sentences (both ambiguous and nonambiguous) such as the following:

(12) a. Be sure that you take the right turn. (lexical ambiguity)
     b. Be sure that you take the left turn.
     c. Be sure that you take the correct turn.
(13) a. The paper presented carefully limited analyses of the problem.
        (surface ambiguity)
     b. The paper presented today limited analyses of the problem.
     c. The paper presented very limited analyses of the problem.
(14) a. The shooting of the Indians bothered the agent. (underlying
        ambiguity)
     b. The shooting from the Indians bothered the agent.
     c. The shooting at the Indians bothered the agent.

The subjects were instructed to interpret each sentence and then add
another sentence to complete the story. The results are indicated in
table 11.1. The figures on the last line are particularly interesting in that
they show subjects responding faster to ambiguous sentences than to
nonambiguous sentences, and in the case of underlying ambiguity the
difference was significant. That there should be no significant increase
in completion time is predicted by the clause-boundary hypothesis,

Table 11.1
Time (seconds) to start the responses to ambiguous and unambiguous sentences in experiment 1

| | Type of Ambiguity | | |
	Lexical	Surface Structure	Underlying Structure
Ambiguous sentences	5.28	9.03	8.83
Corresponding unambiguous sentences	4.93	9.40	9.72
Mean difference of responses (ambiguous − unambiguous)	+0.35	−0.27	−0.89
Percentage of Ss responding faster to ambiguous versions	34%	56%	82%

Source: Bever, Garrett, and Hurtig 1973.

since subjects were instructed to wait until they had interpreted the sentence before continuing. But the finding that underlying ambiguities facilitated completion was unexpected. On the theory that all ambiguities are simultaneously but independently computed up to clause boundaries, since either interpretation of each sentence was acceptable in the experiment, the chances of computing an interpretation faster are actually increased by having more available readings, not decreased.[14] This is on the assumption (p. 280) that once a reading is consciously perceived, further processing on that sentence stops. How can these effects be reconciled with the facts recorded earlier from MacKay (1966) indicating that underlying ambiguity had a retarding effect on completion times? Again the idea of classifying ambiguities by perceptual differences is useful. Suppose we give sentences (12)–(13) Bever, Garrett, and Hurtig's fairly standard transformational analyses as indicated in figures 11.6 to 11.11. One can see that the lexically ambiguous sentences have identical underlying structures, and the superficially ambiguous sentences have underlying structures with "a minor difference, characteristically in placement of a modifier" (p. 282). However, for the sentences involving underlying ambiguity, the deep structures differ in important underlying relations such as subject and object, and the ambiguities cannot be resolved by surface bracketing. In the case of lexical ambiguity (12a) the perceptual operations used to compute the readings are virtually identical, in the surface ambiguity case (13a) they are very similar, but in the deep structure cases (14a) they are quite distinct. Thus the theory predicts that the last case will exhibit more

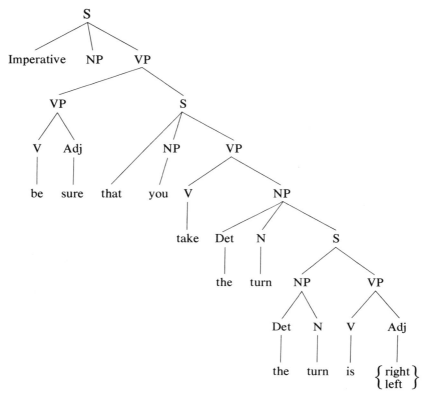

Figure 11.6 Structure underlying (12b) and one reading of (12a)

interference characteristics when tested before a clause boundary, and that is what was found. (See Bever, Garrett, and Hurtig 1976, 219–220, for further discussion.)

A question left unsettled (Bever, Garrett, and Hurtig 1973, 285) is whether the operative notion of a clause should be that of a surface or underlying clause. Intuitively, one would think that surface structure clause is the relevant notion. One reason is that it may be necessary to recover more than one underlying clause to interpret a surface clause, and if short-term memory were emptied at the first deep clause, ambiguity at the underlying level could not be perceived. Since such ambiguity is perceived, the surface clause must be the relevant notion of a clause, though an exact definition of this notion is far from clear.[15] As Carroll (1978, 506) remarks, "In sum, the identity of those sentence perception units remains elusive."

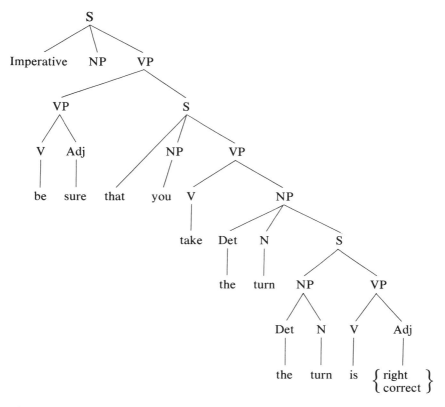

Figure 11.7 Structure underlying (12c) and one reading of (12a)

Stage 3. Evidence for stage 3 of the clausal-closure hypothesis comes from data in both the previous experiments and new ones, as well as from introspection. We have all had the experience of taking one clause in a sentence one way only to encounter a word that forced us to reinterpret the sentence from the beginning. This suggests that we have retained only one reading R1 and must compute the alternative reading R2 the second time around. The problem is to devise a test situation that will distinguish *computing* R2 then and there from *retrieving* R2 from temporary store. It is not clear to us that either the study by Foss, Bever, and Silver (1968) or that by Carey, Mehler, and Bever (1970), which are usually cited as supporting the single-reading theory, actually do distinguish these two possibilities. More recent work supporting a single-reading theory also has problems. For instance, Schvaneveldt, Meyer, and Becker (1976) used a word/nonword sorting task to support

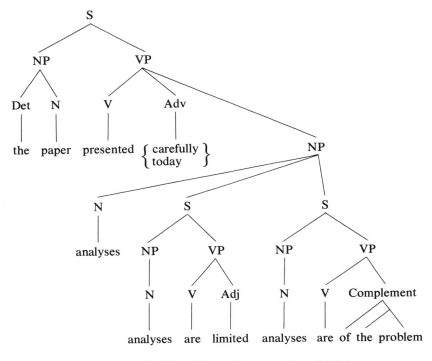

Figure 11.8 Structure underlying (13b) and one reading of (13a)

a single-reading theory, but they did not control for word and meaning frequencies. Tyler and Marslen-Wilson (1977) argue for a single-reading account as well but fail to control for syntactic cues to disambiguation.

We have not yet said anything about exactly how one reading for an ambiguous sentence is, in fact, computed and selected. This problem arises at the end of each clause, and at the end of sentence. At both points factors relating to the plausibility of an interpretation, including its coherence with antecedent and expected events, seem to play a role. To determine experimentally how this works would involve testing for how beliefs, and especially mutual contextual beliefs, affect the computation and selection of alternative readings, and how these beliefs interact with various syntactic strategies (see Fodor, Bever, and Garrett 1974, 328–372). Recent work by Oden and others (see Oden 1978; Oden and Spira 1978) can be brought to bear on the problem, at least as regards literal and direct utterances. They have collected experimental evidence supporting the idea that a semantic processor builds tentative

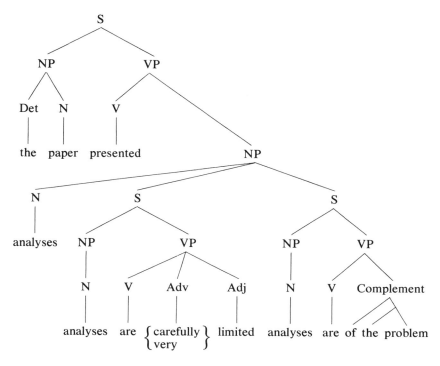

Figure 11.9 Structure underlying (13c) and one reading of (13a)

semantic structures in the course of language processing and applies certain relevant semantic constraints to each of these structures to determine their relative plausibility. This building and evaluation of candidate semantic structures is to take place in parallel for all possible interpretations, just as proposed by the clausal-closure theory. However, Oden's system includes two mechanisms that use "degree-of-sensibleness" information to rule out interpretations, making it unnecessary to process all of them completely:

The first mechanism, absolute judgment, rejects a candidate interpretation whenever its sensibleness value falls below some cut off point . . . the second mechanism, relative judgment, eliminates all but the most sensible interpretation, but only after enough processing has been performed (e.g. at the end of a clause) so that the system has an accurate assessment of the relative sensibleness of the interpretations. (Oden 1978, 35–36)

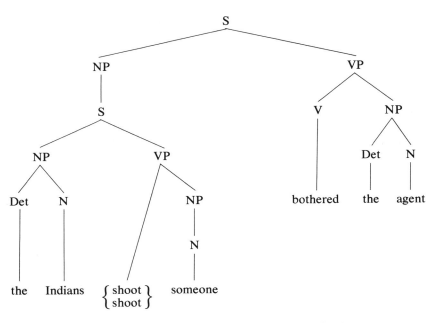

Figure 11.10 Structure underlying (14b) and one reading of (14a)

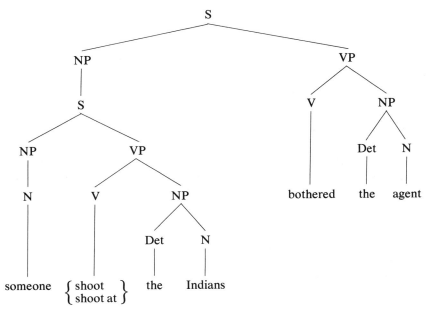

Figure 11.11 Structure underlying (14c) and one reading of (14a)

For us the main support for stage 3 comes from the results in Bever, Garrett, and Hurtig (1973, experiment 2) which results support the clausal hypothesis. Insofar as this model has empirical support, so does our account of the steps from L1 to L2 of the SAS (see section 2.2), whereby the hearer considers the various meanings of the sentence uttered and then rejects all but one as contextually inappropriate.

11.2.2. Propositional Content Stage

Disambiguation takes the hearer only part way to understanding what is said. In addition, he must identify the speaker's referential intents. As Fodor, Bever, and Garrett (1974, 142–170) illustrate, only recently have psychologists given up the idea that all reference involves just resemblance or causation between referent and symbol, and seriously considered the view that reference is in part a relationship involving linguistic rules and conventions. As a result there is virtually no work to report on the psychological reality of the inferences underlying the referential portion of the schema.

In chapter 8 we contrasted what is said with what is implied, entailed, or presupposed. Psychologists have attempted in various ways to test for psychological effects of these different factors. In particular, evidence has accumulated suggesting that some cases of pragmatic presupposition are treated distinctly during comprehension and should be distinguished, psychologically, from entailments. Since we construe pragmatic presupposition in terms of what S presumes H to be aware of, we should examine the work on *new* and *given* information.

According to Clark and Haviland (1974, 1977), upon hearing a sentence like "Was it Margaret that Paul married?" where the given (presumed) information is that Paul married someone, H follows these steps:

Given-New strategy:
GN1. Divide the sentence into presumed and new information.
GN2. Match the presumed information in memory.
GN3. Integrate the new information with material now in memory.

If this is a comprehension strategy, difficulties or complications at any stage should increase appropriate measures of difficulty. Studies have used a variety of linguistic devices including the definite article, personal pronouns, Wh questions, repeating adverbs ("again"), relative clauses, and implicative verbs ("remember"). All tend to support the conclusion that steps GN1 to GN3 are being followed during comprehension.

Haviland and Clark (1974) report a sequence of experiments designed, in part, to provide evidence for step GN2 of the strategy. In experiment 3, subjects were given sentences like (15)–(17):

(15) a. Last Christmas Eugene became absolutely smashed.
     b. This Christmas he got very drunk again.
(16) a. Last Christmas Eugene went to a lot of parties.
     b. This Christmas he got very drunk again.
(17) a. Last Christmas Eugene couldn't stay sober.
     b. This Christmas he got very drunk again.

In example (15) the context sentence (15a) provides an appropriate antecedent for "again" in the second sentence (15b), and the match at step GN2 should be quite direct. In example (16) the context sentence (16a) provides only the basis for an *inference* to an appropriate match, so step GN2 would be less directly or immediately effected. In (17) the context sentence specifies the appropriate condition *negatively;* an inference involving negation is required and thus is also less direct than (15). Subjects were timed from the beginning of reading the second sentence to its being understood; mean latencies are reported in table 11.2. They confirm the plausibility of step GN2 of the strategy.

We mentioned in section 8.4 that some conversational implicatures, unlike most, do not involve flouting a maxim and that H makes an inference on the assumption that S *is obeying* the conversational presumptions. It is plausible that step GN2 summarizes the mechanisms underlying such an inference. Thus, in example (16), in order to maintain the presumption of relevance and apply step GN2, H must infer that Eugene got drunk at a party last Christmas. In this case H applied procedures of inductive inference; in other cases, he might use deductive inference or even have to restructure the utterance itself (see Clark and Haviland 1977, 8).

Further evidence for such inferences comes from Brewer (1977). In this study subjects heard a sentence such as "The safecracker put a match to the fuse" and were given a cued recall test for these and associated implications. Typically, more subjects recalled the pragmatic implication of the sentence ("The safecracker lit the fuse") than the original sentence itself.

In another experiment Just and Clark (1973) investigated pairs like (18) and (19).

Table 11.2
Mean comprehension time (in milliseconds) for target sentences in direct, indirect, and negative antecedent pairs

Antecedent	Adverbs				
	still	either	again	too	means
Direct	1031	1102	984	976	1023
Indirect	1058	1244	1040	1047	1097
Negative	1076	1141	1063	1065	1088

Source: Haviland and Clark 1974.

Table 11.3
Problems and their mean latencies (in milliseconds) for experiment 1

Premise and Question	Component Interrogated	Mean Latency
John remembered to let the dog out.		
Where is the dog?	Implication	1795
Where is the dog supposed to be?	Presupposition	1939
John forgot to let the dog out.		
Where is the dog?	Implication	2199
Where is the dog supposed to be?	Presupposition	2410
It was thoughtful of John to let the dog out.		
Where is the dog?	Presupposition	2015
Where is the dog supposed to be?	Implication	2158
It was thoughtless of John to let the dog out.		
Where is the dog?	Presupposition	2441
Where is the dog supposed to be?	Implication	2426

Source: Just and Clark 1973.

(18) a. John remembered to let the dog out.

    b. John forgot to let the dog out.

(19) a. It was thoughtful of John to let the dog out.

    b. It was thoughtless of John to let the dog out.

In each pair the two sentences have the same (pragmatic) presupposition but opposite entailments. For example, both (18a) and (18b) presuppose that the dog should be let out, but (18b) entails that it was not. Just and Clark presented subjects with premise and question sets as in table 11.3, and obtained the indicated latencies. Although "forget" sentences take 438 msec longer than "remember" sentences, there was no significant interaction effect by questions (1973, 24). The implications of "forget" and "thoughtless" did not take relatively longer to answer than the questions interrogating the positive components. Just and Clark concluded that subjects do not make use of presuppositions and entailments independently of each other.

In experiment 2, Just and Clark attempted to test the hypothesis (the *ordered model*) that subjects look for answers to questions first in the entailments of a sentence and then in the presupposition. Subjects were given premise-conclusion pairs ("If John remembered to let the dog out, then the dog is out") drawn from table 11.4, and asked to judge them true or false. The latencies obtained are indicated in the table. Assuming standard results on verification of positive and negative sentences, Just and Clark conclude that table 11.4 (and table 11.3 as well) provide support for the ordered-model hypothesis.

If that hypothesis is correct, we might ask how it fits into the three steps of the given-new strategy. In that process, presumed material was matched and stored first and then entailments were processed; whereas in the ordered model, entailments are processed first, then presuppositions. Is there an ordering paradox here? Not if one assumes that the ordered model is in fact an elaboration beyond step GN3 of the given-new strategy. That is, we should continue the strategy in such a way that when further access to the presumptions or implications of the sentence is required, there is a step-wise procedure for carrying this out:

Given-New strategy continued:
GN4. Search new information for an answer to a question.
GN5. If GN4 fails to be satisfactory, search the presumed information.

Additional evidence for inferential operations underlying communication at this level comes from the studies of Harris (1974), Singer (1976), and Harris and Monaco (1978), though we will not review their results. We conclude that insofar as such processing operations have psychological support, the sorts of inferences leading to L3 of the SAS can be ruled plausible.

11.2.3. Illocutionary Force Stage

We turn now to the later stages of the comprehension process—identifying the speaker's illocutionary intent. For us the obvious initial hypothesis concerning what underlies this identification is provided by the information flow contained in the SAS, which can be summarized as:

Table 11.4
Problems and their mean latencies (in milliseconds) for experiment 2

Premise and Conclusions	Component Interrogated	Mean Latency
John remembered to let the dog out.		
The dog is out. [true]	Implication	2814
The dog is in. [false]	Implication	3252
The dog is supposed to be out. [true]	Presupposition	3564
The dog is supposed to be in. [false]	Presupposition	4100
John forgot to let the dog out.		
The dog is in. [true]	Implication	3670
The dog is out. [false]	Implication	3536
The dog is supposed to be out. [true]	Presupposition	4183
The dog is supposed to be in. [false]	Presupposition	4664
It was thoughtful of John to let the dog out.		
The dog is out. [true]	Presupposition	3647
The dog is in. [false]	Presupposition	3964
The dog is supposed to be out. [true]	Implication	4162
The dog is supposed to be in. [false]	Implication	4539
It was thoughtless of John to let the dog out.		
The dog is out. [true]	Presupposition	3939
The dog is in. [false]	Presupposition	4527
The dog is supposed to be in. [true]	Implication	4657
The dog is supposed to be out. [false]	Implication	4673

Source: Just and Clark 1973.

4. c. *Direct act:* Determine the literal meaning of *e* and then the literal illocutionary act being performed, if any. If no literal act is being performed, determine the nonliteral act being performed.

   d. *Indirect act:* If *S* is not just performing a direct act (literal or nonliteral), determine what indirect act is being performed as well.

   e. *Communicative intent:* On the basis of 4(c) and 4(d) determine *S*'s communicative intent.

If this represents a psychologically real process, one can expect that (i) *H* computes the literal meaning first and (ii) if *H* infers a nonliteral or indirect intent, reaching that conclusion should take longer than computing the literal meaning.

There is some evidence for inferences underlying the identification of the direct force of an utterance, or at least its immediate storage in memory. For instance Schweller, Brewer, and Dahl (1976) report the results of two experiments on illocutionary force. In experiment 1, subjects heard sentence triples such as the following:

(20) a. *Implicit:* The weatherman told the people about the approaching tornado.

b. *Control:* The weatherman told the people about the approaching warm weekend.

c. *Explicit:* The weatherman warned the people about the approaching tornado.

Given the evidence that pragmatic implications and assertions can be conflated in memory, it was predicted that there would be a shift in recall of the (a) sentences in the direction of the explicit (c) sentences, but no such shift for the (b) sentences. The results (1976, 329) substantiate the prediction with a 35 percent shift for the first type of sentence and a 2 percent shift for the second type. Since inferences underlie the pragmatic implications on which the prediction is based, we may tentatively conclude that inferences underlie these misidentifications of illocutionary force on recall, and so are available to play a role in comprehension. For more direct evidence we must look at nonliteral and indirect acts.

An experiment by Brewer, Harris, and Brewer suggests that predictions (i) and (ii) are correct for *nonliteral* utterances. In their experiment subjects were given pairs of sentences from proverb sets such as:

Original Proverb: It's a silly fish that is caught twice with the same bait.

Literal-Same paraphrase: Only a foolish fish is captured more than once on the same hook.

Figurative-Same paraphrase: Only a fool does not learn from experience.

Literal-Different paraphrase: A wise fish and a foolish fish, both caught, are equally dead.

Figurative-Different paraphrase: Wise men as much as fools do not learn from experience.

The reasoning was that if a hearer heard a literal paraphrase-plus-proverb sequence then there should be little discernible difference between this order and the reverse order of proverb-plus-literal paraphrase. However, for the figurative paraphrase-plus-proverb the hearer will first have to calculate the literal meaning of the proverb and then its figurative meaning before being able to match it with its correct paraphrase. This extra step should consume extra time, so there should be, and was, a significant interaction between order of proverb presentation and (speed of) recognition of literal versus figurative paraphrase. The authors concluded that the processing of literal and figurative meaning occurs in two stages and that the comprehension of the literal meaning precedes the comprehension of the figurative meaning.

Because only proverbs unfamiliar to the subjects were used, we interpret the experiment as providing evidence for the psychological reality of the presumption of literalness (PL). In effect, subjects were first reacting to the proverbs as if they were literal, then processing them figuratively when the task demanded it. Under the circumstances that means that they were presuming that the sentence should be taken literally until the task proved that assumption wrong, and this is tantamount to conforming to PL. It might be interesting to compare these results with similar tests involving familiar proverbs, which would probably override the PL and so not add significantly to response times.

Clark and Lucy (1975), using the familiar three-feature pattern for negative and positive sentences, found that at least sometimes predictions (i) and (ii) are true for *indirect* acts as well. The three characteristics of this pattern are that, other things being equal, (1) positives are judged true faster than false, (2) negatives are judged false faster than true, and (3) positives are easier to process, overall, than negatives. Subjects were presented with displays consisting of a sentence like (21a) or (21b) followed by a circle colored either pink or blue (sentence pairs used are listed in table 11.5).

(21) a. Please color the circle blue. (positive indirect force)
     b. Please don't color the circle blue. (negative indirect force)

Subjects were to respond "yes" (true) or "no" (false) by pushing an appropriate button, on condition that the displayed circle fulfilled the directive conveyed by the sentence. Since each pair of sentences contained a negative element, it was possible to see whether the three-feature pattern emerged with respect to the indirect force of the sentence. The pattern did emerge (p. 62):

True: average of 346 msec faster for positive requests.
False: average of 308 msec faster for negative requests.
Overall, positives average 222 msec faster than negatives.

These results, as well as analysis of the individual pairs of sentences given in table 11.5 indicate that subjects did represent the indirect force of the sentence in the course of comprehension.

Table 11.5
Mean latencies and percent errors[a] for pairs 1–10[b]

		Response		
Pairs	Basic sentences	True	False	Mean
1.	(a) Please color the circle blue.	1213 (0)	1610 (5)	1411
	(b) Please don't color the circle blue.	1799 (10)	1644 (12)	1722
2.	(a) Can you make the circle blue?	1473 (0)	1990 (1)	1731
	(b) Must you make the circle blue?	2082 (16)	1810 (2)	1946
3.	(a) Why not color the circle blue?	1510 (1)	2060 (5)	1785
	(b) Why color the circle blue?	2047 (11)	1856 (6)	1951
4.	(a) I would love to see the circle colored blue.	1537 (0)	1771 (0)	1654
	(b) I would hate to see the circle colored blue.	2014 (5)	1778 (1)	1896
5.	(a) You should color the circle blue.	1613 (11)	1662 (3)	1637
	(b) You shouldn't color the circle blue.	1978 (3)	1669 (8)	1824
6.	(a) Shouldn't you color the circle blue?	1723 (2)	2047 (2)	1885
	(b) Should you color the circle blue?	2510 (16)	1945 (16)	2228
7.	(a) The circle really needs to be painted blue.	1544 (3)	1916 (5)	1730
	(b) The circle doesn't really need to be painted blue.	2156 (5)	2122 (2)	2139
8.	(a) Doesn't the circle really need to be painted blue?	2098 (5)	2373 (7)	2236
	(b) Does the circle really need to be painted blue?	2251 (9)	2087 (6)	2169
9.	(a) I'll be very happy if you make the circle blue.	1779 (0)	2103 (3)	1941
	(b) I'll be very sad if you make the circle blue.	2362 (7)	1880 (2)	2122
10.	(a) I'll be very sad unless you make the circle blue.	2357 (2)	2798 (10)	2577
	(b) I'll be very happy unless you make the circle blue.	2692 (11)	2322 (8)	2507

a   In parentheses.
b   Latencies are given in msec.
Source: Clark and Lucy 1975.

This experiment provides evidence for predictions (i) and (ii). Evidence that H computes literal meaning first comes, for example, from sentence pairs 9 and 10 (table 11.5). On the assumption that "unless" is inherently negative (= "if not"), it should take longer to encode "unless" than to encode "if," and it did take over ½ sec longer to verify pair 10 than pair 9. This suggests that literal meaning was computed in the course of carrying out the verification task, which of course took longer. Moreover, this time difference in verification cannot be attributed to a difference in indirect force, since it is plausible to assume that verification of corresponding members of pairs 9 and 10 is task-equivalent:

(a) I'll be very *happy if* . . . ≈ I'll be very *sad unless* . . .
(b) I'll be very *sad if* . . . ≈ I'll be very *happy unless* . . .

Further evidence that literal meaning is computed is that interrogatives consistently took longer than their corresponding declaratives. It is difficult to attribute this always to differences in the length of the sentences or differences of indirect force (Clark and Lucy 1975, 66ff).

Although this study supports the SAS in broad outline, it leaves most details open. For instance, by instructing subjects at the outset to look for directive force, most of the inferential apparatus of the SAS was by-passed. After all, the SAS comprises numerous lines of inference, with citations of a variety of presumptions and mutual contextual beliefs. The Clark and Lucy study taps only two of these: the literal meaning of e and the indirect force of its utterance. It even leaves open the question of whether or not H infers that S has performed a literal illocutionary act.

We have not yet said anything about the perlocutionary act from a psychological point of view. Schweller, Brewer, and Dahl (1976) report results of experiments on perlocutionary acts. In one experiment (experiment 4) subjects were presented with sentences describing an illocutionary act such as (22a).

(22) a. *Illocution:* The angry farmer threatened the trespassing boys.
b. *Appropriate perlocution:* The farmer frightened the trespassing boys.
c. *Inappropriate perlocution:* The farmer calmed the trespassing boys.

Asked later to recall what they had seen, many subjects who had in fact seen an illocutionary description such as (22a) instead reported the appropriate perlocution (22b) but not, of course, the inappropriate perlocution (22c). Subjects conflated in memory the illocutionary description with the appropriate perlocutionary description, and this suggests that there is a readiness to infer from the original illocution what we call (in chapter 3) the associated perlocution. Schweller, Brewer, and Dahl conclude:

The overall results of these four experiments demonstrate the highly active nature of a hearer's processing of sentences and the effects this active processing has on memory for sentences. Subjects are clearly able to use content and context to elaborate sentences they have heard in terms of illocutionary forces and perlocutionary effects . . . earlier work . . . has shown that a number of different kinds of inferences can become confused in memory with the material originally presented. The results of the present experiments extend this range of inference types affecting memory to include illocutionary forces and perlocutionary effects, thus lending further empirical support to the general theory that human memory is not a passive, isolated system, but rather an active one in which knowledge from one domain interacts in a very systematic fashion with knowledge from other domains. (1976, 336)

Although we have been able to survey only briefly some of the relevant literature, the limited evidence currently available supports several steps of the speech act schema. In particular, we found evidence for contextual selection of one reading of an expression from among possible readings, even when subjects were not aware of the ambiguity. We also found evidence for representation of the nonliteral and indirect force of an utterance, as well as for inferential operations connecting them to the literal and direct force. Finally, we noted some evidence against total decomposition of lexical items during comprehension, evidence thus favoring the inferential semantics tentatively endorsed in chapter 8. Considered as a whole, this evidence is encouraging for the inferential approach to linguistic communication, but it would be rash at this time to claim more than preliminary empirical support for our theory. The SAS represents much more information than current experimental literature touches on, and it encompasses a variety of inference patterns. Research on the psychological implications of the speech act schema has only just begun.

Appendix   Mutual Belief and Social Concepts

The notion of mutual belief has figured prominently in our account of illocutionary acts. There are mutual contextual beliefs, which facilitate various steps of the hearer's inference to the speaker's communicative intention, and the several presumptions, which assure the hearer that there is an inference to be drawn. The speaker relies on these mutual beliefs to make his communicative intention recognizable. The notion of mutual belief was central also to our discussion of conventional illocutionary acts. The concept of convention was explicated in terms of mutual belief, and the institutional facts that conventional acts affect or effect are matters of mutual belief.

We wish to broaden our perspective and explain the systematic role of mutual belief in the analysis of various sociological concepts. These concepts enable us to represent a variety of institutional facts and phenomena of social interaction, of which communication is a special case. We will be concerned with two kinds of sociological concepts, social regularities and social collectivities. Among regularities we will distinguish norms, practices, rules, and roles, and these notions will be subdivided further. Social collectivities can be distinguished by degree of structure: types, groups, and organizations.

The underlying point of using the notion of mutual belief to analyze sociological concepts is to resist reifying *society*. Society is not an autonomous entity to which people are subject, even if they often experience it that way, so we must be careful not to abstract it from the people who make it up. On the other hand, society does not exist in the privacy of people's heads, as wishes and worries do, any more than it exists "out there," as tigers or trees do. In some sense it is intersubjective, and the concept of mutual belief enables us to explain precisely how. We can think of society as a system regulating and organizing people's behavior. Our strategy will be to analyze the concepts in terms of which this regulation and organization can be represented and to do so in terms of mutual belief. There would be no social system if people had nothing to do with one another, but more than that, their actions interlock and exhibit patterns in virtue of the beliefs and attitudes they share. In fact, a great part of what people know about one another is that they share a great many beliefs and attitudes. Knowing this requires a shared conceptual scheme, which, besides its elaborate categorization of things in the natural world, includes a catalog of what there is for people to be and to do. When we refer to social regulation and organization, we imply that the resulting patterns of behavior are not merely statistical, meeting the expectations of detached scientific observers, but are in large measure socially recognized, meeting the expectations of members of society themselves. At least in part, the system of regulation and organization that explains these patterns is internalized in people's beliefs and attitudes and is part of their shared conceptual scheme.

The sociologists Klapp (1957) and Scheff (1967) first put forth the provocative philosophical suggestion that the basic concepts of sociology can be derived from what they called the notion of *consensus*. They and other writers (many cited by Scheff) have thought this notion relevant to such diverse topics as public opinion, mass action, norms and roles, communication, games, culture and tradition, socialization, and social cohesion. Use of the concept of consensus is widespread in social science, but little effort has been made to formulate that concept as anything more than individual agreement. Scheff cites numerous examples of experimental and theoretical work in which this simplistic conception is implicit. The trouble with viewing consensus simply as agreement, Scheff points out, is the failure to allow for the possibility of *pluralistic ignorance* (people agree but don't realize it) and *false consensus* (people mistakenly believe that they agree). Pluralistic ignorance satisfies the simple definition but lacks the behavioral effects of genuine consensus, whereas false consensus may have the same effect on behavior as genuine consensus even though agreement is lacking. Various turns of phrase have been used, Scheff notes, to take these phenomena into account—*perceived consensus, the generalized other, interpenetration of perspectives,* and *reciprocity of perspectives*—but these do not constitute an explication of consensus.

Scheff proposes an analysis in terms of levels of agreement. Among a group of people with opinions on a given issue, a majority can agree or fail to agree at the first level, that is, on the issue itself. At the second level they could understand or fail to understand that they agree (or disagree); pluralistic ignorance is a lack of understanding about agreement, and false consensus is misunderstanding about disagreement. At the third level there can be realization or lack of realization about understanding (or lack of it) about agreement (or disagreement). Theoretically, further levels could be brought in, but practically, on Scheff's analysis, consensus consists in majority agreement, understanding, and realization. Assuming the majority to be a determinate part of the whole group and taking three levels into account, Scheff notes that consensus is but one of eight possible situations.

The trouble with Scheff's account of consensus is its implicit assumption that there is a determinate majority, which agrees or disagrees at any of the three levels. This difficulty can be avoided and consensus defined more perspicuously, we suggest, in terms of belief rather than agreement. For us consensus in the sense important to social scientists is mutual belief. In our formulation (as well as in our later analyses), the usual *if and only if* of philosophical definitions will be supplanted by *to the degree to which,* represented for convenience by $\propto$, the mathematical symbol for proportionality. In this way we accommodate the fact that the phenomena under consideration admit of degree and that no clear line is to be drawn between cases where the concept in question does apply and cases where it does not. We recognize, however, that since multiple dimensions are involved, a metric needs to be specified. At any rate, we define mutual belief (over a collectivity G with respect to a proposition p):

DF$_1$: It is *mutually believed* in G that $p \propto$ the members of G believe:
i. that p,
ii. that the members of G believe that p, and
iii. that the members of G believe that the members of G believe that p.[1]

This definition clearly captures such ideas as the interpenetration or reciprocity of perspectives. And without itself reifying society, it suggests how people can reify society when, in Laing's words (1968, ch. 4), they conform "to a presence that is everywhere elsewhere": the members of G may think of the members of G as *society* rather than as *everyone else,* and those who think this may include everyone.

This notion of mutual belief figures centrally in our definitions of various concepts of social regularities and of social collectivities; their definability in terms of mutual belief is meant to demonstrate and explicate the intersubjective character of these concepts. We often speak of something's being psychologically real to someone if he believes it exists, if it exists for him, irrespective of whether it really does exist. Similarly, we may use the phrase *socially real* to apply to anything that exists for a given society or collectivity G. However, for something to be socially or intersubjectively real for G, it must be not merely psychologically real for each member of G. After all, each might fail to realize this and perhaps even believe that it exists for him alone. Even if that is not the case and the members of G believe it to be psychologically real for one another, they might not believe or might even disbelieve that others believe that. To be socially real, something must be mutually believed to exist. This is the status of the regularities and collectivities to be defined.

Our employment of the notion of mutual belief should not give the impression that people's second- and third-level beliefs are automatically uniform and stable. It is an empirical question, beyond the scope of philosophical analysis, how people acquire the beliefs they do and why there is the uniformity there is in a given culture. Many topics in social psychology bear on this question: socialization, conformity and deviance, mass communication, and the social self. Moreover, mutual beliefs don't come into existence all at once; they develop over a period of time. In the United States mutual belief in the wrongness of American involvement in the Vietnamese war took years to be realized. Indeed, the Administration's stratagem of singling out the so-called silent majority created a long period of false consensus. Fads, fashions, and crazes seem to involve flowing and ebbing waves of mutual belief. Such phenomena as social movements, political backlashes, trends in the stock market (panic selling), landslide elections resulting from the bandwagon effect, keeping up with the Joneses, generation gaps, and religious revivals all seem to involve upsurges of mutual belief. There is no telling the degree to which mass media and the astute exploitation thereof may foster a state of pluralistic ignorance about the need for change and, further, a state of false consensus concerning the status quo.

SOCIAL REGULARITIES

Three kinds of social regularities may be distinguished: norms, practices, and rules. The reasons for distinguishing them will be explained—in fact they are embodied in the definitions we will offer—

and subconcepts and kindred concepts of each will be singled out. The key notion of mutual belief figures in each definition.

Norms

What is a social norm? Landis (1971, 228) defines a norm as "the accepted or required behavior for a person in a particular situation." According to Secord and Backman (1974, 300), "a social norm is an expectation shared by group members which specifies behavior that is appropriate for a given situation." They note (p. 402) that expectations are both anticipatory and normative in nature, and thus social norms are also. This descriptive/evaluative ambiguity is suggested by the adjectives "normal" and "normative," so a norm is both a regularity and a regulation. Landis's definition mentions merely the normative aspect of norms; but it seems that to count as a norm, the behavior in question must be generally performed and not merely a generally unfulfilled standard. However, we will follow Landis in calling the expected behavior rather than the expectation itself the norm. Nothing crucial rides on this terminological preference, but it will facilitate the formulation of our definition.

Our definition must embody the idea that a social norm is neither merely a statistical regularity nor merely a standard that people may hardly ever observe; thus, the definition must exclude behavior like people's putting on their pants before their shoes and standards like never showing temper. Our definition must express the social reality of norms. We let A designate the kind of behavior in question,[2] C the kind of recurrent situation to which the norm applies, and MB 'mutually believed.'

DF_2: A (in C) is a *social norm* in G $\propto$:
i. the members of G do A in C,
ii. it is MB-ed in G that (i), and
iii. it is MB-ed in G that the members of G should do A in C.

It follows from this definition that when C arises, the mutual beliefs specified will be activated in the people involved, and so, assuming they identify one another as members of G, they will mutually expect one another to do A. In specific instances the specification of A may designate only a certain kind of agent, such as children, drivers, or guests. In this case only the specified kind of agent can fulfill or violate the norm, but still the mutual beliefs are shared by all.

Among the types of action that the variable A ranges over are negative actions, such as not picking your nose or not embracing strangers. When such a description is plugged into the definition, what the members of G do is not to perform a certain action. For such negative norms, as we might call them, we may formulate a separate definition.

DF$_3$: There is a *social norm* in G *against A* (in C) $\propto$:
i. the members of G do not do A in C,
ii. it is MB-ed in G that (i), and
iii. it is MB-ed in G that the members of G should not do A in C.

Logically speaking, this definition is superfluous, provided we allow A in DF$_2$ to range over negative actions. Nevertheless, it is worth formulating this definition of negative social norms, for a great many social norms are of this type, proscriptions rather than prescriptions. (For subsequent definitions the negative forms will be omitted.)

It is possible, indeed common, for just some of the clauses in DF$_2$ to be satisfied. Several cases are worth labeling:

DF$_4$: A (in C) is a *statistical regularity in G* $\propto$:
i. the members of G do A in C.

Sometimes the term *norm* (as opposed to *social norm*) is used to designate statistical regularities.

Statistical regularities need not be recognized by the people to whom they apply, and social scientists have discovered a great many such regularities (including many pertaining to topics other than behavior). We should single out the case where the members of G themselves are aware, indeed mutually aware, of such a regularity, for in this event, when C arises there will be a mutual expectation that A be done.

DF$_5$: A (in C) is a *social regularity*[3] in G $\propto$:
i. the members of G do A in C, and
ii. it is MB-ed in G that (i).

Since clause (iii) of DF$_2$ is absent from DF$_5$, the mutual expectation that arises in C need not be normative in nature but merely empirical. Notice that clause (ii) might hold without (i) holding, in which case the MB would be false. Such a socially imagined regularity might have occurred—such a false mutual belief might have prevailed—as to sexual behavior when it was a hush-hush subject.

Finally, we might define the case where a certain type of behavior is mutually recognized as the standard even when people generally don't live up to it.

DF₆: A (in C) is a *social standard* in G ∝:
iii. it is MB-ed in G that the members of G should do A in C.

Of course a standard may also be a statistical regularity, and if it is a social regularity as well, then it is a social norm. A social standard is a special case of a social value, which might be defined as anything (not just behavior) that is mutually believed in G to be of value.

Behavior that is the standard, including that which is the norm, is mutually believed in G to be what people should do—or should not do, in the case of negative norms. In between is the entire range of things that are socially acceptable, neither required nor forbidden. Accordingly, we can say that a type of behavior is socially acceptable if there is no standard that requires not doing it, that is, no standard against it.

Having defined some of the concepts that fall under it, let us return briefly to the concept of social norm itself, as analyzed in DF₂. Even though the definition implies that when C arises people mutually expect A to be performed, it implies nothing about people's reasons for doing A. A person utilizing the expectations implied by the definition might do A to receive approval, to avoid being socially rejected (or punished), to appear mentally normal, to avoid suspicion. He may have no reason at all and do A out of habit. Why people conform to norms depends on the norm and on the person, but this is a topic for social psychology not philosophical analysis.

DF₂ does not imply that there must be a sanction for every norm— some norms are more serious than others, and some people are more serious than others about norms. Nevertheless, because norms are mutually expected to be followed, it is not surprising that when someone violates a norm, other people may react accordingly. As Hart (1961, 54–56) puts it, norms have an "internal aspect," in that they provide a basis for "criticism of others and demands for conformity" that should yield "acknowledgement of the legitimacy of such criticism and demands when received from others." In short, norms are not only followed but applied. Indeed, there are norms regarding the violation of norms. Depending on the seriousness of the offense, there may be a norm for others to criticize the violator and to demand amends or at least apology. But in some cases there is a norm against saying anything—it would be impolite, cause embarrassment, or create a scene. And of course, again depending on the case, there are norms for violators: to apologize, to offer a legitimate excuse, and where possible to make amends. Still again, there is sometimes a norm against the offender saying anything.

Practices

That a type of act is the norm does not determine what people's reasons are for doing it. Even if a person believes he should do it, that may not be his reason for doing it. However, a special case of social norms, which we label *social practices,* has a reason for action built into its definition. There is a definitional connection between the existence of a practice and people's reason for following it: a practice is a norm that people follow in order to conform, in order to be like others or at least to seem to be. Norms in general can be followed for this reason, but practices by definition are.

DF$_7$: A (in C) is a *social practice* in G $\propto$:
i. A (in C) is a social norm in G, and
ii. people's reason for doing A in C is, at least partly, that it is generally done.

The definition of norms (DF$_2$) implies that people who follow a norm recognize that others do, but it does not imply that this is their reason for doing so, even if part of their reason is that following the norm must be the right thing to do because others do it—that's not the reason specified in clause (ii) of DF$_7$. Typical examples of practices include dressing in accordance to one's sex (or class or age), social drinking, and standing for the national anthem.

It might be objected that a vicious circle is built into the definition of practices: the members of G do A partly because the members of G do A. However, this is not a vicious circle but an endless chain. Each does A partly because others have been doing A (and can be expected to continue to). Naturally, that could not have always been everyone's reason, but the definition does not require that A was originally a practice. During the period in which a practice comes into being, as people begin performing the action in question, their reasons for doing it and their beliefs about the extent of its being done may be unclear and in flux, whereas once the practice is established and stable, mutual belief in its existence and continuation prevails.

Rapidly changing practices, such as fads and fashions, are an interesting special case. Dance crazes, hair styles, and dress fashions are practices that people follow in order to do what is "in," to be "with it" (these locutions are no longer in fashion). Most people don't want to appear "out of it," and as styles periodically change, the idea is to be neither too far ahead of the game nor too far behind it (style setters are a special type). Notice, by the way, that the collectivity G in which a fad or fashion prevails may be specifiable only as that in which the fad or fashion prevails—the in crowd consists of those who do what is in.

Rules

The term *social rule* will be used to designate any social norm that entails some special social obligation (in addition to the general obligation to follow norms).[4] Four different kinds of rules warrant being defined here. Since there is no precedent (to our knowledge) for terminology that marks these distinct kinds, we call them, for reasons that will become evident, *coordinative rules, cooperative rules, collective rules,* and *regulations.* These categories are not mutually exclusive.

Coordinative rules are social rules like driving on the right, speaking in turn, and going to the end of the line, whose point is to coordinate the activity of a number of people who are trying to do more or less the same thing with a minimum of interference from others. Each person who follows such a rule is doing his part in a joint effort to coordinate the activities (driving, communicating, buying a ticket) of all involved.

DF_8: A (in C) is a *coordinative rule* in G $\propto$:
i. A (in C) is a social norm in G, and
ii. it is MB-ed in G that general performance of A in C enables the members of G each to do some act B with a minimum of interference from one another.

The definition requires only that general performance of A be mutually believed to minimize interference—whether it does so is another matter.

Cooperative rules. There are many actions whose performance by one person makes sense only if many others do the same thing: recycling cans and bottles, conserving energy, going out on strike. If one has good reason to believe that hardly anyone else will do A, one has little reason to do it oneself. These cumulative actions (see Bach 1977) yield collective goods or prevent collective evils. Collective goods are goods that everyone enjoys if anyone does, such as clean air, quiet in a library, or higher wages (in a union shop). Collective evils hurt everyone (not that a few don't benefit from them also) if they hurt anyone, as with air pollution and oil shortages. The free-rider problem arises when people refuse to perform a cumulative action (conserving energy or not littering) because enough others will do it anyway. The problem is that if too many people think this way, too few will perform the cumulative action—unless there is a rule requiring each person to contribute his effort. Such a rule is a cooperative rule.

DF$_9$: A cumulative action A is a *cooperative rule* in G $\propto$:
i. A is a social norm in G, and
ii. it is MB-ed in G that general performance of A tends to produce some collective good or prevent some collective evil.

Clause (ii) requires only a mutual belief not the truth of it, so conceivably general observance of a cooperative rule could turn out to be detrimental to G.

Collective rules organize collective action out of individual efforts. Rules that divide labor in a family, a tribe, or a company are collective in this sense. In general, a collective rule apportions assignments to different members of G, whose combined action is presumed to further the interests of G or its members. Thus, to follow a collective rule is to do one's part.

DF$_{10}$: A set of actions $A_1, \ldots, A_n$ is a *collective rule* in G $\propto$:
i. to do one's part is the social norm in G,
ii. there is a mutually recognized procedure for determining each person's part, and
iii. each person's part is one of $A_1, \ldots, A_n$.

The definition does not require each member of G to be aware of what everyone else's assignment is but only that everybody has one (several might have the same). In a formal organization (to be defined later), there are people whose part is to determine others' parts, whereas in an informal group the apportionment of parts could be arrived at by mutual agreement rather than executive edict. We will see that a formal organization can be thought of as governed by a system of collective rules.

Regulations are standards that are enacted, promulgated, or otherwise imposed on G by some mutually recognized authority (who may or may not be legitimate—having power does not imply having the right to exercise it). Generally a regulation is codified or otherwise made official, but this is not required by our definition.

DF$_{11}$: A (in C) is a *regulation* in G $\propto$:
i. A (in C) is a social standard in G, and
ii. by virtue of some mutually recognized authority, A (in C) is required in G.

Political regulations are laws, and regulations generally (but not necessarily) have sanctions enforcing their observance, but the definition requires only that they be standards, not norms. Nevertheless a regulation can be a norm—or even a coordinative, a cooperative, or a collective rule.

SOCIAL COLLECTIVITIES

People can be grouped either in the sense of being categorized together or in the sense of interacting with one another. Sociologists generally call the first sort of grouping a *category,* reserving the term *group* for the second. The only relationship members of a category have, generally, is that of having something in common, the feature that places them in that category; the relationship among members of a group is their pattern of interaction. Further distinctions must be drawn here, and they will be the subject of our detailed analysis. A *role category* is a socially recognized category whose behavior is subject to specific expectations. Role categories include both *positions* and *social types.* The notion of *role* itself must be explained; there are ambiguities in the notion of role (akin to those in the notion of social norm) that have to be resolved. Under the heading of *groups* we will distinguish, in increasing order of structure and complexity, *face-to-face groups, crowds, social groups,* and *organizations.* The notion of mutual belief will have a central place in all our definitions.

Role categories

People can be classified in all sorts of ways: by age, sex, race, height, personality, nationality, profession. Some categories are not recognized by the general public but only by social scientists, and of course among them there is divergence, for instance, on the categorization of personality types. Not every category is worth singling out, either because it is nearly vacuous (blue-eyed teen-aged businesswomen) or because no significant empirical generalization can be made over it (left-handed pawnbrokers born on odd-numbered Thursdays). We should distinguish categories that are socially recognized, and over which there are social expectations, from those recognized only by social scientists and over which there are merely statistical regularities. We will follow Secord and Backman (1974, 402) and use the term *role category.* Sociologists commonly use *status* to designate a position in a group or in a social structure. People also classify one another by personality traits and behavioral idiosyncrasies; these *social types* include fools, egotists, heroes, nice guys, creeps, bigots, big shots, and cheapskates. We will use the term *position,* rather than *status* with its evaluative connotations, to designate a place in a group or social relation; *role category* will cover both positions and social types, depending on the features (F) involved.

DF_{12}: A set of people with F is a *role category* in G $\propto$:
i. it is MB-ed in G that F is used to classify people in $G,$ and
ii. there is some social regularity, standard, or norm applying to people with F.

Clause (i) says that it is mutually recognized in G that people classify one another in terms of F and not-F (American/foreign) or along a dimension on which F lies (Italian, on the dimension of nationality). Clause (ii) requires that F not be some idle category that doesn't pertain to the behavior of people with F and to people's mutual beliefs about the behavior of people with F. In this way, role categories are relevant to people's social behavior and awareness of it, for they apply to people about whom there are special mutual expectations.[5] In discussing roles, we will explain why clause (ii) requires either a social regularity, a standard, or a norm to apply to people with the features defining a role category.[6]

The term *social role* (or simply *role*) is highly ambiguous. Secord and Backman (1974, 405) note that it can refer to a role category, to the expectations associated with that category (role expectations), or to the expected behavior itself. We will restrict the term *role* to the expected behavior, although this is not to be confused with what Secord and Backman (pp. 405–406) call "role behavior," which is whatever a person in a given role category actually does relevant to the role expectations, whether or not he fulfills them.

If this isn't ambiguity enough, restricting the term *role* to the expected behavior must allow for the fact that expectations can be normative or merely anticipatory (as we observed in discussing norms). Our account of the notion of role should reflect this distinction, since some roles are expected (anticipated) but hardly required to be played. Everybody expects a boor to act rudely, but nobody (besides himself) thinks he should. Accordingly, the use of the term *role* must be restricted further and other terms introduced to fully resolve the ambiguities inherent in standard usage. We will distinguish between *roles* as social regularities, *role standards* as social standards, and *normative roles* as combinations of both. Thus we let R range over patterns of behavior (since roles typically include a cluster rather than a single kind of behavior).

DF_{13}: R is a *role* for people of role category F in G $\propto$:
i. in G people with F exhibit R, and
ii. it is MB-ed in G that (i).

DF_{14}: R is a *role standard* for F in G $\propto$:
iii. it is MB-ed in G that in G people with F should exhibit R.

DF_{15}: R is a *normative role* for F in G $\propto$:
i. in G people with F exhibit R,
ii. it is MB-ed in G that (i), and
iii. it is MB-ed in G that in G people with F should exhibit R.

Generally speaking, roles but not role standards apply to *social types*, like fools, bigots, and cheapskates; whereas *positions*, like parents, preachers, and politicians, have role standards (or even normative roles, if it is mutually believed that they meet their standards and they do). It is important to make the distinctions embodied in these definitions, because the expectations (mutual beliefs activated in particular situations) that are directed at people of a given type or position can be anticipatory, normative, or both. Which they are depends on the type of position and on people's associated mutual beliefs.

The reason social types are generally associated with roles and positions with role standards is that roles generally define social types whereas positions generally define role standards. In other words, a person belongs to a type (fool, hot shot, ladies' man) in virtue of what he does; a person does certain things because of his position (coach, custodian, columnist). However, there are exceptions to this generalization. Social types like nudists and cigar smokers are subject to role standards; other social types, like ladies and heroes, are defined by the standards they live up to (normative roles).

Roles (and role standards) often interlock in the sense that they may specify how people of one position (or type) act (or are to act) with regard to people of the same or of some other position (or type). Organizations (DF_{17}) are a complex instance. A final point about our definitions is that when clause (ii) is satisfied without clause (i), we have the case of a social *stereotype*, where there is a (usually) false mutual belief in G about some minority's behavior.

Groups

In the broadest sense of the term, a group can be a category, an aggregate, or a role category, but here, following general usage in social science,[7] the term *group* will be more restrictive. Even so, groups can range from strangers in brief, perfunctory interaction to a formal organization. Despite the variation on this continuum, groups all have the feature that their members have some sort of structured relationship, be it mutual expectations based on social norms that are applied anonymously or a rich set of mutual beliefs based on personal acquaintance. We distinguish four kinds of groups: *face-to-face groups, crowds, social groups,* and *organizations.*

No special definition (in terms of mutual belief) is needed for a *face-to-face group,* which is any combination of people engaged in any kind of direct interaction, however brief, casual, and routine. The persons involved may be acquaintances or members of the same social group or organization, in which case specific norms and role standards apply. But even unacquainted and unrelated participants in the most fleeting random encounter have mutual expectations based on general social norms and on contextual mutual beliefs as to their respective identities and the definition of the situation.

Not just any aggregate of people in proximity constitutes a group. Pedestrians on a busy mall, passengers on a commuter train, and shoppers in a department store do not constitute a group—there need not be any interaction or structured relationship among co-present persons over and above that following from the observance of general social norms, such as common courtesies. There is no action as a group or as members of a group. However, in the event of a sudden emergency or anything which captures everyone's attention, collective action quickly becomes possible. Suddenly they become aware—indeed mutually aware—of the same thing. Then they become a *crowd,* which Landis (1971, 211) defines as 'a temporary collection of people in close physical contact reacting together to a common stimulus.' We add the requirement that members of a crowd be mutually aware of the stimulus; the phrase "reacting together" does not imply this awareness—they might be reacting simultaneously but without being mutually aware of the stimulus or of each other. There are many kinds of crowds, including audiences, mobs, and social gatherings.

People having something in common need not have any common

interest or mutual awareness. They need not have any special pattern of interaction. What we call a *social group* has these features. This accords fairly well with the common sociological idea of a social group as entailing consciousness of kind (or a we feeling) together with patterned interaction. Our definition is meant to explicate this idea.

DF_{16}: *G* is a *social group* $\propto$:

i. the members of *G* have some feature *F* in common, together with an associated interest *I*,

ii. it is MB-ed in *G* that (i),

iii. partly because of (i) and (ii), the members of *G* think of *G* as "we," and

iv. partly because of (i), (ii), and (iii), there is a pattern of interaction in *G* governed by a set of norms (including cooperative rules) and normative roles, MB-ed in *G* to further *I*.

Social groups range from friendships, families, and cliques to clubs, unions, and professional associations (the latter groups have organizations within them). DF_{16} is intended to capture the idea of a collection of people mutually regarding themselves as a unit (we) to which they belong, united by having something in common, including a mutual interest that is presumably furthered in their group activities. All four clauses are necessary because, for example, clauses (i) and (ii) can be satisfied without (iii) or (iv), as in the case of social types like baseball fans or fat people. Indeed, the first three clauses can be satisfied without the fourth, as illustrated by an oppressed class (or race) with what Marxists call class consciousness but with no organized activity. A social group, at least in the restricted sense defined here, must have the features specified by all four clauses.

The mutual beliefs associated with social types and positions (see DF_{12}) prevail in the community at large, whereas those associated with social groups need not extend beyond the group itself. In other words, membership in a social group, as opposed to a role category, is determined by the members themselves. To become a member of an existing social group, a person must be regarded by the established members as a member; to be so regarded he may have to fulfill some membership requirement over and above sharing the feature *F* and the interest *I* (required by the definition). Otherwise, he won't be regarded by the members as "one of us," and won't join in the group activity (or won't be allowed to). A membership requirement is a convention in *G* of the form: If a person with F does A, then he becomes a member of G. Sometimes A is going through a ceremony or receiving some kind of initiation.

In the case of a social group being formed, its existence and membership in it are a matter of mutual acknowledgment. This is true for a primary group, where there is intimate face-to-face contact between members throughout its existence. Members all know one another on an individual basis, and it is the we feeling itself more than anything else that determines membership. In this respect such groups as consanguine families and athletic teams are borderline cases between primary and secondary groups.

Our definition of social groups should be consistent with the fact that groups can persist even though the membership changes (this is true mainly of secondary groups). The definition does not indicate how at different times different sets of people could constitute the same group. It seems that the main condition of identity over time is continuity of membership. At the very least, this means that at no time after its inception is it composed of all new members. In practice, groups have names, symbols, meeting places, traditions, and the like to provide continuity over time. In theory, however, there is no sure-fire way to settle all questions of identity. It is easy to imagine situations where it is impossible to decide whether the same group still exists or, after a group divides into two, which (if either) is the original group and which the splinter group.

Organizations

A formal organization is much more structured than DF_{16} requires a social group to be. Its members are clearly differentiated by position, to which specific duties and responsibilities are attached. Collective rules (DF_{10}) with the status of regulations (DF_{11}) prescribe interconnecting normative roles (DF_{15}) that organize the activity of people in the same and in different positions. Unlike in a social group, in an organization the members need not have anything in common (other than being members) or any common interest, and they need not share any we feeling. Rather than identifying with the organization, they may be motivated only extrinsically, by rewards or threat of punishment.[8] An organization may have features of a social group, just as a social group may have those of an organization (or contain an administrative organization within it). DF_{16} and the following definition of organizations are not mutually exclusive:

DF_{17}: G is an *organization* $\propto$ there exist in G:
i. a differentiated set of positions defined by conventions, and rules for filling them,
ii. collective rules determining normative roles for each position (duties and responsibilities),
iii. collective rules for how and when to follow (ii) (procedures),
iv. lines of authority between positions and channels of communication for exercising authority, and
v. conventions for recognizing (i)–(iv).

The first four clauses specify the distinct elements of structure that constitute a formal organization, the rule-governed patterns of action and interaction of people in differentiated positions with specified duties and responsibilities (and procedures for carrying them out). Strictly speaking, clause (iv), referring to lines of authority and channels of communication, is redundant, in that the rules specified in the previous clauses must, in any real organization, cover authority and communication. In order to differentiate official from unofficial patterns of interaction, organization theorists often distinguish authority from influence. In our terminology the official rules specifying authority relations, indeed the official rules generally, are regulations in the sense of DF_{11}, whereas influence relations are governed by informal social norms and further determined by particular personal relationships and norms of groups within the organization.

Clause (v) refers to what Hart (1961, 92ff) calls rules of recognition, but since they determine what count as rules, we will call them conventions. In an organization such conventions require not merely that rules be mutually recognized but that they meet special conditions, such as being enacted and codified. In effect, clause (v) stipulates a mutually recognized means for determining what the rules are.

CONCLUSION

The analysis of basic social concepts attempted here is meant to elucidate their meanings and spell out their connections. The central concept, mutual belief, refines the notion of consensus, which sociologists have recognized to be central not only to the description of a great many social phenomena but also to the analysis of key social concepts. By systematically defining these concepts in terms of mutual belief, we make explicit their intersubjective character. The social reality of the regularities and collectivities thus defined is constituted by people's mutually dependent actions, beliefs, and attitudes. Thus, we need not succumb to the reification advised by Durkheim of "considering social facts as things." Nevertheless, we are in a position to understand why social facts can strike people as things—their being socially real is sufficient for that.

Apart from whatever theoretical understanding they provide, our definitions of basic social concepts have definite empirical possibilities. They are formulated in terms of people's behavior and beliefs, both of which are subject to empirical investigation. Moreover, the definitions do not state *if-and-only-if* relationships, as philosophical analyses generally do, but *to-the-degree-to-which* ($\propto$) relationships. Properly quantified, these can become determinate functional relationships characteristic of scientific propositions. The existence of norms, roles, groups, and the rest is a matter of degree, as our formulations reflect, and empirical investigation can determine the degree to which particular norms, roles, and so on, do exist and how that degree varies over time, as they gradually come into and go out of existence, their scopes broadening and narrowing.

Definitions are not theories and do not explain the phenomena whose concepts they formulate. However, we think the concept of mutual belief and the more general concept of the social distribution of belief, including the cases of pluralistic ignorance and false consensus, have great explanatory potential. Phenomena come to mind like socialization, person perception, public opinion, social cohesion, and mass action, to name but a few topics of sociology and social psychology.

Notes

Notes to Chapter 1

1. In due course we will specify the ranges of the variables *so-and-so, such-and-such*, and *a certain way*. Except for the term *utterance act*, our terminology is Austin's (1962). Utterance acts for us are what Austin calls *phatic acts*, which necessarily involve the performance of what he called *phonetic acts*, a notion unnecessary for our purposes. Utterance acts involve producing certain sounds belonging to (and as belonging to) a certain language, and are reported by direct quotation. Austin characterizes the *rhetic act* as the use of a sentence "or its constituents with a certain more or less definite 'sense' and a more or less definite 'reference'" (1962, 93), and is reported by the familiar device of indirect quotation. Although Austin speaks of the locutionary act as comprising the phonetic, the phatic, and the rhetic acts, generally what he says about locutionary acts applies to them qua rhetic acts. For us locutionary acts are rhetic acts in Austin's sense. See section 2.1.

2. A comprehensive treatment of this second issue would require solving some very hard problems in the (general) theory of action—in particular, problems of identity, individuation, and the part–whole relation of acts. We do not propose (nor presuppose) a general theory, and the reader is invited to try to subsume our discussion of speech action under such a theory, e.g. Goldman (1970) or Thomson (1977).

3. Besides, as Austin noted (lecture X), there are uses of "by" that mark off illocutionary, locutionary, and miscellaneous other redescriptions of an (utterance) act.

4. *A* and *B* mutually believe that *p* if and only if each believes (1) that *p*, (2) that the other believes that *p*, and (3) that the other believes that the first believes that *p*. The idea (as "mutual recognition" and as "mutual expectation") originated with Schelling (1960, ch. 3), who also speaks of a matter of fact as being "obviously obvious." For more discussion see the appendix.

5. Although there are some questions about how much leeway one has in reporting what has been uttered (can we report "I vant a banana" as "I want a banana"?), differences between utterances of the same sentence do not seem to matter semantically. However, there is an utterance-act difference between

whispering something, speaking it, and shouting it, a difference between mumbling something and articulating it clearly, and a difference between uttering something slowly, normally, and fast; each of these utterance-act differences can make an illocutionary difference. A whispered "Leave" might be taken as a plea, a spoken one as a request, and a shouted one as an order or even threat. See Miller and Johnson-Laird (1976, sect. 7.4.1, and references therein) for more discussion.

6. This point does not apply to certain special cases. If S and H are learning a language together, it might well be that S utters e knowing H understands e just because S has seen H use or understand e previously. Or if technical terminology without wide currency is used, then special beliefs to the effect that H is acquainted with that vocabulary are required on the part of S.

7. Even if, as a matter of empirical fact, people have to use or witness the use of a language in order to learn it, our conceptual claim is not affected. Knowledge of a language is one thing, its being mutual in a community is another.

8. For example, in saying that indirect quotation reports the proposition expressed by the utterance of the sentence, we do not mean to hide the philosophically notorious problems of referential opacity and of the identity of propositions.

9. Not all instances of the blank are related in quite the same way to the interrogative uttered. "What time is it?" involves subject–predicate inversion, whereas "Who discovered the calculus?" simply becomes: S says that H is to tell S who discovered the calculus.

10. Not all illocutionary acts (greetings, for example) have propositional content, but we ignore this complication here.

11. Explicit performative utterances are no exception. As argued in chapter 10, literally they are statements and only indirectly do they have the force of the sort named by the performative verb. For example, a typical utterance of "I order you to leave" is literally a statement and only indirectly an order.

12. Grice (1968, 60–61) seems to recognize this important difference when he argues that with meaningful items, the reflexive intention can be replaced by a simple intention. See also Schiffer's discussion of this point (1972, 133ff).

13. The reason for this choice of examples is the strategy of analyzing linguistic meaning in terms of speaker meaning. See Grice (1968), Schiffer (1972, ch. 6), and Bennett (1973, 1976).

Notes to Chapter 2

1. Depending on how S pronounces e, there can be problems in even reaching L1. We have made allowances (chapter 1, note 5) for utterances involving mispronunciation, foreign accents, and faltering speech.

2. *Pace* Humpty Dumpty, there is no limit to what S can mean by e. However, ordinarily if S means ... by e, S believes that e means ... in L (or at least in some dialect of L shared by H).

3. This example is in the singular, but what follows applies, mutatis mutandis, also to plural cases.

4. The way H represents to himself the referent (as "the such-and-such") may in some cases be identical to the description S uses to refer to it (as the "so-and-so").

5. As Donnellan has observed (1966), there is another way in which definite descriptions can be used to refer even when they don't apply to what they are being used to refer to. S might utter "The diamond necklace looks magnificent on her" and yet be referring to a certain glass necklace. Even if S himself does not believe the necklace to be made of diamonds, he may believe that H believes this or that H believes that he (S) believes this, and so on. Whatever the case, S succeeds in referring to the glass necklace if S and H mutually believe of the glass necklace, however each thinks of it, that it is what S is talking about. On our view, what Donnellan means by "referential" as opposed to "attributive" uses of definite descriptions is not a special semantic feature of definite descriptions but rather a special case of the general phenomenon of successful communication despite discrepancies between what the speaker says and what he intends to be thereby doing. Essentially the same point is made by Castaneda (1977, note 7) and by Kripke (1977, especially 263–264), who distinguishes "speaker's reference" from "semantic reference" and uses this distinction to supplant Donnellan's.

6. Although the schema contains parameters for speaker, hearer, and expression (S, H, and e), it does not reflect variations in time. However, L3 could be interpreted as having a time parameter as well:

L3. S is saying at t (to H) that *(...p...).

By providing parameters for time, the schema is able to represent some uses of the tenses and time reference: In uttering "I am tired now," S is saying at t (to H) that S is, at t, tired. In uttering "You left," S is saying at t (to H) that H left, at some time earlier than t. In uttering "(You will) leave!" S is saying at t, that H is to leave at some time later than t. However, for the purposes of the schema this time parameter may be omitted inasmuch as, at least in ordinary oral communication situations, the time at which the hearer represents to himself what the speaker is saying is approximately the time at which the speaker is saying it. For other situations—hearing a tape or reading a memo—the time parameter could readily be included.

7. These two interpretations are not intended to mark all the existing theories of sense, some of which are discussed in chapter 8. As for theories of proper names, among current rivals are the theories of Kripke (1972), Loar (1976), and Katz (1977a).

8. Alternatively, S is saying that H is to make it be the case that H closes the door. It is sometimes suggested that what be made the case is: the door is closed. Although that might work for this example, it is very awkward for others. Consider: in uttering "Give me two nickels for a dime" S is saying that H is to make it be the case that S has two nickels for a dime.

9. Some acknowledgments (e.g. apologies) can be performed with constatives. For example, uttering "I am sorry for that" can be used both to state that one is sorry and to apologize. Our discussion of acknowledgments in section 3.4 will make clear the difference. There seems, incidentally, to be no particular type of saying associated with literally performed acknowledgments.

10. The main types of intonation that would have to be considered are contrastive stress and rising intonation on declaratives. It is not clear that the latter should be treated like interrogatives, since they are not used to perform analogous locutionary acts. It is very odd to say: In uttering "John admires Vilas?" *S* was asking *H* whether or not John admires Vilas (or *S* was saying that *H* was to tell *S* whether or not John admires Vilas).

11. Searle (and Katz by implication) denies the existence of locutionary acts altogether, at least as Austin characterizes them. Searle remarks, "Every sentence has some illocutionary force potential, if only of a very broad kind, built into its meaning. For example, even the most primitive of the old-fashioned grammatical categories of indicative, interrogative, and imperative sentences already contain determinants of illocutionary force. For this reason there is no specification of a locutionary act performed in the utterance of a complete sentence which will not determine the specification of an illocutionary act" (1968, 412).

Searle is correct that every sentence has some illocutionary force potential built into its meaning, and it is true that Austin neglected this point. However, since any sentence can be used nonliterally in all sorts of different ways, what Searle means must be restricted to the sentence's *literal* illocutionary force potential. The specification of the locutionary act performed in the utterance of a sentence used nonliterally does *not* determine the specification, even approximately, of the illocutionary act. Nonliteral utterances show that meaning does not determine the *identity* of force. More fundamentally, meaning does not guarantee the *existence* of illocutionary force. For example, without any illocutionary intention *S* might say that Jesus was a Jew, with the perlocutionary intention of offending *H*. Thus, since a locutionary act can be performed without any illocutionary act being performed, the distinction between the two types of acts must be preserved.

Katz's (1977c) theory depends on ignoring this distinction. He believes that a portion of speech act information should be represented in the grammar of a language, that is, in the semantic component. Although he recognizes the contribution of context to illocutionary force and that this contribution must be handled by pragmatics (which is "performance theory at the semantic level" (p. 15)), he thinks that semantic competence, "what an ideal speaker would know about a sentence when no information is available about its context, that is, when it is used in the 'null context'" (p. 14), includes considerable illocutionary force information. However, contrary to what Katz says, the null context is not an idealization like a frictionless plane, but a fiction, for there is no situation, even ideally, in which context contributes nothing to what is being done. When Katz says that sentence "meaning is the information that determines use in the null context" (p. 21), he implies that use is determined even when (by his definition of "null context") no information is available about its context. But clearly, if no such information is available, there is no such determination. At most, what is determined is the literal illocutionary force, if any, but not that there is any. Perhaps because he does not acknowledge this point, Katz develops a theory of *propositional types* which goes far beyond what we include at the level of sentence meaning.

Notes to Chapter 3

1. In addition to Austin's and Searle's, taxonomies have been proposed by Vendler (1972), Fraser (1973), McCawley (1975), and Schiffer (1972). Vendler's and McCawley's are variants of Austin's; Fraser's and Schiffer's are substantially different. Katz (1977, 195–222) classifies a variety of types of what he calls "performative propositions" (a semantic category we do not use) and claims that his scheme can be adapted to illocutionary acts.

2. Of course, the same verb may name several types of illocutionary acts, e.g. "suggest" and "insist."

3. The analysis of advisories has the superficial form of that of constatives—in particular, confirmatives; the difference is that in advising, S is providing H with a reason to act rather than a reason to believe. Thus, like directives in general, literal advisories are imperative in form. Advisories performed using declaratives like "You should" or "It would be a good idea to" are performed indirectly.

4. In his "How to derive 'ought' from 'is'," Searle (1964; 1969, ch. 8) claimed, quite correctly, that promises are not only acts of undertaking an obligation but acts that create obligations. His view is that it is in virtue of being a successful illocutionary act that a promise creates an obligation. This is apparently a consequence of his theory of illocutionary acts as governed by constitutive rules, which theory we discuss in chapter 7. On our view, the most that a promise creates qua illocutionary act is the mutual belief between S and H that S's utterance obligates S to do A. That it does so in fact is another matter, be it a matter of moral or of institutional fact. Whatever it is, it is not an illocutionary fact.

5. Regarding this intention, the speaker's obvious insincerity results from the obvious futility of trying to get the hearer to change his mind.

6. It might be objected that our broad interpretation of what it is to provide a reason by one's utterance lets too much into the concepts of expressing an attitude and of performing an illocutionary act, in particular, that it blurs, indeed obliterates, the distinction between nonliteral and indirect illocutionary acts by making seemingly direct, nonliteral acts into indirect acts. For example, if S says to H, "I don't have any wheels," thereby telling H that he doesn't have a car (available), clearly he is not telling H that he has no wheels, although he would be if he were speaking literally. Yet, the objection continues, our conception of expressing an attitude seems to imply that S is expressing the belief that he doesn't have any wheels and thereby telling this to H. For his

utterance surely provides *a* reason, rather than no reason, for *H* to think this, albeit a reason that is immediately overridden by the nonliteral reading of the utterance. If providing a reason is compatible with, indeed suggested by, obvious insincerity, then it would seem that *S* is being obviously insincere with respect to the literal reading. Indeed, since he relies on this fact to get his nonliteral intention recognized (compare an utterance of "I need to get my wheels aligned"), there would be no basis for saying that *S*'s utterance is nonliteral rather than indirect.

This elaborate objection is based on a misunderstanding of just what our conception of expressing an attitude is. In expressing an attitude, the speaker *R-intends* his utterance to be taken as reason to believe he has the attitude. In cases of obvious insincerity, even though *S* knows that his utterance will not be taken as sufficient reason to believe he has the attitude, and knows that *H* knows that *S* knows this (because there is a mutually believed reason to the contrary), still *S* knows that his attitude toward the propositional content of his utterance is at issue. Therefore, *S* can reasonably R-intend his utterance to be taken as relevant to this issue. Even though he knows that it will not be taken as (intended to be) sufficient reason to believe that he has the attitude in question, still he can reasonably R-intend it to be taken as a reason, a reason which, under the circumstances, is overridden by other matters of mutual contextual belief. However, in the case of a clearly nonliteral utterance, when *S* says to *H* (under suitable circumstances) that he doesn't have any wheels, his having or not having wheels (literally) is not at issue and indeed is R-intended to be recognized to be not at issue. *H* in turn infers (in accordance with L5′ of the SAS as elaborated in chapter 4) that *S* could not be telling him that he has no wheels. Accordingly, *H* seeks a nonliteral reading.

Thus the case of direct nonliteral utterances has not been ruled out by our conception of expressing an attitude. For it is precisely in this case that *H* is R-intended not to take *S*'s utterance as reason to believe that *S* has the attitude he would be expressing if he were speaking literally.

When *S* is speaking *indirectly,* he is expressing certain attitudes over and above those expressed literally. Moreover, the hearer is to identify the attitudes expressed indirectly in terms of those expressed literally. In other words, he recognizes that *S* is *F*-ing that *P* by recognizing that *S* is F^*-ing that *p* but not merely F^*-ing that *p*. In the case of direct nonliteral illocutionary acts, however, *H* is intended to rule out *S*'s F^*-ing that *p* and to recognize that *S* is *F*-ing that *P* instead. And *H* is to do this on the basis of what *S* is saying, not on the basis of *S*'s would-be literal act, F^*-ing that *p*. When a person is speaking nonliterally, he is using his words, some of them anyway, as if they meant something different from any of their meanings in *L,* and he intends *H* to recognize just how. In order to express an attitude other than one that would be expressed literally, he intends his words to be taken differently from the way they could be literally taken, in any of their senses, so that in effect he doesn't mean what he says. But what he means instead must be identifiable, namely, in terms of taking certain words differently in a way that is plausible under the circumstances. This does not happen with indirect acts, because an indirect act must be identified in terms of the literal act being performed; therefore, the words of the utterance are to be taken literally.

If one still has misgivings about our way of handling the case of obviously obvious insincerity, we offer an alternative formulation of what it is to express an attitude, which we believe to be equivalent to, but more perspicuous than, our original one. Instead of saying that expressing an attitude is R-intending H to take one's utterance as reason to believe that one has that attitude, we can say that it is R-intending H to take one's utterance as sufficient reason, unless there is mutually believed reason to the contrary, to believe that one has that attitude. In this way we can sidestep the issue of whether an overridden reason is still a reason, while at the same time making it clear that communicating attitudes is one thing and having attitudes is another.

The case of acknowledgments may seem troublesome even for our revised formulation of the notion of expressing an attitude. This is because our definitions already allow for perfunctory acknowledgments, which are obviously insincere with respect to the feeling expressed. In these instances S intends his utterance to satisfy, and intends H to take it to satisfy, the social expectation that the appropriate feeling be expressed. Could an acknowledgment performed with this intention be obviously insincere? Clearly it could be: for example, S might be apologizing for something for which a perfunctory apology is not enough. If this is mutually believed, then S cannot reasonably intend his utterance to satisfy the social expectation that one express regret, nor could he reasonably intend H to take it as satisfying that expectation. S would have succeeded in apologizing, but H would surely not accept the apology.

7. Of course, he could be speaking nonliterally *and* be obviously insincere. In the drinking example, instead of saying that he hadn't been drinking, S could have said that he hadn't touched a drop; it would be mutually obvious that S was speaking nonliterally, claiming, however insincerely, that he hadn't been drinking.

Notes to Chapter 4

1. Though Grice (1975) was not the first to note all of these maxims of conversation (see Harnish 1976b, 341), he was the first to bring them together as part of a coherent and compelling theory of communication.

2. Recently R. Kempson (1975, 160–161) has attempted to formulate this maxim more precisely, but the result is implausibly strong.

3. This accounts for Searle's generalization 1 over speech acts (1969, 65) without appealing to constitutive rules.

4. In the case of questions, this amounts to not asking a question like "Have you stopped beating your wife?" unless you have reason to believe what is assumed.

5. Grice (1975) does not elaborate on the maxim "Be polite." Politeness is a very tricky concept; part of the reason may be that it acts in many ways like an *excluder* (see R. Hall, 1959).

6. Thus, it could be argued that understatements involve literal acts.

7. We have left open a number of issues surrounding R1–R3. For instance, what exactly is the *opposite* of a term or expression, as mentioned in R1? One natural answer is that the opposite is the *antonym*. However, the notion of antonymy is not much clearer than the notion of oppositeness and is often characterized in terms of it. As for R2, various figurative relations fall under the umbrella term *metaphor*. What counts as a metaphorical or figurative connection? These vary in perhaps unpredictable ways and we have mentioned only two of the types that have received labels:

(R2) a. *Synecdoche:* a salient, distinctive whole/part if a part/whole is mentioned.
b. *Metonomy:* a salient, distinctive associated object, property, or relation.

8. Note that in this case of sarcasm negation goes to the embedded sentence, and is thus not simple external negation.

Notes to Chapter 5

1. Because the LP and the CP are applicable to normal communicative situations, the mere fact of utterance warrants H to think that S has some communicative intention identifiable by what is uttered. Only where the CP (or the LP) is inoperative is it necessary for H to infer from the nature of S's utterance the existence of some communicative intention. In effect, then, we are saying that linguistic communication, at least as normally accomplished, requires the LP and the CP. Nonlinguistic communication does not and thus requires a more complex inference by H. On some occasions (see note 4) nonlinguistic communication can be performed using language.

2. It is not clear what such a claim would amount to anyway. Rational reconstructions (in science and philosophy) are usually axiomatizations of less explicitly formulated working theories. Conditions of adequacy on such an enterprise include preservation of theorems, minimal redundancy in primitive terms, etc. None of these characteristics is appropriate to the present case, unless nothing more is meant by "rational reconstruction" than 'idealization.' See Suppes (1957, ch. 12) and references therein for more discussion.

3. See Fodor (1975, ch. 3) for a discussion of these kinds of cases from the point of view of cognitive psychology.

4. Suppose during the rehearsal of a play, wherein the CP is suspended, S, following the script, says to H "Tonight is the night, my love." H's husband happens to be the director, and it happens that he, as mutually believed by S and H, will be spending the evening with the producer. Moreover, there is a certain special twinkle in the eye of S that only H can observe. In this context, despite the suspension of the CP, S could reasonably have uttered the line with the communicative intention that H take it as an invitation to see him that night. H relies not on the CP but on the twinkling in S's eye to infer that S has some communicative intention.

5. Many of the published counterexamples to the various versions of Grice's account of speaker meaning rely on there being no CP operative (see Strawson 1964; Grice 1969; Schiffer 1972). What is in question in those cases is not the identity but the existence of S's communicative intention. These examples generally involve nonlinguistic communication, where there is nothing about the "utterance" analogous to being a sentence of English that activates the CP. For this reason, we suggest, discrepancies between the intended inference and the inference made produce counterexamples—cases that don't seem to be instances of communication. Finally, there are linguistic counterexamples; even if they are cases of communication, they are not linguistic communication, since S does not intend H to rely on the meaning of the words he utters. In Searle's oft-discussed example (1969, 44f) of "Kennst du das Land wo die Zitronen blühen?" used to communicate that S is a German soldier, S intends H merely to rely on the fact that the sentence is in German.

6. In general S also has a perlocutionary intention, recognition of which would further explain his utterance. However, perlocutionary intentions need not be recognized to be fulfilled; therefore H need not be able to explain S's utterance at this level.

7. It is not, to use a catch-phrase in contemporary philosophy, an inference to the *best* explanation (see Harman 1973). Rather, H takes the fact that he has found a *plausible* explanation of the speaker's utterance as good reason to believe this explanation to be the right one.

8. The inference is usually made routinely, but when the speaker is particularly obscure or subtle, explicit inference may be necessary before the hearer is confident (if he ever is) that he has things right.

9. For example, S might ask H "What are you doing tonight?" intending it to be taken as an invitation only if the answer is "Nothing" or something to that effect.

Notes to Chapter 6

1. See section 7.1. Rawls' (1955) *practice conception of rules* and Searle's (1969) *constitutive rules* are similar to our conventions. Unfortunately, their accounts do not clearly distinguish rules as requirements from the conventions defining the actions required. Another possible confusion is to think that every act that is part of a ritual, ceremony, or other formalized procedure is conventional. Of course it is in one sense, but not necessarily in the relevant sense. Such an act is conventional in the relevant sense only if the description it falls under makes reference to institutional facts such as the position of the act in the procedure.

2. These are essentially the same as Searle's (1975b) *declarations* and *representative declarations*, although for him all illocutionary acts are conventional in the sense of being governed by constitutive rules. His labels are slightly misleading, since representative declarations are not declarations (on his account).

3. Strictly speaking, we should say that an institutional fact is anything expressed by a proposition that is true in virtue of being mutually believed in

some collectivity, or anything expressed by a proposition that follows from a proposition expressing one or more institutional facts (possibly together with other true propositions).

4. Even if some self-made autocrat makes the basic decisions that determine the major institutional facts in his society, these institutional facts, including the fact that what he says goes, are still matters of mutual belief. It is not a political but a conceptual point that the existence of these facts (their describability in institutional terms) depends on mutual belief, even if one person has the power to cause these facts to obtain.

5. We don't mean to imply that every fact about an institution is an institutional fact. To be sure, every fact describable only in terms that are applicable in virtue of mutual belief (whether about acts, persons, procedures, policies, rules, or objects) is an institutional fact. However, what we have in mind as noninstitutional facts are those that might describe social cohesion, social mobility, stability, power distribution and various other matters of concern to sociologists. In general, sociological facts about institutional facts are not institutional facts.

Notes to Chapter 7

1. Of course, here we are not using "express" in our technical sense of 'R-intend the hearer to infer.' In our imaginary situation, the speaker has a simple intention for the hearer to infer his attitude on the basis of his utterance's falling under a communicative convention of the sort we are imagining.

2. Still, it might seem that the very utterance of appropriate words in the right circumstances automatically counts as an acknowledgment, regardless of S's (R-)intention. Greeting is especially troublesome. It would seem that to say "Hi" or "Hello" upon encountering someone for the first time on a given occasion could not but count as a greeting and therefore does not require an R-intention or recognition thereof. Indeed, no intention at all seems required. But suppose that H believes S is not aware of him and so cannot be acknowledging his presence. Since uptake has not been achieved, has S succeeded in greeting H? Uptake involves attributing to S a communicative (R-)intention. And if S realizes that H believes he (S) is unaware of H, S cannot expect his utterance to be taken as a greeting. To be a greeting, an utterance of "Hi" or "Hello" must at least be addressed to someone and be intended to be taken as so addressed. But that is hardly enough. Part of what makes such utterances seem automatically to be greetings, irrespective of intention, is that it is difficult to imagine nonliteral uses of such terms. But it is not impossible. S and H might not be on speaking terms. For days they pass each other without exchanging a word. Finally, tired of sidelong glances, S says "Hi" to H. Relying on the mutual contextual belief, which is likely to have developed by this time, that their dispute was too petty to be permanent, S R-intends his utterance to be taken as a proposal to resume normal relations. He relies also, of course, on the standard use of "Hi" to greet friends but not necessarily enemies. We con-

clude, then, that there is more to greeting than saying "Hi." Even a per-functory greeting is R-intended to be taken as such.

3. Strictly speaking, for Searle only some constitutive rules take this form, which he contrasts with the characteristic form of *regulative rules* like " 'Do X' or 'If Y do X' " (1969, 34). Mysteriously, he says in the very next sentence, "Within systems of constitutive rules, some will have this form," but he never explains why rules (within a system of constitutive rules) that take the form of regulative rules are not themselves regulative rules, albeit regulative rules that govern the behavior defined by constitutive rules (see section 7.1). Accord-ingly, our discussion focuses on constitutive rules that take the counts-as form.

4. Searle notes this feature (1969, 61, note 1), but does not seem to consider it as severe and artificial a limitation as we think it is.

5. This seems to be a consequence of the if-clause in R(g). Supposing that conditions 1–8 do obtain, R(g) requires that S utter e if S is to speak sincerely and correctly. But suppose that (in the dialect) some other sentence e' means the same thing as e and (so) has the same semantic rules as e. Then conditions 1–8 will be sufficient for the correct and sincere utterance of e' also. Since 1–8 define what it is to promise (in uttering something so used), it seems to follow that if one is to promise in this dialect one must utter e and utter e'. Also, the only-if clause leaves the problem of ambiguous sentences unresolved. If a sentence is ambiguous, then on Searle's account the utterance of e could have incompatible necessary conditions if p were true and q were false:

i. Utter e only if p.
ii. Utter e only if q.

Under such circumstances one could not utter e without violating a rule of the language.

6. For instance, Grice (1969) has this as a consequence of a principle governing intentions to the effect that one must suppose that there is at least some chance that one's intention will be fulfilled in order to have that intention.

7. He does analyze a notion of convention relevant to coordination problems and points out that this is not the sense in which utterance types are conven-tional. By the way, his formulation of this other notion of convention comes close to our notion of a practice (see appendix).

Notes to Chapter 8

1. See Kempson (1975, ch. 8) for some excesses of this sort.

2. It might use a simple, unambiguous syntax and subscript all ambiguous lexical items.

3. Given this connection between decomposition and prediction of semantic properties and relations, it was very prudent of Davidson (1967) as a non-decompositionalist to deny the necessity of accounting for such properties/relations as ambiguity, synonymy, entailment, etc. His subsequent (1970) re-versal on some of these matters jeopardizes his nondecompositional position.

4. The merits of inference over decomposition from the point of view of psychology of language will be discussed further in chapter 11.

5. Fodor, Bever, and Garrett (1975, 180) give the following as a sample of what they call a "rule of inference": "A formula of the form P *and* Q entails a formula of the form P and a formula of the form Q." But this is not a rule of inference, it is a statement about a semantic relation.

6. This is not necessarily to say that it has some other form or forms, at least on the view that only sentences that are (or express something that is) true or false have a logical form.

7. Moreover, what it is for an expression to have a meaning is not specific to a language, though grammars are.

8. "Mean" can also be used for 'intend to refer to' as in "He meant Connors when he said he met a famous tennis player."

9. Grice himself seems to have conflated these last two uses in his original (1957) article, but distinguishing them (Grice 1969) renders his analysis immune to criticisms like Ziff's (1967).

10. When not speaking literally or not seriously (see (1) and (2)), for S to mean (5) that p may be for him to *imply* that p.

11. Our points about simple sincerity and about intended hearer response can be strengthened by being tied together. Whereas any form of subtle deception involves the speaker having an intention he intends the hearer not to recognize or not having an intention he intends the hearer to think he has, simple deception is straightforward insincerity—the speaker does not believe what he seemingly wants the hearer to believe, or he does not want the hearer to do what he seemingly wants the hearer to do. Now it will not do to say that the notion of speaker meaning does not preclude insincerity, because insincerity is not meaning what one says in the wrong sense (1) of the word "mean." At least it won't do if, as Schiffer argues, to mean something is to intend to cause, in the way specified by Shiffer's analysis, H either to actively believe something or to do something. And these are, according to Schiffer (1972, 80–87), the only types of response that are tied to meaning something. Nothing in Schiffer's final analysis (1972, 63) precludes insincerity, and yet according to that analysis S, in meaning something, issues an utterance with the intention of realizing a certain state of affairs E that, if realized, is sufficient for S and H to mutually know that E obtains and that it is conclusive evidence that S has the primary intention of causing H to believe or to do something (in the way specified by the further details of the analysis). But how can S reasonably expect his primary intention to be fulfilled if H thinks S is insincere? To be sure, Schiffer's analysis requires that H's response be for an intended reason, and that this be achieved, at least partly, by H's belief that S's utterance be related in a certain way to the intended response (these requirements are given in clauses (1) and (2) of Schiffer's analysis), so it might be thought there wouldn't be a reason if H thought S was insincere. In this case, Schiffer's analysis implies that S at least intends H to have taken him to be sincere. However, by not being explicit about S's

sincerity, or at least about S's intention for H to take him to be sincere, Schiffer's analysis obscures the fact that the only way S's utterance can cause, in the required way, H to believe something or to do something (except for cases like reminding) is for H to take S's utterance as evidence that S believes that p or that S wants H to Ψ. Otherwise, the intended connection that S intends H to recognize between his utterance e and the intended response will only reveal S's insincerity, not incline H to respond as intended. Schiffer's analysis fails to make explicit *why* H actually responds as he does, when he does as he is meant to do. H's reason for so responding is based on what he thinks S thinks or wants, not merely on deciphering S's primary intention about what H is to believe or do. However, once we make explicit that H's response (except for reminding cases) is mediated by his attributing a certain belief or want to S, it is clear that S's intention that H attribute to him (S) a certain attitude is distinct from his intention that H respond in a certain way. It then becomes clear that once H identifies what S believes or wants, the primary intended response is clearly perlocutionary. For once H identifies S's belief or desire, as expressed by S's utterance, no recognition of any further R-intention is required for H to respond appropriately to that belief or desire, which is the primary response required by Schiffer's analysis. Instead, H responds as intended, reasoning as follows:

Declarative cases:
1. S believes that p (by recognition of R-intention).
2. S wants me to believe that p.
3. Therefore, I will believe that p (unless there is strong reason to the contrary, i.e., unless I am not convinced).

Imperative cases:
1. S wants me to Ψ (by recognition of R-intention).
2. Therefore I will Ψ (failing a strong reason to the contrary).

Recognition of S's R-intention figures only in step 1. H's primary response is not a further matter of recognizing S's R-intention, for there isn't any further R-intention to recognize.

12. Besides offering various informal conceptions of presupposition, numerous authors fail to apply their pet conceptions consistently to their own examples and even shift conceptions within (and between) articles without notifying the reader. As a result there is a variety of ways to categorize these observations: lexical vs. sentential, sentential vs. speaker, semantic vs. pragmatic, logical vs. psychological, etc., depending either on the examples, the conceptions of presupposition espoused, or the conception of presupposition that actually applies to the examples.

13. Frege did not rigidly maintain a distinction between what a SMU of a sentence presupposes (vs. what a sentence means—its sense) and what a speaker presupposes (vs. what a speaker asserts). Frege contrasted presupposition with both sense (hence with entailment) and assertion. It was not necessary for his purposes to keep these distinct since for Frege, what a speaker asserts and the content of a declarative sentence are (indexicals aside) the same

thing: the thought that p. (See Harnish 1977, and in preparation, for more discussion.)

14. Strawson (1950) also seems to have entertained the doctrine that no statement is made if the presuppositions are not satisfied, but this theory would not accord well with our definition of asserting in terms of expressing propositional attitudes, nor with the plausible view that a statement can be *what is asserted*.

15. Frege actually says (1892, 69) that (13a) presupposes that the name "Kepler" refers to something, which conflicts with other doctrines he holds and conclusions he draws. (See Harnish, in preparation, for further discussion.)

16. Strawson (1952, 176) continues by saying that in general, "There are many ordinary sentences beginning with such phrases as 'All . . . ', 'All the . . .', 'No . . .', 'None of the . . .', 'Some . . .', 'Some of the . . .', 'At least one of the . . .', which exhibit, in their standard employment, parallel characteristics to those I have just described in the case of a representative 'All . . .' sentence. That is to say, the existence of members of the subject-class is to be regarded as presupposed (in the special sense described) by statements made by the use of these sentences; to be regarded as a necessary condition, not of the truth simply, but of the truth or falsity, of such statements."

17. Not every negation forms a contradictory. Usually internal negation creates a contrary, not a contradictory sentence. Whereas an external negation such as "It is not the case that . . ." always does. Thus external negations should be used in tests calling for contradictories. The contradictory of s is not-s, true if and only if s is false.

18. Keenan's example does not seem to fit his characterizations. It is not obvious that a perfect stranger (adult) of equal social status could not say (in French) to H "Tu es dégoûtant" after seeing H spit on the sidewalk, and be taken to mean literally exactly what he said.

19. From S's standpoint sometimes the relation can be weaker; S believes H believes that p and S believes that H believes that S believes that p.

20. The external negations give a similar, but weaker understanding; compare (31b) and (32b) with "It is not the case that John realizes that his car has been stolen" and "It is not the case that John has stopped playing tennis." Perhaps when the negative element is placed next to the verb "realize" (internal negation) it tends to attach more firmly to the belief condition because it is that condition that adds new information to the complement of the verb—the complement could itself be negated if that were all one wanted to communicate. When the negative element is distant from the verb, the conditions are more on a par and thus the negation can go to the conjunction, though the belief condition is still favored.

21. It seems, incidentally, that the theory of *semantic* presupposition cannot handle these cases without postulating ad hoc ambiguities.

22. See section 7.1 for the definition of a rule.

23. It might be thought that there is a way of taking (46) so as to be consistent—assume that x is completing someone else's ϕ-ing. But (43b) cannot really be used to communicate *that*.

24. See Harnish (1976b, 373–389) for some discussion of additional cases from this perspective, and D. Wilson (1975, ch. 6) for additional data.

25. This diagram is meant only to be suggestive; no readily apparent interpretation of the domination lines is coherent. It is an interesting and important question how these notions are related. We will not discuss Grice's theory of meaning any further, but it is important to know how utterer's meaning and utterance-type meaning are related to saying and implying. Especially vexing is the relation between utterer's meaning and implicature. We would argue that what one implicates (as well as what one says) is always a species of what was meant, differences being traceable to different ways in which various intentions are to function and different reasons the audience is intended to have. It is important for this strong view that one not be able to imply that p and not mean that p, from which it follows that one could not imply unintentionally.

26. The reason for the disjunction is that Grice's terminology has shifted from the first of each pair to the second. The shift to *implicature* frees him from the restrictive logical use of *implies*, and the shift to *said* is a generalization from *state*. One can report what someone said without reporting what was stated, for instance, when one reports that he said that you are to leave the room.

27. In an early paper (1961) Grice discusses four cases "in which . . . something might be said to be implied as distinct from being stated." Although his main concern is to decide on the vehicle of implication in each case, Grice does suggest a pair of useful diagnostic tests (p. 446):

Nondetachability (of the implication from what is asserted): "*Any* way of asserting what is asserted . . . involves the implication in question."
Noncancelability (of the implication without canceling the assertion): "One cannot take . . . [another] form of words for which both what is asserted and what is implied is the same as [the first] . . . and *then* add a further clause withholding commitment from what would otherwise be implied, with the idea of annulling the implication without annulling the assertion."

Suppose S has said that p, and we wonder whether S has thereby *said* or *implied* that q. If S can consistently claim p, but not q, then S did not say that q, so but could only have implicated it.

28. Some have been misled by Grice's remarks. For instance, Elinor Keenan's interesting paper (1976) is somewhat marred by the supposition that her data from Madagascar are counterexamples to Grice's theory of conversation. She assumes that for maxims to be universal, they must be categorically observed. But this need not be so. Grice's theory of implicature requires just that the speaker and hearer(s) be observing the cooperative maxims. This assumption is necessary for Grice's theory of implicature to work, but it is also sufficient. Grice nowhere says, nor would want to say, that all conversations are governed

by the cooperative maxims. There are too many garden-variety counter-examples: social talk between enemies, diplomatic encounters, police interrogations of reluctant suspects, most political speeches, and many presidential news conferences. These are just some of the cases in which the maxims of cooperation are not in effect and are known not to be in effect by the participants, notwithstanding pretenses to the contrary.

Since Grice's theory is basically conditional (if any conversation is governed by the cooperative maxims, then implicatures can be explained in a certain way), falsifying the theory takes more than showing the antecedent sometimes to be false. What must be done to falsify the theory, and what Keenan does not report doing, is to find examples of cooperative exchanges where the maxims are violated in the requisite way and none of the predicted implicatures are present. Keenan does ask the important question: why don't the Malagasy cooperate with information? Apparently the Malagasy are so closely knit that possessing information another lacks gives one status over the other; reluctance to cooperate on information could be a natural consequence of the general reluctance to relinquish advantages in status.

29. Fragmentary accounts of various maxims can be found in the literature. On *quantity* see Strawson (1964b), on *quality* see Ross (1930, 21) and Urmson (1952, 224–230). This fact does not diminish Grice's achievement of widening these observations and integrating them into a theory.

30. The maxim of relation (our presumption of relevance) turns out to be so central and important in conversational implicature that it is not clear that it belongs on equal footing with the others. We suspect that maxims are (at least partially) ordered with respect to weight, etc., and that relevance is at the top, controlling most of the others.

31. The general question arises of how to discover new maxims and how to justify the claim that some maxim governs discourse. On our view of course, conversational presumptions (maxims) have the status of contextual mutual beliefs. As such they contribute to the explanation not only of implications but also of other conversational phenomena. See chapter 4.

32. We want to emphasize that these are not mutually exclusive ways of infringing a maxim. Clashes seem to be a special case of violation in which the violation is forced, or seen as forced, by maxims that conflict under the circumstances.

33. In this reasoning H makes use of at least the following information: (1) the conventional meaning of the words, (2) the identity of the referents, (3) the conversational maxims (or CooP), (4) the context of utterance, (5) background knowledge, and (6) the mutual belief that S and H share knowledge of (1)–(5). These items correspond to items in the SAS. Items (1) and (2) correspond to L2 and L3 of the SAS; item (3) to the communicative presumption; items (4) and (5) to the mutual contextual beliefs (MCBs) cited in the SAS. Item (6) makes it clear that the other items are matters of mutual belief.

34. Notice that the explanation cannot turn on a difference in the verbs, because the same verb in different sentences can have different implications (see Harnish 1976b).

35. Clause (4) is not clearly true and seems to conflict with (2). In (4) Grice seems to be invoking his old criterion of cancelability as the test for whether what is said is the vehicle of the implication. But since (nonconventional) implicature is not entailment and can always be canceled, it is not clear why truth and falsity are relevant.

36. It was this narrow, strongest notion of conversational implicature that we used in effect in section 4.3.

37. Grice (1975, 51) seems to deny this by classifying two examples of implicature as "examples in which no maxim is violated, or at least it is not clear that any maxim is violated." However, one paragraph later he writes, "In both examples, the speaker implicates that which he must be assumed to believe in order to preserve the assumption that he is observing the maxim of relation." If so, then the speaker has infringed the maxim of relation at the level of what is said. We think that Grice's latter characterization is right, and that the examples differ from the flouting examples only in the degree of irrelevance.

38. And more generally, what is it for e to mean something?

Notes to Chapter 9

1. See Sadock (1972). This locution suggests these senses are not compositional, but Sadock himself proposes underlying structures for them similar to those for imperative sentences literally used to make requests, and these are surely compositional. One problem is that it is not clear whether, or how, generative semantics can define compositionality—the meaning of a complex expression being a function of the meaning of its meaningful constituents and their grammatical relations.

2. Sadock modifies this eventually (1974, 114) to "I *indirectly* request you to . . ." But since indirection (on Sadock's account) consists of a disparity between form and function it is unclear what this could amount to as a piece of *semantic* representation.

3. Question mark indicates rising intonation on the tag.

4. Exclamation point indicates falling intonation on the tag: "The tag has approximately the same intonation as the imperative *kiss me*" (Sadock 1974, 133).

5. The sentence may be grammatical if "please" is read as short for "please tell me." But in that case "please" does not modify the verb denoting the requested action in the main clause—contrary to the generalization used.

6. But notice that in spite of (8d) and (14b), we do have "When will someone please wash the car?!"

7. But we do get "When are you going to buzz off?!" In general the more vulgar forms ("fuck off") work better in this argument.

8. Following Green (1972), Sadock applies the term to sentences used for issuing directives in general. We limit it to the three forms given earlier. (Here, however, we will ignore the third form: "How(s) about . . . ?")

9. Another use of such constructions as "Step on my other foot, why don't you?" is sarcastic and not literal.

10. For some people it is progressively more odd to say ?"Yeah" and ??"Yes."

11. If this is correct, "Can we go now?" as a *suggestion* will have to be indirect off of the question reading.

12. Searle (1975a, 67–68) misses this point. An ambiguity theorist will argue that a second meaning is a necessary part of the best available explanation of certain linguistic facts.

13. This seems to be the view of Searle (1975a, 64, 68, 76, 77) who says, "there can be conventions of usage that are not meaning conventions" (76). Since Searle has no analysis of conventions (other than as systems of constitutive rules, which he cannot invoke on pain of collapsing conventional meaning and conventional use), it is impossible to evaluate this proposal on his terms; consequently, we evaluate it on ours.

14. Presumably the speaker is not force-punning, simultaneously using both readings.

15. There are some internal difficulties. For instance, "?(the hearer can pass the salt)" is not the same proposition as "the hearer is to pass the salt"; thus the formulation would have to provide machinery for forming the propositional content of the standardized illocution.

16. Think of ordering paradoxes, or the Bach-Peters paradox (see E. Bach 1970).

17. We are not here addressing the question of characterizing the various types of sentences that instantiate T. This is a research problem for any account of illocutionary standardization. Whether speakers have to know extra meanings (as the ambiguity thesis requires), illocutionary conventions (as the conventionality thesis requires), or merely illocutionary precedents, whatever this knowledge is it must somehow include a specification of the types of sentences it concerns.

18. By dropping (ii) we get the related notion of *having a standardized use for F-ing that p*. An expression can have a standardized use without ever actually being used that way—though it could be so used. For instance, it could very well be the case that no one has ever actually used a long compound sentence like "Could you change the tint on the TV, and turn down the boiler on the still, and . . . ?" Yet in appropriate circumstances we would know what was being done in the utterance of such a sentence. This said we can concentrate on the stronger notion of *being* standardly used.

19. This does not even appear to be the case with standardized forms used literally to express the speaker's desire. An indirect request made by uttering "I'd like you to take me home now," is also, uncontroversially, a statement of the speaker's preference. Clearly the ambiguity thesis could not be plausibly suggested for cases like these.

20. See our discussion of this point in section 3.6.

21. In some cases A may be a necessary condition for doing what is indirectly requested, A'. S might ask H, "Can you reach the buzzer?" in order to request him to push it.

22. "You can A" can also be used as a permissive, but then "can" means 'may' rather than 'is able.'

23. These forms don't take the preverbal or postsentential "please" because the action whose necessity or compulsoriness is literally questioned is the negation of the action indirectly requested. "Must you A?" is an indirect request for H *not* to (continue to) A, and "Mustn't you A?" is an indirect request for H *to A*. Therefore, if "please" is read as "if it pleases you (to do what I'm requesting you to do)," the action referred to is not the one mentioned in the literal question. The same point applies to literal questions like "Can you reach the salt?" where the indirect request is for the hearer to *pass* the salt (*"Could you reach the salt, please?").

24. In our discussion of illocutionary modifiers and of syntactic liberties (chapter 10) we generalize our claim about "please." We argue that the grammaticality of a sentence is not guaranteed either by its being acceptable or by its being usable. A grammar cannot do everything—if certain linguistic phenomena can be explained without demanding contortions from the grammar, they needn't be regarded as pertaining to grammaticality. This does not mean that anything one's grammar doesn't explain is not a matter of grammaticality— there must be principled reasons for construing such a phenomenon as not one of grammar. In the case of illocutionary modifiers, we argue that the sentences in which they occur are not grammatical although they admit of readily determinable conversational paraphrases by sentences that are fully grammatical. We point out that the higher performative approach could work for only some of these sentences anyway, for that only in some cases do the conversational paraphrases take the form of structures with higher performatives.

25. It seems that the occurrence of "please" is restricted to sentences whose subject is "you" and whose verb phrase is in the simple present or simple future. Thus, instead of (54) and (55), the following examples wouldn't illustrate the right point: *"Did you please pass the salt?" *"I can please pass the salt."

26. A further problem for the ambiguity thesis is presented by interrogatives used as requests for permission. Consider (a) "May I (please) go now?" Without "please" this example can be used literally as a question asking whether S is permitted to go. It needn't be used to request permission, for H might not be the one empowered to give it. However, (a) can be used as a request for permission as well, and with "please" it could only be so used. No doubt an ambiguity theorist would say that it derives from an underlying imperative that, on the performativist story, would look something like "I request that you permit me to go now." On that account "please" would be grammatically no different from what it is in imperative and whimperative contexts. On our view an utterance of (a) is a literal question and an indirect request for permission, and "please" must be handled paragrammatically.

Now consider (b) "May I (please) have a beer?" Its utterance (with or without "please") could be either an indirect request for *H* to give *S* a beer or an indirect request for *H* to permit *S* to get a beer. As a literal question it is unambiguous. The problem for the ambiguity thesis is to account for both indirect uses. Does the sentence have three meanings? It seems that these examples further illustrate the difficulty of trying to incorporate the "please" phenomena into grammar.

Finally, compare (b) with (c) "I'd like some beer, please." Without "please," used literally (c) would be a statement of *S*'s preference, and with or without "please" it can be either an indirect request for *H* to give *S* a beer or an indirect request for *H* to give *S* permission to help himself. For the same reason we denied that (b) has two meanings, we deny that (c) has three.

27. Notice that an indirect report of (52) could not include "please," just as, in general, illocutionary modifiers cannot be included in indirect reports of what the speaker said: *"He asked ₗₒc me whether I could please pass the salt."

Notes to Chapter 10

1. For instance, Sadock (1974, 12) says "No theory of grammar can completely avoid treating illocutionary force because of the existence of explicit performatives."

2. The first-person plural can be used performatively, as when a spokesman speaks for a group; and the second-person passive can be used performatively, as in "You are commanded . . ." We follow Austin's general usage of "performative" as meaning explicit rather than primary performatives, a distinction he "introduced rather surreptitiously" by p. 69.

3. Such sentences need not be used performatively, as when one is speaking in the historical present or describing one's habitual behavior. See Austin (1962, 64, 68).

4. Most English verbs normally take the progressive (continuous) present, rather than the simple present. Zeno Vendler (1972, chs. 1, 2) notes that like performatives, statements of mental acts and of mental states also take the simple present. He draws some interesting parallels between them and performatives. See also discussions by Katz (1977c) and Ginet and Ginet (1976).

5. We are sticking with Austin's provisional performative/constative distinction. His subsequent general theory of illocutionary acts collapsed that distinction, since constatives are performative in the sense that they involve doing something. But they are also true or false ("I state that . . ."). Still, he never came to hold that all performatives can be true or false.

6. That this regress does not follow is argued in Harnish (1976a).

7. Another flaw is the vagueness of "something slightly less than full conventional force."

8. Austin (1962, 69–70) gives a similar variety of cases to show what "making explicit" conveys, but he claims that a performative is not a statement only because it could not be true or false. This passage is the closest he comes to an argument.

9. Katz (1977, 175f) rejects this supposition (hence our argument) because he thinks performativity must be explained semantically, not pragmatically. (See also our note 11, ch. 2.)

10. Austin (1962, 57) uses a legalistic locution to describe the force of "hereby" as serving to indicate that the utterance "is, as it is said, the instrument effecting the act."

11. Lemmon (1962) includes performative sentences among those to which his title, "Sentences Verifiable by their Use," applies. We applaud his recognition, by implication, of the constative character of performatives, but we would characterize them, unlike most of Lemmon's other examples, as "true in virtue of their use."

12. This claim does not apply to conventionalized performatives.

13. Fraser indicates that hedged performatives are to be accounted for differently from simple performatives when he points out that the speaker can cancel the illocutionary force of hedged performatives but not of simple performatives. Compare "I must ask you to leave, but I won't" with "I hereby ask you to leave, but I'm not (asking you to leave)." Only in the second case, involving a simple performative, does the speaker contradict himself. On our view this is accounted for by the fact that he is both asserting and denying that he is asking the hearer to leave. However, in the first example, the speaker is asserting that he must ask, not that he is asking, the hearer to leave, whereas he is denying that he has any intention of asking the hearer to leave. Clearly there is no contradiction in this case. Our account of hedged performatives will thus be different from our account of simple performatives. For example, in "must" cases the speaker's statement is not of what he's doing but only of what he must do.

14. Fraser claims (1975, 196) that in hedged performatives the "use of 'must' implies a sense of helplessness" with respect to what the speaker says he must do: he is doing it not because he wants to but because he has to. Fraser's point is that the speaker in using "must" is trying to relieve himself of some of the onus of responsibility for what he is doing. But compare the hedged request (7) with the hedged admission "I must confess that I forgot your name." To cover both sorts of cases we suggest describing the speaker as reluctant. Being helpless because obligated is but one route to reluctance. One can be reluctant to harm the hearer but also reluctant to harm (embarrass) oneself.

15. Insofar as the locutions are of standardized form, such inferences can be short-circuited in practice.

16. What kind of phenomenon is calling attention—as done by stress, paraphrase, and other devices like clefting, preposing, inverted word order? Are these phenomena matters of meaning and therefore part of the subject of semantics? Or are they relevant only to pragmatics?

17. Schreiber thinks this fact supports the performative analysis. However, at best it is consistent with the performative analysis. To support that analysis, it must be explainable in terms of higher performatives. Schreiber's data are cases like the following:

(a) Sam $\left\{\begin{array}{l}\text{admitted}\\\text{discovered}\\\text{noted}\end{array}\right\}$ that $\left\{\begin{array}{l}\text{possibly}\\\text{unfortunately}\\\text{apparently}\end{array}\right\}$ the earth is flat.

(a) *Sam $\left\{\begin{array}{l}\text{admitted}\\\text{discovered}\\\text{noted}\end{array}\right\}$ that $\left\{\begin{array}{l}\text{candidly}\\\text{confidentially}\\\text{bluntly}\end{array}\right\}$ the earth is flat.

The (a) cases are grammatical (and more or less acceptable) instances of sentence adverbs as clause modifiers in predicate complement constructions, whereas the adverbs of manner in the (b) cases produce, in the same environments, ungrammatical sentences. (This is Schreiber's claim—it is a matter of considerable theoretical dispute just what sorts of unacceptability constitute ungrammaticality; we are inclined to regard some sorts of semantic nonsense as grammatical.) The performative analysis accounts for the difference between (a) and (b) because the (b) cases would have to be derived from impossible structures like (bP), which violate the rule that performative clauses cannot be freely embedded in other structures.

(bP) *Sam $\left\{\begin{array}{l}\text{admitted}\\\text{discovered}\\\text{noted}\end{array}\right\}$ that I tell you $\left\{\begin{array}{l}\text{candidly}\\\text{confidentially}\\\text{bluntly}\end{array}\right\}$

that the earth is flat.

Unfortunately, this rule is nothing more than an ad hoc device to rule out counterexamples to the performative analysis. A more straightforward explanation of the unacceptability of (b) and of (bP) would be in terms of conceptual nonsense, not (linguistic) ungrammaticality.

18. Presumably, an account can be given of why, on the performative analysis, (39) is not derived from *"I request truthfully that you tell me whether you lied to me."

19. Presumably, an account can be given on the performative analysis for why (42) and (43) are not derived, respectively, from "I tell you fortunately that you lied to me" and "I tell you clearly that you lied to me."

20. See Chomsky (1965, ch. 1.2) for the classical elaboration of the distinction between grammaticality and acceptability.

21. *H* may not realize consciously that the locution is not a grammatical sentence. Nevertheless, he can augment the locution with the parts that would make it complete. He knows the meaning of this complete sentence and can thereby determine what *S* meant to say at the locutionary level, something of the form *(...p...)*. In this way the SAS is unblocked.

22. There are also *lexical liberties,* such as using "He was stabbed by three nameless inmates" instead of "He was stabbed by three inmates whose names we do not know." We do not pursue lexical liberties here, though they seem to be related to nonliteral uses of language such as metaphor.

23. What would a theory of pronominalization look like that had to cover, in the same way, "He looks like he could lift a ton and throw *it*" and "He looks like he could lift a ton but not spell *it*."

24. Reported by Associated Press, Nov. 11, 1973, under the curious title: "South African Motorists Mangle Facts in Accidents."

Notes to Chapter 11

1. Also, it does not tell us certain things we would like to know. What exactly are these messages and how are they related to such things as the semantics of the language and the intentions, beliefs, and desires of the communicants? How can the picture be extended to other speech acts like promises, apologies, verdicts, and greetings?

2. See Harnish (1977b), Dennett (1977), and Morton (1978).

3. Such a system can include a number of distinct but intertranslatable sub-systems. See Harnish (1977b, 174) for further discussion and references.

4. Fodor (1975, 28–29) gives a similar schema for the case of considered action in general.

5. Fodor, Bever, and Garrett (1974, 375) mention three kinds of factors that can contribute to the determination of the PI: what the speaker is attending to, his motivational state, and the contents of his memory. We do not dispute any of these; indeed we will try to flesh them out, for they are not very informative.

6. The idealizations to the effect that alternatives are not always considered and consequences computed remain in effect for SP. In many (most?) cases $PI_i = PI_1$ and $e_i = e_1$. That is, the speaker's actual pragmatic intent PI_i is the first and only one formed, and the expression uttered e_i is the first and only one constructed. In these cases most of the decision-theoretic structure of the model is idle.

7. Osgood (1971) discusses a number of other correlations as well, concerning pronouns, articles, and negations.

8. Fodor, Bever, and Garrett do not seem to be consistent in their description of these conclusions. They often describe the model as working "left to right, top to bottom" (pp. 418, 434). This makes a difference in that they also endorse (p. 418) the claim that at least the studies by Forster (1967, 1968) "provide the clearest evidence so far available for the theory that surface trees are elaborated roughly in the order that Yngve's model requires." But as Fodor, Bever, and Garrett note earlier (p. 407), Yngve's model (and Forster's experimental design) requires that these trees be constructed from top to bottom and left to right in order to get structures in memory having the shape of the tree in figure 11.2. In view of this endorsement it is extremely puzzling why Fodor, Bever, and Garrett comment (p. 419), "The Yngve model would have such bizarre consequences as the following: since the tree is elaborated from top to bottom, its general structure must be chosen before its lexical contents." They do not say why, especially in light of Forster's work, this is bizarre.

9. See V. Valian (1977) for a review of some of the current theories that do not stress these structural parameters of speech production and, because they do not, are in various ways inadequate.

10. Of course there may be such asymmetries which are too small to be detected by introspection. At this point the evidence would become experimental, not intuitive.

11. Fodor, Fodor, and Garrett (1975, fn. 4) acknowledge this possibility but their alternative, which is simply to "acknowledge a class of negative primitives that includes both the explicit and the implicit negatives" strikes us as weak. It suggests, counterintuitively, that there is no direct connection between the syntactic facts involving these negatives and their semantic representation as negatives.

12. Katz (1977c, 61) represents "bachelor" in essentially this way.

13. MacKay bases some of his conclusions on the functioning of a well-studied amnesiac known as H.M. As a result of bilateral removal of mesial parts of the temporal lobes and the hippocampus, H.M. is thought to be unable to form new long-term memory traces but has normal short-term memory. According to MacKay (1973, 37), H.M. was able to disambiguate lexical and surface ambiguities but not underlying ambiguities; MacKay concluded, "We suggest that hippocampal patients will be unable to learn or fully process the underlying relations of syntactic structures they have not encountered in the past." This explanation is suspect. If H.M. can understand normal sentences constructed out of familiar lexical items, then he must be using his knowledge of underlying syntactic relations just to get subject and object correct in sentences like "He is easy (eager) to please." So if H.M. has access to this grammatical information in comprehension, why should he not also have access to it in disambiguation? If the answer is supposed to involve the notion of "unencountered underlying relations of syntactic structures" then the answer is obscure at best. What *is* an "unencountered" underlying relation for a mature speaker of a language? Finally, recent work on organic brain disease patients with severe long-term memory dissolution shows no tendency to favor lexical and surface disambiguation over the disambiguation of underlying ambiguities (see Bayles 1979).

14. The probability that at least one of two independent states will be picked is generally greater than the probability of picking one in isolation: P_1 or $P_2 = (P_1 + P_2) - (P_1 \cdot P_2)$. However, we should be very suspicious of the assumptions required to make the mathematics fit this case, e.g., that the "space" at hand needs to be searched for a reading. If both readings are being computed, then both readings are available to the hearer.

15. Another part of the problem of identifying the type of clausal unit has to do with the notion of a main clause. For example, many grammars give the sentence "John wanted to leave" the underlying structure:

$[_{S_1} [_{NP_1} \text{John} _{NP_1}] [_{VP_1} [_V \text{wanted} _V] [_{S_2} [_{NP_2} \text{John} _{NP_2}] [_{VP_2} [_V \text{leave} _V] _{VP_2}] _{S_2}] _{VP_1}] _{S_1}]$

The surface form of the sentence results when NP_2 is deleted under identity with NP_1. We can see that "John leave" in S_2 might be construed as a clause. But how about "John wanted" in S_1? Is this an underlying clause? Or is the whole complex "John wanted John leave" the main underlying clause? We have assumed in the text that each underlying occurrence of S defines an underlying clause. If that position is not adopted and instead one says that subordinate S nodes (or labeled brackets) are part of one single underlying clause, then it is possible for the underlying clause to be the unit of comprehension. Indeed, Carroll and Bever (1976, 324) suggest that this latter position is the only one when they write, "We have suggested that the deep sentoid, and *therefore* its surface realization, the clause, is the primary unit of sentence perception" (emphasis added). So it seems that the matter is both empirical and terminological.

We have ignored, so far, a purported third alternative to these views, namely, the position of J. Carroll et al. (see for instance Carroll 1978), wherein the relevant notion of a clause is said to be "functional" as well as structural. However, on inspection it turns out that the notion of *function* at work is, from the point of view of language use, pretty thin: "We refer to linguistic sequences which provide the listener with an intact subject-verb-(object) group as *functionally complete* sequences, and we predict that such sequences will be 'good' sentence perception units" (p. 507). From a speech act point of view this looks like a version of the surface structure conception tentatively endorsed in the text, restricted to certain forms.

Notes to Appendix

1. Lewis (1969, 52ff) and Schiffer (1972, 30ff) use the terms *common knowledge* and *mutual knowledge,* respectively, which needlessly imply the truth of what is mutually believed. Their definitions are not limited to three levels of belief but go on indefinitely. Higher-level beliefs are in principle possible, and indeed among spies or deceptive intimates there could be divergence at level four or higher without divergence at the first three levels, but we think such higher-level beliefs are not possible for a whole community or large group. Nevertheless, to allow for this possibility our definition could be amended to require that no higher-level belief, if there are any, be false.

2. *A* may be any of a wide range of behaviors rather than one particular kind, which have some feature in common. We might speak of *A* (in *C*) as the range of a norm and *G,* the collectivity to which it applies, as its scope. Also, note that in section 7.1 we used DF_2 to define *rule,* but here we reserve that term for the special cases covered by $DF_8 - DF_{11}$.

3. In general when "social" modifies any of our defined expressions, it implies 'socially real by virtue of mutual belief.'

4. In effect each type of rule to be defined contains a special reason that amplifies the *should* clause (iii) in our definition of social norms.

5. A subcategory of a role category may fail to be a role category. Subcategories like 24-year-olds or 158-pounders are too specific to have their own regularities or standards.

6. The concept of social class is a special case of social position. In speaking of classes, whether economic, political, racial, or otherwise, we imply that the

society in question is as a whole divisible into classes, such that each person is a member of one and only one class. Of course there may be borderline cases where the society does not divide up neatly or where there is social mobility. Furthermore, the social stratification of classes is associated with a value scale reckoned by power, wealth, or prestige. Accordingly, there are norms for the behavior and for the treatment of members of each class.

7. Even in social scientific contexts, the term *group* is sometimes used so broadly as to include role categories or even categories simpliciter, as in *ethnic group, age group, opinion group,* and *reference group.* Members of such groups need not share any degree of structured relationship, although they could form groups in the narrower sense of social group defined in DF_{16}.

8. Group identification (and alienation) are discussed in Bach 1973, ch. 2.

Bibliography

Akmajian, A., R. Demers, and R. Harnish. 1979. *Linguistics: An Introduction to Language and Communication.* Cambridge, Mass.: MIT Press.

Akmajian, A., and F. Heny. 1975. *An Introduction to the Principles of Transformational Syntax.* Cambridge, Mass.: MIT Press.

Anderson, S. 1971. "On the linguistic status of the performative-constative distinction." Bloomington: Indiana University Linguistics Club.

Austin, J. L. 1962. *How to Do Things with Words.* Cambridge, Mass.: Harvard University Press.

Bach, E. 1970. "Problominalization." *Linguistic Inquiry* 1:121–122.

Bach, K. 1970. "Part of what a picture is." *British Journal of Aesthetics* 10:119–137.

Bach, K. 1973. *Exit-Existentialism.* Belmont, Calif.: Wadsworth.

Bach, K. 1975a. "Performatives are statements too." *Philosophical Studies* 28:229–236.

Bach, K. 1975b. "Analytic social philosophy—basic concepts." *Journal for the Theory of Social Behavior* 5:189–214.

Bach, K. 1977. "When to ask, 'What if everyone did that?'" *Philosophy and Phenomenological Research* 37:464–481.

Bach, K. 1978. "A representational theory of action." *Philosophical Studies* 34:361–379.

Bates, E. 1976. *Language and Context: The Acquisition of Pragmatics.* New York: Academic Press.

Bayles, K. 1979. *Language Profiles of a Geriatric Population,* Doctoral dissertation, University of Arizona.

Bennett, J. 1973. "The meaning nominalist strategy." *Foundations of Language* 10:141–168.

Bennett, J. 1976. *Linguistic Behavior.* Cambridge, England: Cambridge University Press.

Bever, T., M. Garrett, and R. Hurtig. 1973. "The interaction of perceptual processes and ambiguous sentences." *Memory and Cognition* 1:277–286.

Bever, T., M. Garrett, and R. Hurtig. 1976. "Projection mechanisms in reading." *Journal of Psycholinguistic Research* 2:215–226.

Bever, T., J. Katz, and T. Langendoen, eds. 1976. *An Integrated Theory of Linguistic Ability*. New York: Crowell.

Bierwisch, M. 1970. "Semantics." In J. Lyons, ed., *New Horizons in Linguistics*. Baltimore: Penguin.

Boer, S., and W. Lycan. 1976. "The myth of semantic presupposition." Bloomington: Indiana University Linguistics Club.

Brewer, W. 1977. "Memory for the pragmatic implications of sentences." *Memory and Cognition* 6:673–678.

Brewer, W., R. Harris, and E. Brewer. "Comprehension of literal and figurative meaning." Unpublished manuscript, n.d. University of Illinois.

Cairns, H., and C. Cairns. 1976. *Psycholinguistics*. New York: Holt, Rinehart & Winston.

Carey, P. W., J. Mehler, and T. Bever. 1970. "When do we compute all the interpretations of an ambiguous sentence?" *Advances in Psycholinguistics*, 61–75.

Carroll, J. 1978. "Sentence perception units and levels of syntactic structure." *Perception and Psychophysics* 6:506–514.

Carroll, J., and T. Bever. 1976. "Sentence comprehension: A case study in the relation of knowledge and perception." In E. Carterette and M. Friedman, eds., *Handbook of Perception*, vol. 7. New York: Academic Press.

Castaneda, H.-N. 1977. "On the philosophical foundations of the theory of communication: Reference." *Midwest Studies in Philosophy* 2:165–186.

Chomsky, N. 1957. *Syntactic Structures*. The Hague: Mouton.

Chomsky, N. 1965. *Aspects of the Theory of Syntax*. Cambridge, Mass.: MIT Press.

Chomsky, N. 1977. *Essays on Form and Interpretation*. Amsterdam: Elsevier North-Holland.

Clark, H., and E. Clark. 1977. *Psychology and Language*. New York: Harcourt Brace Jovanovich.

Clark, H., and S. Haviland. 1974. "Psychological processes as linguistic explanation." In D. Cohen, ed., *Explaining Linguistic Phenomena*. New York: Hemisphere Publishing Co.

Clark, H., and S. Haviland. 1977. "Comprehension and the given-new contract." In Freedle.

Clark, H., and P. Lucy. 1975. "Inferring what was meant from what was said." *Journal of Verbal Learning and Verbal Behavior* 14:56–72.

Cohen, L. J. 1974. "Speech Acts." In T. Sebeok, ed., *Current Trends in Linguistics*. The Hague: Mouton.

Cole, P., and J. Morgan, eds. 1975. *Syntax and Semantics*, vol. 3. New York: Academic Press.

Davidson, D. 1967. "Truth and meaning." *Synthese* 17:304–323.

Davidson, D. 1970. "Semantics of natural languages." Reprinted in Davidson and Harman, eds., *The Logic of Grammar*. Encino, Calif.: Dickenson, 1975.

Davidson, D., and G. Harman, eds. 1972. *Semantics of Natural Language*. Dordrecht, Holland: Reidel.

Davison, A. 1975. "Indirect speech acts and what to do with them. In Cole and Morgan, eds., *Syntax and Semantics*, vol. 3.

Dennett, D. 1977. Review of J. A. Fodor, *The Language of Thought*. *Mind* 86:265–280.

Donnellan, K. 1966. "Reference and definite descriptions." *Philosophical Review* 75:281–304.

Evans, G., and J. McDowell, eds. 1976. *Truth and Meaning*. Oxford, England: Oxford University Press.

Field, H. 1978. "Mental representation." *Erkenntnis* 13:9–61.

Fillmore, C. 1971. "Verbs of judging." In Fillmore and Langendoen, eds., *Studies in Linguistic Semantics*. New York: Holt, Rinehart & Winston.

Fillmore, C., and T. Langendoen, eds. 1971. *Studies in Linguistic Semantics*. New York: Holt, Rinehart & Winston.

Fodor, J. A. 1975. *The Language of Thought*. New York: Crowell.

Fodor, J. A., T. Bever, and M. Garrett. 1974. *The Psychology of Language*. New York: McGraw-Hill.

Fodor, J. D. 1977. *Semantics: Theories of Meaning in Generative Grammar*. New York: Crowell.

Fodor, J. D., J. A. Fodor, and M. Garrett. 1975. "The psychological unreality of semantic representation." *Linguistic Inquiry* 6:515–531.

Forster, K. 1967. "Sentence completion latencies as a function of constituent structure." *Journal of Verbal Learning and Verbal Behavior* 6:878–883.

Forster, K. 1968. "Sentence completion in left-and-right branching languages." *Journal of Verbal Learning and Verbal Behavior* 7:296–299.

Foss, D. J., T. Bever, and M. Silver. 1968. "The comprehension and verification of ambiguous sentences." *Perception and Psychophysics* 4:304–306.

Fraser, B. 1971. "An analysis of 'even'." In Fillmore and Langendoen, eds., *Studies in Linguistic Semantics*, New York: Holt, Rinehart & Winston.

Fraser, B. 1973. "A partial analysis of vernacular performative verbs." Austin: Texas Performadillo Conference.

Fraser, B. 1975. "Hedged performatives." In Cole and Morgan, eds., *Syntax and Semantics*, vol. 3.

Freedle, R., ed. 1977. *Discourse Production and Comprehension*, vol. 1. Norwood, N.J.: Ablex Publishing Co.

Frege, G. 1892. "On sense and reference." In P. Geach and M. Black, eds., *Translations From the Philosophical Writings of G. Frege*, Oxford: Blackwell.

Frye, M. 1973. "Force and meaning." *Journal of Philosophy* 70:281–294.

Garrett, M. 1970. "Does ambiguity complicate the perception of sentences?" *Advances in Psycholinguistics*, 48–60.

Ginet, S., and C. Ginet. 1976. Review of Z. Vendler, *Res Cogitans*. *Philosophical Review* 85:216–224.

Goldman, A. 1970. *A Theory of Human Action*. Englewood Cliffs, N.J.: Prentice-Hall.

Green, G. 1975. "How to get people to do things with words." In Cole and Morgan, eds., *Syntax and Semantics*, vol. 3.

Greenbaum, S. 1969. *Studies in English Adverbial Usage*. Miami, Fla.: Miami Linguistics Series.

Grice, H. P. 1957. "Meaning." *Philosophical Review* 66:377–388.

Grice, H. P. 1961. "The causal theory of perception." *Proceedings of the Aristotelian Society*, Supplementary Volume 35:121–152.

Grice, H. P. 1967. *William James Lectures*. Unpublished.

Grice, H. P. 1968. "Utterer's meaning, sentence-meaning and word-meaning." *Foundations of Language* 4:225–242.

Grice, H. P. 1969. "Utterer's meaning and intentions." *Philosophical Review* 78:147–177.

Grice, H. P. 1975. "Logic and conversation." In Cole and Morgan, eds., *Syntax and Semantics*, vol. 3.

Hall, R. 1959. "Excluders." *Analysis* 20:1–7.

Harman, G. 1973. *Thought*. Princeton, N.J.: Princeton University Press.

Harnish, R. 1972. *Studies in Logic and Language*. Doctoral dissertation, Massachusetts Institute of Technology.

Harnish, R. 1975. "The argument from lurk." *Linguistic Inquiry* 6:145–154. Reprinted in Bever, Katz, and Langendoen, eds., *An Integrated Theory of Linguistic Ability*, New York: Crowell.

Harnish, R. 1976a. "Two consequences of transparent subject position." *Philosophical Studies* 30:11–18.

Harnish, R. 1976b. "Logical form and implicature." In Bever, Katz, and Langendoen, eds., *An Integrated Theory of Linguistic Ability*, New York: Crowell.

Harnish, R. 1977. Review of M. Dummett, *Frege: Philosophy of Language*, 1973. *General Linguistics* 17:47–58.

Harnish, R. 1977a. "Searle on Katz's semantic theory." *The Southwestern Journal of Philosophy* 8:23–32.

Harnish, R. 1977b. Review of J. A. Fodor, *The Language of Thought*. *The Journal of Psycholinguistic Research* 6:172–184.

Harnish, R. 1978. Review of J. Sadock, *Toward a Linguistic Theory of Speech Acts*. *Lingua* 44:288–301.

Harnish, R. "A projection problem for pragmatics." To appear in F. Heny and H. Schnelle, eds., *Syntax and Semantics*, vol. 10. New York: Academic Press (in press).

Harnish, R. *Fregean Semantics* (in preparation).

Harris, R. 1974. "Memory and comprehension of implications and inferences of complex sentences." *Journal of Verbal Learning and Verbal Behavior* 13: 626–637.

Harris, R., and G. Monaco. 1978. "Psychology of pragmatic implication: Information processing between the lines." *Journal of Experimental Psychology* 107:1–22.

Hart, H. L. A. 1961. *The Concept of Law*. Oxford, England: Oxford University Press.

Haviland, S., and H. Clark. 1974. "What's new? Acquiring new information as a process in comprehension." *Journal of Verbal Learning and Verbal Behavior* 13:512–521.

Heringer, J. 1972. *Some Grammatical Correlates of Felicity Conditions and Presupposition*. Bloomington: Indiana University Linguistics Club.

Holmes, V., R. Arwas, and M. Garrett. 1977. "Prior context and the perception of lexically ambiguous sentences." *Memory and Cognition* 5:103–110.

Hungerland, I. 1960. "Contextual implication." *Inquiry* 3:211–258.

Hutchinson, L. 1971. "Presupposition and belief-inferences." Chicago Linguistic Society 7.

Jackendoff, R. 1972. *Semantic Interpretation in Generative Grammar*. Cambridge, Mass.: MIT Press.

Just, M., and H. Clark. 1973. "Drawing inferences from the presuppositions and implications of affirmative and negative sentences." *Journal of Verbal Learning and Verbal Behavior* 12:21–31.

Karttunen, L. 1973. "Presuppositions of compound sentences." *Linguistic Inquiry* 4:169–193.

Katz, J. J. 1966. *The Philosophy of Language*. New York: Harper & Row.

Katz, J. J. 1972. *Semantic Theory*. New York: Harper & Row.

Katz, J. J. 1975. "Logic and language." In K. Gunderson, ed., *Language, Mind and Knowledge*. Minneapolis: University of Minnesota Press.

Katz, J. J. 1977a. "A proper theory of names." *Philosophical Studies* 31:1–80.

Katz, J. J. 1977b. "The real status of semantic representations." *Linguistic Inquiry* 8:559–584.

Katz, J. J. 1977c. *Propositional Structure and Illocutionary Force*. New York: Crowell.

Katz, J. J., and J. A. Fodor. 1963. "The structure of a semantic theory." *Language* 39:170–210.

Katz, J. J., and T. Langendoen. 1976. "Pragmatics and presupposition." *Language*. In Bever, Katz, and Langendoen, eds., *An Integrated Theory of Linguistic Ability*, New York: Crowell.

Keenan, E. 1971. "Two kinds of presupposition in natural language." In Fillmore and Langendoen, eds. *Studies in Linguistic Semantics*, New York: Holt, Rinehart & Winston.

Keenan, E. 1976. "On the universality of conversational implicatures." *Language in Society* 5:68–81.

Kempson, R. 1975. *Presupposition and the Delimitation of Semantics*. Cambridge, England: Cambridge University Press.

Klapp, O. E. 1957. "The concept of consensus and its importance." *Sociology and Social Research* 41:336–342.

Kripke, S. 1972. "Naming and necessity." In Davidson and Harman, eds., *Semantics of Natural Language*, New York: Humanities Press.

Kripke, S. 1977. "Speaker's reference and semantic reference." *Midwest Studies in Philosophy* 2:255–276.

Lackner, J. R., and M. Garrett. 1973. "Resolving ambiguity: Effects of biasing context in the unattended ear." *Cognition* 1:359–372.

Laing, R. D. 1968. *The Politics of Experience*. New York: Ballantine Books.

Lakoff, G. 1970. "Linguistics and natural logic." *Synthese* 22:151–271.

Lakoff, G. 1972. "Performative antimonies." *Foundations of Language* 8:569–572.

Lakoff, G. 1975. "Pragmatics and natural logic." In E. Keenan, ed., *Formal Semantics of Natural Language*. Cambridge, England: Cambridge University Press.

Landis, J. R. 1971. *Sociology: Concepts and Characteristics*. Belmont, Calif.: Wadsworth.

Lemmon, E. 1962. "Sentences verifiable by their use." *Analysis* 12:86–89.

Lewis, D. 1969. *Convention*. Cambridge, Mass.: Harvard University Press.

Lewis, D. 1970. "General semantics." *Synthese* 22:18–67.

Loar, B. 1976. "The semantics of singular terms." *Philosophical Studies* 30: 353–378.

Locke, J. 1691. *An Essay Concerning Human Understanding.*

MacKay, D. 1966. "To end ambiguous sentences." *Perception and Psychophysics* 1:426–436.

MacKay, D. 1973. "Aspects of the theory of comprehension, memory, and attention." *The Quarterly Journal of Experimental Psychology* 25:22–40.

MacKay, D., and T. Bever. 1967. "In search of ambiguity." *Perception and Psychophysics* 2:193–200.

Marslen-Wilson, W. 1975. "Sentence perception as an interactive parallel process." *Science* 189:226–228.

McCawley, J. 1973. "Remarks on the lexicography of performative verbs." Austin: Texas Performadillo Conference.

Miller, G. A., and Johnson-Laird, P. N. 1976. *Language and Perception.* Cambrige, Mass.: Harvard University Press.

Montague, R. 1974. *Formal Philosophy.* Edited by R. Thomason. New Haven: Yale University Press.

Morton, A. 1978. Review of J. A. Fodor, *Language of Thought. Journal of Philosophy* 75:161–169.

Muraki, M. 1972. "Discourse presupposition." In *Papers in Linguistics* 5.2.

Oden, G. 1978. "Semantic constraints and judged preference for interpretations of ambiguous sentences." *Memory and Cognition* 1:26–37.

Oden, G., and J. Spira. 1978. "Influence of context on the activation and selection of ambiguous word senses." Wisconsin Human Information Processing Program, report number 6.

Osgood, C. 1971. "Where do sentences come from?" In Steinberg and Jakobovits, eds., *Semantics,* Cambridge, England: Cambridge University Press.

Partee, B. 1977. "Possible worlds semantics and linguistic theory." *The Monist* 60:303–326.

Quine, W. 1960. *Word and Object.* Cambridge, Mass.: MIT Press.

Rawls, J. 1955. "Two concepts of rules." *Philosophical Review* 64:3–32.

Rosenberg, J. 1974. *Linguistic Representation.* Dordrecht, Holland: Reidel.

Ross, Sir D. 1930. *The Right and the Good.* London, England: Oxford University Press.

Ross, J. 1970. "On declarative sentences." In R. Jacobs and P. Rosenbaum, eds., *Readings in English Transformational Grammar.* Lexington, Mass.: Ginn.

Ross, J. 1974. "Three batons for cognitive psychology." In W. Weimer and D. Palermo, eds., *Cognition and the Symbolic Process.* Hillsdale, N.J.: Earlbaum.

Russell, B. 1905. "On denoting." *Mind* 14:479–493.

Sadock, J. 1972. "Speech act idioms." Chicago Linguistic Society 8.

Sadock, J. 1974. *Toward a Linguistic Theory of Speech Acts*. New York: Academic Press.

Scheff, T. 1967. "Toward a sociological model of consensus." *American Sociological Review* 32:32–46.

Schelling, T. 1960. *The Strategy of Conflict*. Cambridge, Mass.: Harvard University Press.

Schiffer, S. 1972. *Meaning*. London, England: Oxford University Press.

Schreiber, P. 1972. "Style disjuncts and the performative analysis." *Linguistic Inquiry* 3:321–347.

Schvaneveldt, R., D. Meyer, and C. Becker. 1976. "Lexical ambiguity, semantic context, and visual word recognition." *Journal of Experimental Psychology: Human Perception and Performance* 2:243–256.

Schweller, K., W. Brewer, and D. Dahl. 1976. "Memory for illocutionary forces and perlocutionary effects of utterances." *Journal of Verbal Learning and Verbal Behavior* 15:325–337.

Searle, J. 1964. "How to derive 'ought' from 'is'." *Philosophical Review* 73: 43–58.

Searle, J. 1965. "What is a speech act?" Reprinted in J. Searle, ed., *The Philosophy of Language*. London, England: Oxford University Press, 1971.

Searle, J. 1968. "Austin on locutionary and illocutionary acts." *Philosophical Review* 77:405–424.

Searle, J. 1969. *Speech Acts*. Cambridge, England: Cambridge University Press.

Searle, J. 1975a. "Indirect speech acts." In Cole and Morgan, eds., *Syntax and Semantics*, vol. 3.

Searle, J. 1975b. "A taxonomy of illocutionary acts." In K. Gunderson, ed., *Language, Mind and Knowledge*. Minneapolis: University of Minnesota Press.

Secord, P., and C. Backman. 1974. *Social Psychology*, 2nd ed. New York: McGraw-Hill.

Singer, M. 1976. "Context inferences in the comprehension of sentences." *Canadian Journal of Psychology* 30:39–46.

Steinberg, D., and Jakobovits, L., eds. 1971. *Semantics*. Cambridge, England: Cambridge University Press.

Stenius, E. 1967. "Mood and language game." *Synthese* 17:254–274.

Strawson, P. 1950. "On referring." *Mind* 59:320–344.

Strawson, P. 1952. *Introduction to Logical Theory*. London: Methuen.

Strawson, P. 1964a. "Intention and convention in speech acts." *Philosophical Review* 73:439–460.

Strawson, P. 1964b. "Identifying reference and truth values." *Theoria* 30:96–118.

Strawson, P. 1971. "Meaning and truth." In *Logic-Linguistic Papers*. London: Methuen.

Suppes, P. 1957. *Introduction to Logic*. New York: Van Nostrand Reinhold.

Tannenbaum, P., and F. Williams. 1968. "Generation of active and passive sentences as a function of subject or object focus." *Journal of Verbal Learning and Verbal Behavior* 7:246–250.

Thomson, J. 1977. *Acts and Other Events*. Ithaca, N.Y.: Cornell University Press.

Tyler, L., and W. Marslen-Wilson. 1977. "The on-line effects of semantic context on semantic processing." *Journal of Verbal Learning and Verbal Behavior* 16:683–692.

Urmson, J. 1952. "Parenthetical verbs." Reprinted in C. Caton, ed., *Philosophy and Ordinary Language*. Urbana: University of Illinois Press.

Valian, V. 1977. "Talk, talk, talk: A selective critical review of theories of speech production." In Freedle, ed., *Discourse Production and Comprehension*, Norwood, N.J.: Ablex Publishing Co.

Vendler, Z. 1972. *Res Cogitans*. Ithaca, N.Y.: Cornell University Press.

Weiser, A. 1974. "Deliberate ambiguity." Chicago Linguistic Society 10, 721–730.

Weiser, A. 1975. "How to not answer a question: Purposive devices in conversational strategy." Chicago Linguistic Society 11.

Wilson, D. 1975. *Presupposition and Non-Truth-Conditional Semantics*. New York: Academic Press.

Ziff, P. 1967. "On H. P. Grice's account of meaning." *Analysis* 28:1–8.

Index

DATE DUE